ARTIFICIAL INTELLIGENCE

ARTIFICIAL INTELLIGENCE

PATRICK HENRY WINSTON
Massachusetts Institute of Technology

Addison-Wesley Publishing Company
Reading, Massachusetts — Menlo Park, California
London — Amsterdam — Don Mills, Ontario — Sydney

This book is in the Addison-Wesley Series in Computer Science.

Michael A. Harrison
Consulting Editor

Second printing, April 1979

ISBN 0-201-08454-6
DEFGHIJKL-MA-8987654321

PREFACE

It is possible to race through this book in one term, but it requires determination
and not much else to do. There are several better alternatives, all of which exploit
the division of the material into two parts, one without programming and one
concentrating on programming. Part One consists of Chapter 1 through Chapter 9,
and Part Two, of Chapter 10 through Chapter 16.

- Use the first part of the book as a one-term introduction to the key ideas. The
  first five chapters should receive most of the attention inasmuch as they examine
  basic ideas like elementary representation, symbolic constraint exploitation,
  search, and control. These can be followed by selected topics from the next four
  chapters which deal with understanding natural language, representing
  common sense meaning, computer vision, and expert problem solving.

- Use the second part of the book as a one-term course on LISP, its uses, and
  derived language concepts like those in PLANNER and CONNIVER.

- Take advantage of the correspondence between the programs described in the
  first and second part of the book to make a one-year, two-term sequence. Some
  may prefer to do Part Two first.

- Treat the ideas and the programs which support them simultaneously, doing
  material from Parts One and Two alternately. One way to do this is to treat
  the concepts from Part One in lectures and the programming in Part Two in
  smaller group meetings. Using this scheme the first three chapters of Part One
  can be done in parallel with the first three of Part Two. Then Chapter 4 and
  Chapter 13, both on search, mesh nicely. Finally, Chapter 5 on control and
  Chapter 6 on language dovetail with Chapter 15 on interpreting Production
  Systems and compiling Augmented Transition Networks. The parallel scheme,
  by bringing material from the remaining chapters, again becomes a two-term,
  one-year sequence.

P.H.W.

ACKNOWLEDGEMENTS

The drawings in this book are by Suzin Jabari.

The cover design is by Karen Prendergast.

The book was set through the courtesy of Information International, Incorporated, Culver City, California. Robert Woodham made it possible to use the author's computer-prepared magnetic tapes with Information International's high-quality typesetting systems.

The following people helped by offering suggestions about content or style: Thomas O. Binford, Richard Brown, Daniel Chester, Max Clowes, Randy Davis, John Donovan, Edward Feigenbaum, Tim Finin, Ken Forbus, Edward Fredkin, Eugene Freuder, Jim Gillogly, Ira Goldstein, Carl Hewitt, Berthold K. P. Horn, Margareta Hornell, Mark Kahrs, Eva I. Kampits, Mark Lavin, Tomas Lozano-Perez, Alan Mackworth, Stavros Macrakis, William A. Martin, Drew McDermott, David McDonald, Marvin Minsky, Allen Newell, Nils Nilsson, Paul Okunieff, Richard Rosenberg, Neil Rowe, Ried Smith, Guy Steele, Steve Tanimoto, David Waltz, and Milt Waxman.

A willingness to help is not an implied endorsement, of course.

CONTENTS

5 CONTROLLING ATTENTION

6 THE MEANING OF MEANING

PART TWO

10 UNDERSTANDING PROGRAMMING

11 BASIC LISP PROGRAMMING

17 PROBLEMS TO THINK ABOUT

1
THE
INTELLIGENT
COMPUTER

This book is an introductory textbook for a new field which has come to be called Artificial Intelligence. The purpose of this first chapter is to explain why knowing about Artificial Intelligence is important, to outline the field, and to give some examples of what progress has been made.

THE FIELD AND THE BOOK

Artificial Intelligence is the study of ideas which enable computers to do the things that make people seem intelligent. But then, what is human intelligence? Is it the ability to reason? Is it the ability to acquire and apply knowledge? Is it the ability to manipulate and communicate ideas? Surely all of these abilities are part of what intelligence is, but they are not the whole of what can be said. Indeed, a definition in the usual sense seems impossible because intelligence appears to be an amalgam of so many information-processing and information-representation talents.

Nevertheless, one can define the goals of the field of Artificial Intelligence:

■   The central goals of Artificial Intelligence are to make computers more useful and to understand the principles which make intelligence possible.

Since one goal is to make computers more useful, computer scientists and engineers need to know how Artificial Intelligence can help them solve difficult problems. And since the other goal is to understand general intelligence better for its own sake, psychologists, philosophers, linguists, and other people who want to understand human intelligence also need to know and evaluate what is learned. The purpose of this book is to provide all of these people with a picture of what is going on. Thankfully no special background is required, not even computer programming experience or sophisticated mathematical training.

1

Smarter Computers Can Help Solve Some of the Problems of Today's World

Do we really need to make our computers smarter? It seems so. Everyone knows we must use our energy, food, and human resources wisely, and we must have high-quality help from computers to do it. As the world grows more complex, the computers must help not only by doing ordinary computing, but also by doing computing that exhibits intelligence.

It is easy to think of applications in tomorrow's world which seem like science fiction by today's standards. Here are a few:

- In farming, computers should control pests, prune trees, and enable selective harvesting of mixed crops.
- In mining, computers should work where the conditions are too dangerous for people, and they should recover the manganese nodules from the bottom of the sea.
- In manufacturing, computers should be doing assembly and inspection jobs of all kinds.
- In offices, computers should schedule people and groups, refer problems to the right people, summarize news, and polish draft documents, freeing them of spelling and grammatical errors.
- In schools, computers should consider their students' problems as bugs to be fixed, and they should provide students with computerized superbooks in which microprocessors display orbiting planets and play musical scores.
- In hospitals, computers should help with diagnosis, monitor patients, manage treatment, and make beds.
- In households, computers should give advice on cooking and shopping, care for the floors and lawn, do the laundry, and deal with maintenance.

Certainly none of these things are possible now, but Artificial Intelligence can help make them possible.

Understanding Computer Intelligence Is a Way to Study General Intelligence

Artificial Intelligence enthusiasts believe that using computers to understand the central issues and the dimensions of intelligence is a powerful addition to the traditional methods of psychology, philosophy, and linguistics. Here are some reasons for their commitment:

- Computers invite experiment. Computers are ideal experimental subjects. They exhibit unlimited patience, they require no feeding, and they do not bite. Moreover, it is usually simple to deprive a computer program of some piece of knowledge in order to test how important that piece really is. It is impossible to carve up animals' brains with the same precision.

■ Computer science offers rich metaphors. Work with computers has led to a rich new language for talking about how to do things and how to describe things. Metaphorical and analogical use of the concepts involved enables more powerful thinking about thinking.

■ Computer models are precise. Implementing a theory uncovers conceptual mistakes and oversights that ordinarily escape even the most meticulous researchers. Often major roadblocks appear that were not even recognized as problems at all before beginning the cycle of thinking and experimenting.

■ Computer theories bound task requirements. Once a program performs a task, statements can be made about how much information processing the task requires. In general these are upper bounds since there is rarely any way of guaranteeing that no better idea can make the job easier.

Note that wanting to make computers *be* intelligent is not the same as wanting to make computers *simulate* intelligence. Artificial Intelligence excites people who want to uncover principles that apply to all intelligent information processors, not just those that happen to be made of wet nervous tissue instead of dry electronic gadgetry. Consequently, there is neither an obsession with mimicking human intelligence nor a prejudice against using methods that seem involved in human intelligence. The overall result is a new point of view which brings along a new methodology and leads to new theories.

One result of this new point of view may be new ideas about how to help people become more intelligent. Just as psychological knowledge about human information processing can help make computers intelligent, theories derived purely with computers in mind often suggest possibilities for how to educate people better. Said another way, the methodology involved in making smart computer programs may transfer to making smart people.

The Chapters of the Book Cover the Basic Ideas of the Field

To understand Artificial Intelligence or work in the field, one must understand basic ideas for organizing knowledge, exploiting constraints, searching spaces, and controlling attention. Chapters 2 through 5 of this book are directed at defining and explaining these basics:

Chapter 2, recognizing analogies and learning simple concepts. Everyone knows that hard problems often look simple from a different point of view. The need for good ways of describing problems is therefore familiar. This chapter illustrates the point in a computer intelligence context by explaining a computer program that does geometric analogy problems and a program which learns to identify toy-block structures.

Chapter 3, exploiting natural constraints. Once essential facts are well described, constraints may emerge that make solving problems easy. This is true of problems in basic algebra, for example. In this chapter, the constraints limit how lines can fit together in drawings and how words can fit together in sentences.

Chapter 4, exploring alternatives. Sometimes there is no way to solve a problem without exploring some alternative routes to a solution. Useful examples are the problems involved in traversing various kinds of mazes and the problems involved in playing games like chess and checkers.

Chapter 5, controlling attention. The problem of searching interacts strongly with the problem of passing attention around a computer problem solver's internal collection of methods. In this chapter the focus turns directly to the question of attention, and we consider two well-known paradigms — the General Problem-Solver paradigm and the Production-System paradigm — in an effort to establish some useful techniques.

Given that the basic ideas of these chapters provide some of the information-processing strength needed to produce intelligent behavior, the next question is: How can they be combined into task-oriented computer programs? Chapters 5 through 9 look at this question by concentrating on how computers can be made to converse in human language, know common sense things, see the world, and solve difficult problems expertly:

Chapter 6, the meaning of meaning. For a computer to deal with a sentence it is sometimes necessary to translate the sentence into an internal description suited to solving some problem. We will look at what is needed to do this in the context of a world consisting of toy blocks in order to work on some of the problems of natural language.

Chapter 7, representing knowledge in frames. To really understand language seems to require considerable common-sense knowledge of the world, including knowledge about how people interact with each other. The representation schemes studied in previous chapters are not adequate, it seems, and a better one is investigated here.

Chapter 8, points of view on vision. Better representation seems to be the key to computer understanding of visual images as well as to computer understanding of language. To really get very far with vision, it is also necessary to be serious about the way light is reflected from surfaces.

Chapter 9, knowledge engineering and teaching people thinking. Good applications make any science more exciting. To close the first part of the book, we look first at one program that helps with a form of medical diagnosis and another that does a certain kind of chemical analysis. Then, having suggested that the principles behind intelligent programs constitute something that could be called knowledge engineering, we see how programming ideas can be introduced usefully into elementary education.

One reason to be optimistic about future progress in all of these areas lies in the fact that basic ideas find frequent application. Thus the basic ideas are a channel for cross fertilization. A good idea about vision soon supports progress on expert problem solving, and vice versa.

Moreover, there is help from outside. Many disciplines contribute ideas to this new field. Since intelligence requires so many strengths, the problems faced in many established disciplines intersect the natural concerns of people doing Artificial Intelligence. Linguistics, Pattern Recognition, Decision Theory, and Automatic Theorem Proving are such disciplines with important things to say. None of these particular four is stressed in this book, however, for two reasons: each is a well-developed field deserving full book treatment, not just a one-chapter precis; and each requires a mathematical background which is not presumed here.

One contribution to the field that should be understood, however, is Artificial Intelligence's computer programming heritage. To understand the ideas introduced in the first nine chapters in depth, there is a need to see some of them embodied in program form. A study of LISP, with examples drawn from the earlier material, addresses that need.

Chapter 10, understanding programming. This is a discussion of why programming is important and what can be learned from doing it.

Chapter 11, basic LISP programming. Next comes an introduction to the LISP programming language and the idea of symbol manipulation.

Chapter 12, the blocks world. The purpose of this chapter is to display an example of goal-oriented programming as well as to explain something about the manipulation of property lists. The sample program makes plans for moving toy blocks from one place to another, taking care to move obstructions when necessary. Automatic answering of questions about goals and data-driven programming are also described.

Chapter 13, the games world. Some search strategies from the earlier search chapter are implemented with a view toward further exposition of both the search strategies and the recursion involved in programs that implement them.

Chapter 14, symbolic pattern matching. Programming becomes much easier and more efficient if symbolic pattern matching is provided. Here we see how to implement a matching program, partly in order to exercise LISP and partly for its own sake. Included is a sample toy program that solves high school algebra problems given in simple English.

Chapter 15, implementing embedded languages. Matching is very important in natural language as well as elsewhere, but the matching must be fairly sophisticated. This chapter begins by showing how to do part of the job by embedding an Augmented-Transition-Network matching language in LISP. Then a Production-System interpreter is implemented as another example of embedding a language in LISP, thereby giving more perspective on the general process of creating higher-level languages.

Chapter 16, data bases and demons. Triggering programs on the basis of traffic into and out of a warehouse of facts has become an important feature of popular languages embedded in LISP like PLANNER, CONNIVER, and PLASMA.

WHAT COMPUTERS CAN DO

Having listed the ideas to be examined in this book, let us look at some representative examples of what computers can do once they are programmed using such ideas. Be cautious, however! It is as easy to become a rabid believer as it is to remain dogmatically pessimistic. Much remains to be discovered, and when talking about what computers can do, it is often appropriate to preface claims with "To some extent..." In most cases basic research is only now becoming engineering practice.

Computers Can Do Geometric Analogy Intelligence Tests

Figure 1-1 shows an example typical of the analogy problems that appear on intelligence tests. The person being tested must identify the answer figure that best fits the relation, A is to B as C is to X. Evans wrote a program capable of high-school-level performance. Its success demonstrates the role of good, purposeful descriptions. This program, as well as many others in this section, will be explained later.

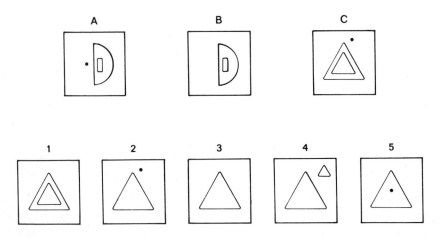

Figure 1-1 Evans' analogy program easily handles this problem, reporting that 1 is the best answer. The program, written in the early 1960s, performs at high-school-sophomore level.

Computers Can Learn

Several programs now demonstrate learning talent. One learns new concepts from sequences like the one shown in figure 1-2 for learning about arches. Another by Lenat deals with concepts like multiplication, factorization, and prime number. It

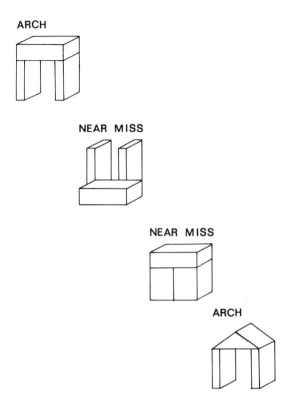

Figure 1-2 Winston's concept-learning program learns about arches from a series of samples. The program decides that an arch is a brick or wedge that must be supported by two bricks which do not touch.

demonstrates that a program can invent mathematics that even some professional mathematicians find interesting and exciting. In particular, Lenat's system stumbled across the obscure idea of maximally divisible numbers, even though Lenat himself, and evidently most other mathematicians, had never thought about them before. The powerful mathematician Ramanujan had, however, so Lenat's program is in distinguished company.

    Other representative examples of learning focus on the acquisition of procedural knowledge. One system, conceived by Fikes, Hart, and Nilsson, makes more and more complicated plans for a robot which pushes boxes, opens doors, and switches lights. It works by recalling and adapting old plans for new situations. Other systems by Sussman and by Goldstein learn by debugging almost correct programs.

Computers Can Understand Simple Drawings

Equipped with television cameras, computers can see well enough to deal with the world of toy blocks. They make conclusions about what kinds of objects are present, what relations exist between them, and what groups they form. These programs note that the scene in figure 1-3 consists of eight objects, including three which form an arch in the middle foreground. They further observe that to the left of the arch is a wedge, and to the right is a distorted brick with a hole, and a three-object tower stands in the background.

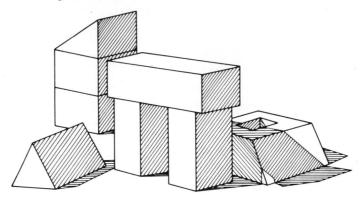

Figure 1-3 Waltz' scene-understanding program uses knowledge about possible vertex configurations to categorize lines. Typical scenes have cracks, shadows, boundaries, concave lines, and convex lines. (From *The Psychology of Computer Vision*, by Patrick H. Winston, copyright 1975 by McGraw-Hill Book Company, New York. Used with permission of McGraw-Hill Book Company and Patrick H. Winston.)

Creating this capability already requires a broad spectrum of ideas about image constraints, knowledge representation, problem solving, and sophisticated control structures. Understanding scenes with curved objects is more difficult, but progress is being made.

Computers Can Understand Simple English

There are now several programs that appear capable of distinguished dialogue on restricted subjects: Winograd's deals with the toy-blocks world, Woods' with Moon rocks. Sample interaction with Winograd's system is given later in a section on language understanding.

Computers Can Do Expert Problem Solving

Mathematics is the first domain requiring intelligence in which computers achieved expert performance. Computers can do arithmetic at unbelievable speed, of course. Slagle showed they can do much more in his classic program for integral calculus. Slagle's program accepts integration problems and produces answer expressions as in the example of figure 1-4. It is simple enough to serve as a programming example even though it comfortably handles problems from university-level examinations. Recent programs, like the one in M.I.T.'s MACSYMA system, do even better because they have more and better knowledge. No human can compete with them.

$$\int \frac{x^4}{(1-x^2)^{5/2}} \ dx \ =$$

$$\text{arcsin } x \ + \ \tfrac{1}{3}\tan^3 (\text{arcsin } x) - \tan(\text{arcsin } x)$$

Figure 1-4 Slagle's integration program, now obsolete, was an early success. Performance is equal to that of very good college freshmen. Newer programs have no human peers.

Feigenbaum and his colleagues also have demonstrated fine examples of computer problem solving competence. One system of programs, DENDRAL, understands mass spectrograms well enough to interpret data like that in figure 1-5 with the skill of graduate students in organic chemistry. Another system, MYCIN, is intended to help physicians diagnose and treat certain bacterial infections. Preliminary tests of MYCIN indicate better-than-average performance moving toward the level of human specialists.

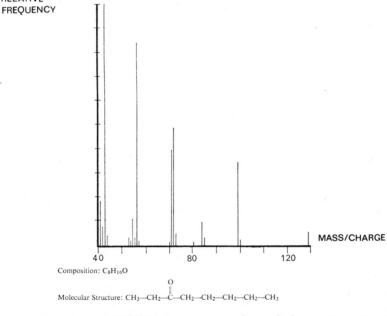

Composition: $C_8H_{16}O$

Molecular Structure: CH_3—CH_2—$\overset{\overset{O}{\|}}{C}$—$CH_2$—$CH_2$—$CH_2$—$CH_2$—$CH_3$

Figure 1-5 Feigenbaum's DENDRAL, a program for analyzing mass spectrogram data, accepts mass spectrograms and chemical formulas and finds molecular structures. The program does specialist quality work. (From "Heuristic DENDRAL" by Buchanan, Sutherland, and Feigenbaum, *Machine Intelligence 4,* copyright 1969 by American Elsevier Publishing Company, New York. Used with permission of Donald Michie, Editor-in-Chief, Machine Intelligence Series, University of Edinburgh, Scotland.)

Sussman and Stallman have created still another advanced program, this one capable of understanding electronic circuits. Their program reaches conclusions about a diagram like the one in figure 1-6 using human-like reasoning, rather than brute-force attack on the network equations. An advantage lies in the system's ability to talk about what it has done in terms human engineers can understand.

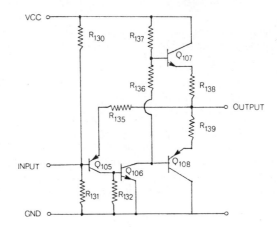

Figure 1-6 Sussman's and Stallman's circuit-understanding program uses human-like reasoning to determine network voltages and currents. Its explanations of complicated electronic devices are in terms that are easily understood by electrical engineers. (From "Heuristic Techniques in Computer-Aided Circuit Analysis" by Gerald Sussman and Richard Stallman, *IEEE Transactions on Circuits and Systems,* vol. CAS-22, no. 11, November, 1975, copyright 1975 by the Institute of Electrical and Electronics Engineers, New York. Used with permission of the Institute of Electrical and Electronics Engineers.)

Computers Can Do Useful Industrial Work

It is fortunate that computers may eventually do work that people increasingly refuse to do — jobs that are dirty, dangerous, demeaning, hopelessly boring, or poorly rewarded. As society advances, such jobs must be done by flexible, intelligent systems or by an armamentarium of specially built machines using brute force methods. So far the special machines dominate. Hardly anyone has shoes made to order even though one person's two feet rarely indicate the same shoe size. Tailor-made suits similarly give way to the standard item off the rack.

Although the assembly shown in figure 1-7 hardly resembles shoes or a suit, it nevertheless symbolizes an alternative to production line uniformity. An eight-piece radial-bearing assembly is shown under construction by a computer-controlled, variation-tolerant arm and hand. Curiously, only simple programming ideas are needed. By feeling what it is working with, the computer has less need to work with strictly uniform parts, deadly accurate assembly machinery, and elaborate jigs, clamps, and vises.

Figure 1-7 Inoue's mechanical assembly program uses force sensing to handle tight, 12 micrometer tolerances.

Computers Can Model Psychological Processes

Some psychologists work on Artificial Intelligence because they want to understand human thought from an information-processing point of view. Associative concept memory is one area studied. Another is human problem solving involving models which illuminate such short-term memory phenomena as chunking, latency, and overflow. Such models are tested using both programs and people as the experimental subjects.

Of course it is possible to exploit the similarities of human and computer intelligence in another way by noting that if computers and people must depend on the same fundamentals to be intelligent, then intelligent computer programs must be a rich source of metaphors and analogies relevant to studying and increasing natural intelligence. Many believe that the methodology involved in making smart programs transfers to making smart people.

SUMMARY

■ Artificial Intelligence has tremendous potential for applications in many socially relevant areas. Leaders in a wide variety of fields need to know its ideas.

■ As a means for studying intelligence, working with computers offers certain clear advantages. Theories so developed are more likely to be precise and they provide bounds on the information processing required.

■ There are several dimensions along which intelligent behavior can be displayed. These are made possible by strength in information handling capability associated with certain basic areas. Knowledge representation is perhaps the most important. Others are constraint exploitation, search, and control.

■ Computers can already do many things that seem to require some intelligence. They can solve many problems like experts, reason geometrically, solve problems in mathematics, learn simple concepts, understand simple drawings, engage in simple dialogue, and do useful work.

REFERENCES

Most of the work cited in this chapter will be discussed and referenced in more detail later.

■ Gerald Jay Sussman and Richard Matthew Stallman, "Heuristic Techniques in Computer Aided Circuit Analysis," *IEEE Transactions on Circuits and Systems,* vol. CAS-22, no. 11, November 1975.

■ B. Buchanan, G. Sutherland, and E. A. Feigenbaum, "Heuristic DENDRAL: A Program for Generating Explanatory Hypotheses in Organic Chemistry," in *Machine Intelligence 4,* American Elsevier, New York, 1969.

■ Randall Davis, Bruce Buchanan, and Edward Shortliffe, "Production Rules as a Representation for a Knowledge-Based Consultation Program," AIM-266, The Artificial Intelligence Laboratory, Stanford University, Stanford, California, 1975. A good overview of work on the MYCIN program for medical diagnosis and treatment of certain bacterial infections.

■ Thomas G. Evans, "A Heuristic Program to Solve Geometric Analogy Problems," PhD thesis, in *Semantic Information Processing,* edited by Marvin Minsky, The M.I.T. Press, Cambridge, Massachusetts, 1968.

■ James R. Slagle, "A Heuristic Program that Solves Symbolic Integration Problems in Freshman Calculus," in *Computers and Thought,* edited by Edward A. Feigenbaum and Julian Feldman, McGraw-Hill Book Company, New York, 1963.

■ Richard Bogen *et al, MACSYMA Reference Manual,* Laboratory of Computer Science, Massachusetts Institute of Technology, Cambridge, Massachusetts, 1975. Details about the state-of-the-art system developed by Joel Moses and William A. Martin and their group.

■ David Waltz, "Understanding Line Drawings of Scenes with Shadows," in *The Psychology of Computer Vision,* edited by Patrick Henry Winston, McGraw-Hill Book Company, New York, 1975.

■ Patrick Henry Winston, "Learning Structural Descriptions from Examples," PhD thesis, in *The Psychology of Computer Vision,* edited by Patrick Henry Winston, McGraw-Hill Book Company, New York, 1975.

■ Richard E. Fikes, Peter E. Hart, and Nils J. Nilsson, "Learning and Executing Generalized Robot Plans," *Artificial Intelligence,* vol. 3, 1972.

■ Gerald Sussman, *A Computer Model of Skill Acquisition,* PhD thesis, American Elsevier, New York, 1975.

■ Ira P. Goldstein, "Summary of MYCROFT: A System for Understanding Simple Picture Programs," *Artificial Intelligence,* vol. 6, no. 3, 1975.

■ Terry Winograd, *Understanding Natural Language,* PhD thesis, Academic Press, New York, 1972.

■ William A. Woods and R. M. Kaplan, "The Lunar Sciences Natural Language Information System," BBN Report No. 2265, Bolt, Beranek and Newman Inc., Cambridge, Massachusetts, 1971.

■ Hirochika Inoue, "Force Feedback in Precise Assembly Tasks," AI-M-308, The Artificial Intelligence Laboratory, Massachusetts Institute of Technology, Cambridge, Massachusetts, 1974.

■ A. P. Ambler, H. G. Barrow, C. M. Brown, R. M. Burstall and R. J. Popplestone, "A Versatile System for Computer Controlled Assembly," *Artificial Intelligence,* vol. 6, no. 2, 1975. This particular paper by the Edinburgh group is a good introduction to many of the difficult issues involved in putting intelligent computers into assembly work. A number of laboratories around the world have serious efforts aimed at this kind of productivity technology. Those at Stanford, Stanford Research Institute, M.I.T., Edinburgh, and Japan's Electro-Technical Institute are particularly interested in exploiting the ideas of computer intelligence.

■ Peter H. Lindsay and Donald A. Norman, *Human Information Processing,* Academic Press, New York, 1972. A great introductory psychology textbook with an emphasis on ideas of the sort championed by people in Artificial Intelligence.

■ Allen Newell and Herbert A. Simon, *Human Problem Solving,* Prentice-Hall, Englewood Cliffs, New Jersey, 1972.

■ Seymour Papert and Cynthia Solomon, "Twenty Things to do with a Computer," AI-M-248, The Artificial Intelligence Laboratory, Massachusetts Institute of Technology, Cambridge, Massachusetts, 1971.

There are now a number of textbooks on Artificial Intelligence. Like this book, each of the others expresses a point of view by choosing to focus on a characteristic collection of tools and issues.

■ Nils J. Nilsson, *Problem-Solving Methods in Artificial Intelligence,* McGraw-Hill Book Company, New York, 1971. A good book, albeit somewhat narrow in the light of subsequent work. Nilsson's concentration on search and theorem proving makes his book and this one nicely complementary.

■ Richard Duda and Peter Hart, *Pattern Recognition and Scene Analysis,* Wiley, New York, 1973. The first half of this book is a good introduction to pattern recognition, and the second is a good introduction to the artificial intelligence of scene understanding.

■ Phillip C. Jackson, *Introduction to Artificial Intelligence,* Mason and Lipscomb, New York, 1974. A broad survey-style book touching on many topics.

■ Earl B. Hunt, *Artificial Intelligence,* Academic Press, New York, 1975. Hunt's book is distinguished in part by its stress on statistical pattern recognition and theorem proving.

■ Bertram Raphael, *The Thinking Computer,* W. H. Freeman, San Francisco, 1976. An interesting, easy-to-read introduction.

There are also several collections which contain much valuable material. The following are representative:

- Edward A. Feigenbaum and Julian Feldman, *Computers and Thought,* McGraw-Hill Book Company, New York, 1963.

- Marvin Minsky, *Semantic Information Processing,* The M.I.T. Press, Cambridge, Massachusetts, 1968.

- Rodger Schank and Kenneth Colby, *Computer Models of Thought and Language,* W. H. Freeman, San Francisco, 1973.

- Daniel G. Bobrow and Allan Collins, *Representation and Understanding,* Academic Press, New York, 1975.

- Patrick H. Winston, *The Psychology of Computer Vision,* McGraw-Hill Book Company, New York, 1975.

- Yorick Wilks and Eugene Charniak, *Computational Semantics,* North Holland, Amsterdam, 1976.

There is, in addition, a series of books with titles of the form *Machine Intelligence —,* edited by Bernard Meltzer and/or Donald Michie, and published by American Elsevier, New York.

2 RECOGNIZING ANALOGIES AND LEARNING SIMPLE CONCEPTS

A representation is a set of conventions about how to describe things. We will see that thinking seriously about intelligent behavior of any sort requires thinking seriously about what representation is best suited to the domain in which the intelligent behavior is exhibited. Indeed, this chapter's principal purpose is to demonstrate the central importance of finding good representations capable of bearing good descriptions.

The chapter's secondary purpose is to introduce theories of geometric-analogy problem solving and of elementary learning. These particular examples are used because they show that simple representations, couching simple descriptions, can produce interesting behavior. More complicated representations will be introduced from time to time throughout the book.

REPRESENTATION ALTERNATIVES

We will take up analogy and learning presently. First, two general points about representing knowledge deserve stress.

There Is a Spectrum of Representation Alternatives

Usually knowledge is in the form of collections of facts describing either concrete physical objects or less tangible abstractions. Alternatively, the knowledge may be in the form of programs if the knowledge is intimately tied up with performing some process. This powerful notion of procedural description will come to center stage later. The illustrations of this chapter stick to two nonprocedural representations: assertion collections and semantic nets.

Representations Vary in Power Considerably

In some *un*interesting theoretical sense, all representations are equivalent in that they all are imbedded ultimately in the symbolic structures available in some computer language like LISP and thence down into arrangements of bits in memory. In a practical sense, however, some representations emphasize things that are important to solving a class of problems. One scheme, therefore, is more powerful than another because it offers more convenience to the user even though both can do the job theoretically. *Convenience,* however, is perhaps too weak a word. In general, the much greater perspicuity and the inherent thinking aids that come with the more powerful representations enable research progress that would be impossibly difficult with anything less adequate. People familiar with basic computer science will understand that the word *power* is used in the same sense as it is when one says a computer equipped with a high-level programming language is more powerful than one with only a basic assembler. In an uninteresting theoretical sense, both are, after all, Turing-machine equivalents.

ANALOGY INTELLIGENCE TESTS

Geometric analogy problems like the one in figure 2-1 are typical of those that appear on human intelligence tests and typical of those solved routinely by a computer program finished in 1963. The problem is to select some answer figure, X, such that A is to B as C is to X gives the best fit. Or said in another way, we are after the rule describing how C becomes some X which most closely matches the rule describing how A becomes B. The key to doing such problems lies in good descriptions of the rules. Once we have such descriptions, working the problems

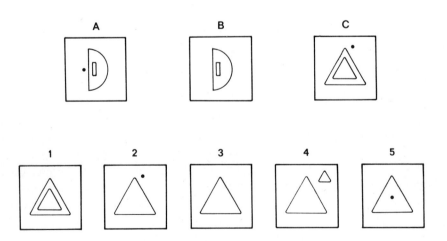

Figure 2-1 A typical input for Evans' geometric analogy problem program.

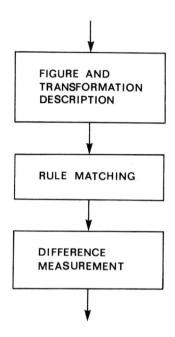

Figure 2-2 Evans' program consists of three important modules.

becomes a simple matter of matching rule descriptions together and keeping track of some measure of similarity. We therefore think of the analogy process as consisting of the three fundamental modules shown in figure 2-2.

The Rules Consist of a Three-Part Table

The rules describe how one figure, the source, becomes another, the destination. The rules have three parts:

- A description of the source figure in terms of how the subfigures in it relate to one another. The possible relations are ABOVE, LEFT, and INSIDE.
- A description of the destination figure, again in terms of how the subfigures relate to one another.
- A description of how the subfigures in the source figure become changed in the destination figure. Typically a subfigure may become smaller, larger, rotated, reflected, or some combination of these things. Also possible are additions and deletions of subfigures.

Figure 2-3 shows a typical rule that has been translated from the form a computer would use internally to a form that is easy for people to read. Note that the labels *l, m,* and *n,* appear in both figures and in both descriptions. Placing these labels correctly is the job of a preliminary matching operation that identifies similar subfigures.

Note also that the changes in the relationships of the subfigures are locked up in the source and destination figure descriptions, part 1 and part 2 of the rule description. There is nothing explicit that says *n* has moved from inside *m* to the

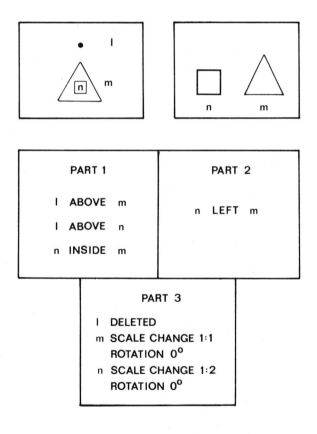

Figure 2-3 Evans' program constructs rule descriptions describing how A becomes B and how C becomes each of the given answer possibilities. The rules consist of three parts. Two describe relationships between subfigures, and one describes how subfigures change.

left of *m*. Changes in individual subfigures are given directly, however, and they are described in part 3. Soon we will see how all three parts contribute to solutions, but first we need to assure ourselves that the descriptions can be derived from the drawings.

Subfigure Relationships Are Simple

Given the particularly simple domain of two-dimensional geometric figures, finding the spatial relationship between one subfigure and another requires no sophistication. As shown in figure 2-4, a program computes the center of area of the two subfigures, imagines diagonal lines through the center of area of one of them, and notes which sector so defined contains the center of area of the other subfigure. Since the relationships used are symmetric, it is not necessary to note both left and right relationships: the relationship Y RIGHT-OF X is redundant, given that X LEFT-OF Y.

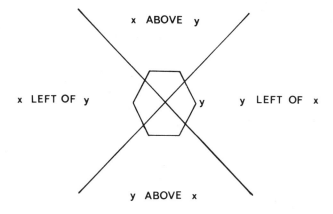

Figure 2-4 Relationships between subfigures are computed by comparing centers of gravity.

In deciding INSIDE is the existing relation rather than either LEFT-OF or ABOVE, the first step is to make sure that the subfigures do not touch. Then the description program constructs a line from any point on one figure to the drawing boundary in any direction as shown in figure 2-5. If the imaginary line intersects the second figure an odd number of times, then the second figure surrounds the first. Happily this method involves only line-intersection formulas, and it works even if the figures are extremely convoluted.

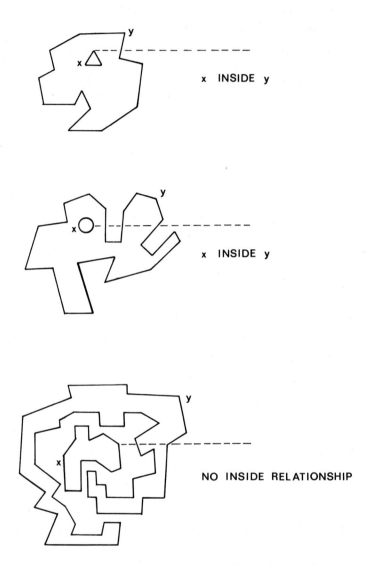

Figure 2-5 One subfigure is judged to be inside another if a line drawn to infinity crosses the boundaries of the alleged surrounding subfigure an odd number of times.

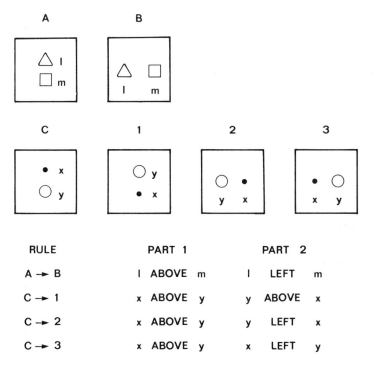

Figure 2-6 Only subfigure descriptions are relevant to this problem; subfigure changes are not. Examination of the rules verifies that 3 is the best answer.

Part 1 and Part 2 Concentrate on Subfigure Relationships

We have seen how relationships among subfigures are specified by part 1 and part 2 of each rule. The example in figure 2-6 is contrived so as to involve only part 1 and part 2. Part 3 is not relevant because no subfigures are altered in the move from source figure to destination figure.

It is clear that the best matching rule is rule 3, since if we associate *l* with *x* and *m* with *y*, the two match exactly. Note however that there is no a priori reason to associate *l* with *x* rather than with *y*. In going from source figure to destination figure, we do indeed want to be sure that squares go to squares, circles to circles, triangles to triangles and so on. But this need to match one subfigure to a similar one does not hold in comparing two rules. In the example, answer figure 3 is to be selected even though the subfigures in A and B are a triangle and a square, whereas in C and in all the answer figures, the subfigures are a circle and a dot. In general the matching program must try all possible ways of associating the variables together when matching up rules. In the example we have both

$$l \longrightarrow x \qquad\qquad l \quad\quad x$$
$$\text{and} \quad \times$$
$$m \longrightarrow y \qquad\qquad m \quad\quad y$$

This one-for-one association of variables implies that the number of subfigures undergoing change must be the same in both of the two rules being matched. This is true also of the number of additions and deletions. Any attempt to match two rules for which the numbers are different fails automatically. This means that in the problem shown in figure 2-7, 3 wins immediately by default, as 3 is the only answer figure with the same number of subfigures as B, and hence the rule describing the relationship between C and 3 is the only one that can possibly match the A to B rule.

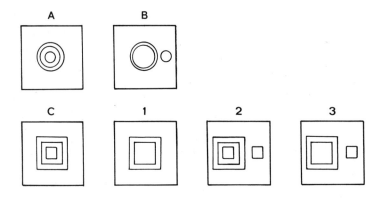

Figure 2-7 Variable matching between rules cannot begin unless B and the answer figure have the same number of subfigures. Answer 1 and answer 2 are rejected for this reason, leaving 3 as the only choice.

If n subfigures move from the source figure to the destination figure in each of two rules being compared, there will be $n!$ ways of associating the variables together in searching for the best way to match the rules. More generally, if n_1 subfigures are changed, n_2 are added, and n_3 deleted, in going to the destination figure, then the number of possible associations is $n_1! \times n_2! \times n_3!$. Each must be tried.

Rule Part 3 Concentrates on Subfigure Changes

Since there was no possible influence from part 3 of the transformation rules, we could concentrate on part 1 and part 2. Similarly, the problem in figure 2-8 allows concentration on part 3 alone. Since there is never more than one subfigure, there can be no relations between subfigures, and part 1 and part 2 can contribute nothing to the results. Using part 3 generates an immediate solution since only answer figure 1 corresponds to a simple 45° rotation with no scale change.

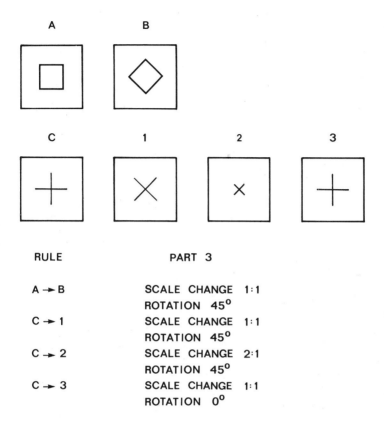

RULE	PART 3	
A → B	SCALE CHANGE	1:1
	ROTATION	45°
C → 1	SCALE CHANGE	1:1
	ROTATION	45°
C → 2	SCALE CHANGE	2:1
	ROTATION	45°
C → 3	SCALE CHANGE	1:1
	ROTATION	0°

Figure 2-8 Since each figure has only one subfigure, rule part 1 and part 2 are completely empty. Answer 1 is correctly selected using part 3 only.

A Simple Scoring Mechanism Compares the Rules

How should the similarity of two rules be measured? So far the problems have been so simple that the best answer rule matches the A to B rule exactly. But if an exact match cannot be found, then it is necessary to use a score-keeping mechanism. One way to do this is to count the number of individual entries in the two rules that are identical — that is, to find the size of the intersection of the two rules. Another idea is to find how much must be thrown out of the A to B rule in order that the remainder consists only of elements found in the rule compared with it. Curiously,

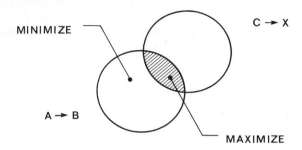

Figure 2-9 Rule differences are measured by degree of overlap. Answers are determined by finding the C to X rule with the maximum number of elements in common with the A to B rule. Finding the C to X rule which requires the least deletions from the A to B rule amounts to the same thing.

both of these different-sounding theories are equivalent, as demonstrated by the diagram in figure 2-9. Since the size of the circle representing the elements in the description of the A to B rule is fixed and is the same for all rule comparisons, finding the rule which maximally intersects with the A to B rule is equivalent to finding the rule which minimizes what must be thrown out of the A to B rule.

In order to tune the process a bit, various possibilities to be found in part 3 of the rule can be counted less strongly than the elements in part 1 and part 2. If each match of elements in part 1 and part 2 scores one point, then something like the scores shown in figure 2-10 works out well for adding in part 3 items to the total rule comparison score. A radically different set of numbers could reflect a different judgment about how the various possibilities should be ordered. The given set is

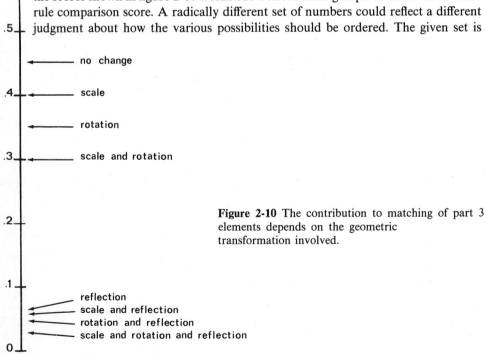

Figure 2-10 The contribution to matching of part 3 elements depends on the geometric transformation involved.

biased against reflections, but another might very well prefer reflections to rotations. The corresponding programs would occasionally disagree with one another about the answers!

Further Rule Refinement Is Needed

The technique developed so far is adequate for many analogy problems, but the one in figure 2-11 causes trouble. Matching the A to B rule with the C to 1 rule, x must be associated with l and y with m. Similarly for C to 2, the opposite pairing is forced and we have x associated with m and y with l. But note that under the associations given, both C to 1 and C to 2 give exact match against A to B. So far there is no way to capture the idea that going from A to B and from C to 1 is to remove the triangle.

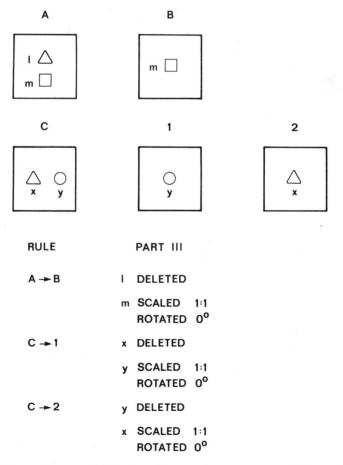

Figure 2-11 When rules are matched, the subfigures of one are paired with those of the other. The pairs need not consist of geometrically similar items, but if they do, the match receives some slight extra credit. For the problem shown, the two given answers tie without the extra credit. With it, answer 1 wins.

The trouble is that no attention is paid to whether the variables matched between rules correspond to similar geometric figures. Giving some extra credit to certain matches of one rule against another solves the problem. The extra credit goes to matches in which variables corresponding to similar subfigures are paired. Something like a bonus of .3 for each such pair works well. In this particular case, the C to 1 score would be augmented by .3, while the C to 2 score would stay the same. Thus 1 would be correctly selected as the best answer.

Subfigure Matches May Not Be Unique

So far the subfigures in the source and destination figures have been individual and distinct and there has been no problem in deciding how to form the rule describing the transformation. But in cases like the one in figure 2-12, there is ambiguity. Which of the two triangles has disappeared? Surely the larger one is gone. But has the smaller one been deleted and the larger shrunk?

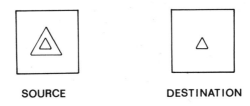

SOURCE   DESTINATION

Figure 2-12 Description variations are introduced when there is more than one instance of a subfigure. Here the large triangle may have been deleted, or alternatively, the small one may have been deleted and the large one shrunk.

In fact neither theory can be judged the superior without context from the rest of the problem. Consequently two rules should be constructed, one corresponding to each way the triangles in the source figure can be identified with triangles in the destination. Thus for each source and destination pair there may be many rules, and for each rule there may be many ways of matching it against another rule. Indeed for some problems, as many as forty or fifty rule-pair associations might be candidates for the highest matching score.

The Program Works Well

Examine figure 2-13. It shows some examples drawn from intelligence tests which are clearly within the grasp of the program.

In the first example, 3 is the correct answer, and 3 is indeed the only answer figure that the program seriously considers because 3 alone among the answer figures has the same number of subfigures as B has. Remember that requiring the same number of subfigures is an indirect consequence of permitting match only between rules for which the number of additions, deletions, and transformations are the same.

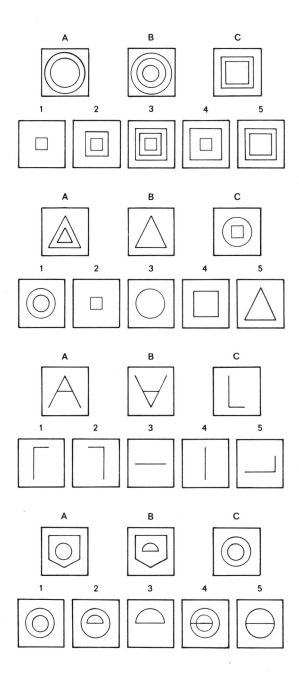

Figure 2-13 Some problems successfully solved by the geometric analogy program.

In the second example, the most reasonable theory about the rule for going from A to B is that the inside subfigure is deleted. The rule for C to 3 is the same and 3 would be selected by our process. But note that for the A to B rule, another theory would be that the outside figure is deleted and the inside one enlarged. Given this theory the correct answer would be 4. But since subfigure transformation descriptions involving change in scale score less than those in which there is no change at all, then 3 is the answer of choice, with 4 a close second. Answer 4 would be the clear winner if 3 were not present.

In the third example, the A to B rule could be described as either a rotation or a reflection, with 2 being the best answer if the process prefers rotations, and 1 if it likes reflections better. Rotations are preferred and 2 is judged best.

In the fourth example, the central subfigure seems to be truncated in going from A to B, but there is no way for the program to handle truncations, and if the program is to succeed, it must succeed through some other way of looking at the problem. Certainly answer figures 3, 4, and 5 are eliminated immediately from consideration since they do not have the proper number of subfigures. Only 1 and 2 are plausible. The C to 1 rule indicates that both subfigures are carried from the source to the destination and both are unchanged. In the C to 2 rule, however, there seems to be a deletion of the central circle and an addition of a half-circle, just as is the case in going from A to B. Answer 2 is therefore the best choice. Its selection is reinforced by the bonus points awarded when two rules are matched together for which the associated variables correspond to geometrically similar subfigures.

The Geometric-Analogy Process Demonstrates the Worth of Good Descriptions

For the geometric-analogy process, as with many others, there are several answers to the question of importance:

- The geometric-analogy program demonstrates the importance of good, purposeful description.
- It demonstrates a need for good description matching machinery.
- It demonstrates that computers can do things normally understood to require intelligence.

Particular processes are worth studying in detail because they demonstrate such general principles or because they serve as generalized metaphors which simplify the description and understanding of new problems. This is self-evident. Yet inability to say why something is important in a few words is a common bug in people. It is usually idle to know how something works without knowing why it is important. There is no effective substitute for always ready, brief *because* answers to the *why* questions.

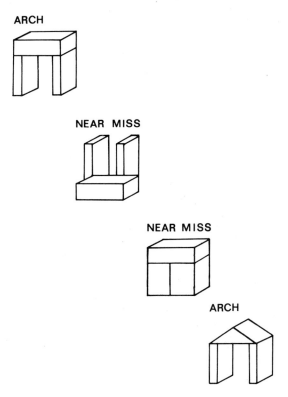

Figure 2-14 A learning sequence for the arch concept. The first sample conveys the general idea. The others reinforce it by emphasizing that there must be support, that the sides must not touch, and that the top need not be a brick.

LEARNING SIMPLE DESCRIPTIONS

Our next objective is to focus on description in the context of learning, showing that with good descriptions available, a program can learn from samples selected by a teacher.

In figure 2-14, the samples illustrate particulars of what we humans think of as an arch. (Properly speaking, the structure shown is a lintel and pair of posts, but for our purpose, that does not matter.) Note that the series starts with a typical arch. From it the computer derives a very general idea of what an arch is — the computer learns that an arch involves two standing bricks which together support a third brick lying on its side.

Each subsequent sample builds on this by driving home some particular point. In the second sample the computer sees the same objects as before but in a different configuration. It is told that the pieces no longer form an arch. Since the principal change is that the support relationships have disappeared, the computer concludes that the support relations must be an important aspect of the general arch concept. Note that this correct idea is conveyed by a single well-chosen sample rather than by extended training through a tedious statistical exercise.

In the third sample the two standing bricks touch. Again the computer is told that the structure is not an arch. Nothing else is significantly different from the first arch in the sample sequence. Evidently the standing bricks must not touch if there is to be an arch. Progress is made once again by way of a good sample and the knowledge that it is not an arch.

The teacher may or may not assert the fourth sample to be an example of an arch according to personal taste. If it is given as an arch, then the computer notes that having a brick on top is not essential. At the very least, either a brick or a wedge will do; it is even reasonable to guess that any simple parallelepiped is acceptable.

Networks Facilitate Better Description

There is a gulf between a rough scenario and the precise detail required to create a working program. To make this learning theory work, considerable strength is needed in the dimension of knowledge representation. The simple unordered listing of facts that served adequately in the world of geometric-analogy problems is not sufficiently perspicuous. We replace it with a scheme by which knowledge is recorded in the links and nodes in a network.

Suppose there is a wedge on top of a brick forming a sort of toy house as in figure 2-15. The objects and the nodes that represent them are labeled A and B so that the correspondence is clear. Both are represented by nodes. The fact that A is supported by B is carried by a labeled pointer between those nodes.

In general a description will contain information about individual objects as well as information about how they relate to one another. Hence there will be pointers like those in the second part of figure 2-15 indicating such properties as class membership. The terminology of sets could be used to name the pointers involved, but informal labels like IS-A are used instead because the informal terms are more comfortable to use, being closer to ordinary language.

So far, of course, the only gain over the straightforward listing of relationships used in the geometric-analogy representational system derives from the fact that the two-dimensional graph helps us perceive the way the relations are grouped together. Now, however, we go a small step further. In the third part of figure 2-15 the new pointers explicitly make note of the fact that the two objects are part of a whole. This introduces hierarchical grouping into our formalism, something definitely absent in the geometric-analogy program.

It Is Easy to Learn the Idea of a House

Already we have enough descriptive power to understand existing computer learning programs on a deeper level. Consider the problem of learning about a house, for example. It is important that there be a brick and a wedge and a support relationship between them. How can a computer learn these facts?

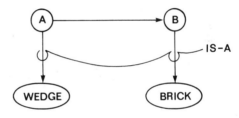

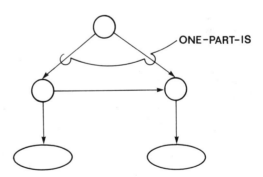

Figure 2-15 Scenes can be represented as networks of linked concepts. In the first network, two concept nodes are shown to be related by the **IS-SUPPORTED-BY** pointer. In the second network, the same nodes are connected by IS-A pointers to general concepts, **WEDGE** and **BRICK**. In the third network, ONE-PART-IS pointers tie the two nodes together and show that they are part of a single concept, an instance of a house.

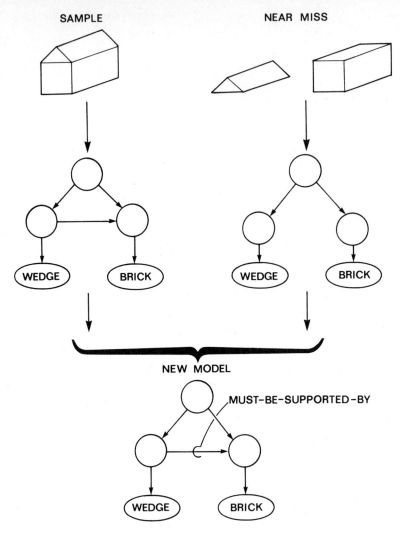

Figure 2-16 Giving an instance of a concept is always the first step in teaching it. Here an instance of a house is followed by a near miss wherein the support relation is gone.

To begin, the teacher shows a good typical example from which the computer derives an initial, unrefined model in the form of a network description as shown in the first part of figure 2-16.

Next the example shown in the second part of figure 2-16 teaches the importance of the support relation. This sample is not a house, but since it falls short of being a house only by a little, it will be called a near miss.

■ A *near miss* is a sample which does not qualify as an instance of the class being taught for some small number of reasons.

The description for the near miss indeed differs from the initial description of the house in one detail only: the **IS-SUPPORTED-BY** pointer is missing.

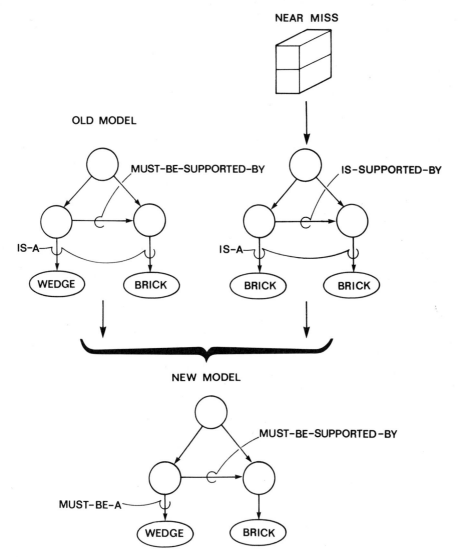

Figure 2-17 The fact that the top of a house must be a wedge is taught through a near miss wherein the top is something else.

Comparing the two descriptions leads naturally to the conclusion that the IS-SUPPORTED-BY pointer is *de rigueur* for a house. Thus the synthesis of the two descriptions is a new, refined model in which the IS-SUPPORTED-BY pointer is replaced by its emphatic form, MUST-BE-SUPPORTED-BY. Henceforward no configuration will be identified as a house unless there is an IS-SUPPORTED-BY pointer.

It is equally straightforward to give near-miss samples designed to convert the IS-A pointers into MUST-BE-A emphatics. Comparing the description of the brick on a brick in figure 2-17 with the model as developed so far does this job for the upper part of the house. From here it is easy to select near-miss samples that convert other pointers to emphatic forms as desired.

Descriptions and Near Misses Are Important

Two fundamental points bear emphasis:

■ To teach a new concept, it is important that both the teacher and the student can describe things properly in the domain in which the concept exists.

■ To teach a new concept, it is important that the teacher use near-misses as well as examples.

Keeping these ideas firmly in hand helps in understanding this learning theory in more complicated situations.

Learning about an Arch Requires More Elaborate Difference Handling

Sometimes a sample may differ from the current model by way of two very similar differences. This happened in the case of the arch. Let us take a second look at the arch-learning sequence in order to see how the ideas work at the level of differences between network descriptions.

Already in the initial sample and the first near-miss shown in figure 2-18 there are two differences, both of which involve a missing IS-SUPPORTED-BY pointer. A sensible reaction is to suppose the teacher intended the two differences and supposes they will be handled simultaneously and in the same way. Thus both IS-SUPPORTED-BY relations are replaced by MUST-BE-SUPPORTED-BY through the single sample.

The next near-miss, that of the second part of figure 2-18, similarly involves two differences of the same sort, namely two new TOUCH pointers relate the posts. Now, however, the near miss fails because pointers are added rather than subtracted. It must be that the new pointers should be forbidden. This is accomplished through the device of a negative emphatic, MUST-NOT-TOUCH.

So far each near miss restricts what can be an arch. Positive examples take the model the other way. Consider the final configuration with a wedge on top. If this is to be an arch, some change in the model should reflect a loosening of constraint. At the very least the IS-A connection between the top of the arch and BRICK should be cut away and replaced by an IS-A pointer to a more general class as shown in figure 2-19. Going for SIMPLE-RIGHT-PARALLELEPIPED represents a conservative position with respect to how much induction to allow on the basis of a single example. Figure 2-19 shows that there is a chain of more and more general concepts related to BRICK and WEDGE leading all the way to the universal THING category. The new target for the top's IS-A pointer could be anything along the chain of A-KIND-OF relations, depending on how impetuous the program wishes to be.

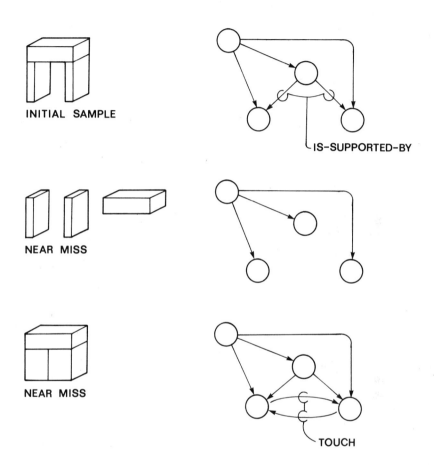

Figure 2-18 Teaching the arch concept begins with showing an arch example to convey the general idea. The first near miss brings out the importance of the support relations. Next, a near miss with touching sides shows that the sides must not touch. Both near misses involve two differences of the same kind which are handled together.

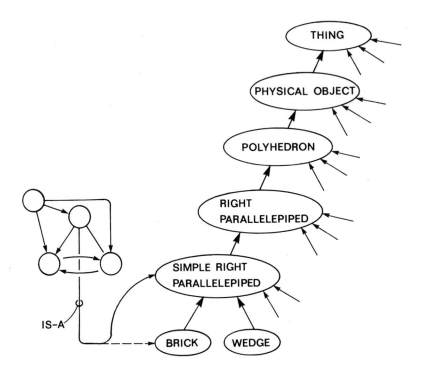

Figure 2-19 An example with the top brick replaced by a wedge moves the evolving model toward generality. The amount of generalization depends on how far up the A-KIND-OF chain the learning procedure goes.

There Are Only a Few Principal Difference Types

Categorized differences between descriptions drive the learning process. Another pass through the system uncovers still more detail. Consider the two simple network fragments in figure 2-20. The goal is to describe the difference between them. First it is necessary to match them up deciding how nodes in one network correspond to nodes in another. Once this has been done, once a matching program has succeeded in linking together pairs of nodes, then the description of differences can begin with the creation of a skeletal framework which reflects the common structure contained in both networks.

Next, individual differences are described by commentary hanging from the skeleton. One such commentary announces that one network exhibits a relationship which the other does not. This difference note, handily enough, has the same form as other nodes in the network. Figure 2-21 shows a skeleton and a difference note.

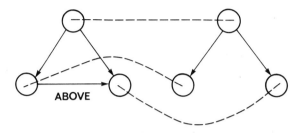

Figure 2-20 Building symbolic descriptions is the first step in learning from samples. Next, each sample description is matched with the model to bring out differences and similarities. The matching process attempts to pair up the nodes in two networks.

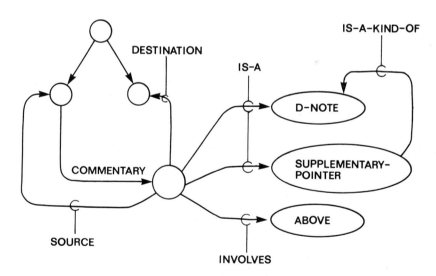

Figure 2-21 Successful match creates a two part result: a central skeleton reflects on how the two networks are similar, and a collection of difference notes comments on how they are different.

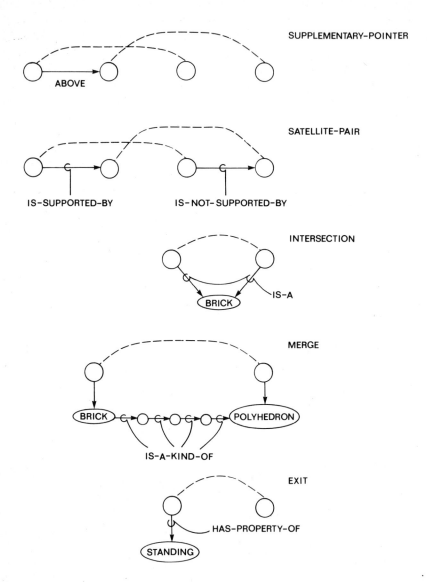

Figure 2-22 Many kinds of difference and similarity notes are possible, some of which are shown here.

Difference notes hang about the skeleton like grapes on a cluster. It is useful to have several types. Those illustrated and defined in figure 2-22 are convenient. Both SATELLITE-PAIRs and SUPPLEMENTARY-POINTERs deal with relationships between linked nodes in the two matched networks. The SATELLITE-PAIR could of course be handled by two separate SUPPLEMENTARY-POINTER connections, but in general it is sensible to explicitly demonstrate the closely related nature of such pairs. The other difference types deal with the relations that the linked nodes shoot out into the general plexus. INTERSECTION and MERGE differences actually reflect more in the way of similarity than difference. An EXIT, however, is a genuine difference in that one net extends a pointer while the other does not. Of course the particular pointers appearing in the difference examples are only representative — there are no particular restrictions on what they might be.

Now some important aspects of the description and learning processes can be expressed more crisply:

■ Differences between two scenes can be expressed in terms of a few types of difference notes describing the relationship between two networks: the SUPPLEMENTARY-POINTER, the SATELLITE-PAIR, the MERGE, the INTERSECTION, and the EXIT. These split into subcategories according to the specific pointers involved.

■ Learning happens when the skeleton and its difference notes are transformed into a new model. This is done in accordance with a small set of rules contained in a table.

Figure 2-23 gives the table of differences and responses to them. The table is not large. Note that some differences are subject to multiple interpretations. When such a difference is encountered, the first interpretation is assumed permanently unless some later information forces reconsideration.

Difference Description May Include General Commentary

Although the description devices introduced already are sufficient for many purposes, occasionally it is good to have some anchor for general commentary on the differences observed. It might be that only INTERSECTIONs are seen or perhaps only INTERSECTIONs and symmetry suggesting SATELLITE-PAIRs involving LEFT and RIGHT pointers. To include such observations is straightforward. The skeleton with the difference notes becomes half, rather than all of the difference description because it is complemented by a structure that gives more direct and organized access to the differences. As shown in figure 2-24, individual difference notes can be accessed either through the skeleton or through the difference commentary. This provides explicit organization of differences within the difference description, something the geometic-analogy program did not have.

Action of Concept Generator given a Near Miss

Situation	Response
Supplementary-Pointer or Exit appears in the Model	Replace Pointer by Must-Be Satellite
Supplementary-Pointer or Exit appears in the Near Miss	Place Must-Not-Be Satellite in Model
Supplementary-Pointer or Exit appears in the Model; Pointer is a Negative Satellite	Replace Pointer by Must-Not-Be Satellite
Supplementary-Pointer or Exit appears in the Near Miss; Pointer is a Negative Satellite	Place Must-Be Satellite in Model
Negative-Satellite Pair	Replace Pointer by Must-Be Satellite
Must-Not-Be-Satellite Pair	Do Nothing
Merge at Model's Node	Replace Pointer by Must-Not-Be Satellite to the Near Miss' Node
Merge at Near Miss' Node	Replace Pointer by Must-Be Satellite
Other Merge; First Option	Replace Pointer by Must-Not-Be Satellite to the Near Miss' Node
Other Merge; Second Option	Replace Pointer by Must-be Satellite

Action of Concept Generator given an Example

Situation	Response
Supplementary-Pointer or Exit appears in the Model	Drop Pointer
Supplementary-Pointer or Exit appears in the Example	Do Nothing
Supplementary-Pointer or Exit appears in the Model; Pointer is a Must-Be-Satellite	Contradiction
Supplementary-Pointer or Exit appears in the Model; Pointer is a Must-Not-Be Satellite	Do Nothing
Negative-Satellite Pair	Drop Pointer
Must-Not-Be-Satellite Pair	Contradiction
Merge; First Option	Move Pointer to Merge Point
Merge; Second Option	Drop Pointer

Figure 2-23 Each difference possibility corresponds to a specific action on the model. If the sample is a near miss, one difference is presumed responsible and one action is taken. But if the sample is an example, action is taken on all differences observed.

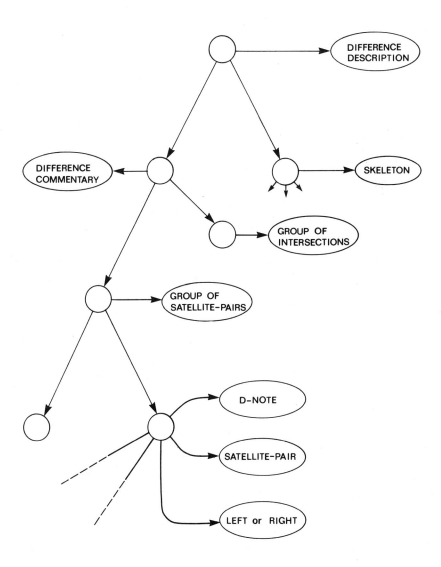

Figure 2-24 A difference commentary adds strength to a difference description by focusing on the differences directly, rather than through the skeleton.

Identification May Be Done in Several Ways

Identification is the implied purpose for learning. If the learning is to be considered successful, then identification power should follow from it. This power may be required in several somewhat different ways. Two particularly simple examples are these:

■ It may be required to identify an object or configuration in isolation by marching through a group of candidate models until a satisfactory match is found.

■ Alternatively, it may be better to go completely through the group of models to find the best match.

A first approximation to a satisfactory match concentrates on the handling of the emphatic relations found in the model. Clearly any pointers with names prefixed by MUST-BE- signal positions where the importance of a relation has been established by some learning experience. Should a corresponding pointer be absent from the unknown, the match fails without further consideration. Similarly, model pointers prefixed by MUST-NOT-BE- cause match failure if the unknown exhibits a positive form of the pointer specified.

Going beyond this to find the best match, rather than just the first satisfactory match, requires more evaluation of the degree of difference between the unknown and each model. It is necessary to translate the abstract notion of difference, d (<unknown>, <model>), into a concrete scheme. A simple way of doing this is to count up the number of differences. Should this be too coarse a measure, each type of difference can have an adjusted influence on the result through the use of some importance reflecting coefficients:

$$
\begin{aligned}
d\,(&\text{<unknown>}, \text{<model>}) \\
&= \quad W_{IN} \text{ <number of INTERSECTIONs>} \\
&\quad + W_{EX} \times \text{ <number of EXITs>} \\
&\quad + W_{ME} \times \text{ <number of MERGEs>} \\
&\quad + W_{SU} \times \text{ <number of SUPPLEMENTARY-POINTERs>} \\
&\quad + W_{SA} \times \text{ <number of SATELLITE-PAIRs>}
\end{aligned}
$$

Further refinements give the measure sensitivity to the level on which the difference is found and to the names of the pointers involved. It must be said, however, that this weighted sum scheme for combining evidence is limited. For one thing, all information is compressed into a singularly inexpressive number. This is fine unless it should be necessary to understand what happened later on. When identification through selection of a model is the top-level goal, the approach does no particular damage.

The Student and the Teacher Share the Work

Where does learning by seeing samples of blocks world structures fit into a general theory of learning? Is it an isolated and tangential phenomenon or is it something which affords insights into central questions? We must climb out of our study of details and face such questions squarely. Our purpose, after all, is to understand general principles of intelligence. Understanding particular systems is useful primarily as a means toward that end.

Consider figure 2-25. According to the view offered there, no piece of apparatus is abandoned as one moves up the learning hierarchy. At each step something is added to those mechanisms already in hand. Learning by being told is simpler than learning by seeing samples since there is no need to decide what difference is most important and what to do about it. But on both levels there is a need for a data structure into which information about what is important can be assimilated. To learn by being told, there is a need to match descriptions that constitute the telling with the model as so far evolved in order to determine where to make a change.

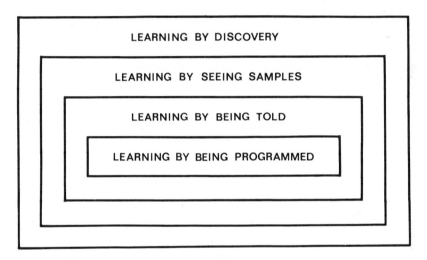

Figure 2-25 Learning by seeing samples is only one kind of learning. Moving from the simple kinds to the hard kinds transfers some burdens from the teacher to the student without changing the total process much.

Thus even below the level of seeing samples we see a need for familiar mechanisms. Thinking about going the other way suggests that these mechanisms persist. Learning by discovery requires all of the talents of learning by seeing samples with the additional requirement that some new procedure must take on the burden of generating near misses.

The progression is one in which the student assumes more and more of the work from the teacher. The work involved seems more or less the same: either student or teacher must create examples and near misses; and one or the other must compute differences, decide priorities, establish reactions, and change the model.

SUMMARY

■ Descriptive power is an essential prerequisite to such diverse tasks as solving geometric-analogy problems and genuine, participative learning. With adequate descriptive power, both tasks are simple; without such power, approaching either invites foolish, *ad hoc* thinking.

■ Geometric-analogy problems and learning from sample sequences both require description matching: for geometric-analogy problems, rules must be matched; for learning, the current model and the current sample must be matched.

■ Strictly speaking, graphical networks are equivalent to lists of facts, but in practice, grouping implied by graphical form is helpful in seeing what is going on.

■ The notion of the near miss is vitally important in teaching through sequences of samples.

■ Learning may take place on different levels. A student may learn by being programmed, by being told, by seeing samples, or by discovery. In all cases the work involved is shared by the student and the teacher.

REFERENCES

■ Thomas G. Evans, "A Heuristic Program to Solve Geometric Analogy Problems," PhD thesis, in *Semantic Information Processing,* edited by Marvin Minsky, The M.I.T. Press, Cambridge, Massachusetts, 1968. Early classic work on which all of the geometric analogy section is based. One of the first programs demonstrating that computers can do things normally considered intelligent.

■ M. Wertheimer, *Productive Thinking,* Harper, New York, 1945. Develops an antecedent to the learning theory presented.

■ Patrick Henry Winston, "Learning Structural Descriptions from Examples," PhD thesis, in *The Psychology of Computer Vision,* edited by Patrick Henry Winston, McGraw-Hill Book Company, New York, 1975. Source of the material on learning.

■ J. Moore and Allen Newell, "How Can Merlin Understand?" in *Knowledge and Cognition,* edited by L. Gregg, Lawrence Erlbaum Associates, Potomac, Maryland, 1974. One of the very few papers addressing the process of analogy and how it can be involved in learning. The theory gropes importantly toward a mechanism that would permit a new piece of knowledge to be constructed by transforming an old one, rather than just by specialization or generalization.

The next two items present other important works on learning which similarly stress the importance of description. They focus on the learning of procedures rather than on physical structures.

■ Gerald Sussman, *A Computer Model of Skill Acquisition,* PhD thesis, American Elsevier, 1975.

■ Ira P. Goldstein, "Summary of MYCROFT: A System for Understanding Simple Picture Programs," *Artificial Intelligence,* vol. 6, no. 3, 1975.

3
EXPLOITING
NATURAL
CONSTRAINTS

When a domain is well understood, it is often possible to describe the objects in the domain in a way that uncovers useful constraints on how the objects interact with one another. This is true both for understanding scenes in the world of vision and for understanding discourse in the world of human language. We will look first at the scene analysis of line drawings of toy blocks because the subject demonstrates the power of description-based constraints. Then we will turn to one kind of sentence-level linguistics to see the same phenomena in a different setting.

EXPLOITING CONSTRAINTS IN SCENE ANALYSIS

The simplest goals for a computer with an electronic eye are discovering how many objects there are in view, the spacial relationships between objects, and the properties of individual objects. Reaching even these goals has proved difficult, however, and only a few of the problems seem solved.

In the restricted world of toy blocks, computer programs now can convert the signals from an electronic eye into a line drawing and can translate a line drawing into statements about the number of objects, their relationships, and their properties. Only the second problem, that of using finished line drawings, can be said to be well understood, however. The other problem, that of producing line drawings, is not fully solved even now.

Here we discuss how a finished line drawing like the one in figure 3-1 can be analyzed by a program. We will find that crack, shadow, boundary, and interior line types combine at junctions in only a few ways. Then we will see that this constraint determines the type for each line in a scene. Once line types are known, it is easy to use those lines known to be boundaries to divide the scene into objects, thus reaching one of the stated goals.

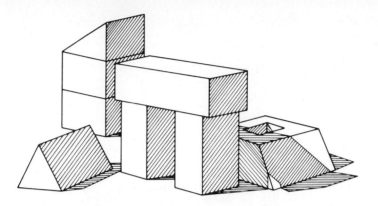

Figure 3-1 Scene analysis decides how each line in a drawing should be interpreted. Scenes like this are easy for Waltz' program. (From *The Psychology of Computer Vision,* by Patrick H. Winston, copyright 1975 by McGraw-Hill Book Company, New York. Used with permission of McGraw-Hill Book Company and Patrick H. Winston.)

Lines Fall into a Few Classes

To begin, think about polyhedra with lighting arranged to eliminate all shadows. The lines in drawings of this world are representations of various physical edge types. A simple, natural partitioning of these lines is shown here:

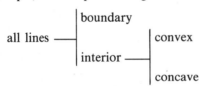

First, all lines are divided into boundary lines and interior lines. Boundary lines separate regions belonging to different objects and interior lines separate regions belonging to the same object. Then the interior-edge category is broken up into those lines which represent concave edges and those which are convex. For notational convenience, the line types are identified on drawings by some symbol conventions. Since these conventions will be used liberally, it is important to memorize them now:

■ Convex lines bear a + label.

■ Concave lines have a − label.

■ Boundary lines have a > or a < label.

The direction of the small arrows placed on boundary lines is determined by which side of the line corresponds to a face of the obscuring object. Imagine taking a stroll along the line keeping the obscuring object on the right. The arrow is placed in the direction of walking.

Now by interpreting the drawing in figure 3-2 in the natural way as an L-shaped solid, it is easy to label each line in a way that properly reflects its physical origin. Labeling a drawing in this way exploits an understanding of the physical situation

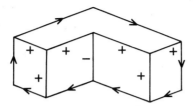

Figure 3-2 An L-shaped solid illustrates the three basic line interpretations: convex lines, marked with + labels; concave lines, marked with − labels; and boundary lines, marked with > or < labels.

in order to arrive at interpretations for the lines. The key idea to pursue now is that of turning the process around and using knowledge about line interpretations to derive an understanding of the physical reality. To do this it is necessary to understand the interpretation constraints imposed by the physical world.

The world's physical vertexes cause junctions which can be divided into categories according to the number of lines coming together and the angles between the lines. Figure 3-3 assigns mnemonic names to the common categories. Thankfully some simple assumptions shrink this list down to ARROWs, Ls, FORKs, and Ts,

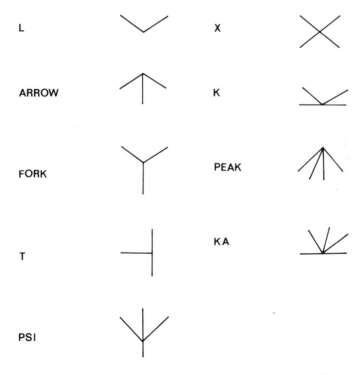

Figure 3-3 The common junctions. Most are excluded if vertexes are all trihedral and there are no shadows.

thus simplifying explanation. These assumptions are in force only temporarily; later they will be relaxed:

■ There are no shadows or cracks.

■ All vertexes are the intersection of exactly three object faces. This excludes the objects in figure 3-4.

■ The choice of viewpoint is such that no junctions change character with a small movement of the eye. The viewpoint in figure 3-5 is therefore forbidden.

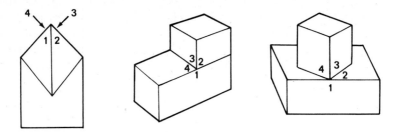

Figure 3-4 The trihedral vertex criterion excludes all of these objects. Four faces meet at each of the junctions indicated.

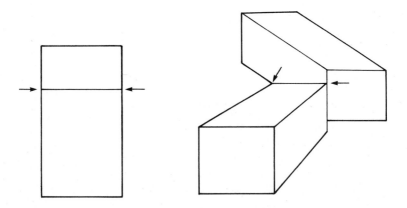

Figure 3-5 The general position criterion excludes both of these configurations because slight perturbation of the viewing positions radically changes the junctions indicated.

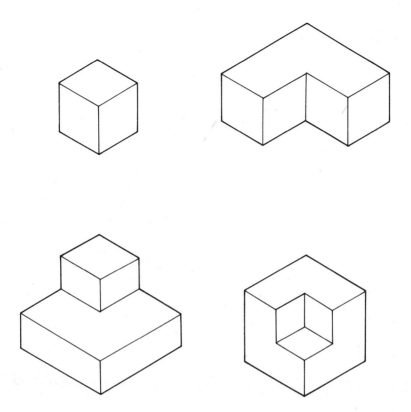

Figure 3-6 Some objects formed exclusively with trihedral vertexes.

The reason these assumptions help is that they reduce the number of junction types and hence the number of combinations possible for line labels surrounding the junctions to a manageable size. The most important assumption is that all vertexes in space are places at which exactly three faces meet, as on the corners of a cube. These are the trihedral vertexes. Everything in figure 3-6 is formed exclusively from trihedral vertexes. Note that the junctions seem restricted to just four types, L, FORK, ARROW, and T. By restricting the initial inquiry to trihedral vertexes, we have apparently avoided K, PSI, X, PEAK, and KA vertexes. Soon we will see that this must be so.

Since there are four ways to label any given line, there must be $4^2 = 16$ ways to label an L. Similarly there must be $4^3 = 64$ ways to label FORKs, ARROWs, and Ts. This gives an upper bound of 208 on the number of junction combinations that can occur naturally in line drawings. Curiously only 18 of these arrangements of line labels can possibly result from physical vertexes. It is not possible, for example, to find the junction labelings of figure 3-7 in drawings of real polyhedral objects. Our next job is showing such junction arrangements are nonrealizable and collecting the arrangements that are all right. There are only six for Ls, five for FORKs, four for Ts, and three for ARROWs. Having them, analyzing scenes is like working easy jigsaw puzzles.

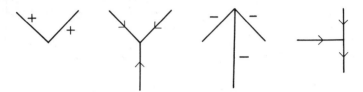

Figure 3-7 Some junction labelings not found when scenes are restricted to objects with trihedral vertexes.

The Trihedral World Exhibits Only 18 Legal Junction Arrangements

We proceed by looking at every possible physical vertex from every possible direction in order to enumerate all ways in which line labels can be placed around drawing junctions. This sounds crazy and horrifying. How could it be possible to handle all the alternatives? The assumption that scenes contain only trihedral vertexes provides the answer. The three faces of any trihedral vertex define three planes, and three planes divide space into eight compartments as in figure 3-8, and

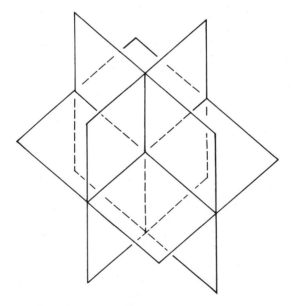

Figure 3-8 The three faces of a trihedral vertex divide space into eight octants. The planes need not meet at right angles as shown here.

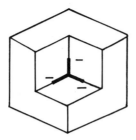

Figure 3-9 The junction seen when seven octants are filled. The three concave lines are seen no matter where the viewer stands within the one available viewing octant.

an object forming a vertex manifestly must fill up one or more of the eight compartments so formed. We therefore can be sure of getting at all junction possibilities by a two step process: consider all ways of filling up eight octants with object material, then view each of the resulting vertexes from the unfilled octants.

Of course if all eight octants are filled, then there is no vertex and consequently nothing to consider. But suppose only seven of the eight are filled as in figure 3-9. Evidently the seven-octant situation validates a FORK junction arrangement in which each of the three lines involved bears a — label. Note that the only junction of interest in the drawing is the one in the center. The surrounding drawing is only a visual aid to understanding how the seven filled octants produce a drawing junction. Note further that since seven octants are filled, there can be only one octant from which to look at the vertex. The junction type seen is a FORK no matter what particular position is taken within the viewing octant. Thankfully, invariance within a viewing octant holds in general. The junction type does not change as the viewpoint moves within one viewing octant even though the angles between lines do vary considerably.

So far the catalogue of possible junctions has but one entry, a FORK. If only one octant is filled, there are new entries. This is illustrated in figure 3-10, again with the junction of interest surrounded by a drawing which provides a visual aid to establishing the context of the filled octant. From one point of view, the vertex

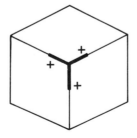

Figure 3-10 If one octant is filled, the view from the diagonally opposite octant yields a FORK surrounded by convex labels. Standing in the six other octants gives a different result.

appears as a **FORK** with each line labeled with a +. But since only one octant is filled, there must be seven from which to look, and so far we have only the junction arrangement derived from the octant diagonally opposite the stuff of the object. Positions must be taken in the six other octants. Three of these are the positions occupied by the stick figures in the first part of figure 3-11.

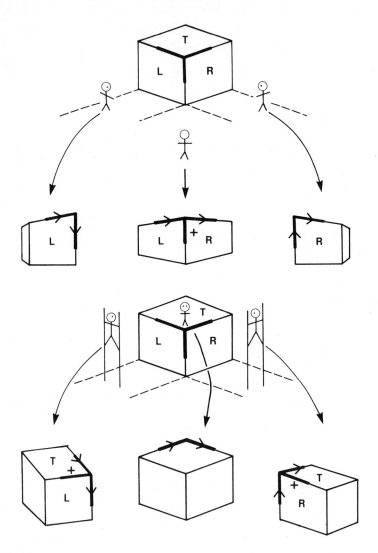

Figure 3-11 Stick figures help to show what a one-octant vertex looks like from various viewpoints. Because of symmetry, the seven viewing octants yield only three different labelings, one **L**, one **FORK**, and one **ARROW**.

For two of the three remaining octants, we put two stick figures on stilts to boost them up over the plane defined by the top of the cube. The final viewpoint is defined by a stick figure on top. See the second part of figure 3-11. All six stick figure views provide only two new junction label arrangements since three of the views produce one kind of **ARROW** arrangement and the other three produce only one kind of L. Actually, this was to be expected from the inherent symmetry of the situation.

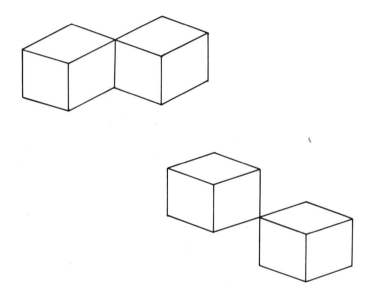

Figure 3-12 Both of these two-octant vertexes are forbidden by the trihedral vertex criterion (which is really a three-face criterion). In both, six faces meet at the vertex.

Now consider the situations with two, four, or six octants filled. All are excluded by the initial trihedral presumption. Suppose, for example, that two octants are to be filled. If the two are adjacent, then the edges between them would be cracks, there would be four object faces at the central vertex, and the vertex would be nontrihedral. If the two filled octants are not adjacent, then they would meet either along an edge or at a common point. Either way, as shown in figure 3-12, there would be more than three faces at the central vertex. Similar arguments exclude the four and six octant filled cases, leaving only three and five to be considered.

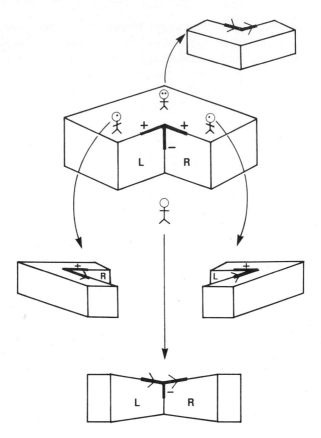

Figure 3-13 If three octants are filled, the remaining five viewing octants each supply a unique junction labeling. There are three distinct Ls, one FORK, and one ARROW.

For three octants, see figure 3-13. Each of the five viewing octants provides a unique arrangement. Of course one of the viewing octants is represented by the view given. There the vertex is seen as an ARROW. In one of the other octants, the vertex looks like a FORK, and in each of the other three remaining, an L. Each of the L type arrangements observed is unique.

Adding the new FORK labeling requires some care because any of the three arms of an isolated FORK may be the one properly labeled with the — symbol. This is why the observed FORK configuration generates three entries for the list of legal junctions, even though any one of them can be rotated to look like any other.

Figure 3-14 illustrates what derives from five filled octants. There are three junction arrangements, each of which is different from the ones seen before.

Finally, there are four T type labelings which derive from partial occlusion of the four basic line types. This brings the total to 18, all of which are collected together in figure 3-15.

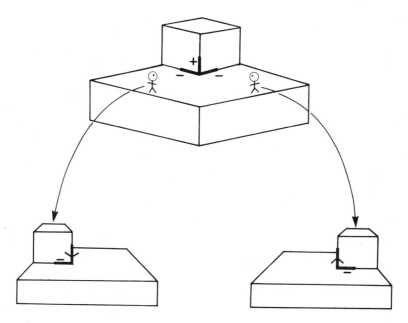

Figure 3-14 If five octants are filled, the three viewing octants supply two Ls and one ARROW.

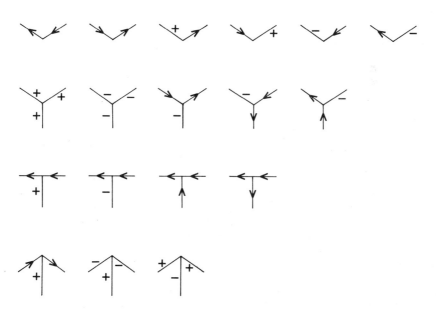

Figure 3-15 Eighteen junction configurations are possible. Were it not for physical constraints, there would be 208.

Note that we have now enumerated all possible ways in which trihedral vertexes can be formed, and we have viewed each such vertex from all possible directions. It must be that the 18 junction arrangements are all that there can be. Any arrangement not on the list cannot correspond to any real trihedral vertex!

Part of Scene Analysis Is a Search for Correct Junction Labels

When examining some sample scenes, keep in mind three facts evident from initial assumptions and from inspection of the table:

■ There are only > labels on the border separating a collection of objects from the background. They form a clockwise ring.

■ There is only one kind of ARROW with > labels on its barbs. For such an ARROW the shaft must be labeled with a +.

■ There is only one kind of FORK with any + label. For this FORK, all the lines are in fact forced to be labeled with + labels.

Now how can knowledge about possible junction arrangements be useful in analysis? The process can be illustrated using a drawing of a cube. To begin with, the lines bordering on the background can certainly be uniformly labeled with boundary labels as in figure 3-16. Next, each of the ARROW's shafts is forced to be a + since the barbs are already known to be boundary lines. This leaves only the central FORK to investigate. Since all the junction's lines already have + labels assigned through previous considerations, it remains only to check that a FORK with three + labels is in the list of physically realizable junctions, which of course is the case.

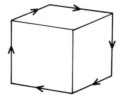 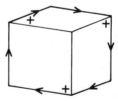

Figure 3-16 Scene labeling begins by placing boundary arrows pointing clockwise on the scene's border. Next it is usually convenient to label the shafts of the ARROW junctions whose barbs lie on the border.

So far we have used only the particularly useful facts listed above for ARROWs and FORKs. They are enough to show how the known constraints force each line to be interpreted in a way consistent with the natural, intuitive interpretation. Now

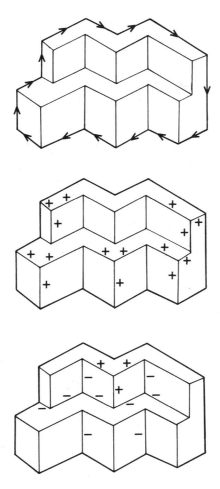

Figure 3-17 Labeling of this two-tiered figure begins with the background border as usual. Next the shafts of the border ARROWs begin a propagation of convex symbols that continues through all FORKs encountered. Miscellaneous junction labelings finish the job.

consider the slightly harder example in figure 3-17, a sort of two-tiered, double L-shaped figure. Again it is useful to begin by labeling the background boundary. Then it is easy to move toward the interior using the special fact about ARROWs with boundary labels on their barbs, together with the fact that a + on a FORK forces two more + labels. To move still further requires returning to the label table, finding that the only ARROW with a + on a barb has a second + barb and a − shaft. Similarly the only ARROW with a − on a barb has a second − barb and a + shaft. These force all of the remaining labels as shown.

Starting from interior junctions is more difficult because they lack the *a priori* labeling of two lines with boundary symbols. In general more than one interpretation is possible until the analysis reaches a boundary, at which point the ambiguity is usually resolved. This seems true of human performance as well and accounts for a class of visual reversal phenomena. Consider an enlarged version of the last illustration in figure 3-18. Concentrating on the center, one can see either a series of steps or a row of thick saw blades, particularly if the top, bottom, and both ends are covered up. This may be because interior junctions which are separated by distance or occlusion from the powerful boundary constraints undergo reversals in which concave, − edges seem to switch with convex, + types.

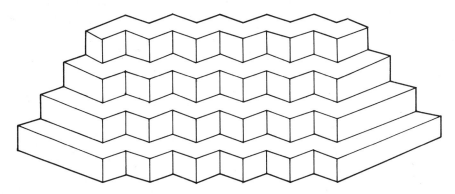

Figure 3-18 The background border contributes considerable constraint to scene analysis efforts. By covering the sides of this object, the disconnected central portion is perceived alternately as a series of ledges and as a row of thick saw blades.

■ Thus the theory not only provides mechanisms by which computers can analyze scenes, but also provides a plausible explanation for a standard human phenomenon. Something is being said about the nature of the problem domain which has little to do with the individual that is working in that domain, be it human or computer.

It is also interesting to note that the theory is useful not only in analyzing normal scenes but also in identifying illegal scenes, those which cannot ordinarily be real objects. The drawing in figure 3-19 is illegal and this conclusion can be reached through a labeling argument. Proceeding as before, background lines, background ARROW junctions, and FORK junctions with + labels can be exploited as shown. But now there is no way to label line *z*. The ARROW on one end insists on a − label while the L on the other demands a boundary label! (Incidentally the same conclusion drops out of the observation that two faces meet along two different lines, *x* and *y*.)

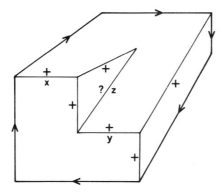

Figure 3-19 An impossible object. There is no way to label line z such that the junctions on both ends are in the table of legal configurations.

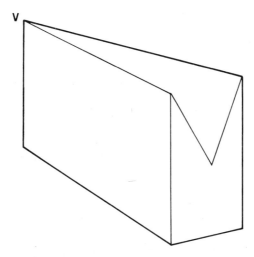

Figure 3-20 Some reasonable-looking drawings cannot be labeled and therefore cannot correspond to objects made of trihedral vertexes alone.

Some care must be taken in using this idea for detecting illegal drawings, however. For one thing the theory as described so far handles only the trihedral vertex world. Drawings like the one in figure 3-20 can represent legal objects, but they are not recognized as legal because nontrihedral vertexes are needed. In this case, four faces come together at vertex *v* in the natural interpretation.

Going the other way, even a correctly labeled drawing may not represent a legal object. All physically realizable objects with only trihedral vertexes surely must have drawings that can be labeled, but while having a labelable drawing is a necessary condition for realizability, it is not a sufficient one. In figure 3-21 the drawing can be labeled and even seems alright to human viewers at first, but it certainly is illegal, again because supposedly planar faces A and B meet along two different lines, x and y.

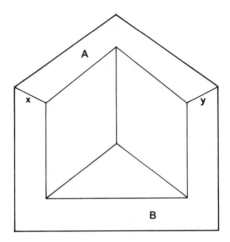

Figure 3-21 Some drawings cannot correspond to realizable objects even though they can be labeled consistently.

The Nontrihedral World Requires More Line Interpretations

So far drawings have been analyzed as if suspended in isolation. But if a cube, say, may be resting on a table, it can be argued that a better interpretation recognizes that the bottom lines are probably concave edges rather than boundaries. Such an interpretation is not unique, however, since the cube might just as well be stuck against a wall as figure 3-22 shows. Without some additional clue or assumption, several interpretations are equally plausible.

Note, however, that introducing shadows resolves the ambiguity. The blocks in the middle of figure 3-23 definitely seem supported by a horizontal surface while the ones to the left and right, although less familiar, seem attached vertically. Evidently expanding the theory to include labels for shadows adds further constraint and simplifies analysis. Indeed, shadows do add power to the repertoire of labels, and given this move toward generality, it is time to add cracks as well.

Take note that both boundary and shadow labels indicate a direction: boundary labels mark the region to the right as the one physically connected with the boundary edge while shadow labels are small arrows placed so that they point into the shadowed region. Cracks are labeled with cs.

Thus, the list as it stands now has seven labels, two each for boundary and shadow edges, one each for concave, convex, and crack edges. It would be

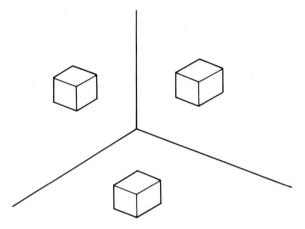

Figure 3-22 Without shadows, there are several ways to interpret a cube: it may be suspended or it may be attached by one of its hidden faces.

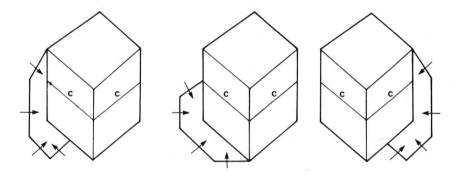

Figure 3-23 Shadows determine where an object rests against others. Note the shadow and crack labels.

straightforward, but tedious, to derive the legal junction arrangements again for this expanded set of line labels. Having done the job, examples would illustrate that the description refinement increases the number of constraints with consequent improvement in speed and directness of analysis. Rather than do this, we ask if there might be still further ways to divide up the line types. Indeed there are. Two particularly good ways are described in a moment. First, however, there is a caution about purpose. We are racing headlong toward big numbers because the set of legal junction combinations will grow considerably with the impending expansion of the set of line interpretations. There will be several thousand legal junction combinations, not just 18 as before, and it is impossible to develop the list of them here or to attempt to simulate what a computer can do with them. Instead we will first inquire about how the number of legal combinations grows relative to the number of illegal combinations, and then we will look at experimental results to help answer questions about what improvements the expanded label set yields and why.

Two line-type refinements have been promised. The first recognizes that objects often come together at concave and crack edges. The concave and crack labels, — and *c,* can be split into subcategories indicating the number of objects involved and which is in front. Suppose a concave edge represents a place where two objects come together. Then imagine pulling the two apart slightly. The concave edge becomes a boundary edge with the label pointing in either of two directions as shown in figure 3-24. The two possibilities are indicated by compound symbols made up of the original label and the new label. If by chance there are three objects, again a compound symbol is used as shown.

Cracks are treated analogously, giving a total diagram of figure 3-25 which illustrates the eleven possible ways any particular line may be interpreted.

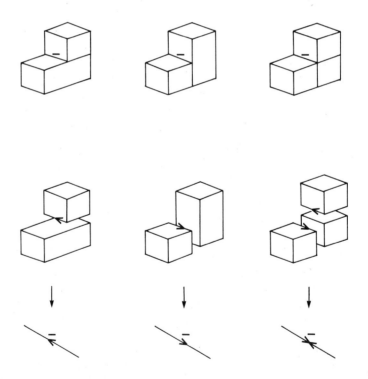

Figure 3-24 Concave edges often occur where two or three objects meet. It is useful to distinguish among the possibilities by combining the concave label with what would be seen if the objects were separated.

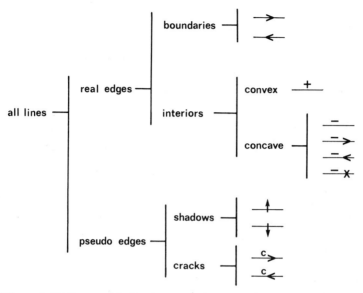

Figure 3-25 The possible line interpretations and the corresponding labels.

Illumination Adds Constraint

The second way of refining the line descriptions has to do with lighting. One approach is to suppose that the state of illumination on any face falls into one of three categories illustrated in figure 3-26: the face may be directly illuminated, it

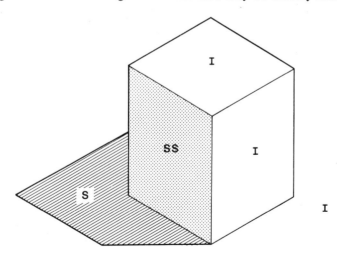

Figure 3-26 Illumination information often provides useful constraint. If there is a single light source, it is convenient to recognize three surface categories: directly illuminated, I; shadowed by intervening objects, S; and self-shadowed by virtue of facing away from the light source, SS.

may be shadowed by another object, or it may be shadowed because it faces away from the light. The three possibilities are denoted by I, for directly *i*lluminated, S for *s*hadowed by another object, and SS for facing away from the light, that is, *s*elf-*s*hadowed.

Labels can carry knowledge about these illumination states in addition to basic information about edge type. If the illumination states and line types were to combine freely, there would be $3^2 = 9$ illumination combinations for each of the 11 line types, giving 99 total possibilities. But only about fifty of these are possible: there cannot be, for example, a combination in which the lighting state varies from one side to another across any sort of concave edge. Such a situation would require an excludable coincidence in which a shadow line projected exactly onto the concave edge.

Manifestly each of the line interpretation refinements has contributed to a great expansion:

- Initially only basic types of lines were proposed: boundary lines and interior concave and convex lines.
- These were augmented by including shadows and cracks.
- Cracks and concave lines were split up according to the number of objects coming together and how they obscure one another.
- Finally, line type information was combined with illumination information. About fifty types emerge from this final expansion.

These changes make the set of physically realizable junctions large, both for the original L, ARROW, and FORK types and for the new K, PSI, X, KA, and other vertex types allowed by relaxation of the original trihedral and general position constraints. What is gained? What are the results of working out and using the new junction arrangements?

VERTEX TYPE	APPROXIMATE NUMBER OF COMBINATORIALLY POSSIBLE LABELINGS	APPROXIMATE NUMBER OF PHYSICALLY POSSIBLE LABELINGS;	APPROXIMATE RATIO
L	16	6	37.5 %;
FORK	64	5	7.8 %;
T	64	4	6.2 %;
ARROW	64	3	4.7 %

Figure 3-27 Working with only the basic concave, convex, and boundary line interpretations, the number of junction arrangements used in labeling scenes is a fraction of the combinatorial possibilities. Evidently Ls offer the least constraint, ARROWs the most.

VERTEX TYPE	APPROXIMATE NUMBER OF COMBINATORIALLY POSSIBLE LABELINGS	APPROXIMATE NUMBER OF PHYSICALLY POSSIBLE LABELINGS;	APPROXIMATE RATIO
L	2.50×10^3	80	3.20 %;
FORK	1.25×10^5	500	4.0×10^{-1} %;
T	1.25×10^5	500	4.0×10^{-1} %;
ARROW	1.25×10^5	70	5.6×10^{-2} %;
PSI	6.25×10^6	300	4.8×10^{-3} %;
K	6.25×10^6	100	1.6×10^{-3} %;
X	6.25×10^6	100	1.6×10^{-3} %;
MULTI	6.25×10^6	100	1.6×10^{-3} %;
PEAK	6.25×10^6	10	1.6×10^{-4} %;
KA	3.12×10^8	30	9.6×10^{-6} %

Figure 3-28 Expanding the set of interpretations to include shadows, cracks, separable edges, and illumination brings about more constraint. The number of physically possible junctions is an incredibly tiny fraction of the combinatorial possibilities, especially for the junctions with many lines.

First consider how the physically possible junctions measure up as a fraction of the constraint-free arrangements. Figure 3-27 gives the results for the original set of four label possibilities. The percentages indicate firm, but not extraordinary constraint. When the line categories are expanded, however, all numbers grow large and the constraint becomes incredible. By patient enumeration, Waltz derived the results in figure 3-28. The evident constraint in some cases restricts the legal fraction of junction arrangements to as little as 9.6×10^{-6} % of the total! To be sure, the total number of arrangements has increased to a size too large to apply and use by hand, but still the constraints are so extreme that a computer using the large set can converge on a solution for a complicated drawing that is less ambiguous and more quickly derived than before.

The details of the process of using the labels are described later in the chapter on search strategy alternatives. Let it suffice here to draw analogy to the process of solving simultaneous algebraic equations:

■ In equations there are a number of variables whose values are to be determined; in scenes there are lines whose interpretations are to be found. Values for algebraic variables are determined using the equations as the source of constraint. Interpretations for lines are found using the junctions in the same sort of constraint role.

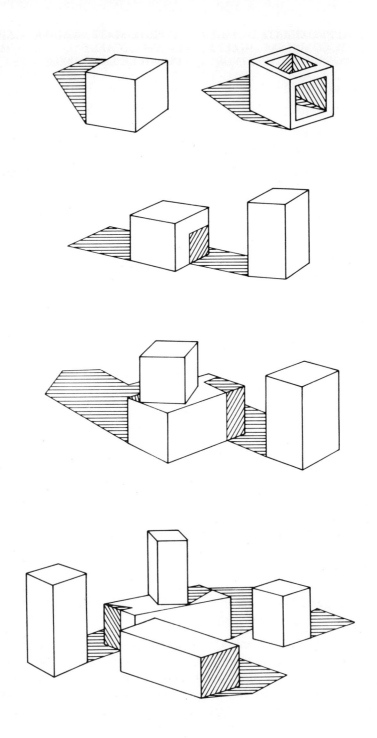

◀ **Figure 3-29** Extensions to the basic Waltz scheme enable analysis of scenes with holes, lighting direction coincidences, vertex alignments, and nontrihedral vertexes. (From *The Psychology of Computer Vision,* by Patrick H. Winston, copyright 1975 by McGraw-Hill Book Company, New York. Used with permission of McGraw-Hill Book Company and Patrick H. Winston.)

Experiments Provide Insight into What Theory Can Do

One thing is sure: programs based on Waltz' labeling set succeed on complicated scenes. The scenes in figure 3-29, for example, are analyzed even though they exhibit holes, lighting direction coincidences, viewing angle special cases, and nontrihedral vertexes. The end result is a labeled scene with each line known to be a particular line type or at least restricted to a few alternatives.

From this, it is easy to divide the scene into objects. To see why, recall that the basic set of eleven line interpretations contained seven boundary lines,

and four nonboundary lines,

Boundary lines completely partition scenes into their constituent objects. Tracing over the boundary lines in the last illustration brings the objects into relief, as shown in figure 3-30.

The procedure not only solves hard problems, it also demonstrates that the work required to do a scene grows in roughly linear proportion with the size of the scene. If the size of a scene is measured in terms of the number of objects in it, then this experimentally observed relationship between computation and complexity suggests that the influence of particular lines and junctions tends to be confined to the locality in which they reside.

To see why, suppose scenes can be split up somehow into compartments of more or less fixed size in terms of the lines and junctions contained in each compartment. If the compartments are such that constraint does not flow across their frontiers, then the total time required to analyze a scene is surely linear with the number of compartments and hence with the number of junctions. That such a compartmentalization should occur makes sense since the T junctions that most often separate one object from another have very little ability to transmit constraint because an obscuring boundary can lie in front of any kind of edge. Knowing nothing

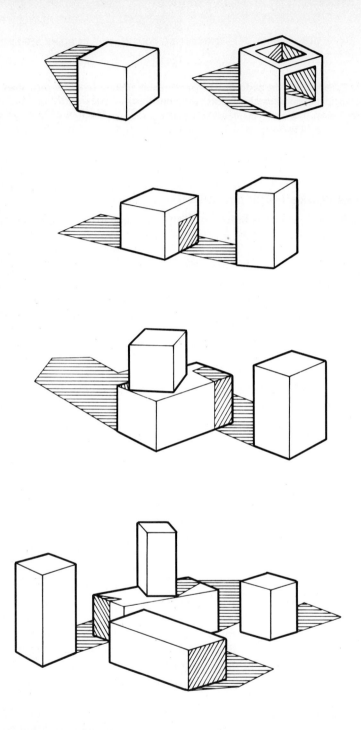

Figure 3-30 Since analysis identifies all object boundary lines, including the concave and crack types, object separation is simple. (From *The Psychology of Computer Vision,* by Patrick H. Winston, copyright 1975 by McGraw-Hill Book Company, New York. Used with permission of McGraw-Hill Book Company and Patrick H. Winston.)

Figure 3-31 Knowing that the crossbar of a T is two boundary lines says nothing about the upright.

about the T junction in figure 3-31 and then learning that the crossbar is two boundary lines says nothing new at all about the upright. It must be that local constraints are usually sufficient to unambiguously interpret the lines if they are to be unambiguously interpreted at all. This suggests that if the theory succeeds in doing analysis, it should succeed in time proportional to the size of the scene. Fortunately, experiment verifies both success and proportional time.

Experiments Show Where Theory Breaks Down

So far the results of refined line interpretations excite and encourage. Scene analysis seems possible. There are some problems beyond the practice of the analytic programs based on the theory, however. These problems tend to require global considerations.

The first drawing in figure 3-32 looks innocuous, but it gave quite a fright when tried. Somehow two interpretations came through, the sensible one with boundary

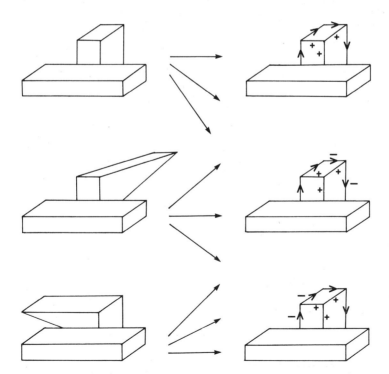

Figure 3-32 Without shadows, some drawings stubbornly refuse to produce a unique labeling. For the example given, all labelings are reasonable, because junction-preserving distortions produce scenes for which the odd labelings feel correct.

AMBIGUOUS   UNAMBIGUOUS

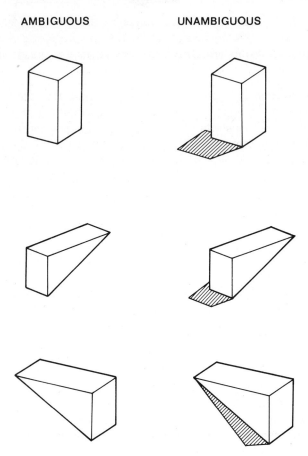

Figure 3-33 Shadows add constraint and reduce ambiguity. Without the shadows, more than one interpretation is possible for each object.

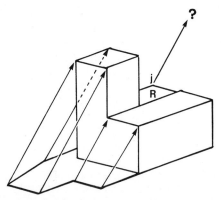

Figure 3-34 Some scene analysis problems require global reasoning. The Waltz labeling procedure cannot decide if region R is a shadow or a block.

arrows surrounding the standing brick, and two foolish ones in which separable edge labels replace two of the boundary arrows. Has the program gone berserk?

No. In fact, it would be serious if the separate interpretations failed to appear. The last two drawings in figure 3-32 explain why. Each of the scenes is constructed by stretching the drawing of the standing brick in such a way that it becomes a lying wedge. Note that no new junction appears, no old one disappears, and none change type. Consequently nothing influences the result of labeling. The process is completely blind to changes unless the changes modify junction types or connections. The program must propose the same answers before and after the brick becomes one or another of the wedges. Yet for the wedges, the separable edge — interpretations are clearly suitable. Now the reason why the original scene produced three interpretations is clear. If the program gave only the standing brick interpetation, it would necessarily blunder with the wedges since they look just the same as far as the program is concerned!

One reason this simple scene causes such trouble lies in the absence of shadows. There is no ambiguity for any of the objects in figure 3-33. The shadows supply sufficient constraint.

In any event, it is clear that programs which ignore details of line direction and length cannot always decide the exact interpetations for all lines as well as humans do. Figure 3-34 shows another problem supporting this conclusion. The question concerns the nature of region R. Is it an object or a shadow? Some thought makes the conclusion obvious. It must be an object, for if it were a shadow, there would be a shadow-causing vertex associated with junction j. Yet there is none. We know the direction of light from other junction pairs, and there is no appropriate shadow-causing vertex in that direction from j. Here again is a problem involving reasoning with angle and direction and requiring application of knowledge gained at some quite distant place. A program using only knowledge about local line combinations, although powerful indeed, cannot do these things.

Waltz' Results Illustrate a General Constraint Phenomenon

It is generally true that more description yields better, faster performance. And more precisely, it is generally true that concentrating on the description of the atomic entities in a domain brings out constraints that substantially help analysis. By turning to language, we will develop some confidence that this "Waltz effect" embraces a variety of intelligent information-processing tasks. In scene analysis, the atomic entities were lines and junctions. In understanding language, they will be word groups and sentences.

EXPLOITING CONSTRAINTS IN SENTENCE ANALYSIS

A noun group is a noun together with any auxiliary words that accompany it, such as adjectives and determiners like *a* and *the*. In the simplest sentences the noun groups satisfy particular needs with respect to explaining the action specified by the verb. The sentence, "Robbie hit the ball with a bat," for example, carries information about how Robbie, a ball, and a bat relate to the verb *hit*. A program that understands such a sentence must discover that Robbie performs the action of hitting, he does it to the ball, and he uses the bat as a tool. In technical terms, the program must discover that Robbie is the agent of the action, the ball is the object, and the bat is the instrument.

Robbie, incidentally, will appear in various forms throughout this book, usually as an aspiring robot.

Our present purpose is to speculate about how the constraint-exploitation idea can help with this small part of natural language analysis, thereby supporting the argument that constraint exploitation is a generally useful tool. As before, we jump into the middle of a big puzzle, one which is far from completely worked out. A constraint-oriented process is described, but a total language system is not. For now we even presume the existence of a program that can digest raw sentences and separate the words into the individual groups.

Simple Sentences Focus on State Description and State Change

What does a sentence do? If we refrain from looking too hard for special cases and esoterica, most sentences of ordinary dialog fall into only a few categories: along one dimension there is the declarative, imperative, interrogative division that everyone learns about in elementary grammar; along another, there is one class of sentences that deal with the description of objects and another that deals with descriptions of actions in which objects participate. "The block is red," for example, is a declarative sentence relating the block and the general property of being red. "The red block supports a pyramid," is also a declarative sentence, but differs from the other example in that it gives a relationship between two objects rather than between one object and a property. "The red block exploded," is an action sentence. "Did the red block explode?" is an interrogative form. "Blow up the red block," is imperative.

For both object-focused sentences and action-focused sentences, the notion of state is fundamental to the point of view under development here:

■ Description sentences describe or ask about the state. Action sentences describe, ask about, or demand some change in state.

■ The world the state refers to may be as concrete as an arrangement of blocks or as abstract as a collection of ideas, for even abstract objects may be thought to reside in places, have properties, and be subject to changes in state.

For action sentences there is some analogy between sentences and objects on one hand and functions and arguments on the other. This analogy is not entirely misadvised. Many sentences do seem strongly action centered. No claim is made about paragraphs and other extended units of communication structure, but for many sentences the objects behave as if they were an assortment of function arguments, each with its own particular semantic role. They are sorted out by assigning objects to various purposes. How? Soon we will come to an enumeration of the primary constraints that seem useful.

The Case of a Noun Group Is a Property Specifying How It Relates to Its Target Verb

There is considerable flexibility in noun-group construction: a group may be preceded by a preposition; a group may be introduced by a determiner like *a* or *the* or *these;* there may be a collection of adjectives; the noun may be followed by descriptive prepositional phrases; and the noun even may be missing as in the sentence, "These are too big."

Although interesting, the detailed structure of noun groups is not the primary concern here. Instead we are seeking answers to two simple questions:

■ What role does a noun group play?

■ How is it possible to determine the role?

It is customary to use the word *case* instead of *role* when referring to what a noun group does. One speaks, for example, of the agent case or the instrument case. In a way these names are unfortunate because these cases are only remotely related to the nominative, accusative, and genitive cases studied in elementary English grammar. Those cases deal with the surface syntactic role of a noun group, not the deeper semantic relationship between the noun group and the action.

The number of cases embraced by any particular theory varies considerably. Filmore, an early champion of the semantic-case idea, wrote in terms of half-a-dozen basic cases. Others use considerably more. The exact number does not matter much as long as there are enough to expose natural constraints on how verbs and case instances form sentences. For now, consider the list of case possibilities given below and illustrated by figure 3-35:

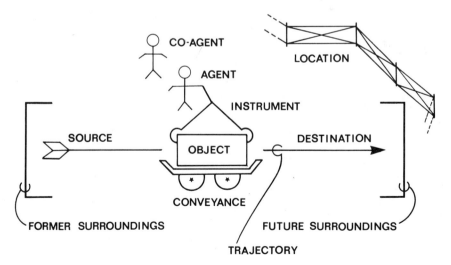

Figure 3-35 Case grammar focuses on how noun groups relate to actions. These are some of the more common possibilities.

Object. The object is the thing the sentence is really all about, typically the thing undergoing a state change. Often the semantic object is the same as the syntactic direct object as in "Robbie hit *the ball.*" On the other hand it may appear as the syntactic subject as in *"The ball* was hit by Robbie."

Agent. The agent is the thing that causes the action to occur. Volition is generally implied as in *"Robbie* kissed Suzie," but there are exceptions as in *"The moon* eclipsed the sun." The agent is often the surface subject but may also appear in a prepositional noun group: "Mary was kissed *by John.*"

Instrument. The instrument, at this level of analysis, is a tool used by the agent. The preposition *with* typically introduces instrument type noun groups as in "Robbie assembled Suzie *with a screwdriver.*"

Co-agent. The word *with* may also introduce a noun group which serves as a slightly subordinate partner to the principal agent. They carry out the action together: "Robbie assembled another robot *with Suzie.*"

Source and destination. State changes are often simple changes in physical position. The source is the initial position and the destination is the final position: "Robbie went *from the dining room to the kitchen.*" The movement which involves a source and a destination need not necessarily occur in physical space: "Robbie's mood went *from bad to worse.*"

Conveyance. The conveyance is just that, the thing in which or on which one travels. "Robbie always goes *by train.*"

Trajectory. Motion from source to destination takes place over a trajectory. In contrast to the other case possibilities, several prepositions can serve to introduce trajectory noun groups: "They went in *through the front door.* Robbie carried her *over the threshold.*"

Location. The location is where an action occurs. As in the trajectory case, several prepositions are possible, each of which conveys meaning in addition to serving as a signal that a location noun group is coming: "He studied *in the library, at a desk, by the wall, under a picture, near the door.*"

Other cases not illustrated in the figure include the following:

Beneficiary. The beneficiary is the person for whom an action is performed: "Robbie cleaned the house *for mother.*"

Raw material. If a substance disappears into a product, then it is an instance of the raw material case. *Out of* typically introduces the raw material: "Robbie made a calculator *out of integrated circuits.*"

Time. Time specifies when an action occurs. The prepositions *during, while, before,* and *after* introduce noun groups serving as time case fillers.

If a noun group is preceded by a preposition, the combination is called a prepositional group. Note that the case identity of the noun group inside a prepositional group is highly constrained by the flagging preposition:

from ➤ source

to ➤ destination

by ➤ agent or conveyance or location

with ➤ instrument or co-agent

for ➤ beneficiary or duration

For example, given the preposition *by,* it is reasonable to expect an agent, a conveyance, or a location, but not an instrument, raw material, or beneficiary.

Many Kinds of Constraints Help to Determine a Noun Group's Case

As suggested by figure 3-36, constraints flow into noun groups from the surrounding context:

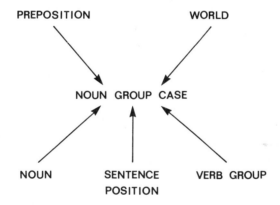

Figure 3-36 Many constraints help determine noun group case.

■ Sentence position gives good clues about the case identity of some noun groups, particularly the agent, object, and time noun groups.

■ Preceding prepositions limit a noun group's case possibilities.

■ Each verb meaning carries strong preferences about what cases appear in combination with it.

■ For most cases only one instance is allowed in any sentence. If, somehow, the case of one noun group is determined, then the others in the sentence are forced to be something else. Time, trajectory, and location are some exceptions in the sense that more than one noun group may be involved in their description.

■ The noun itself often prevents otherwise possible case identifications. We get a different picture from "Robbie was sent to the scrap heap by parcel post," than from "Robbie was sent to the scrap heap by Marcel Proust," because parcel post is more likely to be a conveyance rather than an agent while Marcel Proust has opposite tendencies.

None of the impinging constraints need be particularly strong since there are so many of them. The situation is the same as with junction labeling: the constraint offered by one particular neighbor may not be overwhelming, but taken together the community of neighbors swiftly drives analysis to inexorable conclusions.

Languages Rely on a Variety of Constraint Sources

Strength in one dimension allows flexibility in another. It is easy to imagine how a language might have a larger number of prepositions that flag cases than English with an offsetting reduction in the number of ordering rules. This is true, for example, of Russian relative to English.

Resolving Case Identity Helps Resolve Verb Ambiguity

Verbs and verb groups in isolation exhibit meaning ambiguity just as noun groups have purpose alternatives. Thankfully, delimiting constraints again seem to flow in and resolve the ambiguity.

For verbs there are several meaning-selection constraints. In particular the noun group in the object case can help considerably. Consider the following examples:

He shot the rabbit.

He shot the picture.

Shooting a rifle and shooting a camera are very different kinds of shooting, even though there are similarities at a certain level of abstraction. The words *rifle* and *camera* are not specifically mentioned. Information found in the words *rabbit* and *picture* are apparently enough to pick out the verb's proper meaning. There is no other evidence, after all.

A suspicious circularity lurks here, of course. If the noun group in the object case helps select a meaning for the verb, how is it that information peculiar to each verb meaning helps to find the object in the first place? Have patience. This will be sorted out when we speculate about an overall algorithm for exploiting all the constraints.

Particles Help Select Verb Meaning As Well

Another way verb meanings are selected is through a small family of selector words. By custom, selector words used in combination with verbs are called *particles* rather than *prepositions,* but the same words do both jobs. Some classic examples involve particle selection of meanings for *throw* and *pick:*

He *threw* some food.

He *threw away* some food.

He *threw up* some food.

She *picked up* some candy.

She *picked out* a nice assortment.

Contexts Add Further Constraint

One final strong influence on meaning derives from the overall context. Curiously, quite a lot can be gained from a very coarse categorization of life's subjects into a few worlds like these:

The physical world. This is the primary one. Things change state by changing position and by losing or acquiring properties and relationships. All other worlds relate strongly to the physical world through analogy.

The mental world. This is the world in which the objects are facts, ideas, and concepts. We think about them with verbs, properties, and relationships borrowed from the physical world, just as if the abstractions were physical things capable of changes in location and other state parameters. Consider these examples:

The theory is supported by facts.

The overall concept is solid.

The idea was exposed in the class.

Truth poured out of the book.

The ownership world. In the ownership world the objects are abstract certificates of control, possession, or ownership whose locations are in the hands of people or organizations. Again the happenings of this world are communicated in language strongly analogous to that of the physical world:

The bank took the car back.

Robbie took the ball away from Spot.

Note that transfer of a physical thing is often, but not necessarily, implied. We assume Robbie is holding the ball he took control of, but the bank probably never sees the physical car.

Knowledge about the identity of the world can influence the meaning of both verbs and noun groups. Consider this:

Robbie was killed by the bank.

If the physical world is the context, then poor Robbie has just died next to a river. If the communication is about the ownership world, however, then Robbie's fate is some major ruin caused by a financial institution.

Sentences Succumb to a Constraint Resolution

Since we now have an interplay of constraints as figure 3-37 shows, it is time to postulate an algorithm for using them. The algorithm will not be perfect since much of the linguistics of the sentence remains an active arena for death-grip debates. We will nevertheless try to give an idea of how most simple sentences can be understood by presenting the simple overall strategy shown by figure 3-38.

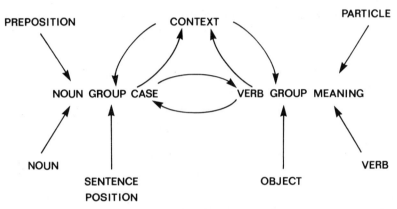

Figure 3-37 A sentence's noun groups and verb group stand among many constraints. The object is a particular noun group distinguished by its invariable lack of a preposition and by its strength in determining the meaning of the verb.

We assume, for the sake of simplicity, that all noun groups support and help describe the action. We ignore the existence of noun groups which modify other noun groups. We further assume, as stipulated earlier, that an available program has the talent required to split up simple sentences into a verb group and noun groups, some of which are introduced by prepositions. Later we will look at such a program in detail. For now it is enough to assume its existence and work with its capabilities.

The first step, that of finding the main verb, is therefore accomplished by an assumed program. That program returns with a verb group that may very well contain a verb with many possible meanings. Several steps offer opportunities to successively hack away at the collection of meanings, ultimately yielding a unique interpretation, or at worst, a small number.

Noting the presence or absence of a particle helps considerably. Verb meanings inconsistent with an observed particle or inconsistent with the absence of a particle are thrown out immediately.

The next step is to locate the object among the noun groups without flagging prepositions, but the proper choice depends on whether the verb group is passive. Suppose it is. It is then a sure bet that the semantic object, the thing the sentence

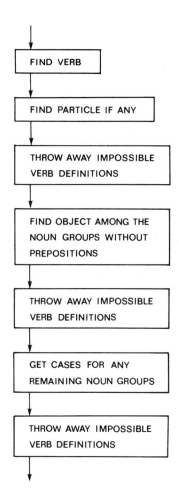

Figure 3-38 For simple sentences the verb meaning and case assignments can be found straightforwardly.

is about, must occupy a spot in front of the verb. It is what one learns to call the subject of the sentence in grammar school, so keep in mind the distinction between syntactic and semantic cases. The object of interest here is the semantic object.

If the verb is active, the most likely possibility is that the object follows the verb. If there is only one preposition-free noun group after the verb, the odds are that it is the object, given that it does not show signs of specifying time. Normally time noun groups are easily recognized on the basis of their constituent words. If there are two preposition-free noun groups following the verb after time and place noun groups are discarded, then hopefully the verb dictionary says something about whether the first or second one is the object by default. Otherwise, the second is probably the object. All this is directly derailed if the verb does not require an object. Assume that it does, just so things can be kept manageable.

With the object in hand, there is again an opportunity to weed out noxious verb meanings, namely those whose stored definitions are incompatible with the now known object.

At this point it is conceivable that more than one verb meaning remains, possibly with more than one of the noun groups serving as potential objects. Although unlikely, provision must be made. The understanding process must go forward with more than one interpretation in parallel. It is an empirical fact, however, that human communicators do not seem to permit branching to get out of hand. Just as the number of interpretations seems to explode, some constraint or another comes in and keeps things manageable.

In any event, it is now appropriate to nail down the cases for other noun groups, starting with those without prepositions. Again the surviving verb meanings may state preferences about what they want and where they want it. Many active verbs, for example, demand an overt agent and prefer to find it in the syntactic subject position. Such verb-carried demands are ordinarily enough to fix the case for the one or two preposition-free noun groups that may be found in addition to the object. Knowing the cases for the noun groups without prepositions then greatly simplifies identifying the cases for those with prepositions by virtue of the powerful constraint dictating that only one instance of a case can appear per sentence. Consider, for example, a sentence containing a noun group introduced with the word *by*. This word typically introduces either the agent case or the conveyance or the location. If the agent role is already spoken for by the syntactic subject, then only the conveyance and location possibilities remain. Generally this remaining ambiguity can then be resolved either by knowledge about the words in the noun group or by deference to the dictionary-stated needs of the verb.

Finally, knowing that certain cases are present may help resolve any remaining ambiguity of verb meaning.

Whew! It is done, sort of. The procedure is *not* completely trustworthy, but it does suggest that the use of constraints is a reasonable approach to analysis in natural language. The next section solidifies the important points by way of some examples.

Examples Using TAKE Help Explain How Constraints Interact

Suppose Robbie and Suzie are robots that communicate using a very simple and very limited subset of English that includes the objects shown in figure 3-39. The verbs in their subset of English may have more than one meaning, but they certainly do not have all of the meanings possible in unrestricted English.

Robbie and Suzie move things, get sick, engage in business activities, and date. Consequently the verb *take* has a variety of meanings:

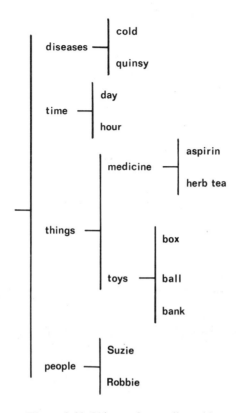

Figure 3-39 Objects of a small world.

TAKE1 means transport. Either source or destination or both should appear.

TAKE2 means swindle. The destination case is absent when this meaning is intended. Only people can be swindled as there are no institutions.

TAKE3 means to swallow medicine. The available medicines include aspirin. The beneficiary is the same as the agent.

TAKE4 means to steal. People are not stolen.

TAKE5 means to initate and execute a social event with another person. The particle *out* is always used.

TAKE6 means to remove. The particle *out* is always used. People cannot be removed.

TAKE7 means to assume control. The particle *over* signals this meaning.

TAKE8 means to remove from the body. The particle *off* is always used.

These various meanings combine with noun groups according to the rules of a simplified case grammar. Assume all passive sentences have exactly one prepositionless noun group (the traditional syntactic subject) and it appears before the verb. All active sentences have one such preposition-free noun group before the verb and one or two following it (the traditional indirect and direct objects).

Case	Flag	Restriction on case fillers
object	----	----
source	from	----
destination	to	----
agent	by	must be PEOPLE
conveyance	by	must not be PEOPLE
co-agent	with	must be PEOPLE
instrument	with	must not be PEOPLE
beneficiary	for	must be PEOPLE
duration	for	must be TIME
raw material	out of	must not be PEOPLE
old surround	out of	----
new surround	into	----

Now we can examine a few sentences with a view toward better understanding the way various constraints interact.

Robbie took aspirin. The verb meanings TAKE5 through TAKE8 are eliminated because there is no particle. Evidently Robbie is the agent and aspirin is the object by virtue of word order and the lack of alternatives. TAKE1 is unlikely because there are no noun groups that can be either the source or the destination of a transporting action. TAKE2 is out because aspirin is not a subclass of people and hence cannot be swindled. Thus the sentence means that either Robbie swallowed aspirin or he stole some.

Robbie took aspirin for Suzie. Robbie is the agent and aspirin is the object by the same word order argument used before. Again only TAKE3 and TAKE4 survive particle and object considerations. *For* can flag either the beneficiary or duration, but since Suzie is not time, she must be the beneficiary. This in turn eliminates the TAKE3, swallow medicine definition because it requires the agent and beneficiary to be the same. Robbie has stolen. (Of course Robbie may have swallowed aspirin because Suzie begged and pleaded him to, but that depth of semantic analysis is beyond the capability of this system.)

Robbie took out Suzie. The particle limits the verb meaning to TAKE5 and TAKE6, to date or to remove. TAKE6 requires an inanimate object, so Robbie dated Suzie.

Robbie took out the garbage. Garbage is inanimate, hence removed, not dated.

Robbie took the ball to Suzie. Given the ball is the object, TAKE1 and TAKE4, to transport and to steal are the alternatives. Since there is a destination case given, TAKE1, to transport is preferred.

Robbie took Suzie the ball. Again the ball is the object but the lack of a flagging preposition makes the role of Suzie unclear and there is no ready way to decide between TAKE1 and TAKE4.

Robbie took Suzie. Suzie being the object, TAKE1 and TAKE2, to transport and to swindle are possible. Since there is no source or destination, Robbie has probably swindled Suzie.

Robbie took Suzie to the ballet. With a destination, the swindle conclusion is unlikely. Robbie has transported.

The ball was taken out of town by Robbie by car for a day for Suzie. Since the sentence is passive, the ball is the object. This limits the verb meaning to TAKE1 or TAKE4. This ambiguity remains. The compound preposition *out of* can flag either raw material or old surround. Knowing about what can be a raw material or that *take* is not a form of *construct* should, resolve the two possibilities, but that sort of information is not available in this simple analysis. *Car* is an unknown word so it could be either the agent or a conveyance. But since Robbie is animate, he must be an agent, thus filling the agent slot, forcing car to be a conveyance. Finally, a day and Suzie are easily resolved into duration and beneficiary by way of the usual constraint check.

Instantiated Case Slots Help Answer Questions

Once the case structure of a sentence is worked out, many questions about the indicated activity are answered by simple reference to the occupants of the case slots. Consider this statement:

> *Robbie made coffee for Suzie with a percolator.*

There are four noun groups, each of which fits into a particular case:

object	➤	coffee
agent	➤	Robbie
instrument	➤	a percolator
beneficiary	➤	Suzie

Four corresponding questions can be answered now:

What was made?	➤	object	➤	coffee
Who made it?	➤	agent	➤	Robbie
With what was it made?	➤	instrument	➤	a percolator
For whom was it made?	➤	beneficiary	➤	Suzie

Similar results follow from another sentence:

Robbie went to the theater with Suzie by car.

Who went?	➤	agent	➤	Robbie
With whom did he go?	➤	co-agent	➤	Suzie
To where did he go?	➤	destination	➤	the theater
By what did they travel	➤	conveyance	➤	car

Thus cases roughly correspond on a one-to-one basis with some of the simple questions one is likely to ask about an action. This is not surprising. After all, the cases are alleged to be a nearly exhaustive categorization of the things which can describe the action specified in general terms by the verb. It is only natural for the set of categories to be sufficiently refined to offer a clean correspondence to the aspects of an action that are generally of enough interest or importance to be asked about.

Such question answering is important, but keep in mind that it is only one of the functions of first-line semantic analysis. Presumably the results of case partitioning are the fodder for still deeper mechanisms that understand the relationships between individual sentences, evolving contexts, and global knowledge about the world. This comes later. For now we rest content with the demonstration that understanding the interplay of constraints is a powerful way for us to approach some difficult problems. It is not the only way, but it is as important as any. We will look at alternatives presently.

SUMMARY

■ Improving and refining descriptions often mobilizes powerful constraints that force conclusions directly, without sophisticated problem solving and reasoning mechanisms. Both scene analysis and sentence understanding bear this out.

■ For the scene analysis of line drawings, Waltz ends up with a need to enumerate a few thousand junction possibilities. Although large, the number is still manageable.

■ Generally the Waltz procedure produces exactly one interpretation for each line in a scene. Only a few lines will have more than one interpretation, and then usually only two or three. The constraint contributed by observed shadows is partly responsible — supposing shadows were only an annoying complication actually made early work more difficult!

■ Potentially, constraints could propagate over a considerable distance. They do not for two reasons: first, influence does not readily pass through the many T joints found on object boundaries; and second, most lines are fully disambiguated after only a few nearby vertexes are explored; constraint cannot pass through. To a large extent, this part of scene analysis is a local phenomenon.

■ Identifying the case role of the noun groups in a sentence is similar to scene analysis in that solid conclusions can often come through simple use of catalogues of constraint properties.

■ Simple sentences consist of a verb group and some number of noun groups supporting the verb group by filling case slots. In any given sentence there is normally not more than one instance of most case types.

■ Some common cases are object, agent, instrument, co-agent, source and destination, conveyance, trajectory, location, beneficiary, raw material, and time. Most of these are associated with particular prepositions which have the sole right to introduce them.

■ Constraint-based sentence analysis makes use of knowledge about the cases and their prepositions; the verbs, their particles, and the cases they require; the world under discussion; and some facts about standard ordering.

REFERENCES

■ Aldolfo Guzman, "Computer Recognition of Three-Dimensional Objects in a Visual Scene," PhD thesis, AI-TR-228, The Artificial Intelligence Laboratory, Massachusetts Institute of Technology, Cambridge, Massachusetts, 1968. Early *ad hoc* methods for scene analysis, particularly those developed by Guzman, stimulated much of the subsequent work.

■ David Waltz, "Understanding Line Drawings of Scenes with Shadows," in *The Psychology of Computer Vision,* edited by Patrick Henry Winston, McGraw-Hill Book Company, New York, 1975. The *tour de force* in scene analysis. The work deals not only with the labeling scheme explained here, but also with similar schemes involving line and surface directions.

■ A. K. Mackworth, "Interpreting Pictures of Polyhedral Scenes," *Artificial Intelligence,* vol. 4, no. 2, 1973. Important work showing how Waltz-like constraints can be derived automatically.

■ C. J. Filmore, "The Case for Case," in *Universals in Linguistic Theory,* edited by E. Bach and R. Harms, Holt, Rinehart, and Winston, New York, 1968. The classic paper on the case concept.

■ William A. Martin, "A Theory of Grammar," technical report in preparation, Laboratory of Computer Science, Massachusetts Institute of Technology, Cambridge, Massachusetts. Source of many of the ideas in this chapter.

■ Beth Levin, "Uses of *Under,*" B.S. Thesis, Electrical Engineering and Computer Science Department, Massachusetts Institute of Technology, Cambridge, Massachusetts, 1976. An exhaustive treatment of the use of *under* from the point of view of case grammar.

Huffman and Clowes, working independently, devised labeling schemes directly antecedent to Waltz'. Their work was limited to the simplified domain in which there are no shadows and only trihedral vertexes.

■   David Huffman, "Impossible Objects as Nonsense Sentences," in *Machine Intelligence 6,* edited by B. Meltzer and D. Michie, Edinburgh University Press, Edinburgh, Scotland, 1971.

■   Maxwell Clowes, "On Seeing Things," *Artificial Intelligence,* vol. 2, no. 1, 1971.

4
EXPLORING ALTERNATIVES

While solving problems, it is often necessary to find paths through network or tree structures. Map traversal has this flavor since going from one city to another involves moving over a sequence of intervening city *nodes* through the available highway *branches*.

When computer programs deal with such problems, the result is two paths, one being a trace through the explored situations or places, the other being a trace through the methods that the computer program itself chooses to use. Figure 4-1 shows this. What happens depends jointly on the structure of the domain and on the structure of the problem solver.

■ If we concentrate on how a system works through a network or tree structure natural to a target domain, we are studying *search*. If we concentrate instead on how the system selects among its internal methods, we are studying *control*.

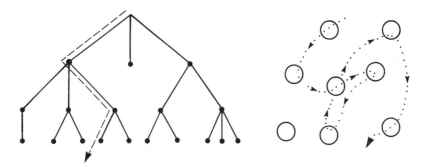

Figure 4-1 Search focuses on methods for exploring the tree stuctures that frequently describe problem domains. Control topics focus on how the problem solver chooses to shift attention among its subprocesses.

Clearly there is no solid boundary dividing search from control. The question is one of focus or point of view. One requires the other to make sense, just as hard work and brains are different, but required jointly for successful scholarship. Moreover, some people prefer to regard control as that special case of search for which the search locus moves through a problem solver's individual methods.

There continues to be argument about whether search is more important than control, particularly with respect to playing games like chess. Probably the extremists on both sides are wrong, and both search strategy and control decisions can be simple, given good problem descriptions. But it is premature to pursue this argument now. In this chapter search is the focus, control will be next, and later on we will return to descriptions and representations.

Figure 4-2 is a roadmap indicating our objectives. As shown, three topics lie under the general heading of search techniques. The first, basic search, includes such

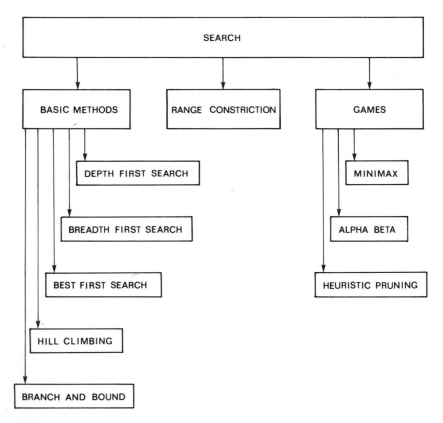

Figure 4-2 The principal divisions of search technology. Many basic methods address the problem of finding acceptable solutions efficiently. Some concentrate on the harder problem of finding optimal solutions efficiently. Waltz' labeling procedure is perhaps the clearest example of the range constriction approach. Techniques for games differ considerably from others because of the additional adversary feature.

classic notions as depth-first and breadth-first searches as well as various hill-climbing and optimal-path methods. Next, the general subject of search by range constriction will be discussed using the special case problem of propagating line labels through line drawings. And finally, there is game-playing in which the notion of search takes on special meaning.

BASIC SEARCH METHODS

We begin with the map-traversal problem. Consider figure 4-3. Suppose we want to move from city S, the starting point, to city F, the final goal, without wasting fuel. Properly speaking, the problem of determining a good path is a search problem in which two kinds of effort are involved:

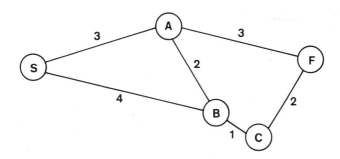

Figure 4-3 A basic search problem. A path must be found from the start node to the finish node. Since the problem solver has no roadmap initially, it must do its own exploring to learn about connections and distances.

■   First, there is the effort expended in *finding* either some path or the best path.

■   And, second, there is the effort actually expended in *traversing* the network.

If it is necessary to go from S to F often, then it is worth a lot to find a really good route. On the other hand, if only *one* trip is required, and if the network is such that hard work is required to force a way through it at all, then it is proper to be content as soon as *some* route is found, even though better ones could be found with more work. For the moment we will consider only the problem of finding one path. We will return to finding optimal paths later.

The most obvious way to find the optimal solution is to devise some bookkeeping scheme that allows orderly exploration of all possible paths. It is useful to note that the bookkeeping scheme must not allow itself to cycle in the network. It would be

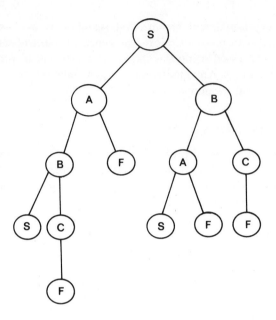

Figure 4-4 Terminating paths leading to previously visited nodes turns networks into trees.

senseless to go through a sequence like S-A-B-S-A-B-... over and over again. Thus networks to be searched are equivalent to trees like the one shown in figure 4-4. The tree shown there is made from the network in figure 4-3 by following each possible path outward from the network's starting point until it runs into a node already visited.

Note that if no city is to be visited twice, there can be no more than n levels, where n is the total number of cities, five here. Each path's total distance would be calculated and the minimum noted. In the example, the destination is reached at the end of eleven distinct paths, each of which has a total length given by adding up just a few distances.

Depth First Searches Dive Deeply into the Search Tree

Given that one path is as good as any other, one no-fuss idea is to pick some alternative at every node visited and work forward from that alternative. Other alternatives at the same level are ignored completely as long as there is any hope of reaching the destination using the original choice. This is the essence of the *depth-first search* idea. Using a convention that the alternatives are tried in left-to-right order, the first action in working on the situation in figure 4-5 would be a headlong dash to the bottom of the tree along the left-most branches.

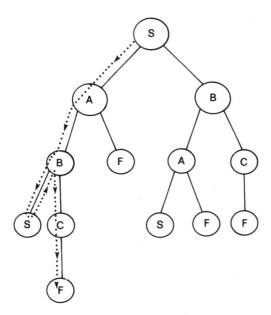

Figure 4-5 In depth-first search, some alternative is selected and pursued at each decision point until forward progress is blocked. Then forward progress begins again from the nearest decision point with unexplored alternatives.

But since this original set of decisions regarding alternatives fails to lead to the F node, the next step is to back up to the nearest node with an unexplored alternative. The last such node is B. The remaining alternative is better, bringing eventual success through C as shown. If the path through C had not worked out, then the process would move still further back up the tree seeking another viable decision point to move forward from. On reaching A, movement would go down again reaching the destination from there.

Warning: depth-first search is an aggressive but dangerous procedure. Imagine a more complicated tree with many more levels than in the sample tree illustrated. A process doing depth-first movement through such a tree is likely to slip past the level at which the F node appears and waste incredible energy in exhaustively exploring parts of the tree lower down. For such trees, depth-first search, while easily implemented, is the worst possible approach.

Breadth-First Searches Push Uniformly into the Search Tree

When depth-first search is a poor idea, breadth-first movement may be useful. Breadth-first searches look for the destination among all nodes at a given level before using the branches descending from those nodes to push on. In the situation shown in figure 4-6, B would be checked just after A. The process would then move on to the next level and discover the F node just after noting that A leads to B as well. This will work even if the tree were infinite or effectively infinite. Although the breadth-first idea is careful and conservative, it can be wasteful. If all paths lead to the destination node at more or less the same depth, then breadth-first search works harder than depth-first search.

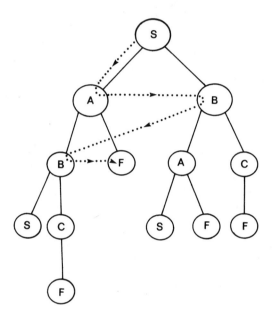

Figure 4-6 In breadth-first search, all alternatives at each decision point receive equal attention. Investigation spreads through the tree layer by layer.

Exhaustive Search Can Be Too Exhausting

Unfortunately, the size of search trees is often very large, making both the depth-first and breadth-first exhaustive enumeration techniques extremely unpalatable. Suppose that instead of a few levels there is a moderately large number. Suppose further that the branching is completely uniform and that the number of alternative branches at each node is b. Then in the first level there will be b nodes. For each of these b nodes there will be b more nodes in the second level or b^2. Continuing this leads to the conclusion that the number of nodes at the bottom must be b^n. In following through the lines of play in chess, for example, one deals with b values on the order of 35 and n values of 100 or more. This must mean that the number of situations found at the bottom of the tree of all possible chess moves would be on the order of $35^{100} = 2.5 \times 10^{154}$. If the distance for the path associated with each terminal node were computed in a nanosecond, it would take 10^{138} years to do the work! Fortunately, there are some situations that allow alternative strategies which trim off a great deal of work.

Local Measurements Turn Depth-First Search into Hill Climbing

Search efficiency may improve spectacularly if there is some way of ordering the branches under each node so that the most promising are explored first. In many situations, measurements can be made to determine a reasonable ordering. Here are some examples:

■ On entering a room we find the temperature uncomfortable. Walking over to the thermostat, we find to our horror that we cannot tell which way to move the setting because the temperature markings have been obliterated.

■ The picture on our TV set has gone bad over a period of time. We must adjust the tuning, color, tint, and brightness controls for the best picture.

■ Halfway up a mountain a terrible fog comes in. Of course we have no map or trail to follow but we do have a compass and a determination to get to the top.

Each of these problems conforms to an abstraction in which there are some adjustable parameters and a way of measuring the performance associated with any particular set of values for the parameters. In one example, the adjustable parameter is the thermostat setting, and the goodness is the resulting degree of comfort. In the TV set there are various knobs, each of which interacts with the others to determine overall picture quality. And, of course, in the mountaineering example, position is adjustable, and movement is either up or down as it changes. It is the mountaineering example that gives hill climbing its name since in each situation the measure of performance, P, is dependent on some set of parameters analogous to east-west and north-south position. See figure 4-7.

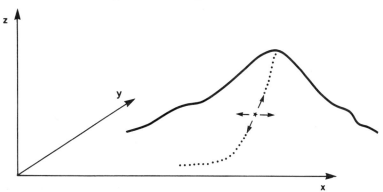

Figure 4-7 Hill climbing is depth-first search plus a method for ordering the alternatives at each decision point. In hill climbing, movement proceeds through the alternative which offers the best improvement to the situation in one step. The required measurements may be absolute or relative, precise or approximate.

■   The hill-climbing metaphor dictates that the way to maximize performance is
    to take one step in each of the standard directions, to move to the highest point
    found, and to repeat until a spot is reached which is higher than all four of the
    surrounding points reached by the one-step probes.

Hill Climbing Hits Many Snags

Nothing could be simpler than hill climbing. But the hill-climbing idea is not
universally useful. The most tragic problems are the foothill problem, the ridge
problem, and the plateau problem.

■   The *foothill problem* occurs whenever there are secondary peaks as in the first
    part of figure 4-8. The secondary peaks draw the primitive hill-climbing
    mechanism like magnets. An optimum point is found, but it is local, not global,
    and the user is left with a false sense of accomplishment.

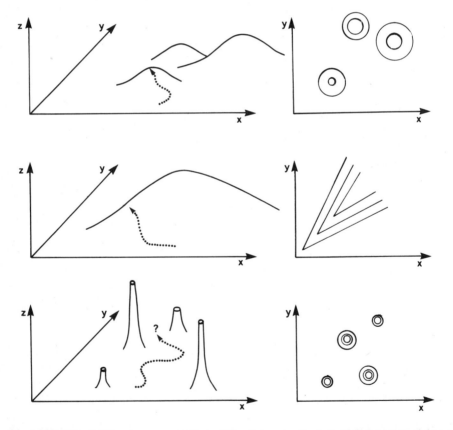

Figure 4-8 Hill climbing is a poor guide in difficult terrain. Each foothill is a potential trap.
Any point on a ridge can look like a peak because movement in all probe directions is
downward. Broad plains cause aimless wandering. In each situation, myopia is the culprit.
A more global view or a better space helps.

■ The *ridge problem* is more subtle, and consequently all the more frustrating. Suppose we are standing on what seems like a knife edge running generally from northeast to southwest as in the second part of figure 4-8. A contour map shows that each standard step takes us down even though we are not at any sort of maximum, local or global. Increasing the number of directions used for the probing steps may help. On a TV set, this would amount to turning the horizontal and vertical hold controls together whenever turning them individually makes the picture strangely worse, rather than better.

■ The *plateau problem* is even harder to handle. It comes up when there is mostly a flat area separating the peaks. In extreme cases the peaks may look like telephone poles sticking up in a football field as in the third part of figure 4-8. The local improvement operation breaks down completely. For all but a vanishingly small number of positions, all standard-step probes leave performance unchanged.

Hill Climbing Breaks Down When There Are Many Dimensions

Hill-climbing problems are not too serious in one-dimensional parameter spaces — we can usually find some channel on a TV set even if the picture is uniformly nonexistent over most of the tuning control's range. But if we had to have two or more controls almost exactly right to tune in, there would be more cursing than entertainment. When 20, 30, or more features may be involved in a problem, it becomes clear that hill climbing has severe limits.

■ Each of the problems — foothill, ridge, plateau — is greatly exacerbated as the number of parameter dimensions increases.

Some systems use simple performance functions which illustrate this. The purpose of the performance functions is to combine evidence from several aspects of a situation and produce a single number which serves as an overall evaluation. This is often done in simple game playing programs. In checkers, for example, the individual sources of evidence typically include numbers associated with the number of pieces, center control, mobility, and so on. The simplest way of putting them together is to form a weighted sum:

$$
\begin{aligned}
\text{<strength>} \quad = \quad & w_1 \times f_1[\text{<board-situation>}] \\
& + w_2 \times f_2[\text{<board-situation>}] \\
& + \ldots \\
& + w_n \times f_n[\text{<board-situation>}]
\end{aligned}
$$

where the f_i's are the evidence-yielding functions of board situations and the w_i's are the weights.

Hill climbing itself is one way of finding a set of weights. First some initial set of weights is chosen, then the weights are perturbed as play progresses. The problem, of course, is sensibly perturbing the weights. If there are 20 fs, then there are 20 dimensions and $2 \times 20 = 40$ basic directions from each node in weight space.

Experience has shown that the resulting search suffers from all of the hill-climbing problems.

The Hill-Climbing Metaphor Can Deflect Attention from Description and Representation

What are the relevant aspects of a problem? How can these relevant aspects be mapped into a set of numerical parameters? How can performance measures be created for a given set of parameters? These are hard questions about which the hill-climbing metaphors say nothing. Infatuation with them often leads to *ad hoc* schemes for tinkering with awkward spaces rather than to finding spaces for which search is simple or not relevant. Using hill climbing to form weighted sums for evaluating game trees is an example. It is easy to get involved and to work hard within that framework, but the very idea of using weighted sums for evaluating game situations is probably a bad idea.

Hill Climbing in Similarity Space Speeds Recognition

On the other side, hill climbing can be involved in sophisticated, reasonable processes. For an illustration, consider the problem of identifying an unknown blocks-world object, using descriptions and differences between them. Imagine a set of models organized into a kind of network as illustrated in figure 4-9. The links connect pairs which are very similar in the sense of the near miss.

Now suppose that an unknown object is to be identified. What should be done if the first comparison against some particular model in the network fails as it ordinarily will? If the match did not fail by much, if the unknown seems like the model in many respects, then surely other models known to be similar should be

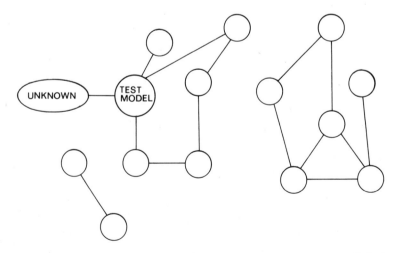

Figure 4-9 Identification of an unknown is faster if similar test models are linked up in clusters. If a trial match fails, but not by much, it makes sense to try nearby models.

tried next. These similar models are precisely the ones connected by links to the original model tested.

In an obvious improvement, the links between models not only convey similarity but also describe the similarity (or more precisely, the difference), as shown in figure 4-10. This not only allows selection of the next test model from a family of likely candidates but also insures selection of the particular member of that family most likely to succeed. The principle is as follows:

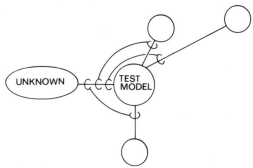

Figure 4-10 In a similarity network, test models are linked up and differences among them are recorded. When a trial match fails, but not by much, the next model tried differs from the current one in the same way the unknown does. Thus progress through the model net is guided by a kind of analogy process.

■ If an unknown differs from a test model in the same way some satellite of the test model differs from it, then that satellite is a good model to test next. In terms of the network metaphors, the initial match is not a failure, it is a knowledge probe.

This is a kind of hill climbing because the movement through the model network is determined by differences between one model and the immediate neighbor that seems most likely to yield an improved match against the unknown.

Note, incidentally, that the process of moving through a network of linked models seems related to solving geometric-analogy problems as well. The analogy metaphor fits because the decision about which neighbor to use is determined by comparing descriptions of differences. In solving analogy problems, one is concerned with descriptions of the differences between drawings A and B and between C and some X:

$d[A,B] \quad d[C,X]$

Each of these expressions represents a rule. To do the problem, the rule taking A into B is compared with all the others. This comparison itself is a description which must be minimized over X.

$d[\, d[A,B] \,,\, d[C,X]\,]$

For moving through a similarity net, the descriptions are between the unknown, U, and the test model, T, and between the various satellites, S, and the test model.

$$d[U,T] \quad d[S,T]$$

To move, these descriptions are compared, minimizing over S:

$$d[\ d[U,T]\ ,\ d[S,T]\ ]$$

The similarity of this expression to the one for solving analogy problems shows that the processes are analogous.

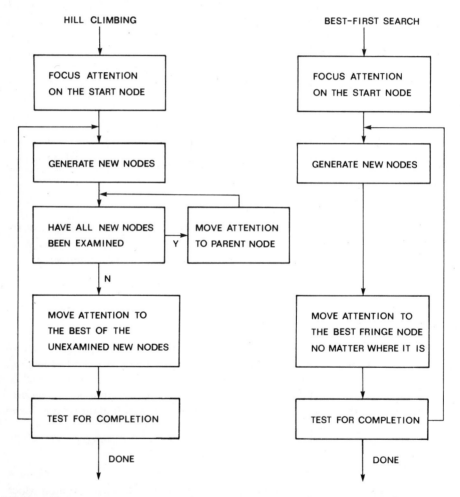

Figure 4-11 Best-first search differs only a little from basic hill climbing. In best-first search, attention moves during each cycle to the best node found globally, whereas in basic hill climbing, attention moves to the best node found locally.

Best-First Search Probes Forward from the Best Partial Path

In classical hill climbing, forward motion is always from the last decision through the seemingly best descendant. A slight, but important variation is illustrated in figure 4-11. Forward motion is from the best node so far, no matter where it is in the partially developed tree. This is called best-first search. It works like a team of cooperating mountaineers seeking out the highest point in a mountain range: they maintain radio contact, move the highest subteam forward at all times, and divide subteams into sub-subteams at path junctions.

Since motion is always in the direction that seems most economical, one might suppose that the total path length of solutions found with this method would tend to be nearer the optimal than those found by pure depth-first or breadth-first searches which move slavishly without regard to the problem. This is correct, in general, but not absolutely certain. Next we examine a way of using a similar idea in a scheme which guarantees discovery of the optimal path.

The Branch-and-Bound Strategy Probes Forward from the Least-Cost Partial Path

The basic idea is simple. Suppose an optimal solution is desired for the trivial tree shown in figure 4-12. Looking only at the first level, the A node is clearly closer than B. Following A to the destination at the next level reveals that the total path length is four. But this means there is no point in calculating the path length for the alternative path through node B since at B the incomplete path's length is already five and hence longer than the path for the known solution through A.

More generally the scheme works like this: During the search there are many incomplete paths contending for further consideration. The shortest one is extended one level, creating as many new incomplete paths as there are branches. These new

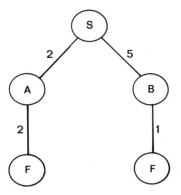

Figure 4-12 The branch-and-bound procedure finds optimal paths by extending the shortest path during each cycle. Here action terminates when the path through node A is extended because the total path length of four is less than the partial path length of five still pending at node B.

paths are then considered along with the remaining old ones and again the shortest is extended. This repeats until the destination is reached along some path. Since the shortest path was always chosen for extension, the path first reaching the destination is certain to be optimal.

The only cause for worry comes up because the last step in reaching the destination may be long enough to make the supposed solution longer than one or more incomplete paths. It might be that only a tiny step would extend one of these incomplete paths to the solution point. To be sure this is not so, all the incomplete paths are extended as before until each is either longer than the supposed solution path or dislodges it.

Now look again at the city traversal problem and see how branch-and-bound works there. Figure 4-13 illustrates the exploration sequence. In the first step, A and B are identified as the descendants of the only active node, S. The partial path distance of A is 3 and that of B is 4, and A therefore becomes the active node. Then B and F are generated from A with partial path distances of 5 and 6. Since F now has a known distance of 6, the algorithm will terminate as soon as all other paths are shown to have a length of 6 or more. Both possibilities are paths extending through B. The one with partial path length 4 is extended first, giving a path ending at A with length 6 and one at C with length 5. Now partial paths ending at B and C have length 5 but extending either leads to partial paths of length 6 or greater and nothing further is to be done. In this example very little is saved relative to exhaustive search.

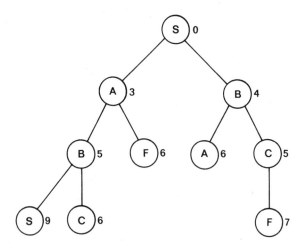

Figure 4-13 The branch-and-bound procedure determines that the path S-A-F is optimal because all other paths have been extended far enough for their lengths to be equal or greater.

In some cases the search can be greatly improved by using guesses about the distances remaining as well as facts about distances already accumulated. After all, if a guess about distance remaining is good, then that guessed distance added to the definitely known distance already traversed should be a good guess about total path length:

<estimated total path length>
  =   <distance already traveled>
       + <estimated distance remaining>

Surely it makes sense to work hardest on developing the path with the shortest estimated path length until such time as the estimate changes upward enough to leave some other path with a lower estimated distance. How well this works depends on how good the guesses are. If they are exact and unfailing, then there is no problem at all. Even at the beginning the distance along the optimal path is known. Wherever there is a choice, the alternative selected is the one that yields the known optimal distance as the *estimated* total path distance. But in general, guesses are not perfect, and a bad overestimate somewhere along the true optimal path may cause it to be permanently overlooked.

But note that *underestimates* cannot cause the right path to be overlooked. An underestimate of the distance remaining yields an underestimate of total path length.

<underestimate of path length>
  =   <distance already travelled>
       + <underestimate of distance remaining>

But if a total path is found by repeatedly extending the path with the smallest underestimate so far, no further work need be done, since it is certain that the real distance along some completed nonoptimal path cannot be shorter than an underestimate of the distance along an incomplete optimal path. If all estimates of remaining distance can be guaranteed to be underestimates, there can be no error in ultimate path selection.

In traveling through networks of cities, the air distance is guaranteed to be an underestimate. Figure 4-14 shows what happens using it on the previous example. As before, A and B are generated from S. Again A is the node to search from since its lower-bound path distance is 6 which is better than that for B. Note that A leads by another route to B again and to F. But now the distance to F, 6, is smaller than the lower-bound path lengths for both of the partial paths. Search stops with a considerable saving effected.

Of course, the closer the underestimate is to the true distance, the better things will work in terms of efficiency, since if there is no difference at all, there is no chance of developing any false movement. At the other extreme, the underestimate may

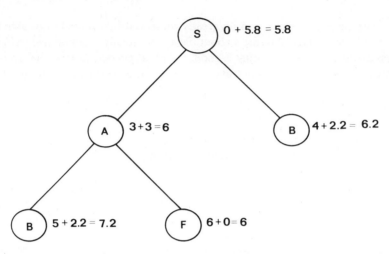

Figure 4-14 An estimate on distance remaining can improve branch-and-bound performance, but the estimate must be certain to be less than the true distance to guarantee the result. Here the estimate is straight-line distance to the finish node. The optimal path is found with less work because the other paths are terminated more quickly by lower-bound estimates on total length than by partial length as accumulated so far.

be so poor as to be hardly better than a guess of zero, which certainly must always be the ultimate underestimate of remaining distance. In fact, ignoring estimates of remaining distance altogether can be viewed as the special case in which the underestimate used is uniformly zero.

AND/OR Trees Make Problem Solving Seem Like Search

To close this section we turn sharply away from map traversal problems in order to see that search ideas can be relevant to more general problem solving as well. In particular, we will develop the AND/OR tree idea which descends from two obvious heuristics:

■ Try to convert a hard problem into one simpler equivalent.
■ Try to convert a hard problem into several simpler subproblems.

Consider the first heuristic. There may be more than one simpler problem that is equivalent to the hard one. Moreover, the best way to solve any one of the possible simpler problems may be to convert it too. The natural result, then, is another tree structure in which each node represents a problem to solve. Such a tree is called an OR tree since at any node, all branches lead to descendent problems which solve the parent problem. Solving any descendent problem is enough. More generally, solving any problem at the bottom of an OR tree solves the original problem at the top as shown in the first part of figure 4-15.

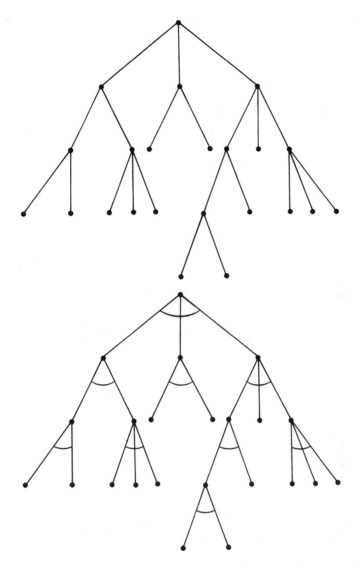

Figure 4-15 An OR tree and an AND tree. To solve the problem at the top of the OR tree, only one terminal problem need be solved, but to solve the problem at the top of the AND tree, all terminal problems must be solved.

The second heuristic complements the first because all the subproblems must be solved before the heuristic does any good. Repeated use of the idea also yields a tree structure, this time an AND tree like the one in the second part of figure 4-15.

By tradition, all the branches at AND nodes are tied together with an arc to emphasize that they help only when they all work together. Note that all the problems at the bottom of an AND tree must be satisfied before the original problem is solved.

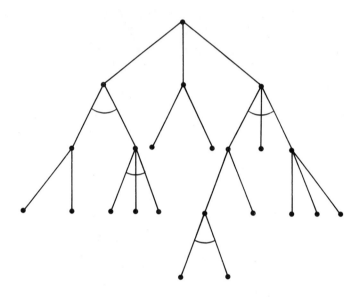

Figure 4-16 An AND/OR tree. Many combinations of terminal problem solutions suffice to solve the problem at the top since the problem solver can choose to follow any branch at any OR node encountered while moving down the tree.

One rarely sees a pure OR tree or a pure AND tree, of course. Instead both types of nodes are freely intermixed, giving trees like the one shown in figure 4-16. Of course it is possible to break up a problem into several different sets of subproblems suggesting a need to have nodes with mixed AND and OR qualities. For the sake of elegance, mixed nodes are avoided by inserting extra OR nodes into the tree. Figure 4-17 shows how this is done.

■ AND/OR trees are mixed collections of pure AND nodes, which show how a problem can be transformed into an equivalent set of subproblems, and pure OR nodes, which show how a problem can be transformed into any one of a set of equivalent problems.

The AND/OR tree typically reveals that many different collections of problems at the bottom suffice to solve the original problem at the top. The structure of an

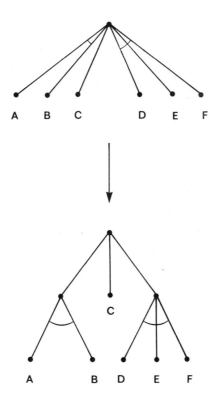

Figure 4-17 Mixed AND/OR nodes can be broken up into combinations of pure OR nodes and pure AND nodes.

AND/OR tree is often studied with interest because it reflects something of the nature of the particular problem at hand as well as the class of problems of which it is typical.

Since the typical AND/OR tree is large, one job of a problem solver is to avoid full development of the AND/OR tree implied by the problem. Therefore as the tree is grown, decisions must be made about which terminal problem to work on or convert into new problems. Since the decisions can be made through techniques resembling hill climbing or best-first search, AND/OR trees make problem solving look like a search problem. Caution is advised however. Looking at problem solving as search can draw attention away from making better problem descriptions which make the search trivial. Consequently, we will defer more talk about problem solving to the next chapter, where the climate is better, and move on to other kinds of search here.

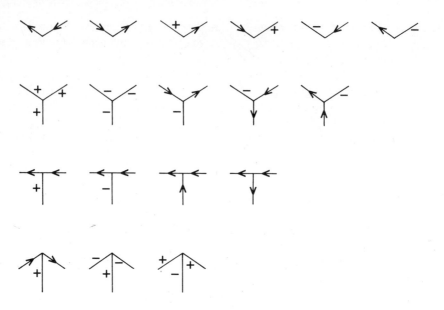

Figure 4-18 The junction combinations for the physically realizable trihedral vertexes. The + symbol labels convex edges; the −, concave; and the arrow, boundaries.

LABEL PROPAGATION IN NETWORKS

The Huffman-Clowes theory of line-drawing analysis provides another useful domain for discussing a kind of search which has quite a different flavor from the tree-oriented methods described so far. Recall that the problem is to determine if all the lines of a given drawing can be interpreted in such a way that the junction arrangements are all found in the list of 18 known to be physically possible, as shown again in figure 4-18. The solution involves an example of the so-called range-constriction search technique.

Ordinary Search Is Poor at Finding Line Labelings for Drawings

In working through arbitrary drawings, occasionally there will be situations in which more than one physically possible arrangement is consistent with the interpretations assumed at previously visited neighboring junctions. There is a choice. One junction labeling may permit finishing the analysis with physically possible junction arrangements, while others lead to disasters wherein some junctions cannot be legally labeled. From one point of view there is a tree of alternatives and a need to search. Note that the shape of the tree is determined by the order in which the junctions of the drawing are examined. Sometimes the junctions can be visited in an order that forces a definite conclusion every time. Each node in the search tree has only one branch!

Tragically, this does not always happen. Suppose, for example, that the unlabeled lines of the drawing fragment in figure 4-19 are to be labeled. There is no junction whose neighbors force a unique configuration choice. At junctions A, B, and C, for example, there are two choices as shown. This being so, suppose the junctions are investigated in lexicographic order, A, B, C, D, E, F, and G. The first

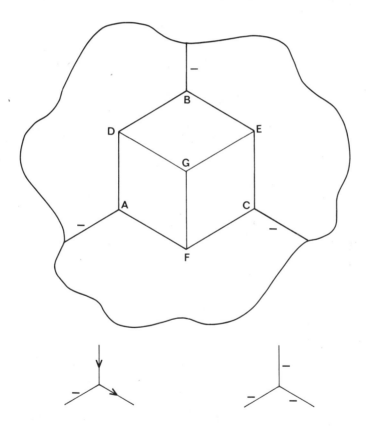

Figure 4-19 There may be no junction where a choice of labeling is forced. Here the drawing fragment presents such a situation because the −labels on all connecting lines are insufficient to force a decision anywhere. Two label combinations remain possible at each of the three FORKs entered. Search is required.

tree in figure 4-20 then reflects the choices inherent in analyzing the situation. This ordering of the junctions creates a branching tree. If the order were A, D, B, E, C, F, and G, then the tree would be the second, simpler one in figure 4-20.

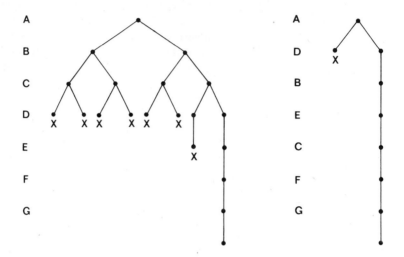

Figure 4-20 For labeling drawings, the size and shape of the search tree is determined by the order in which the junctions are considered. Here one ordering yields considerable branching relative to the other.

Another example is provided by cutting a notch in the edge of a cube as in figure 4-21. After bringing all constraints to bear by propagation from the outer edge, there still remain two choices at both A and B as shown. These choices lead to a tree structure in which two solutions survive.

The Waltz Algorithm Iterates Toward Compatible Junction Labelings

Theoretically, correct solutions could be found by depth-first or breadth-first search, but for scenes of some size, the tyranny of combinatorial explosion prevents those methods from being effective. Fortunately, there is another way of doing things which focuses on the notion of ferreting out and excluding junction arrangements that are demonstrably wrong.

Think of keeping a list of labeling possibilities for each junction. These lists are created when a junction is visited for the first time, and they are maintained each time an adjacent junction is altered. The first visit begins with a look into the table of physically possible labeling arrangements. Each arrangement found in the table is brought into the set of possibilities for the junction under investigation if that arrangement is compatible with at least one possibility in each neighbor's list of possible arrangements.

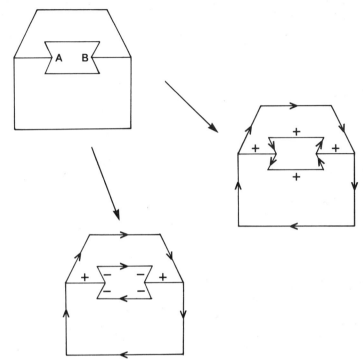

Figure 4-21 Sometimes labeling choices correspond to permanent ambiguity. In this situation, progress is stalled when the facing ARROWs are encountered because each may be labeled with either of the two combinations shown. The search tree and the fully labeled drawings show that both of the two ARROW combinations label satisfactorily even though only one is viable physically.

Suppose, for example, that two ARROWs, a FORK, and an L are buried in a drawing as in figure 4-22. Suppose, further, that these four junctions are lifted out of the drawing and analyzed. The following happens:

■ If ARROW A1 is the first junction visited and none of its neighbors have been visited, then the first step is to bring in all of the possible ARROW junction labels.

■ Suppose the L is the next junction investigated. There are six junction label combinations for Ls in the junction dictionary, but only two of these are compatible with the possibilities known for the adjacent ARROW, A1. The other four are therefore rejected immediately.

■ Having placed labels for the L, the next step is to investigate the neighboring junctions that were previously examined to see if anything can be thrown out because of the new labels at the L. For this situation nothing happens since all three of the ARROW labels at A1 are compatible with something at the L.

■ Moving on to A2, the dictionary supplies three entries as before, but for this ARROW, only one is compatible with the neighbors as already analyzed. The other two are rejected immediately.

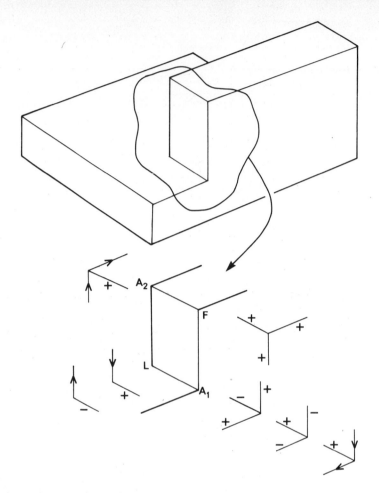

Figure 4-22 Waltz invented a range constriction procedure for labeling scenes. Here the order of investigation is A_1, L, A_2, F. When A_1 is first visited, there are no constraints from neighbors, so all three possibilities from the library are piled up. When L is visited, however, the constraint of living with the existing labelings at A_1 eliminates four L labelings, leaving only the two shown. These in turn permit only one possibility at the next junction, A_2. At A_2 the constant reexamination of neighbors has an effect for the first time, with both L and A_1 being affected.

■   The last time the neighbor of a newly visited junction was revisited, nothing happened. This time, however, looking afresh at the L reveals that only one of the two remaining labelings is compatible with the adjacent ARROW, A2.

■   Having revised the list for L, the adjacent A1 must be revisited as well. Of the three original possibilities, only one is now suitable.

■   Finally, looking at the FORK, the constraints from either of its analyzed neighbors force all but one of the five FORK entries in the junction dictionary to be rejected.

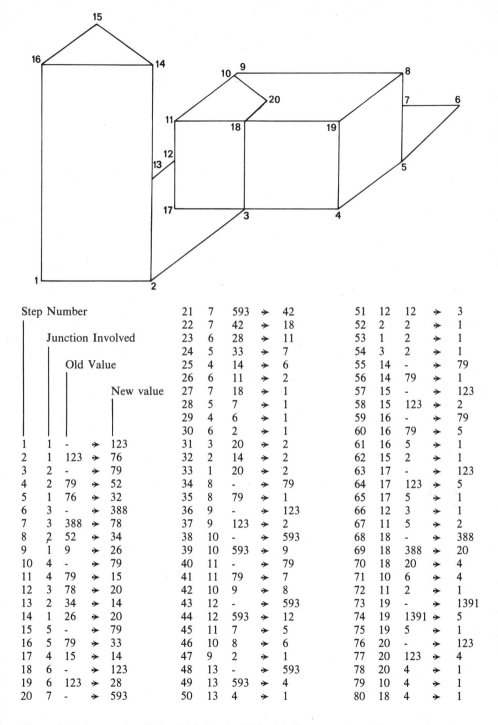

Step Number
| Junction Involved
| | Old Value
| | | New value

1	1	-	➤	123
2	1	123	➤	76
3	2	-	➤	79
4	2	79	➤	52
5	1	76	➤	32
6	3	-	➤	388
7	3	388	➤	78
8	2	52	➤	34
9	1	9	➤	26
10	4	-	➤	79
11	4	79	➤	15
12	3	78	➤	20
13	2	34	➤	14
14	1	26	➤	20
15	5	-	➤	79
16	5	79	➤	33
17	4	15	➤	14
18	6	-	➤	123
19	6	123	➤	28
20	7	-	➤	593
21	7	593	➤	42
22	7	42	➤	18
23	6	28	➤	11
24	5	33	➤	7
25	4	14	➤	6
26	6	11	➤	2
27	7	18	➤	1
28	5	7	➤	1
29	4	6	➤	1
30	6	2	➤	1
31	3	20	➤	2
32	2	14	➤	2
33	1	20	➤	2
34	8	-	➤	79
35	8	79	➤	1
36	9	-	➤	123
37	9	123	➤	2
38	10	-	➤	593
39	10	593	➤	9
40	11	-	➤	79
41	11	79	➤	7
42	10	9	➤	8
43	12	-	➤	593
44	12	593	➤	12
45	11	7	➤	5
46	10	8	➤	6
47	9	2	➤	1
48	13	-	➤	593
49	13	593	➤	4
50	13	4	➤	1
51	12	12	➤	3
52	2	2	➤	1
53	1	2	➤	1
54	3	2	➤	1
55	14	-	➤	79
56	14	79	➤	1
57	15	-	➤	123
58	15	123	➤	2
59	16	-	➤	79
60	16	79	➤	5
61	16	5	➤	1
62	15	2	➤	1
63	17	-	➤	123
64	17	123	➤	5
65	17	5	➤	1
66	12	3	➤	1
67	11	5	➤	2
68	18	-	➤	388
69	18	388	➤	20
70	18	20	➤	4
71	10	6	➤	4
72	11	2	➤	1
73	19	-	➤	1391
74	19	1391	➤	5
75	19	5	➤	1
76	20	-	➤	123
77	20	123	➤	4
78	20	4	➤	1
79	10	4	➤	1
80	18	4	➤	1

Figure 4-23 A scene handled quickly by the Waltz labeling procedure. The vertex numbers give the order in which a heuristic procedure arranges first visits. Note the initial concentration on the boundary and the speed of convergence.

Even when these four junctions are lifted out and analyzed separately, the constraint is sufficient to interpret each line uniquely.

The flow of constraints over a scene full of junctions can be dramatic when the huge Waltz label set is involved instead of the dwarfish Huffman-Clowes set. Increasing the number of choices available at each node makes ordinary depth-first search out of the question, and even constraint propagation is much too involved to effectively hand simulate.

Watching a film is the best way to appreciate what can happen. Lacking that, glancing at the scene and the trace in figure 4-23 provides some feel for how the algorithm works on a small scene. It would be unbearably tedious to follow the trace in detail, but some overall points are obvious without the effort.

Note, for example, that the junction numbering convention indicates that boundary junctions are used first. This exploits the extra constraint available from them. Further inspection of the information shows that convergence is very rapid indeed. After only two or three visits, most of the junctions have only one unique labeling associated with them. Junction 19, for example, starts with 1391 possibilites, then has this reduced to 5 by constraints coming in from one neighbor, and then gets driven to its final unique value by constraints from another.

Note also that after each junction is visited for the first time, its neighbors must be reexamined to see if all the possibilities there are still viable. And if this causes changes at the neighbors, then further checking must be done at their neighbors, and so on until propagating influences stop somewhere at junctions where nothing happens, no previous possibilities being excluded.

DEALING WITH ADVERSARIES

Still another sort of search comes up because of work on games, a subject that remains one of great unrest. For games like chess, checkers, and the oriental game, Go, some people feel that hardly any knowledge is useful beyond whatever is needed to look ahead through many rounds of move and counter-move, imagining the likely consequences of each possible play. Others claim that brilliant strategic play is beyond the capability of approaches based solely on look ahead — much more is required in the direction of understanding and reacting to various sorts of position patterns.

The Adversary Nature of Games Makes Searching Game Trees Different

Thought and practice so far have favored the look-ahead focus, perhaps because the subject of search is relatively tractable. The nodes in the search tree naturally represent board configurations, and they are linked by way of moves that transform one situation into another. Figure 4-24 illustrates. Of course there is a new twist in that the decisions are made by two people, acting as adversaries, each making a decision in turn.

Real games involve quite a few more than the two moves illustrated at any point in the game. The average is given by a statistic known as the branching factor.

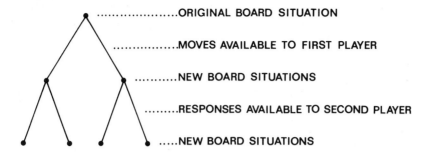

................ORIGINAL BOARD SITUATION

................MOVES AVAILABLE TO FIRST PLAYER

...........NEW BOARD SITUATIONS

.........RESPONSES AVAILABLE TO SECOND PLAYER

.....NEW BOARD SITUATIONS

Figure 4-24 Games provide a search environment with a new twist, competition. As shown, the nodes represent game situations and the links represent the moves that connect them.

■   The branching factor is the average number of legal moves possible at a given position in a game.

It is the combination of branching factor and the average number of moves in a game that generally demonstrates the absurdity of trying to look ahead to the end of the game. In chess, for example, a reasonable estimate for branching factor is about 35 and typically each player makes 50 moves. Certainly 35^{100} is too big.

Less Knowledge Means More Search

If only there were some very good way to rank the members of a set of board situations, it would be a simple matter to use the move which leads to the best situation that can be reached by one move. Unfortunately, no such situation-ranking formula exists. When board situations differ obviously, then some simple measure like piece count can supply a rough guide as to quality, but depending on such a measure to rank the available moves from a given situation produces poor results. Some other strategy is needed.

The obvious generalization is to use a board situation evaluator not immediately, but after play has extended through one or more rounds of move and counter move. This cannot be pursued too far since combinatorial explosion soon leads to unthinkable numbers, but if the development terminates at some reasonable depth, then perhaps the terminal situations can be compared, yielding a basis for more selection. Of course, the underlying presumption of this approach is the notion that the merit of a situation clarifies as it is pursued and that the look-ahead process can extend far enough that even rough board-evaluation formulas may be satisfactory. This presumption is hotly debated.

Using Look Ahead Requires Static Evaluation and Minimaxing

If only the situations reachable in one move are compared, a rank ordering of those situations will do. Unfortunately this is inadequate in the context of look ahead play because an absolute rather than relative standard is needed. The tendency has been to map all considerations into a single, overall quality number. This is forced by the desire to use the simple search strategies we are about to study, but mapping overall quality into a single number has a serious defect.

■ A number can say nothing about how it was determined. It is a poor summary mechanism, often forced on us by what little we know how to do. Too bad.

Positive numbers, by convention, indicate favor to one player, and negative numbers, to the other. The degree of favor goes with the absolute value of the number.

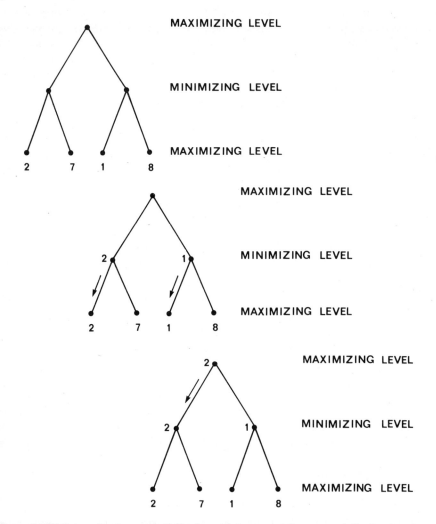

Figure 4-25 Minimaxing is a method for determining moves from a partially developed game tree with a static evaluator which maps situations into a single, advantage-specifying number. One player works toward the higher numbers, seeking the advantage, while the opponent goes for the lower numbers.

■   The process of determining the quality number is called static evaluation. At the end of a limited exploration of move possibilities one finds *static evaluation scores* produced by the *static evaluator.*

The player working toward positive numbers is called the maximizing player. His opponent is the minimizing player. If the player to move is the maximizing player, he is looking for a path leading to a large positive number, and he will assume that his opponent will try to force the play toward situations with strongly negative static evaluations.

Thus in the stylized miniature game tree shown in figure 4-25, the maximizer might hope to get to the situation yielding a static score of 8. But he knows that the minimizer would not permit that since he can choose a move deflecting the play toward the situation with a score of 1. In general the decision of the maximizer must take cognizance of the attitude of the minimizer at the next level down. If the look ahead goes further, then certainly the minimizer moves in accord with choices of the maximizer at the next level down. This continues until the limit of exploration is reached and the static evaluator provides a direct basis for selecting among alternatives. In the example, the static evaluations at the bottom determine that the choices available to the minimizing player yield expected scores of 2 and 1 at the level just up from the static evaluations. Knowing these scores are expected when the minimizer makes his logical moves, the maximizer can determine the best play at the next level up. Clearly he moves toward the node from which the minimizer can do no better than to hold the expected score to 2. Again, the scores at one level determine the action and the summary score at the next level up.

■   The process by which the scoring information passes up the game tree is called the minimax process since the scores at a node are either the minimum or maximum of the scores at the node immediately below.

Note that this can be expensive for two reasons: first, calculating the static value for all possible paths may be expensive; and second, even generating all possible paths can be a stumbling block. Which costs more depends on the details of the static evaluator and move generator used.

The Alpha-Beta Technique Prunes the Search Tree

It might seem at first that the static evaluator must be used on each situation found at the bottom of the tree. But thankfully this is not so. There is a procedure that reduces both the amount of tree that must be generated and the number of static evaluations, thus cutting down on the work to be done overall. It is somewhat like the branch-and-bound idea in that some paths are demonstrably nonoptimal even though not followed to the limit of look ahead.

Consider the situation in the first drawing of figure 4-26 in which the static evaluator has already been used on the first two terminal situations. Minimaxing on the scores of 2 and 7 determines that the minimizing player is guaranteed a situation with a score of 2 if the maximizer takes the left branch at the top node. This in turn ensures that the maximizer can do no worse than direct play toward a score of 2 at the top. This is clear even before any other static evaluations are made since the maximizer can certainly elect the explored branch if others turn out worse. This is indicated at the top node in the second drawing of figure 4-26 .

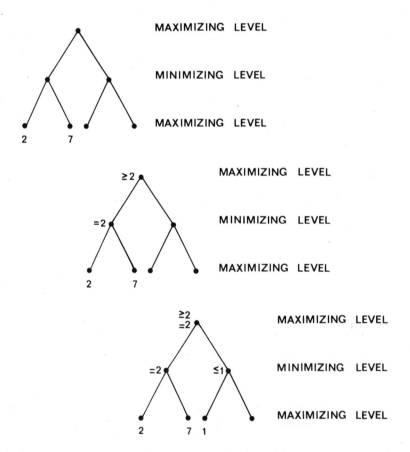

Figure 4-26 Some work can be avoided by augmenting the minimax idea with the alpha-beta procedure. As shown, there is no need to fully explore the right side of the tree because there is no way the result could alter the move decision. Once movement to the right is shown to be worse than movement to the left, there is no need to see how much worse. In general using the alpha-beta procedure means fewer move generations and fewer static evaluations.

Now suppose the next node is evaluated and produces a score of 1. Seeing this, surely the minimizer can do no worse than 1 by the same reasoning that showed that the maximizer can do no worse than 2 at the top. Only the sense of *worse* has changed. At the maximizer levels, worse means toward the smaller numbers, while at the minimizer levels, worse means toward the higher.

Look closely at the tree. Does it make sense to go on to the board situation at the final node? Can the value produced there by the static evaluator possibly matter? Strangely the answer is *No*! For surely if the maximizer knows he can do no worse than 2 along the left branch, he will need to know no more about the right-hand branch other than that he can do no better than 1 there. The last node evaluated could be $+100$ or -100 or any number whatever without affecting the result.

On reflection, it is clear that use has been made of the following key principle:

■ If the opponent has one response that establishes a potential move as bad, there is no need to check any other responses to the potential move. If one is gored, there is certainly no need to find out how many ways or how badly in the worst case.

This principle is the foundation of the *alpha-beta* technique. In practice the actual procedure consists of two activities:

■ Whenever something is discovered about the best that can be hoped for at a given node, check what is known about the parent node. It may be that no further work is sensible below the given node.

■ Whenever the exact game value of a node is established, check what is known about the nodes above. It may be that the best that can be hoped for at the parent node can be revised or determined exactly.

It is appropriate now to see how the alpha-beta technique applies to a larger example. Unfortunately, it is a bit difficult to see how static evaluations intermix with conclusions about node values on paper. A lecture or movie would be better, but lacking that, we make do with circled event numbers placed beside each conclusion showing the order in which they were determined. These are shown in the example of figure 4-27 in which we look at another stylized tree for which three branches descend from every node.

■ *1-2:* Moving down the left branch at every decision point, the search penetrates to the bottom where a static value of 8 is unearthed. This 8 clearly means that the maximizer can do no worse than 8 with the three choices available. A note to this effect is placed by step 2.

■ *3-5:* To be sure nothing better than 8 can be found, the maximizer examines the two other moves available to him. Since 7 and 3 both indicate inferior moves, he concludes that the score achievable is exactly 8 and the correct move is the first one examined.

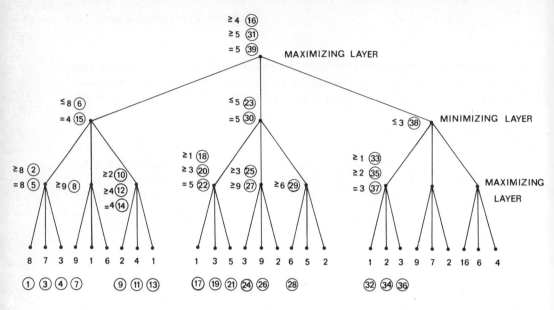

Figure 4-27 A game tree of depth three and branching factor three. The circled numbers show the order in which conclusions are drawn. Note that only 16 static evaluations are made, not the 27 required without alpha-beta pruning. Evidently the best play for the maximizer is down the middle branch.

■ *6:* Nailing down the maximizer's score at the lowest node enables a conclusion about what the minimizer can hope for at the next level up. Since one move is now known to lead to a situation that gives the maximizer a score of 8, then the minimizer can do no worse than 8 here.

■ *7-8:* To see if the minimizer can do better at the second level, his two remaining moves must be examined. The first leads to a situation from which the maximizer can score at least a 9. Here cutoff occurs. By taking the left branch, the minimizer forces a score of 8, but by taking the middle branch, the minimizer will do no better than 9 and could do worse if the other maximizer choices are even more positive. Hence the middle branch is bad for the minimizer, there is no need to go on to find out how much worse it is, and there is consequently no need for two static evaluations. There is no change in the minimizer's worst case expectation — it is still 8.

■ *9-14:* The minimizer must still investigate his last option, the one to the right. This in turn means seeing what the maximizer can do there. The next series of steps bounces between static evaluations and conclusions about the maximizer's situation immediately above them. The conclusion is that the maximizer's score is 4.

■ *15:* Discovering that the right branch leads to a forced score of 4, the minimizer takes the right branch since 4 compares favorably with 8, the previously low score.

- *16:* Now a bound can be placed at the top level. The maximizer, surveying the situation there, sees that his left branch leads to a score of 4. He now knows he will get at least that. To see if he can do better, he must look at his middle and right branches.

- *17-22:* Deciding how the minimizer will react at the end of the middle branch requires knowing what happens along the left branch descending from there. Here the maximizer is in action discovering that the best play is to a position with a score of 5.

- *23:* Until something definite was known about what the maximizer could do, no bounds could be placed on the minimizer's potential. Knowing that the maximizer gets 5 along the left branch, however, is knowing something definite. The conclusion is that the minimizer can do no worse than 5.

- *24-27:* In working out what the maximizer can do below the minimizer's middle branch, it is discovered part way in the analysis that the maximizer can reach a score of 9. But 9 is poor relative to the known fact that the minimizer has one option that insures a 5. Cutoff occurs again. There is no point in investigating other maximizer options, thus avoiding one static evaluation.

- *28-29:* Looking at the minimizer's right branch quickly shows that it too gives the maximizer a chance to force the play to a worse score than the minimizer can achieve along the left branch. Cutoff saves two static evaluations here.

- *30:* Since there are no more branches to investigate, the bound of 5 on the minimizer's score becomes not a bound, but the actual value achievable.

- *31:* The maximizer at the top, seeing a better deal through the middle branch, chooses it tentatively and knows now that he can do no worse than 5.

- *32-37:* Now the maximizer's right-branch choice at the top must be explored. Diving into the tree, bouncing about a bit, leads to the conclusion that the minimizer sees a left branch choice insuring a score of 3.

- *38:* The minimizer can conclude that the left branch score is a bound on how well he can do.

- *39:* Knowing the minimizer can force play to a situation with a score of 3, the maximizer at the top level concludes there is no point in exploring the right branch further. After all, a score of 5 follows a middle branch move. Note that this saves not only six static evaluations but also two applications of the move generator which may be a considerable saving in itself.

It is not unusual to get lost in this demonstration. Even seasoned game specialists feel magic in the alpha-beta technique each time they ponder it after a long interval. Each individual conclusion seems right, but somehow the global result is strange. Later on, when a simple program for doing alpha-beta pruning is demonstrated, the thing may seem more reasonable.

Note, incidentally, that in the example it was never necessary to look more than one level up in order to decide whether or not to stop exploration. This was strictly a consequence of the shallowness of the depth-three tree used. With trees of depth four or more, so-called deep cutoffs can occur which require looking further.

The Alpha-Beta Technique May Not Help Much

It is important to understand just what this alpha-beta technique can be expected to do. One way of addressing this is to ask about the best and worst cases.

In the worst case, alpha-beta does nothing. It is easy to construct a tree in such a way as to ensure that the static evaluator must be applied to all terminal situations.

Analyzing what can come of the best case requires some work. Suppose the tree, by luck or otherwise, is ordered with each player's best move being the left-most alternative at every node. Then clearly the best move of the player at the top is to the left. But how many static evaluations are needed for the top-most player to be sure that this move is optimum? To work into the question, consider the tree of depth 3 and branching factor 3 shown in figure 4-28.

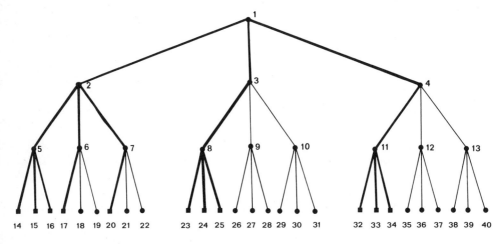

Figure 4-28 In a perfectly ordered tree, the alpha-beta procedure cuts the exponent of combinatorial explosion in half. This is because all of the adversary's options need not be considered in verifying the left-branch choices. Perfect ordering of a tree with depth three and branching factor three reduces the number of required static evaluations from 27 to 11.

Presuming that the best moves for both players are always to the left, then the value of the left-most move for the maximizing player at the top is the static evaluation found for the board situation at the extreme bottom left. Assuming this is correct, then the maximizer has something concrete against which the quality of the alternatives can be compared. He need not consider all of his opponent's replies to those alternatives, however.

■   To verify the correct move at a given node in an ordered tree, it is necessary to consider relatively few of the terminals descendent from the immediate alternatives to the move to be verified. This is true because all terminals found below nonoptimal moves by the opponent can be ignored.

Why is it necessary to deal with all the options of the moving player while ignoring all but one of his opponent's moves? This is a sticky point. The explanation requires close attention to the basic idea: if the opponent has some series of responses that make a move bad no matter what series of moves the moving player might choose, then the move must be bad.

The key to understanding lies in the words *some,* and *no matter what.* The *some* suggests trying one of the opponent's moves wherever he has a choice and hoping that it is good enough to certify the conclusion. But to be sure that the conclusion holds no matter what the moving player might do, it is clearly necessary to check out all of his alternatives wherever he has a choice.

Thus the hope in the example is that only the left-most move from node 3 to node 8 will need exploration. All of the maximizer's counter-responses to that move must be checked, so static evaluations need to be made at nodes 23, 24, and 25.

These establish the maximizer's score at 8, which in turn sets an upper bound on what the minimizer can do at 3, which finally by comparison with the minimizer's score at 2 should show that no further work below node 3 makes any sense. Similar logic applies to node 4 leading to static evaluations at 32, 33, and 34.

But now how can the maximizer be sure that the score transferred up the left edge is valid? Surely he must verify that an intelligent minimizer at 2 would select the left-most branch. This verification can be done by assuming the number coming up the left edge from 5 is correct and then rejecting the alternatives as efficiently as possible. But by the same arguments used at 1, it is clear that not all of the minimizer's opponent's options need be examined. Again branching occurs only at every second level working out from the choice to be verified along the left edge. Static evaluations must be done at 17 and 20.

Finally there is the question of the minimizer's assumption about the number coming up from 5. This requires exploring all of the maximizer's alternatives, the trivial case of the general argument, resulting in static evaluations at 15 and 16 in order to be sure that the static evaluation done at 14 yields the right number to transfer up.

Thus only 11 of the 27 possible static evaluations need be made in order to discover the best move when by luck the alternatives in the tree have been nicely ordered. In deeper trees, with more branching, the saving is more dramatic. In fact it can be demonstrated that the number of static evaluations needed to discover the best move in an optimally arranged tree is given by

<number of evaluations>

$$= \quad 2b^{d/2} - 1 \qquad\qquad \text{for } d \text{ even}$$
$$= \quad b^{(d+1)/2} + b^{(d-1)/2} - 1 \qquad \text{for } d \text{ odd}$$

where b = branching factor
and d = depth of search in moves.

A straightforward proof by induction verifies the formula. One need only generalize the line of argument used in the last example, focusing on the idea that verification of a choice requires full investigation only every second level. Note that the formula is certainly correct for $d = 1$ since it then simplifies to b. For $d = 3$ and $b = 3$, the formula yields an answer of 11, which nicely verifies the conclusion reached for the example.

Warning: the formula is only for the special case in which the tree is perfectly arranged. As such it is an unrealistic estimate of what can actually be expected, for if there were a way of arranging the tree with the best moves on the left, clearly there would be no point in using alpha-beta pruning at all! But this is not to say that the exercise has been fruitless. It establishes the lower bound on the number of static evaluations that would be needed in a real game. It is a lower bound that may or may not be close to the real result depending on how well the moves are in fact arranged. The real result must lie somewhere between the worst case, at which all b^d terminals must be evaluated, and the best case, which still requires approximately $2b^{d/2}$ terminal evaluations.

Either way the number required becomes impossibly large with increasing depth. Alpha-beta merely wins a temporary reprieve from the impact of the explosive, exponential growth. It does not prevent it. See figure 4-29.

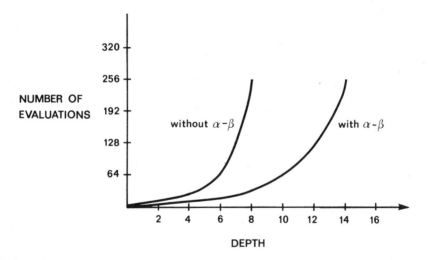

Figure 4-29 The alpha-beta algorithm reduces the rate of combinatorial explosion, but does not prevent it.

Heuristic Search Techniques Also Limit Search

The alpha-beta search speedup technique guarantees as good an answer as can be found by complete, exhaustive minimaxing. Many other techniques have no such guarantee but are used in combination with alpha-beta pruning as additional weapons against explosive tree growth. The following are typical:

Limiting breadth. A brute-force way of reducing the effective branching factor in a game tree is to ignore the less likely possibilities. Since a plausible move generator is generally used anyway in connection with the alpha-beta method, it is easy to single out only the most likely descendants from any node for study.

To generalize slightly, one may arrange for breadth to vary with depth of penetration, possibly even biasing efforts toward moves of greater plausibility through some formula like the following:

<number of descendants>
     =   <number of descendants from parent>
       − <rank in plausibility>

Thus if a node is one of five descendants and ranks second most plausible among those five, then there should be $5 - 2 = 3$ descendants. A complete tree formed using this idea takes on a tapered look as in figure 4-30.

Needless to say a tactical breadth limiting heuristic acts in opposition to lines of play that temporarily forfeit pieces for eventual position advantage. Because they trim off the moves that appear bad on the surface, breadth-limiting programs are unlikely to discover spectacular moves that seem disastrous for a time, but then win back everything lost and more.

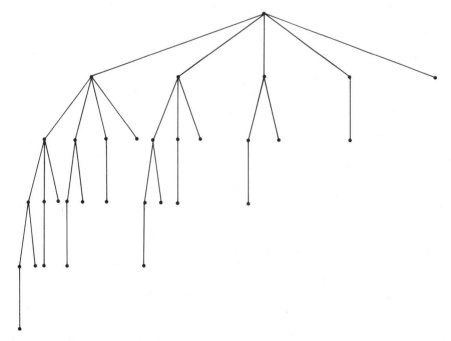

Figure 4-30 Tapering search gives more attention to the more plausible moves. Here the tapering algorithm reduces the search with increases in depth and decreases in plausibility.

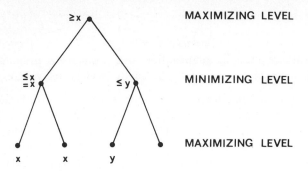

Figure 4-31 Sometimes it makes no sense to explore a branch even though it may be optimal because the potential gain is slight. Here search has shown that the maximizer gets an assured score of x by taking the left branch. Partial analysis of the right branch shows that the maximizer cannot do better than a score of y there. If y is greater than x, there is no alpha-beta cutoff, but if the difference is small, the maximizer may not wish to insist on full evaluation, taking the comfortable left-branch route instead.

Disaster cutoff. Another way of limiting search down through bad moves depends not on the simple position of a move in the plausibility ranking but rather on some accumulating plausibility value. This makes the shape and size of the tree sensitive to the particular situation. If only one line of play makes any sense at all, it would be the only one pursued, and could therefore be followed to greater depth. On the other hand, if many lines of play seem equally plausible, then this method tends to allocate resources among them evenly.

Futility cutoff. Pushing the tree down equally through moves of equal plausibility makes sense. But after some solid evaluations are made, it may well develop that considerable search saving can be had by rejecting partially explored moves that can at best offer only slight improvement on some fully explored move.

Figure 4-31 illustrates the point. The tree as shown has already been partially analyzed. It is convenient to use x and y for the static evaluations rather than sample numbers. Note that the maximizing player at the top has a sure score of x or higher.

Now assume y is bigger than x but only by a little. This is a key point to keep in mind. Down the right branch from the top, the minimizer can hold the maximizer to a score of y or lower — lower if and only if the yet unevaluated node in fact produces a score lower than y.

Now as long as y is greater than x there is no ordinary alpha-beta cutoff because the minimizer cannot demonstrably force the play to a low enough score. But, if the difference between x and y is small, no matter how good the unevaluated node might be, the potential gain achievable by completing the search is small. This is true because if the unevaluated node is very good, the minimizer will simply avoid it, holding the maximizer to a score of y, a meager gain of $y - x$ over what he knew he could get by going down the left side. In this case the decision might well be to move to the left, accepting the certain score of x, and avoiding the extra static evaluation. To be sure, if the value of the unexplored node is bigger than x, then complete analysis would show the absolutely optimal path to be to the right. But

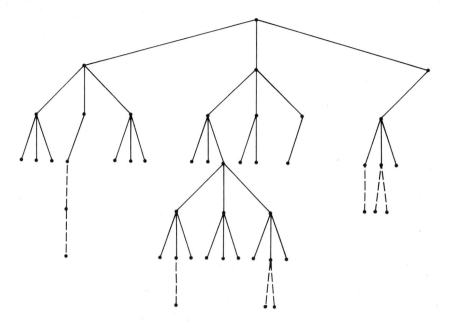

Figure 4-32 Secondary search and feedover procedures may extend exploration beyond normal limits. Dotted lines are continuations of paths which ordinary search had terminated at particularly dynamic situations such as imminent capture. The small search dangling beneath the main tree is done to check the static evaluation of the winning node.

why should a program work like mad for little potential gain? The score found is likely to be lower than x anyway, making the additional work completely futile.

Feedover conditions. So far the techniques limit tree growth. Sometimes it is useful to go the other way and extend the tree when circumstances warrant. If, for example, a chess configuration is particularly dynamic, it makes sense to continue the play until a more quiescent state obtains. There are a number of so-called feedover conditions that can cause a configuration to be considered dynamic and deserving of further exploration:

The king is in danger.

A piece exchange is imminent.

A pawn is about to become a queen.

Secondary search. After all ordinary search is complete with the alpha-beta method, the various heuristic methods and feedover all playing their assigned parts, it is often good to grow a small secondary tree down from the node judged to be at the bottom of the optimal path. Doing this double checks the accuracy of the value assumed for the target node: one estimate comes straight from the static evaluator, and the other from minimax analysis of the secondary search tree. The hope is that the two scores will be roughly the same, confirming that no surprises lie just beyond the limit encompassed by primary search. Presumably the extra depth of search is impractical for the tree in general, but allowable in the singular case of confirming the estimated value of the optimal line of play. Figure 4-32 shows the shape a tree may take on when feedover and secondary search are combined.

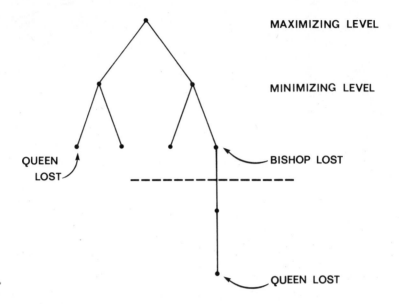

Figure 4-33 The horizon effect foils search-oriented game procedures when disasters can be delayed but not prevented. Here the left-branch move leads directly to queen loss, and the right-branch move leads to a sacrifice followed by queen loss.

The surprises spoken of, incidentally, are often the result of delaying moves that put off, but do not prevent disasters. To illustrate how this can work, suppose there is a combination which leads inevitably to queen capture. Suppose further that the side losing the queen can delay the loss by sacrificing other, lesser pieces somewhere else on the board. As long as the queen loss is inevitable, it is absurd to use delaying moves that sacrifice still more material. But these delaying moves may carry the play beyond the depth limits established for the tree search. In the sample of figure 4-33, the apparent choice is between losing the queen or losing a bishop. But the real choice is between losing a queen or losing the queen *and* bishop. Metaphorically speaking, an inevitable loss is pushed beyond the field of view by a lesser sacrifice. The phenomenon commonly is called the horizon effect. Secondary search helps somewhat, but does not yield a total solution.

SUMMARY

■ The simplest search techniques are depth-first and breadth-first search. Neither finds optimal paths, and both may be inefficient.

■ Hill climbing is an improvement over depth-first search because the branches under any node are explored in the order of their plausibility. Hill climbing still has the same problems inherent in depth-first search, however, in that a wrong decision high up in the tree can lead to endless thrashing low down.

■ Context-sensitive, best-first searches push forward from the most promising node yet encountered.

■ The branch-and-bound technique is a fundamental method for finding optimum routes. The basic idea is to extend the developing tree from the end of the least costly partial path. This is often improved through the use of underestimates of the distances remaining to the goal.

■ Searching for solutions to network constraints is best done by a range-constriction approach that carries each alternative forward until it is definitely out of the running. The method seems applicable in understanding language as well as in understanding scenes.

■ The adversary nature of games makes game tree search a very special subject. The minimax idea is the foundation on which all else rests. Minimax is the procedure by which conclusions about what to do at the lowest nodes of the search tree percolate up to determine what happens at the top.

■ The alpha-beta technique depends on a fact that once the opponent has one way to insure that a move is disastrous, there is no need to explore that move further. While alpha-beta pruning saves considerable work, the optimum line of play is found nonetheless.

■ Alpha-beta pruning may be augmented by a number of heuristic pruning techniques. All of these introduce some danger that the optimum play may not be selected.

REFERENCES

■ Nils J. Nilsson, *Problem Solving Methods in Artificial Intelligence,* McGraw-Hill Book Company, New York, 1971. A thorough textbook treatment of search.

■ David Waltz, "Understanding Line Drawings of Scenes with Shadows," in *The Psychology of Computer Vision,* edited by Patrick Henry Winston, McGraw-Hill Book Company, New York, 1975. Gives a detailed description of the range-constriction search algorithm Waltz uses in scene analysis.

■ Gerald Jay Sussman and Richard Matthew Stallman, "Heuristic Techniques in Computer-Aided Circuit Analysis," AI-M-328, The Artificial Intelligence Laboratory, Massachusetts Institute of Technology, Cambridge, Massachusetts, 1975. Demonstrates that Waltz-like search is useful in expert problem solving by showing that common-sense circuit analysis can be done using constraint propagation.

■   Claude E. Shannon, "Automatic Chess Player," *Scientific American,* vol. 182, no. 48, 1950, and "Programming a Digital Computer for Playing Chess," *Philosophy Magazine,* vol. 41, March, 1950. Classic papers on chess which anticipated most of the subsequent work to date.

■   Allen Newell and Herbert A. Simon, *Human Problem Solving,* Prentice-Hall, Englewood Cliffs, New Jersey, 1972. A thick book containing a long chapter describing many chess ideas developed by the authors since they began thinking about chess in the middle 1950s.

■   Arnold K. Griffith, "A Comparison and Evaluation of Three Machine Learning Procedures as Applied to the Game of Checkers," *Artificial Intelligence,* vol. 5, no. 2, Summer 1974. The idea of search and fancy static evaluation is artfully contested in this paper.

■   James J. Gillogly, "The Technology Chess Program," *Artificial Intelligence,* vol. 3, no. 3, 1972. A good paper showing what can be done by brute force search.

■   Hans Berliner, "Chess as Problem Solving: The Development of a Tactics Analyzer," PhD thesis, Department of Computer Science, Carnegie-Mellon University, Pittsburgh, Pennsylvania, 1975. Deals extensively with chess. Berliner advocates sophisticated, goal-directed plausible move generation, drastically trimmed search trees, and dynamically determined search depth.

The next two papers probe deeply into the alpha-beta idea with a view toward understanding expected performance rather than best or worst case performance. It is shown that the problem is not easy.

■   S. H. Fuller, J. G. Gaschnig, and J. J. Gillogly, "Analysis of the Alpha-Beta Pruning Algorithm," Department of Computer Science, Carnegie-Mellon University, Pittsburgh, Pennsylvania, 1973.

■   Donald E. Knuth and Ronald W. Moore, "An Analysis of Alpha-Beta Pruning," *Artificial Intelligence,* vol. 6, No. 4, 1975.

The next two papers by Samuel are classics which deal extensively with tree-pruning heuristics, schemes for combining evidence, and methods for adaptive parameter improvement.

■   A. L. Samuel, "Some Studies In Machine Learning Using the Game of Checkers," *IBM Journal of Research and Development,* vol. 3, no. 3, 1959.

■   A. L. Samuel, "Some Studies in Machine Learning Using the Game of Checkers II. Recent Progress," *IBM Journal of Research and Development,* vol. 11, no. 6, 1967.

5

CONTROLLING ATTENTION

In studying *search,* we examined some mechanisms that enable systems to explore networks of situations defined by the environment. Now in studying *control,* the focus shifts toward mechanisms that determine how a system shifts attention among its own procedural specialists.

Discussion of control is incomplete without exposition reduced to the level of programming language devices. Fortunately, however, there are some important ideas which are sufficiently abstract that some discussion can begin without the benefit of programming language experience.

In this chapter we take up the General Problem Solver and the Production System ideas in particular because they are both examples of control through so-called demons. In the context of control, a demon is a sort of sentinel that watches for a specific situation and performs some action when it occurs. We will see that the operators of the General Problem Solver and the productions in Production Systems both satisfy this description.

Some people believe that human thought is largely controlled by demons as well. After all, our heads seem full of simple situation-action rules like these:

- Whenever I decide to go to the bookstore, I should see if I need colored pens.
- Whenever I find a problem in mechanics difficult, I should ask if angular momentum is relevant.

To get deeply into the subject of control requires some knowledge of programming. Remember, therefore, that this is only the first pass on selected parts of a subject which must have a second pass later after basic programming is in hand. Here we necessarily stick to abstractions, providing only a feel, not a grip.

CONTROL ISSUES

There is a tendency to assume that complex behavior must require complex answers to basic control questions. Sometimes this is true, but how often is unclear.

Simon's Ant Is Programmed by the Beach

Apparent complexity may descend more from a problem than from the system which solves it. Simon made this point by describing the path of an ant making its way home on a pebbled beach. The path seems complicated. The ant probes, doubles back, circumnavigates, and zigzags. But these actions are not deep and mysterious manifestations of intellectual power. Close scrutiny often reveals that the control decisions are both simple and few in number. An environment-driven problem solver often produces behavior that is complex only because a complex environment drives it. It is easy to overestimate the degree of control sophistication required for intelligent behavior at the same time the description and representation problems are underestimated. This tendency can be avoided by knowing what it means to understand control.

Understanding Control Means Knowing How Procedures Interact

Control schemes can be classified according to how they satisfy three basic needs:

- There must be some method for deciding what procedure to use.
- There must be some way of supplying the active procedure with information.
- There must be some means by which the active procedure can offer a conclusion.

The General Problem Solver is a useful study because it has several ways of deciding what procedure to use next, thus addressing the first big control question.

MEANS-ENDS ANALYSIS AND THE GENERAL PROBLEM SOLVER

Consider an approach to control in which actions depend entirely on the difference between the current situation and the desired situation. In technical terms, we represent the collection of facts that specify the problem and where we are on it as the *current state*. Similarly, where we want to be is the *goal state*. Both are collections of facts about the condition of the world. Here are some examples:

- In a travel situation the current state and the goal state are defined by physical locations.
- In a robot assembly problem the current state might be defined by a pile of bricks and the goal state by a tower.

■ In a geometry problem the current state would be defined by all that is known, both general and specific. The goal state again would be such a collection, but including that which is to be shown.

The General Problem Solver notion embodies a strategy for selecting *operators* to reduce the differences between the current state and the goal state. The General Problem Solver, devised by Newell and Simon, goes frequently by the acronym, GPS, and sometimes by the alias, Means-Ends Analysis.

Operating on Differences Is the Key Idea in GPS

In the travel situation the difference between the current state and the goal state takes on a particularly simple form. It is simply the distance between the place one is and the place one wants to be. Consider a sequence of operators $O_1...O_5$ causing movement through a series of states as in figure 5-1. Each of the operators was selected because it was believed relevant to reducing the difference between the state in which it was applied and the goal state. Operator O_3 actually takes the problem solver further away from the goal. There is no built-in mechanism preventing this in our version of GPS. Thankfully O_4 and O_5 get the system going back in a good direction again.

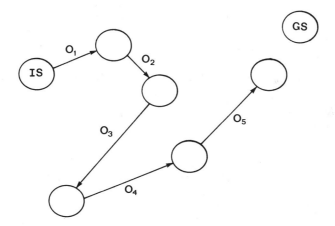

Figure 5-1 The General Problem Solver is a metaphor for problem solving which stresses states, differences between states, and operators for reducing differences. The observed difference determines which operator to try, but forward progress is not guaranteed.

Note also that nothing prevents getting into a state whose apparent distance to the goal is short, but whose actual distance is extreme. This is because the difference measure is often crude and likely to ignore many factors involved in

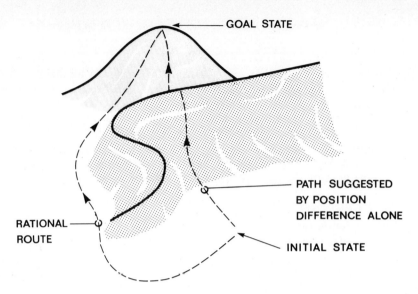

Figure 5-2 Since the difference measure rarely incorporates all relevant aspects of a problem, the General Problem Solver may become committed to difficult solution paths.

getting from one state to another. To see how this can happen, consider a hiker walking toward the mountain shown in figure 5-2. If he walks solely on position differences and moves in the direction which minimizes that difference, he will work his way up the wrong side of the intervening ridge and be forced to climb over.

Sometimes an operator relevant to reducing some measured difference cannot be applied because application requires some state characteristics not exhibited by the current state. If the operator could be applied to a state near the current state, it may be sensible to try to get there. In the diagram in figure 5-3, all this is reflected in the current state, CS, the goal state GS, the difference between them d[CS, GS],

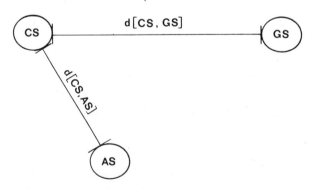

Figure 5-3 If the difference between the current state and the goal state suggests an operator which cannot be applied in the current state, it may be desirable to seek a nearby adjacent state where it can be. Getting to the adjacent state is a new problem for a new copy of the General Problem Solver.

and the adjacent state, AS. State AS is close to CS but has the additional property that an operator suggested by d[CS, GS] is applicable.

Clearly getting to AS is a problem just like any other initial state to goal-state traversal. It makes sense to set up a new problem, and work on that new problem knowing that its solution helps address the original problem of getting to GS. Of course it would not be reasonable to work toward an adjacent state that is actually further away than the goal state. Consequently an operator is rejected if its conditions indicate an adjacent state for which d[CS, AS] > d[CS, GS].

Finally, there may be situations for which no operator can be found that seems relevant to forward motion and a dead end is reached. Whenever this occurs, the last operation is withdrawn, and a new path sought from the previous state. This automatic backup may lead to the repeal of several steps. *Note that the GPS control structure effects a depth-first search of state space.* An example will make this clearer. Motion in the mountains is not quite right for our present purposes, so we will consider a slightly different sort of travel problem.

Robbie Goes to Los Angeles Using GPS Notions

Aunt Agatha lives in Los Angeles and has invited Robbie down from Boston to spend a few days by her pool. There are a number of different ways to travel, and a mechanism is needed to select the proper one at any given point in the trip. Distance seems to be a reasonable criterion. A *difference-operator table* relates the way of traveling with observed distances as well as specifying the *prerequisite conditions.* See figure 5-4.

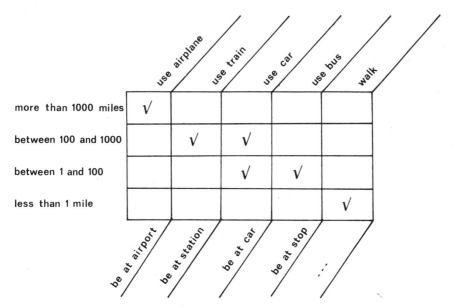

Figure 5-4 Difference-Operator tables record which operators are relevant to each recognized difference. Here transportation alternatives are related to distance possibilities.

The initial distance is clearly greater than 1000 miles so the difference-operator table dictates flying. But prerequisite to using an airplane is being at the airport, and being at the airport becomes an adjacent state relevant to using the flying operator. Thus getting to the airport becomes the goal of a second copy of the process. The distance is less than 100 miles but more than 1 mile so driving is appropriate. This introduces still another prerequisite condition, namely being at the parking garage. To satisfy this condition requires walking which is presumed to have no prerequisite condition.

The following illustrates what has happened so far. Each line is offset to the right in proportion to the number of levels of prerequisite satisfaction involved.

d greater than 1000	Fly	Be at airport
d between 100 and 1	Drive	Be at car
d less than 1	Walk	

At this point something can be done: Robbie walks to the car and drives to the airport. He then faces the problem of getting to the airplane once again, but progress has been made. The distance is now less than a mile and walking is appropriate. Note that this walking step is dictated on a higher level than before.

The walk gets him to the airplane, he flies to the Los Angeles airport, and then tries to get to Aunt Agatha's. But if he follows the directions implied by the difference-operator table, he hits an apparent snag at this point:

d greater than 1000	Fly	Be at airport
d between 100 and 1	Drive	Be at car
d less than 1	Walk (to car)	
d less than 1	Walk (to airplane)	
d between 100 and 1	Drive	Be at car???

The problem of course is that the first operator found in the difference-operator table requires being at the car as a prerequisite condition. But to be at the car would require a silly flight back to Boston. Fortunately, this is prevented automatically by the device that rejects movement to an adjacent state more distant than the goal. Since the car is more distant than Aunt Agatha's when at the Los Angeles airport, the alternative, taking a bus, is selected. The remainder of the trip is straightforward:

d greater than 1000	Fly	Be at airport
d between 100 and 1	Drive	Be at car
d less than 1	Walk (to car)	
d less than 1	Walk (to airplane)	
d between 100 and 1	Take bus	Be at stop
d less than 1	Walk (to bus)	
d less than 1	Walk (to Aunt's)	

Normally GPS Does Forward Chaining Rather Than Backward Chaining

While operating, GPS selects each operator because it spans some distance *from* the current state *toward* the goal state. Since the new location normally lies far short of the goal, a long chain of operators may develop as GPS works forward from the end of the established connections.

■ Working from the initial state toward the goal state is called forward chaining.

With only small changes, it is possible to work backward from the goal state instead of forward from the initial state. As it stands, as shown in figure 5-5, the operator selected really specifies two intermediate states standing between the current state and the goal state. GPS iteratively reduces the distance between the second intermediate and the goal while the distance between the current state and the first intermediate, the adjacent state, is reduced by applying GPS on another level. The distance between the current state and the first intermediate is to be small.

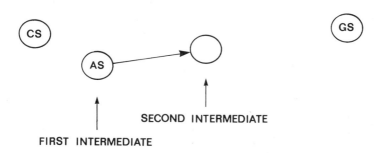

Figure 5-5 Operators specify two intermediate states. When forward chaining, the distance to the first intermediate, the adjacent state, is reduced by recursion. The distance between the second intermediate and the goal is then reduced by iteration.

Reversing everything creates a backward moving GPS with a bias toward keeping the distance between the second intermediate state and the goal small. Iteration fills the gap between the initial state and the first intermediate, and using GPS on another level fills the gap between the second intermediate and the goal.

■ Working from the goal state toward the initial state is called backward chaining.

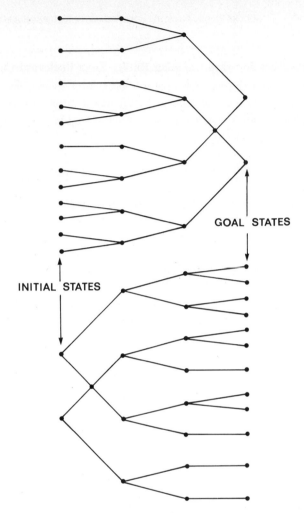

Figure 5-6 The shape of the state space helps determine whether forward chaining or backward chaining is better. Fan in calls for forward chaining and fan out for backward. Otherwise the problem solver can become overcommitted to dead ends.

Deciding whether forward chaining or backward chaining is better depends in part on the shape of the space. Figure 5-6 illustrates by way of two symmetric situations. All possible states are represented along with the operations that can change one state into a neighbor. In the first situation shown, forward chaining is better because there is a general fan in from the typical initial states toward the typical goal states. It is hard to get seriously into a dead end. In the second situation, the shape favors backward chaining since there is fan out instead.

The GPS Notion Involves Several Powerful Control Ideas

Backing away and looking at what GPS does shows several control ideas are inherent.

■   In GPS systems, operators are selected by way of observed difference, not by name.

Implicit, rather than explicit, procedure selection is a key point. Use of a difference-operator table is not. There are other ways of relating differences to operators that avoid the table notion. This is fortunate since using a table would be cumbersome with larger systems.

■   At a given level, GPS iterates through a test-operate sequence until finished.

This too says something about how procedures are selected. The test-operate idea is a sort of abstraction of the ubiquitous notion of feedback.

■   Forward-moving iteration is unwound in depth-first fashion whenever stone walls are encountered.

GPS therefore exhibits automatic backup, an idea that has been fashionable from time to time.

■   GPS applies copies of itself on subproblems. Thus GPS involves the notion of recursion.

Whenever a procedure uses a copy of itself, it is said to recurse. On one level, all GPS procedure selection is done through the difference-operator iteration mechanism. On another level, GPS calls itself recursively and explicitly whenever a subproblem is encountered.

Systems rarely have pedigreed control structures. More often there is a mongrelized mixture. The rule should be to use whatever is required while avoiding sophistication for its own sake.

STRIPS Is an Implementation of GPS

GPS is a seductive metaphor because it is hard to think of a problem-solving activity which does not involve some analysis of where one wants to go in order to determine what to do. But when metaphors are very general, there may be considerable distance between principle and practice. Having GPS in mind is far from having a handbook. Someone must decide how general operators like flying are linked up with particular problems like getting to Aunt Agatha's so that Robbie takes a plane to Los Angeles International rather than just any old airport. That is, someone must face the basic control questions of where the inputs to procedures are found and how the outputs are delivered because GPS, by itself, says nothing about these things.

At the Stanford Research Institute, a research team has done an impressive job of working out answers to the where found and how delivered questions by creating the so-called STRIPS system. Unfortunately, a complete understanding of the details of STRIPS operation requires some experience with automatic proof procedures in the predicate calculus. Still, two projects developed on top of STRIPS provide important illustrations of skill acquisition and planning. It therefore seems sensible to work toward a brief description, even though there may be some whose preparation would allow them to go deeper.

Each operator in STRIPS consists of three lists of facts: the first one is a list of facts that must be true if the operator is to be applied; the second is a list of facts that are no longer true after the operator is applied; and the third is a list of facts that the operator makes true. These lists are called the *prerequisite list,* the *delete list,* and the *add list.* The flying operator, for example, would look something like this:

PREREQUISITE LIST: Robbie is at airport x.
                                 There is a flight from x to y.

DELETE LIST: Robbie is at airport x.

ADD LIST: Robbie is at airport y.

When this operator is used, somehow x and y must be matched to the problem at hand. Once there is a way of doing that, then the procedure input problem is solved and the output problem is too, for the delete list and the add list provide the necessary means to be heard.

There is still one giant problem, however, and that is the problem of knowing implied facts. How, for example, can Robbie know that the deletion of *Robbie is at airport x* implies the deletion of *Robbie is in airport x's city.* This is a problem of deduction which STRIPS solves using a so-called resolution theorem prover. We will not look into that corner of STRIPS for two reasons: first, it requires some understanding of the predicate calculus; and second, many think it is not possible to make a resolution-based theorem prover adequate enough for deduction when there are more than a few known facts. Thankfully the rest of STRIPS can be appreciated anyway with only a little fog hovering about the question of how an operator's various lists manage to be linked up with the difference implied by the current description of the world and the statement of the goal.

Remembered Operator Sequences Help STRIPS Solve Harder Problems

Suppose STRIPS solves some problem, producing a sequence of operators, $O_1...O_n$. Figure 5-7 illustrates a way of describing how an operator's effects survive the application of subsequent operators. All facts added by O_1 are listed in the box immediately below it. The second box contains the same facts except that facts removed by the second operator, O_2, are deleted. Similarly, the third box contains the facts added by O_1 minus any such facts removed by either O_2 or O_3. The arrangement therefore describes the staying power of the first operator in that it shows how that operator's additions survive or fail to survive the deletions of subsequent operators.

Figure 5-8 shows how such survival exhibits for all operators in an entire sequence can go together to form a triangular table. Clearly the construction of the table is such that each row is a collection of all surviving facts placed by operators

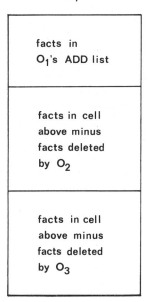

O_1

facts in O_1's ADD list
facts in cell above minus facts deleted by O_2
facts in cell above minus facts deleted by O_3

Figure 5-7 The table shows how some of the facts added by a STRIPS operator are deleted by subsequent operators.

O_1

facts in O_1's ADD list		
facts in cell above minus facts deleted by O_2	facts in O_2's ADD list	
facts in cell above minus facts deleted by O_3	facts in cell above minus facts deleted by O_3	facts in O_3's ADD list

O_2

O_3

Figure 5-8 An elementary triangle table. Each row shows what facts have been added and not yet deleted by the operators so far applied. If the facts in a row resemble the facts required to achieve a new goal, a piece of the old operator sequence table may work well.

appearing above the row. Thus row three, for example, shows what facts are true as a result of the combined effects of operators O_1, O_2, and O_3 appearing in that order. Since these facts may resemble those specified in a new goal, the entire sequence O_1, O_2, O_3 may be a useful way of proceeding. More generally, it is clear that the jth row of the table says something about the way the first j operators affect the world. If this jth row is somehow like what the goal description stipulates, then perhaps the sequence $O_1...O_j$ is a good one to try when seeking the goal. Thus the triangle table created in solving some old problem may be a source of operator sequences that are useful when dealing with new problems. A previous plan which does something in n steps becomes a sequence source capable of offering up operator sequences relevant to n possible goals, one for each row. Conceptually, operator sequences become superoperators with addition lists that are given by the corresponding rows in some triangle table.

Only half of the job is done, however, because only the end of the subsequence is known by row inspection. The question of where to begin the sequence remains. There is no reason to believe O_1 is the best place to start. It may be that the first several operators in the general sequence accomplish only what is already true of the current situation, and the operator sequence can be entered better a bit downstream. In the end, the best operator sequence may be $O_i...O_j$, not $O_1...O_j$.

Getting the proper starting point is not as simple as identifying the proper stopping place. Matching the current world against the rows will not work because the rows only identify how the world has changed, not the total state. A better idea is to focus on operator preconditions and move back from the identified terminal operator, O_j, toward O_i, stopping as soon as the preconditions are satisfied for some operator which then becomes O_i. This idea is not quite bug-free, but it is a good one to work from in order to understand the description of the correct procedure that follows.

As so far described, the triangle table does not help, but with the slight augmentation illustrated in figure 5-9, it does. Each fact in the table is marked if it is a prerequisite to the application of the operator at the end of the row. Any precondition for an operator that is not supplied by an earlier operator is written into a column adjoined to the left side of the table. All of the entries added into this left-side column are marked as essential prerequisites by definition.

Now the question of where an operator sequence can begin has a tight answer: an operator sequence can start if all the facts marked as prerequisites are true in a rectangle to the left of and below the starting operator, O_i, extending down to the terminating operator, O_j.

Why? First, it is clear that all prerequisites to the starting operator O_i, are satisfied since all of them are marked in the true-fact area. Second, it is clear that the prerequisites to the subsequent operators are or will be satisfied because they either lie in the rectangular true-fact area to the left of and below the starting operator or they are supplied by the operator sequence itself as it moves along.

In summary, the way to find a subsequence from a previous plan which is relevant to a new situation involves two steps:

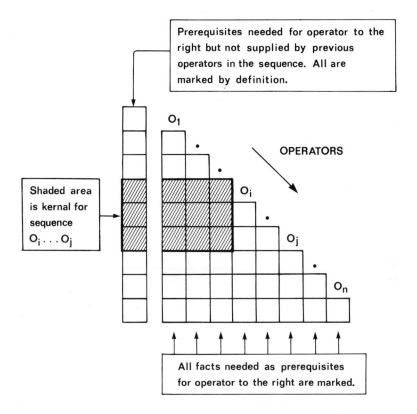

Figure 5-9 An augmented triangle table. All facts which are used as prerequisites by the operator at the end of the row are marked and any other prerequisites are added to the column at the left. The kernel of an operator sequence is then defined to be the prerequisites in the table appearing in the rectangle to the left of the starting operator extending from the row of the starting operator down to the row of the final operator. This kernel enables STRIPS to determine where to enter an old sequence to achieve a new goal in light of the current situation.

■ First, find a row in the triangle table which exhibits facts like those in the goal description. The operator at the end of the previous row is the last operator to be used.

■ Next, move back from the last, terminal operator until an operator is found for which all marked facts to the left of and below it are currently true. This is the first operator to be used.

The marked areas corresponding to the operators are called kernels, incidentally. In addition to their use in subsequence selection, they also aid in monitoring operator sequence execution. The reason is that all of the marked facts in all the kernels should be true just before the corresponding operators are applied.

If the world changed unexpectedly, some fact in a kernel may be turned around, thus interfering with the kernel-true condition and crying stop to the operator executor.

Deferring Recursion Gives STRIPS a Kind of Planning Ability

Sometimes solving a problem can involve deep recursion and considerable effort in satisfying various prerequisite conditions. To avoid wasteful diversions, care must be taken to avoid working on any of the prerequisites for a step if it is clear that the step is bad even before the prerequisites are fulfilled.

Sacerdoti devised a method by which the work of satisfying a step's prerequisites can be avoided automatically when that step is predictably bad. The idea is to determine a solution in broad outline before details are worked out. A form of *planning* is involved which is effected by temporarily dropping concern for prerequisite conditions. To illustrate, suppose Saturday is at hand, Robbie is in Los Angeles, and no arrangements have yet been made about using the free recreation time. Getting a date arranged becomes the goal with the following prerequisite notes seemingly relevant.

■ Mary loves tennis ➤ must arrange for a court and buy new tennis balls.

■ Martha likes expensive food ➤ must take suit to emergency cleaners.

■ Margareta is a bicycle nut ➤ must borrow a second bicycle.

Here it is clear that a lot of work could go to waste if time were spent on prerequisites before checking the viability of the main step. It would be silly to arrange a tennis court or whatever if the girl involved is already engaged. A single phone call is all that is needed, in general, to verify that dealing with prerequisites makes sense.

In the Aunt Agatha example, prerequisites for the very first step, getting on an airplane, required some small amount of recursive problem-solving activity, but not really very much. Still, Sacerdoti's idea can be illustrated.

We can see the scope of the recursion in the diagram in figure 5-10 in which the vertical axis represents recursive depth and the horizontal axis indicates passage

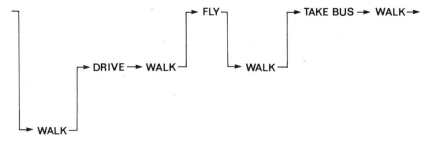

Figure 5-10 The General Problem Solver may dive into deep recursion in order to prepare for operators chosen for relevance to the overall goal. Here one third-level operator and two second-level operators prepare for the first-level operator, FLY.

of time. This is really just a reflection of a previous diagram. In this new form the depth of recursion is clearer since the locus of activity moves down whenever prerequisites call for work on subproblems and up whenever a subproblem has been dealt with. Of course, the times shown are not proportional to actual time used.

In getting to Aunt Agatha's, two planning levels are involved. Each level's activity can be thought of as a planning exercise, with details to be filled in by work at the next level down. The problem is solved first on the top level of main steps only — there would be no concern about getting to the airport until the consequences of getting there are explored. As illustrated in figure 5-11, gaps are filled in later after the overall success of the major operation is apparent. But in filling the gaps, again no attention is paid to prerequisites. The problem of getting to the car is deferred until a third pass.

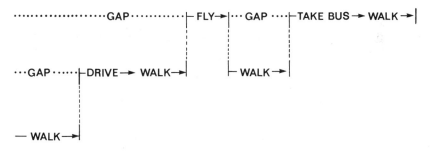

Figure 5-11 The STRIPS version of the General Problem Solver avoids wasted effort spent preparing for bad high-level operators by deferring recursive handling of prerequisite needs. The result is sometimes called length-first search. Here the first business is to be sure that the first-level operators reach the goal. Then the second-level prerequisite problems are investigated, again with details deferred. Finally, the remaining gaps are filled on the third pass.

Why go to this trouble? There is indeed no particular advantage in the example used since each time an operation was fixed on, it proved useful and correct. But if there is a choice between several operators, all with a good, but not certain chance of being useful, then surely the problem solver should avoid wasting effort satisfying the prerequisites of one operator if it will only prove to be a disappointing performer.

SITUATION-ACTION RULES AND PRODUCTION SYSTEMS

Suppose that Robbie wants to spend a day at the San Diego zoo. Aunt Agatha approves, but knows that Robbie will enjoy the visit more if he can recognize the various animals, particularly her favorites. Robbie can see basic features like color, size, and number of legs, but he does not know how to combine such facts into conclusions like, say, this is a cheetah, or that is a giraffe.

Will GPS help? To be sure, GPS fits to some extent: the collection of initial facts is the starting state, another collection of facts with the desired conclusion in it is the goal state, and the operators transform one fact collection into another by adding new, deduced facts. Unfortunately GPS is not fine-grained enough to really help much. Instead, we need a model for going deeper into the process by which salient facts are recognized and resulting facts are deduced.

Production Systems Are Useful for Many Problem-Solving Tasks

Much problem-solving knowlege can be packaged up in the form of little quanta called productions.

■ A *production* is a rule consisting of a situation recognition part and an action part. Thus a production is a *situation-action pair* in which the so-called left side is a list of things to watch for and the so-called right side is a list of things to do.

■ When productions are used in deductive systems, the situations that trigger productions are specified combinations of facts. The actions are restricted to being assertions of new facts deduced directly from the triggering combination. The productions may be called premise-conclusion pairs rather than situation-action pairs.

The restrictions that determine if a production system is a deductive system are satisfied by most of the examples to be given. Although it would be more specific to call them deduction systems, we will usually stick to the more general term.

Robbie Identifies Animals Using a Production System

Robbie needs a fact deduction machine which will take collections of known facts and make new conclusions. Having one production for each animal in the zoo is one strategy, albeit a dull one. The right side of each would be a simple statement of animal name and the left side would be a bulbous enumeration of characteristics large enough to rule out any alternative identification. In operation, the user would first gather up all facts available and then scan the production list for a production which has a matching situation part.

Reasoning from base facts to a conclusion rarely goes through in a single step, however. More often intermediate facts are generated and used, making reasoning a more complicated and interesting process. One consequence is that the productions involved can be small, easily understood, easily used, and easily created. Using this approach, Robbie hopes to produce chains of conclusions leading to the name of the animal he is examining.

Suppose Aunt Agatha directs Robbie to an antechamber of the zoo which contains only seven popular animals. She knows this will simplify her teaching problem because a relatively small number of recognition productions will be needed. Four of them are very simple ones which determine the biological class, mammal or bird:

P1
If   the animal has hair,
then it is a mammal.

P2
If   the animal gives milk,
then it is a mammal.

P3
If   the animal has feathers,
then it is a bird.

P4
If   the animal flies,
      and it lays eggs,
then it is a bird.

The last of these has two elements in the premise collection. Although it does not really matter for the collection of animals in the local zoo, Aunt Agatha evidently knows that some mammals fly and some lay eggs, but only birds do both.

Knowing that an animal is a mammal, one of two productions may be used to determine that it is carnivorous. The simplest has to do with catching the animal in the act:

P5
If   the animal is a mammal,
      and it eats meat,
then it is a carnivore.

If it is not feeding time, a variety of other factors, taken together, are conclusive:

P6
If   the animal is a mammal,
      it has pointed teeth,
      it has claws,
      and its eyes point forward,
then it is a carnivore.

The other animals in the zoo which are mammals all happen to be ungulates:

P7
If   the animal is a mammal,
      and it has hoofs,
then it is an ungulate.

If Robbie has a hard time looking at the feet, he may still have a chance, since any animal which chews cud is certainly an ungulate too:

P8
If   the animal is a mammal,
        and it chews cud,
then   it is an ungulate,
        and it is even toed.

The business about the toes is there just to show an example of productions with multiple conclusions.

Having a way of dividing all mammals into carnivores and ungulates, it is time to look at productions which identify specific animals. For carnivores, two possibilities exist:

P9
If   the animal is a carnivore,
        it has a tawny color,
        and it has dark spots,
then   it is a cheetah.

P10
If   the animal is a carnivore,
        it has a tawny color,
        and it has black stripes,
then   it is a tiger.

Strictly speaking, the basic color is not useful since both of the carnivores are tawny. There is no law saying that the information in productions must be minimal. Often it is better to focus on the individual production, putting in what seems natural, and ignoring the way it compares with others.

For the ungulates, other productions separate the total group into four possibilities:

P11
If   the animal is an ungulate,
        it has long legs and a long neck,
        it has a tawny color,
        and it has dark spots,
then   it is a giraffe.

P12
If   the animal is an ungulate,
        it has a white color,
        and it has black stipes,
then   it is a zebra.

Having worked through the four available mammals, the same can be done for the three birds:

P13
If	the animal is a bird,
	it does not fly,
	it has long legs and a long neck,
	and it is black and white,
then	it is an ostrich.

P14
If	the animal is a bird,
	it does not fly,
	it swims,
	and it is black and white,
then	it is a penguin.

P15
If	the animal is a bird,
	and it is a good flyer,
then	it is an albatross.

Now that all of the animals are on the table, so to speak, note that many features are widely shared. Zebras and tigers have black stripes; tigers, cheetahs, and giraffes have a tawny color; giraffes and ostriches have long legs and a long neck; and ostriches and penguins are black and white.

Now for a case study, suppose Robbie is at the zoo and proceeds to establish certain facts:

■ An animal is observed which has a tawny color and dark spots. Production 9 and production 11 are suggested since both have the tawny color and dark spots requirements. Neither is triggered yet, however, since both have additional premise conditions to be met.

■ While nursing a baby, the animal chews its cud. Evidently the animal gives milk, a fact which triggers production 2, establishing that the animal is a mammal. Knowing that the animal is a mammal combines with the second fact about chewing a cud to trigger production 8, further establishing that the animal is an ungulate and has two or four toes per foot. The conditions for production 11 are nearly all ready.

■ The animal has long legs and a long neck. Production 11 fires. The animal is a giraffe.

Thus the facts flow through a series of productions from left to right until the desired conclusion is reached.

Several Methods Determine Which Production to Use if Many Qualify

In the event many productions have premise or situation specifications that shout for attention, then there must be some way of deciding among them. Here are some of the popular methods:

■ All productions are arranged in one long list. The first matching production is the one used. The others are ignored.

■ The matching production with the toughest requirements is the one used where toughest means the longest list of constraining premise or situation elements.

■ The matching production most recently used is used again.

■ Some aspects of the total situation are considered more important. Productions matching high priority situation elements are privileged.

Deduction Systems Produce AND/OR Trees

A simple deduction-oriented production specifies a single conclusion which follows from the simultaneous satisfaction of the situation recognition elements. Any particular conclusion may spring from many productions. The conclusion specified in a production follows from the AND or *conjunction* of the facts specified in the premise recognition part. A conclusion reached by more than one production is said to be the OR or *disjunction* of those productions.

Conjunction and *disjunction* are thus fancy terms for AND and OR. Depicting these relationships graphically produces an *AND/OR* tree. Figure 5-12 shows an AND/OR tree which reaches from base facts at the bottom through productions to a conclusion at the top. Any collection of productions implies such a tree.

The arrangement of nodes in this tree focuses on how the conclusion can be reached by various combinations of basic facts. As with ordinary AND/OR trees, a conclusion is verified if it is possible to connect it with basic facts through a set of satisfied AND/OR nodes. Different sets of facts can be used to reach a given conclusion by selecting different branches at OR nodes.

Sometimes it is useful to look at the implied tree to get a better feel for the problem space, noting whether the reasoning is likely to be broad and shallow or narrow and deep or (gasp) broad and deep. Again however, caution is in order. When used prominently in discussion of goals and subgoals, they tend to make control look like a search problem with the various search ideas becoming applicable. This position has its good and bad features. One bad feature is that it can create a tendency to fool with an existing problem space rather than to make a better space.

Deduction Systems May Run Forward or Backward

So far the deduction-oriented production system is assumed to work from known facts to new, deduced facts. Running this way, a system exhibits forward chaining. But backward chaining is also possible, for the production system user can

CONCLUSION

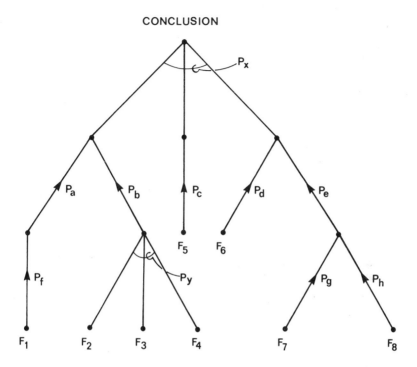

Figure 5-12 A collection of productions defines a tree of conclusions. The tree is equivalent to a so-called AND/OR tree. At AND nodes, all facts on the branches must be true for the AND node to be true, and at OR nodes, any fact is enough. AND nodes are, by tradition, marked with an arc drawn across all the branches while OR nodes have no such marks. Roughly speaking, each OR branch represents a simple production with only one condition in its set of situation conditions. Each AND arc also represents a production with each AND arc corresponding to a situation condition.

hypothesize a conclusion and use the productions to work backward toward an enumeration of the facts that would support the hypothesis.

For example Robbie might hypothesize that a given animal is a cheetah and then reason about whether the hypothesis is viable. The first step is to find a production whose conclusion side identifies an animal as a cheetah. Production 9 is the only one which qualifies. This production's premise side then specifies conditions that must be met if the cheetah hypothesis is correct.

■ It is hypothesized that the animal is a cheetah. To verify the hypothesis, production 9 requires that the animal is a carnivore, that it has a tawny color, and that it has dark spots. There are no productions with tawny color or dark spots on the conclusion side so those facts, if true, must be checked directly by Robbie's sensory system when needed.

■ It is hypothesized that the animal is a carnivore. Two productions may qualify, namely production 5 and production 6. Assume that production 5 is tried first. It requires that the animal be a mammal.

■ It is hypothesized that the animal is a mammal. Again there are two possibilities, production 1 and production 2. Let us try production 1.

■ It is hypothesized that the animal has hair. A sensory system job again. Assume it has hair. This means it must be a mammal and Robbie can go back to working on production 5.

■ It is hypothesized that the animal eats meat. Assume there is no evidence at the moment. Robbie must abandon production 5 and try to use production 6 to establish that the animal is a carnivore.

■ It is hypothesized that the animal is a mammal. True, since this was already established when trying to satisfy the conditions for production 5.

■ It is hypothesized that the animal has pointed teeth; It is hypothesized that the animal has claws; and it is hypothesized that the animal's eyes point forward. Assume the sensory system shows all are true. Evidently the animal is a carnivore allright and Robbie can return to production 9 which started everything done so far.

■ It is hypothesized that the animal has a tawny color; and it is hypothesized that the animal has dark spots. Assume both are true. Production 9 supports the hypothesis that the animal is a cheetah. Evidently it is.

Thus Robbie was able to work backward through the premise-conclusion productions, using desired conclusions to decide what facts to look for. A backward moving chain develops. The chaining ends successfully, verifying the hypothesis, when the implied AND/OR tree is satisfied. The chaining ends unsuccessfully if some required premise facts are left dangling, with no hard facts or production conclusions available to fill them, or if some required premise is actually contrary to known facts.

Purpose Helps Determine How to Run a Deduction System

Knowing that a deduction-oriented production system can run forward or backward, which is better? The question is decided by the purpose of the reasoning and by the shape of the problem space. Certainly if the goal is to discover all that can be deduced from a given set of facts, then the production system must run forward. On the other hand, if the purpose is to verify or deny a particular conclusion, then the production system is probably best run backward from that conclusion. Avoiding needless fact accumulation is one reason. Indeed, no irrelevant facts need be checked at all. The production system can run backward from all premise elements as long as suitable productions exist. Using sensory systems to supply facts is necessary only when no productions apply.

Another reason to run backward is because many, many conclusions irrelevant to the target conclusion can usually come out of an initial, given set of facts. If these facts are fed to a forward running production system, then much work may be wasted in developing a combinatorial nightmare.

Production System Control Seems to Offer Many Features

Champions of production-system ideas cite one or more of the following benefits:

- Production systems provide what some people believe to be a good model of the basic human problem-solving apparatus.

- Production systems enforce a homogeneous representation of knowledge.

- Production systems allow incremental growth through the addition of individual productions.

- Production systems allow unplanned but useful interactions which are not possible with control structures in which all procedure interactions are determined beforehand. A piece of knowledge can be applied whenever apppropriate, not just whenever a programmer predicts it can be appropriate.

Production System Features May Be Flaws in Some Situations

It would seem that production systems allow knowledge to be tossed into systems homogeneously and incrementally without worry about relating new knowledge quanta to old. Evidently production systems should permit knowledge engineers to focus attention on well-constrained premise-conclusion or situation-action combinations, ignoring the question of control. Each production focuses on a particular symbolic constellation of importance and describes an appropriate response.

One must be wary, however. A general truth is that if a problem is simple enough, almost *any* approach will look elegant. Moreover, as King Lear noted, bequeathing control may mean losing control.

Productions Must Be Partitioned into Subsystems If Many Are Required

One particular worry is that production systems may break down if the amount of knowledge is too large, for then the number of productions grows beyond reasonable bounds. The *advantage* of not needing to worry about the interactions among the productions can become the *disadvantage* of not being able to influence the interactions among the larger number of productions.

One possible solution, of course, is to partition the facts and the productions into subsystems such that at any time only a manageable number are under consideration. Within each subsystem, some productions may be devoted to arranging transfer of information or attention to another subsystem. Curiously, some users of Hewitt's ACTORS language produce programs that have a strong resemblance to systems of communicating production subsystems.

The important Carnegie-Mellon HEARSAY II speech-understanding system also looks like a partitioned production system. It consists of a large collection of production-like knowledge sources which operate off of a so-called blackboard. The blackboard really looks like a side view of a Dobos torte inasmuch as it has many layers corresponding to natural speech units like phrases, words, syllables, phonemes, primitive segments, and 10 msec signal slices. These layers tend to produce an implied partitioning of the facts and productions because most of the productions are specific to a particular layer or two.

Many productions are dedicated to forming hypotheses about how to aggregate groups of lower level units into higher level chunks, making big ones out of little ones, so to speak. Thus a syllable-level specialist may spot a favorite group of syllables with the right time arrangement and hypothesize a word. Then this new word may be just the thing a word specialist is waiting for to complete a phrase.

■ Productions may be used to hold grouping knowledge. Such a production is a *piece-group pair.*

Of course many other productions are required to provide administrative support to the basic grouping productions in order to establish priorities, establish effort foci, deal with competing hypotheses, and cope with the thousand difficulties that the real world strikes back with.

PRODUCTION SYSTEMS AND HUMAN PROBLEM SOLVING

Do computational theories of problem solving have promise as psychological models of human reasoning? The answer is Yes, at least to some psychologists who try to understand ordinary human activity using metaphors shared with researchers who concentrate on making smarter computers. Production systems, for example, can be a way of producing new expert problem solvers or a way of explaining certain results in experimental psychology.

One group of experimenters addresses questions about the structure and limitations of the processor, assuming that the production system model is valid. They probe and prod, often trying to invent tasks so unfamiliar that they block out the knowledge that normally interacts with the processor and obscures its nature. This intent explains why some people believe that experiments with cryptarithmetic and sequences of nonsense syllables are a valid no-nonsense approach to basic questions.

Of course, human information processing is an enormous puzzle with many potential starting places. To solve the puzzle, some believe it is best to work from both sides toward the middle with physiological psychology and information-processing psychology progressing together toward an eventual merger. Others feel that only a sequential approach makes sense because one area's solutions are prerequisites for progress on the other area's problems.

Taking an information-processing point of view, they wonder how neural mechanisms provide the basic processing hardware and how accumulated knowledge provides the software. The two questions are not independent, of course, for the hardware-software interface must operate smoothly. Both sides of the boundary are likely to reflect accommodation to the other.

Production Systems Can Model Some Human Problem Solving

Hard-core Production-System enthusiasts believe that humans have productions which key off a small, volatile collection of items collectively called short-term memory.

■   According to human production system theory, *short-term memory* is inhabited by only a few simple symbolic *chunks,* while *long-term memory* holds all the procedures which can be performed. Specific combinations of the short-term memory items activate the long-term memory processes, all of which are buried in *productions.*

■   The productions activated by short-term memory combinations are the only procedures allowed. Control decisions and interprocedure communication are handled exclusively by the short-term memory.

Thus the short-term memory is the key to which procedures are called, what they are given to work with, and how they return results. Each chunk in short-term memory may be a single symbol, like HEADACHE or a small constellation of symbols like PROBLEM: SMOKES CIGARETTES. Evidently the short-term memory contains between five and nine such chunks. One often hears of the seven-plus-or-minus-two phenomenon.

In an *elementary* production system, all operations deal with short-term memory and all are very primitive. Any production may execute any combination of primitive operations once triggered by the proper pattern. If the patterns of more than one production match short-term memory, then some precedence-determining procedure is invoked. The primitives are as follows:

■   A production can *write* a new item into short-term memory. A new item goes in at the front and dislodges an item from the back end. Hence items that have spent some time in short-term memory tend to be forgotten in accordance with human characteristics.

■   A production can *notice* items in short-term memory by moving them from their existing place to the front. This tends to protect noted items from being shoved out of short-term memory by new entries.

■   A production can *mark* an item in short-term memory. Although there is no way to directly delete items from STM, marking an item changes its appearance enough to effect much the same result. Since productions rarely look for marked items, those marked items tend to migrate toward the end of short-term memory and drop off, thus being permanently forgotten. Marking is often used to prevent a goal description from reactivating the same production over and over, a problem that would be something of a plague otherwise.

■ A production can communicate with the environment: a production can *send* a message, thus requesting new information; similarly a production can *receive* a message, placing it at the front of short-term memory. In a human, most communication would be through the attention and analysis mechanisms involved in vision and language. For computer-based simulation, both sending and receiving generally goes through some sort of terminal.

Robbie's zoo productions could be put in this form without much trouble. To really make use of the production idea when dealing with hard problems, however, one must generalize beyond the primitives of the elementary theory. There must be stronger pattern matching options on the left side, and there must be more serious computation on the right side. Once this happens, however, the result can be a production-system shell filled up with a more conventional programming language. One can expect hybrid vigor if the synthesis is well husbanded, a monster otherwise.

Protocol Analysis Produces Production-System Conjectures

To ferret out just what is going on inside people as they solve problems, patient psychologists pore over transcripts of subjects thinking aloud, trying to infer what productions are used. These psychologists use a little jargon to explain:

■ The *state of knowledge* is what the subject knows. Each time the subject deduces something, forgets something, or acquires something through its senses, the state of knowledge changes.

■ The *problem-behavior graph* is a trace of a problem solver through its states of knowledge as it solves a problem.

Typically the problem-behavior graph is important because it helps unravel facts about the subject that produces it. By analyzing the way one state of knowledge becomes another, inferences can be made about the productions that produce the changes. Consider, for example, the following protocol fragment:

> *Let's see, I want to identify this animal, I wonder if it is a cheetah — I have nothing to go on yet, so I think I'll start by looking into the possibility that it is a carnivore — I better check to see if it is a mammal first — yes, that is ok — hair — it doesn't seem to be eating anything so I can't really tell if it is a carnivore — but oh, yes, it has pointed teeth, claws, and forward-pointing eyes, so it is a carnivore all right — now where was I — it's a carnivore, and I also see that it has a tawny color and dark spots — must be a cheetah!*

It would seem that the facts accumulate in the following order: hair, mammal, pointed teeth, claws, forward-pointing eyes, carnivore, tawny color, dark spots, and cheetah. From observations like these, the cryptographic psychologist would probably deduce that Robbie's production system is a backward-running one much like the one used in the other zoo examples. But there is not enough to really be sure about how the facts mentioned are being assembled together, and a longer protocol with more animal identifications is needed.

SUMMARY

■ Search deals with how a system investigates an environment. Control deals with how a system uses its own modules. Behavior is usually determined jointly by the situation, the search strategies, and the control decisions.

■ Understanding a system's control structure implies knowing how the system chooses what to do, how it passes information to the modules it selects, and how it receives results.

■ The means-ends idea is a control idea stressing differences and operator selection aimed at reducing the differences. The General Problem Solver embodiment of the general approach uses operator selection in a depth-first process run by interlocked iteration and recursion.

■ Forward chaining means working forward from the current situation or collection of facts toward some goal state or desired conclusion. Backward chaining goes the other way, working toward the current state or known facts from the goal or conclusion.

■ STRIPS is an implementation of GPS which supports research on the important questions surrounding self-improvement and planning.

■ Production Systems differ from the General Problem Solver in that productions are triggered by the facts available in the current state while GPS operators are triggered by a computed difference.

■ Some production systems correspond to an implied AND/OR tree. The AND/OR tree is a device for showing how the basic facts connect with conclusions. The AND/OR tree may be characterized as deep or wide or both.

■ Production Systems are popular because they seem to offer modularity and incremental growth characteristics.

REFERENCES

■ Herbert A. Simon, *The Sciences of the Artificial,* The M.I.T. Press, Cambridge, Massachusetts, 1969. Source of the metaphor of the wandering ant. This classic little book also contains a discussion of what Simon calls nearly decomposable systems and why science depends on them.

■ G. A. Miller, E. Galanter, and K. H. Pribram, *Plans and the Structure of Behavior,* Holt, Rinehart, and Winston, New York, 1960. Proposes a psychological model of certain kinds of behavior emphasizing the notion of test-operate sequences.

■   G. Ernst and Allen Newell, *GPS: A Case Study in Generality and Problem Solving,* Academic Press, New York, 1969. Early work on GPS with a dozen or so problem domains like integral calculus and plane geometry cast in GPS terms.

■   W. W. Bledsoe, "Non-Resolution Theorem Proving," ATM-29, Departments of Mathematics and Computer Sciences, University of Texas, Austin, Texas, 1975, adapted from a tutorial talk at the Fourth International Joint Conference on Artificial Intelligence. A fine review of automatic theorem proving in general.

■   Randall Davis and Jonathan King, "An Overview of Production Systems," AIM-271, The Artificial Intelligence Laboratory, Stanford University, Stanford, California, 1975. An excellent discussion, treating both features and defects.

■   Lee D. Erman and Victor R. Lesser, "A Multi-level Organization for Problem Solving Using Many, Diverse, Cooperating Sources of Knowledge," *Advance Papers of the Fourth International Joint Conference on Artificial Intelligence,* available through the M.I.T. Artificial Intelligence Laboratory, Cambridge, Massachusetts, 1975. Interesting both because of the view taken on speech understanding and because it is like a dramatically generalized production system. All interprocess communication takes place through a so-called blackboard which all specialists watch and write into as appropriate.

■   Allen Newell and Herbert A. Simon, *Human Problem Solving,* Prentice-Hall, Englewood Cliffs, New Jersey, 1972. The classic work on Production System Theory. It is long. It is important.

The next three references describe work done in the context of the STRIPS problem solver built at the Stanford Research Institute.

■   Richard E. Fikes and Nils J. Nilsson, "STRIPS: A new Approach to the Application of Theorem Proving to Problem Solving," *Artificial Intelligence,* Vol. 2, no. 3/4, 1971. The basic paper on STRIPS.

■   Richard E. Fikes, Peter E. Hart and Nils J. Nilsson, "Learning and Executing Generalized Robot Plans," *Artificial Intelligence,* vol. 3, 1972. Introduction of the idea of triangle tables and superoperators.

■   Earl D. Sacerdoti, "Planning in a Hierarchy of Abstraction Spaces," *Artificial Intelligence,* vol. 5, no. 2, 1974. An insightful piece on planning.

6
THE
MEANING
OF
MEANING

It boggles the mind to think that one day computers will be endowed with the language understanding abilities so far exclusively possessed by human information processors. Hastening that day will take hard work, to be sure, because dealing with unconstrained natural language surely requires strong, as yet undiscovered techniques for representation, constraint exploitation, and other things yet unknown. Still, something is already known, and this chapter's purpose is to show how certain systems of programs exhibit a kind of understanding as they participate in conversations about domains like that of the limited world of blocks, pyramids, and boxes.

THE BLOCKS WORLD

In studying how to make computers understand human language, each question seems invariably to generate another:

■ What can it mean to say that a computer has understood something? Is it enough if the computer offers back an intelligent-sounding response?

■ How much understanding is required to translate from one human language into another? How does this depend on the subject matter?

■ How can a domain of discourse be delineated which is rich enough to be a vehicle for studying the central issues, yet simple enough to facilitate the progress?

Limited Domains of Discourse Are the E. Coli of Language Research

Perhaps the question of domain delineation is the most critical one because understanding language phenomena is like understanding molecular biology.

Neither problem succumbs to frontal assault, and one must work toward limited objectives with the hope that tactical victories will lead to strategic insights. For molecular biology, this means thorough study of very simple organisms, the intestinal organism *E. Coli* in particular. For artificial intelligence, the simple organisms are the strongly limited domains of discourse, the blocks world being an example.

Robbie Converses about the Blocks World

We are about to look at some fragments taken from a conversation between a human and a simulated one-armed robot created by Winograd in his landmark 1971 thesis. Winograd called his robot SHRDLU, but here he will be called Robbie to keep things consistent. Think of SHRDLU as an alias.

Robbie's world is a simulated world of blocks, pyramids, and boxes. It is displayed as in figure 6-1 for the convenience of the human participant. Robbie's responses are actions and upper case English.

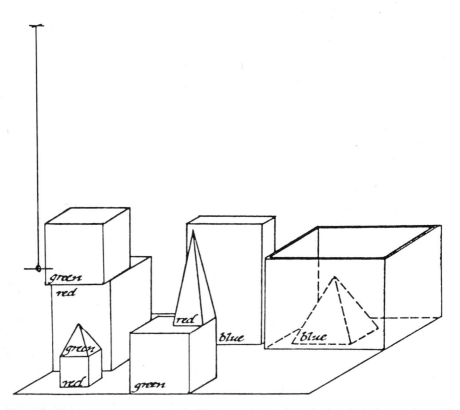

Figure 6-1 For language exposition, the blocks world consists of colored blocks together with a one-armed robot equipped with a magnetic hand. (Figures 6-1 through 6-5 are from *CAES Study Guide on Artificial Intelligence* by Patrick H. Winston, copyright by Center for Advanced Engineering Study, Massachusetts Institute of Technology, Cambridge, Massachusetts. Used with permission of the Center for Advanced Engineering Study.)

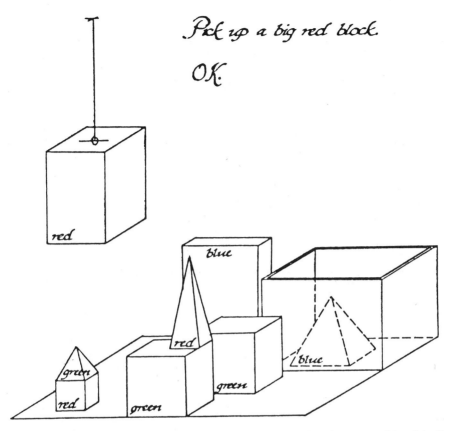

Figure 6-2 A sample command and the resulting action. Note that the green cube, originally on top of the red block, has been laid aside.

■ Pick up a big red block.

OK.

To handle the command, Robbie must decide which block is the big red one and then plan a motion sequence suitable for getting to it. Figure 6-2 shows the result.

■ Find a block which is taller than the one you are holding and put it into the box.

OK.

Robbie must deal with pronoun references.

■ What does the box contain?

THE BLUE PYRAMID AND THE BLUE BOX.

Robbie must decide which objects are in the box and determine how they can be described to the human.

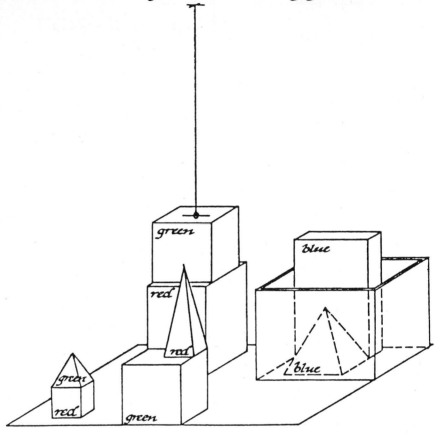

Will you please stack up both of the red blocks and either a green cube or a pyramid.

Figure 6-3 Here the robot had to put aside the green pyramid to get at the red cube required for the stack.

■   What is the pyramid supported by?

THE BOX.

There is more than one pyramid, but Robbie knows that the human must be talking about the same one that was just reported to be in the box.

■   Can a pyramid be supported by a block?

YES.

There is an example, so it must be possible.

■   Will you please stack up both of the red blocks and either a green cube or a pyramid.

OK.

This requires some problem solving.

Does the shortest thing the tallest pyramid's support supports support anything green?

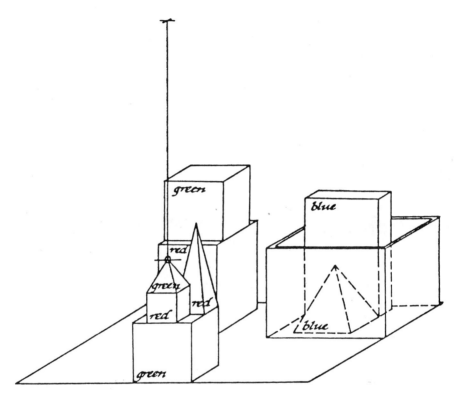

Figure 6-4 Modern language understanding programs can cope with complicated constructions as long as the domain of discourse is limited. The answer to the question is Yes.

■ Which cube is sitting on the table?

THE LARGE GREEN ONE WHICH SUPPORTS THE RED PYRAMID.

Robbie tries to give enough information for a unique determination.

■ Is there a large block behind a pyramid?

YES, THREE OF THEM: A LARGE RED ONE, A LARGE GREEN CUBE, AND THE BLUE ONE.

■ Put a small one onto the green cube which supports a pyramid.

OK.

■ Put the littlest pyramid on top of it.

OK. The result is shown in figure 6-4.

■ Does the shortest thing the tallest pyramid's support supports support anything green?

YES, THE GREEN PYRAMID.

!

■ When did you pick up the green pyramid?

WHILE I WAS STACKING UP THE RED CUBE, A LARGE RED BLOCK, AND A LARGE GREEN CUBE.

Robbie must remember what he has done and in what sequence.

■ Why?

TO GET RID OF IT.

Reasons must be remembered in some sort of goal tree. Here Robbie moves from one goal up to the goal's parent. *How* questions require going from parent to offspring.

■ Why?

TO CLEAN OFF THE RED CUBE.

Continuing with the same question will eventually result in the answer, "Because you told me to."

■ Put the blue pyramid on the block in the box.

OK.

The sentence is ambiguous unless one looks at the scene being discussed. See figure 6-5.

■ Thank you.

YOU'RE WELCOME!

Most people are amazed by this dialogue. There is no doubt that the machine seems to be quite competent with respect to what goes on. Robbie's world view is myopic since Robbie is no good at any question outside the world of the simulation. Nevertheless, Robbie's block world is particularly convenient for studying many issues central to natural language processing, and we shall use it to illuminate some of the resulting ideas. We will only scratch the surface, to be sure — our interest will focus on the process by which object names are derived from their English descriptions.

Robbie Has Very Little to Talk About

The main reason the blocks world is so useful as a framework for beginning a study of natural language is that the things one can talk about are naturally limited. Let us be precise about this. One can talk about the following:

■ *Objects,* such as specific blocks and pyramids;

■ *Relations between objects,* such as IN-FRONT-OF and SUPPORTED-BY;

Put the blue pyramid on the block in the box.

OK.

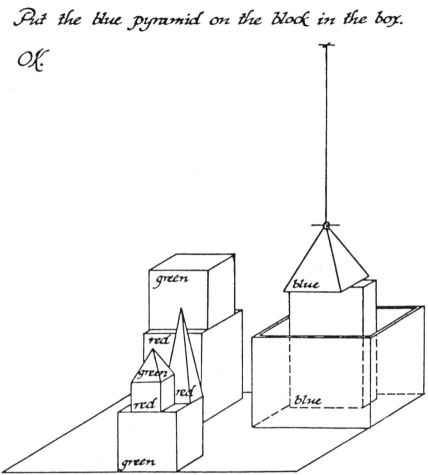

Figure 6-5 Sometimes knowledge of particular situations is required to disambiguate sentences. Here one choice is moving a blue pyramid which is on a block into the box, and the other is moving a blue pyramid onto a block which is in the box. One is eliminated by the known facts.

■ *Relations between objects and intrinsic properties,* such as color and size;
■ *Actions,* such as PICK-UP, PUT-ON, and STACK.

Now, what can be said in connection with these categories? We will look at questions and commands and ignore the problem of assimilating facts. Relations and properties will appear in sentences of two types: questions about whether a relation or a property exists and commands to make a relation exist:

Is the red cube in the box?

Is the red cube big?

Put the red cube on the blue block.

What is needed to handle these and similar sentences? What kind of knowledge? How much? What in particular?

Understanding Requires Multilevel Expertise

Even the simple language of blocks-world questions and commands is hard to deal with. Words must be assembled into groups, groups into sentences, and sentences into coherent histories. There is a need, therefore, for several specialists:

■ The *syntactic specialist* bounces about in a sentence with only the modest goal of segmenting it into meaningful word groups. The syntactic specialist divides each simple sentence into a verb group and one or more noun groups. The verb group consists of a verb together with acompanying auxiliaries and adverbs. Noun groups similarly consist of a noun and various modifiers. To do its job the syntactic specialist must know about how word ordering depends on syntactic word features.

■ The *sentence specialist* determines how the objects described by the noun groups relate to the action described by the verb group. The sentence specialist needs to know how to use both syntactic and semantic information in this analysis.

■ The *scenario specialist* understands how individual sentences relate to one another and to the general story that they collectively tell. In the simple blocks-world situation, the scenario specialist must handle pronoun references and the time order of all actions performed. In less simple situations it must understand how groups of sentences convey implications, evoke expectations, recall memories, establish contexts, create moods, and develop plots.

Thankfully the natural limits on blocks-world conversation permit concentration on the syntactic level, with only brief sorties into the sentence-level and scenario-level problems.

Case Analysis is Straightforward in the Blocks World

The purpose of case analysis is to sort out how the noun groups in a sentence fill various roles. For commands, who is to do the action? For whom? To what? In the blocks world, most of the case slots are easily filled by using tightly bound defaults or by applying very simple syntactic criteria. Robbie, the robot, is the only entity that can do anything, hence Robbie is always the agent. Similarly there is no question about for whom the action is done because the human giving commands is the only possibility. And finally, the object involved in the action must be some sort of block and it is generally the only one inside a noun group lacking an introductory preposition. The instrument and the location are obvious, giving the following overall:

agent: Robbie
beneficiary: human master
instrument: Robbie's hand
location: Robbie's simulated world
object: noun group without a preposition
               containing a block, pyramid, etc.

Indeed there is so much constraint in the blocks world, the problem of sorting the noun groups into cases is not a significant task for most sentences.

Robbie Uses Object Descriptions and Action Names

For the most part, actions, relations, and properties are denoted directly by words like *put, above, and red.* This is not the case with objects. Instead, inspection of the dialogue reveals that quite a number of the words are devoted to specifying the objects by description, not name. What can it mean to understand these specifications? Presumably we humans form some sort of association between the specifying utterance and the visual perception. "A big red block which supports a pyramid," is somehow tied up with an interior model of physical reality built up by our vision apparatus. How this is done is unknown so the statement is admittedly vague. The necessary equivalent for a computer system is not vague, however. There is no external physical world, only the simulated world in memory. To ask about a particular object in this world, one must get at its name, which would be something like BLOCK3 or PYRAMID2 or 31415. The trick then is to derive these names from a description couched in an English utterance. No such trick is required by the blocks world in handling the relations and actions relevant in it because these are named directly, not described. We say *pick up* and *behind.* There is no need to avoid associating unique names with these concepts in our speech because there are few of them. This is true in general. We could not hope to give a unique name to every physical object we deal with in our experience, but we do have names for most of the primitive actions that we can perform and the relations and properties we can perceive.

All of this means that blocks-world understanding involves two semantic steps. The first is the analysis of object description and substitution of object names. The second is the use of these names and the other words of the sentence to do something. In the following example, "Pick up a big red block," ultimately becomes a simple call to the PICK-UP program:

Pick-up a big red block.
↓
Pick up BLOCK3.
↓
(PICK-UP BLOCK3)

We shall see that blocks-world translations of this sort can be effected by cooperating semantic and syntactic programs. The semantic specialist program uses adjectives, nouns, and verbs to supply program fragments which are pasted together under the direction of the syntactic specialist.

Understanding Connects Utterances to the World

Language consists of meaningful groups of words arranged in sentences. Since we can talk about things, there are noun groups. Since we can talk about actions, there are verb groups. Somehow the noun groups become associated with the objects of the physical world. "Note the big block," exhorts the listener to look at a particular object. "Note 27182," would be simpler and less susceptable to ambiguity, but humans denote objects mostly by description, not by name.

Now what can it mean to understand these descriptions? Presumably we humans use our vision hardware to create descriptions of our three-dimensional physical environment. Perhaps these descriptions are symbolic structures with hierarchical levels. Understanding a noun group may correspond to establishing symbolic links between noun groups discovered by language procedures and the symbolic structures developed by vision processing. This is vague. With Robbie we can be much more precise:

■ A noun group is understood by identifying the name of the object described.

What is in a name? Since Robbie uses only an internal simulation, not a real physical world, getting a name from a noun group is all important. If we ask Robbie about the color of the big block, he must work through 27182, the object's name. If we command Robbie to pick it up, again the name is the key to the location information which Robbie needs to position its hand. Indeed almost all of what Robbie knows about objects is accessed by object name just as most of what we know of addresses and telephone numbers is accessed by the names in the telephone book. There is no way to get the telephone number of the beautiful person with the blonde hair.

Translating Noun Groups into Programs Makes Sense in the Blocks World

Let us state a series of claims:

■ Understanding a blocks-world utterance involves a process by which one description is translated into another. The first description is in natural language. The second description is one that is useful in generating a relevant response.

■ Very often the target descriptions for blocks-world sentences are best expressed in the form of programs. These programs, when run, make relevant responses.

■ If the initial utterance is a command, the target can be a program with arguments which accomplishes the required action. If a question is asked, the program can be one that retrieves information, makes deductions, and gives answers.

How can this idea of translation into programs be defended? The explanation depends heavily on the absence of connected dialogue in blocks-world conversations. Each sentence is likely to be independently formulated and independently understood. There are no paragraphs developing an explanation of a situation or arguing toward a conclusion or preparing background context for understanding a cause-effect relationship. Consequently the analogy between sentences and functions made when we discussed the constraints that underlie case grammar are just about the whole story of blocks-world meaning.

What about translating utterances into some sort of interlingua in the form of predicate calculus or networks of concepts or some other representation that does not look much like a program? The answer is that no matter what form the representation takes, there is a program lying camouflaged somewhere. Certainly some representation of a function with arguments may be used which does not look much like a program, but if a response is to be made, then the responder must do something. If the translation goes into something that looks like data, then some program must peruse the data to respond relevantly. But this is a way of saying that the data gives implicit instructions about what to do, an idea that is just one step away from saying that the data is an embodiment of an implied program. Some analysis is required to convert the implicit form into explicit actions perhaps, but the data really does act like a disguised programming language.

Noun Group Programs Find Names

Robbie's ability to deduce object names from descriptions rests on a collection of specialists that look at the noun groups, use them to write search programs, and run those programs to get the names. This involves a beautiful idea:

■ Programs themselves can write and run their own programs.

Thankfully there is no need to put off further discussion until we do some programming. The concepts are handled here and details deferred.

THE STRUCTURE OF NOUN GROUPS

The simplest noun groups consist of only determiners, adjectives, and nouns. Determiners are words like *a, the, this, that, these,* and *those* which help specify which and how many objects are involved.

There are many constraints among the noun group constituents. The determiner, if there is one, comes first. Next comes the adjectives, if any, and finally the noun. After seeing a determiner, the noun group syntactic analyst can look for either an adjective or a noun but not for another determiner. Encountering a noun, the syntactic analyst knows that no further determiners, adjectives, or nouns are very likely. Sometimes a noun is used as an adjective, in which case it is called a classifier, but we will ignore such details for the present.

Grammars Are Mechanisms for Describing Language

Of the many schemes for representing constraints about language, the context-free grammar, the transformational grammar, and the augmented-transition-network grammar are particularly prominent. All are theories of language since all contain descriptions of the constraints that determine if a word sequence is a valid sentence or just disordered garbage. Shortly we will concentrate on grammars represented as augmented transition networks because they suits our purpose best. First however, it is appropriate to look at the other grammars just to know that there are alternative approaches.

To understand both context-free and transformational grammars, think first of a black box which has no input, just an output. From the output come valid English sentences, first the one-word ones, and then progressively longer ones. Inside the box, a typical grammar consists of a set of rules, each of which accepts a word string, modifies it, and delivers the new result. These rules can have a distinctly production-like flavor as shown by these examples:

> R1
> If   the symbol S is present,
> then   replace S with the symbols SUBJECT VERB.
>
> R2
> If   the symbol SUBJECT is present,
> then   replace SUBJECT with the symbols THE PROGRAMMER.
>
> R3
> If   the symbol VERB is present,
> then   replace VERB with the symbol PROGRAMS.

Sentences are generated by applying the rules over and over again to an initial start symbol, S. Following the rules in the example is easy because there is never any point where more than one rule applies to the same symbol. Thus applying rule R1, R2, and R3, in that order, effects the following changes.

> S
> SUBJECT VERB
> THE PROGRAMMER VERB
> THE PROGRAMMER PROGRAMS

While bigger grammars could be written in the same way, linguists habitually use some sort of shorthand notation. This is certainly true when the rules are the so-called context-free rules, those which look for a single symbol and then just replace it. Using the standard shorthand for such rules, the previous grammar can be written as follows:

> GRAMMAR 1:   S ➤ SUBJECT VERB
>   SUBJECT ➤ THE PROGRAMMER
>   VERB ➤ PROGRAMS

In the next, slightly larger grammar, more than one rule frequently applies to the same symbol. More interesting sentences can follow.

GRAMMAR 2:   S → SUBJECT VERB
                       S → SUBJECT VERB OBJECT
                       SUBJECT → DETERMINER NOUN
                       OBJECT → DETERMINER NOUN
                       DETERMINER → A
                       DETERMINER → THE
                       NOUN → COMPUTER
                       NOUN → PROGRAMMER
                       VERB → PROGRAMS
                       VERB → LOVES

Such context-free grammars can become very large indeed, but eventually it becomes clear that to get around a bigger part of language, more general rules are need. The popular extension is to enlarge the situation and action parts of the rules so that more than one symbol determines whether the rule applies and so that symbols can be rearranged and deleted as well as simply replaced. These more general rules are called context-sensitive rules. Studying grammars that use such rules, the so-called transformational grammars, takes one into territory belonging mostly to linguists. Rather than visit there, we will turn to representing facts about language in augmented-transition-network grammars, which are more convenient, it seems, for the development of language-understanding programs.

Recursive Transition Nets Also Can Hold Syntactic Information

A Transition Network is a structure which conveniently captures a variety of facts about syntax. The first part of figure 6-6 gives the basic transition network equivalent for simple noun groups. Each circle represents a state, and labeled arcs show how words of a particular type cause transitions from one state to another. Adjective transitions loop back to the same state since there can be any number of adjectives in a noun group. One can think of a valid noun group as a set of instructions for moving along a path from the starting state to a so-called accepting state represented by a double circle. The node S3 is a double circle because getting there means success. Analysis is complete. A string of words which drives through the network to an accepting state is interpreted to be a noun group. Whenever a sequence of words leads to a state from which all transitions are incompatible with the next word, then analysis is derailed. Such a sequence cannot constitute a simple noun group as defined here.

Prepositional groups are basically noun groups introduced by prepositions. The second part of figure 6-6 shows how to represent them by references to the already defined noun group structure. Note that arcs labeled with names of groups require successful traversal of the named network rather than the presence of a single word. By convention, names of groups appear on arcs in upper case.

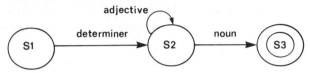

NET FOR BASIC NOUN GROUP

NET FOR PREPOSITIONAL GROUP

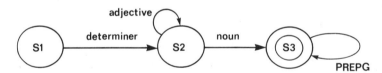

NET FOR NOUN GROUP WITH POSSIBLE
PREPOSITIONAL GROUP OR GROUPS

Figure 6-6 Transition networks describe grammatical constraints. In the first diagram, a simple transition network defines a noun group as a determiner, any number of adjectives, and a noun. In the second diagram, a prepositional group is shown to consist of a preposition followed by a noun group. Upper case arc labels are like subprocedure calls to the named networks. In the third diagram, recursion is introduced by an arc which specifies that optional preposition groups may follow a noun group's noun.

Very often a noun group description is strengthened by one or more prepositional groups following the noun and further specifying it. The third part of figure 6-6 pictures this generalization. An example requiring it is the noun group, "a red pyramid on the big block," which contains the prepositional group, "on the big block."

Since noun groups can contain prepositional groups and prepositional groups can contain noun groups, the combination is recursive. Imbedding can go on to an arbitrary depth:

A red pyramid
 on the big block
  near the empty box
   by the furry purple cube....

Traversing a Transition Net Accumulates Facts

The dictionary of words contains the necessary word-type information needed to use word groups to steer paths through transition networks. Naturally enough, the dictionary contains more information about words than just the basic type. For understanding how Robbie does things, two other kinds of information are important:

■ The word dictionary contains other syntactic features in addition to type.

■ It also contains program fragments.

Let us deal with the features first. The features are properties of a word that determine the word's grammatical role without evoking much of a semantic image. The common possibilities for the *type* feature are DETERMINER, NOUN, VERB, ADJECTIVE, NUMBER, PARTICLE, and PREPOSITION. One of these is in force for each word of a sentence. Others include selections from among SINGULAR and PLURAL for nouns, SINGULAR, PLURAL, DEFINITE, and INDEFINITE for determiners, and PRESENT, PAST, and TAKES-PARTICLE for verbs.

It makes sense to attach features to noun groups too. These are inherited from the words they contain, since only words, not groups of words, have entries in the dictionary.

For the most part the features for a noun group are named for the word types that appear in noun groups. Determiner and number are two important examples. We have seen the *determiner* word type. The *number* word type, not previously introduced, identifies a word or group of words which indicates how many, as in "the three tall pyramids." Thus the terms *determiner* and *number* are used in two ways. For noun groups, *determiner* and *number* are the names of features which have values; for words, *type* is the name of a feature which has some value, DETERMINER and NUMBER being particular possibilities.

■ The *DETERMINER* is DEFINITE or INDEFINITE depending on whether the noun group refers to something definite.

■ The *NUMBER* is usually SINGULAR or PLURAL. More general noun groups may have symbols like NO, ALL, EXACTLY THREE, or MORE THAN FOUR in the number slot.

Transition networks deduce features as a side effect of successful traversal. Here is where information for the noun group features comes from:

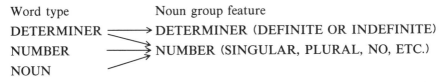

Word type	Noun group feature
DETERMINER ⟶	DETERMINER (DEFINITE OR INDEFINITE)
NUMBER ⟶	NUMBER (SINGULAR, PLURAL, NO, ETC.)
NOUN	

Evidently the number feature for noun groups coalesces and summarizes information from several sources. If the noun group has a number word or group of words, then that usually dominates. Otherwise the determiner or the noun may at least specify singular or plural. The determiners *a* and *this* and *that* are singular while *these* and *those* are plural. *The* is neither. If the number feature of the determiner clashes with that of the noun, the combination is not grammatically correct. Only small children can get away with "this blocks" or "those pyramid."

Augmented Transitions Prescribe Side Effects

Notes hanging on the arcs indicate certain actions to take. These notes and their consequences distinguish augmented transitions from ordinary ones. Figure 6-7 demonstrates how these notes augment the noun-group transition network. As shown, a note on the determiner arc checks the determiner word to see if it is either definite or indefinite. If so, the DEFINITE or INDEFINITE feature is transferred up to the noun group and written into a memory slot reserved for the noun-group's determiner feature. At the same time another note on the determiner arc checks

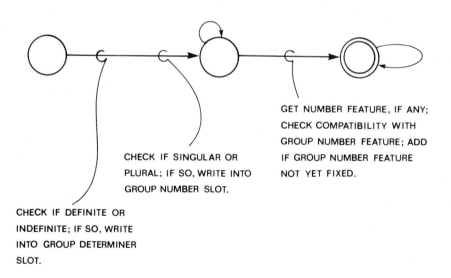

GET NUMBER FEATURE, IF ANY; CHECK COMPATIBILITY WITH GROUP NUMBER FEATURE; ADD IF GROUP NUMBER FEATURE NOT YET FIXED.

CHECK IF SINGULAR OR PLURAL; IF SO, WRITE INTO GROUP NUMBER SLOT.

CHECK IF DEFINITE OR INDEFINITE; IF SO, WRITE INTO GROUP DETERMINER SLOT.

Figure 6-7 Recursive Transition Networks become Augmented Transition Networks when certain memory slots are written after arc traversal and referenced before.

to see if the determiner word is known to be either singular or plural, and if so, writes SINGULAR or PLURAL into a memory slot reserved for the noun group's number feature.

Of course the note on the noun arc can also affect the information in the noun group's number slot, but only if nothing is there already. More specific information that may be there should not be lost. Action is therefore conditional, and the note involves a test as well as an action. Recursive transition networks with notes enabling recording, recall, and testing of facts are called Augmented Transition Networks or ATNs.

Robbie's Dictionary Contains Program Fragments

A world model contains many facts about objects which conform to one of three patterns:

- An object name, a relation name, and another object name.
- An object name, the relation IS-A, and a class name.
- An object name, a property naming relation, and a property.

Here are some examples:

31415	SUPPORTS	27182
TABLE	SUPPORTS	31415
31415	IS-A	BLOCK
27182	IS-A	PYRAMID
31415	HAS-COLOR	RED
27182	HAS-COLOR	BLUE
31415	HAS-LOCATION	(0 0 0)
27182	HAS-LOCATION	(0 0 10)
21415	HAS-SIZE	(10 10 10)
27182	HAS-SIZE	(10 10 15)

Eventually it will be clear how such facts can be recorded in memory in such a way that template-like patterns can be used to retrieve them. A typical retrieval pattern looks like this:

?X HAS-COLOR RED

Thus patterns are like facts in memory except for the possible presence of names that begin with ? symbols. These are special names that serve as anything-goes signals when memory is searched for instances of a pattern. The pattern sample will match the fact

31415 HAS-COLOR RED

just as if 31415 were in the first position of the pattern because names beginning with ? match anything.

Pattern-matching programs allow memory searches which incorporate several basic patterns into a general requirement. Here is an example which differs from actual program form only in unimportant syntactic details:

FIND ALL X SUCH THAT
    ?X HAS-COLOR RED
    ?X SUPPORTS ?Y
    ?Y IS-A PYRAMID

These four lines find all red objects that support pyramids. This is done in two steps. First the patterns are used to retrieve potential values of X and Y from the facts in memory. Then all pairs are tested to see which combinations simultaneously fit all slots.

Much of the program's content comes straight from program fragments stored in memory with each adjective and noun:

Word	Code property
RED	? HAS-COLOR RED
SUPPORTS	? SUPPORTS ?
PYRAMID	? IS-A PYRAMID

The trick is therefore to have a program-writing program which builds search programs out of such fragments. The search programs then come up with the names of objects.

There are many variations which require attention to the number of satisfactory value combinations. The program for the noun-group, "a red object which supports three pyramids," specifies that three pyramids must be found:

FIND > 0 X SUCH THAT
    ?X HAS-COLOR RED
    THERE ARE > 2 Y SUCH THAT
        ?X SUPPORTS ?Y
        ?Y IS-A PYRAMID

Thankfully this introduces a general framework. The expressions > 0 and > 2 fill slots which determine if the search is successful. Filling these slots differently produces many different translations:

Fragment	X slot	Y slot
... a red object which supports a pyramid.	> 0	> 0
... a red object which supports the pyramid.	> 0	= 1
... a red object which supports three pyramids.	> 0	> 2
... a red object which supports exactly three pyramids.	> 0	= 3

... a red object which supports no pyramids.	> 0	= 0
... the red object which supports a pyramid.	= 1	> 0
... the red object which supports the pyramid.	= 1	= 1

Thus the individual pattern lines are retrieved from the word dictionary and the success slot specifications are built out of =, >, <, ALL, and the integers. Combined together in a simple, program-like structure, they express great variety of meaning with precision, clarity, and economy.

Evidently, then, translation from blocks-world noun groups to search programs can be easy, given one basic structure and knowledge about how to fill the slots. A simple program can do the job. Let us see what such a program needs to know.

A Group's Features Determine the Shape of the Corresponding Program

Syntactic analysis gives determiner and number features for noun groups. These features are exactly the information needed to fill the success slots. Here, for example, are the determiner, number, and consequent success slot fillers for various ways of completing the noun group, "... a red object which supports ...."

Determiner	Number	Success slot	Fragment
indefinite	singular	> 0	... a pyramid
definite	singular	= 1	... the pyramid
indefinite	> n	> n	... n pyramids
indefinite	< n	< n	... at most n pyramids
no	plural	= 0	... no pyramids

The patterns supplied by adjectives and nouns are like bricks and the features supplied by other words are like mortar.

INTERPRETING QUESTIONS AND COMMANDS

Once a program understands noun-group translation, many property and relationship questions are easy to answer. They consist of question words like *what* and *how many* in front of a verb and an adjective or a verb and a noun group.

What bricks are blue?

How many bricks are blue?

What bricks support a pyramid?

How many bricks support a pyramid?

Answers to all four questions are found by these two programs:

```
FIND ALL X SUCH THAT
    ?X IS-A BRICK
    ?X HAS-COLOR BLUE
```

```
FIND ALL X SUCH THAT
    ?X IS-A BRICK
    THERE ARE > 0 Y SUCH THAT
        ?Y IS-A PYRAMID
        ?X SUPPORTS ?Y
```

Some WHAT and HOW MANY Questions Are Easy

Of course these programs are exactly like ones that identify objects described by certain noun groups. Indeed, many questions telescope into noun group-programs. This is no surprise since before a noun group can be useful, there is the implied question of what the noun group represents. The difference is in purpose, not construction. For dealing with command sentences, such programs supply arguments to manipulation functions. With questions, the results are enumerated if *what* is the question word, and they are counted if *how many* is used. Direct questions simply bring the answering process up front.

Since question forms seem to translate into program structures in the same way ordinary noun groups did, there is no reason to go into more detail. Simply note that dealing with property and relationship questions also requires enumeration of the English variations that occur and design of the proper programs to go with each. As before, the number of possible combinations is smaller and easier to capture than might be supposed. The only difficulty is that internal object names like 31415 are not well received by human questioners. The enumeration required by *what, which,* and *how many* questions should be done by object description not by object name. Generating suitable descriptions is a chore.

Commands Require Mating Function Names with Object Names

Now Robbie's interpretation of commands can be understood in more detail. Consider

Pick up a red object which supports a pyramid.

Syntactic specialists divide the sentence into verb and noun groups. Since the world is so constrained, there is never ambiguity in a command about what fills the agent, instrument, and object case slots. Robbie is always the agent, its hand is the instrument, and the sentence supplies the object.

The verbs generally specify what is to be done directly. In contrast to the great number of individual objects possible, there are but few actions, and each can therefore have its own unique name. There is no need for intermediate computation in which descriptions become search programs and search programs which then find names. Program names come directly from the verbs that specify them. The *pick up* combination causes reference to a program named PICK-UP, taking one argument, the occupant of the object case slot.

Then comes translation of the noun group, "a red object which supports a pyramid," into program form. Running the program generates a name, something like 31415.

Finally the computed object name is brought together with the retrieved action program producing a function and argument pair, surrounded by parentheses for the sake of the LISP language's syntax: (PICK-UP 31415). This is something that blocks-manipulation specialists can deal with directly. There is no further English analysis. The conversion from English command to an executable function call is complete, and a description suitable for communication has become a description suitable for action. Figure 6-8 summarizes.

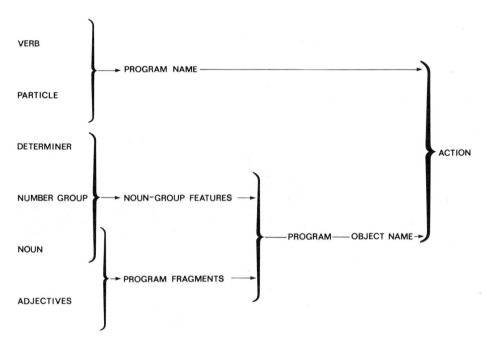

Figure 6-8 In the blocks world verbs often correspond to function calls and noun groups are like arguments. Verbs produce function names directly, but noun groups produce object names only after intermediate construction and execution of search procedures.

SUMMARY

■ It can be argued that making a computer understand language insures its general intelligence because the same issues and the same problems are involved.

■ Understanding natural language is an incredibly complex phenomenon. It seems necessary to start with limited domains to gain a foothold.

- For the blocks world, the problem of translating English descriptions of objects into internal names is a key activity.

- Augmented Transition Networks capture facts about word ordering constraints and provide a convenient, perspicuous way of employing those facts in analysis. The term *augmented* is used because the user is free to write into and later test various memory slots as transitions are made.

- An ATN can assemble together the material for search programs in the course of identifying a noun group. The actual assembly of the program is done by a specialist that uses both the raw material drawn by the ATN from the word dictionary and the structure of the noun group's determiner and number features.

- Having found a way of associating descriptions with internal names, certain questions and commands are easy to handle. Very similar search programs turn up the names with a view toward reciting them, counting them, or passing them as arguments to action programs.

REFERENCES

- Terry Winograd, *Understanding Natural Language,* PhD thesis, Academic Press, 1972. A thesis of very great influence, which unfortunately treated some problems so well that it gave the impression that all problems were solved. It discusses the translation from English to program descriptions in depth along with many other language-understanding issues. A synopsis is available in *Computer Models of Thought and Language,* edited by Rodger Schank and Kenneth Colby, W. H. Freeman, San Francisco, 1973.

- Noam Chomsky, *Syntactic Structures,* Mouton, The Hague, 1957. The classic book on transformational grammar.

Using Augmented Transition Networks for natural language seems to have started with a 1968 paper by Thorne, Bratley, and Dewar, of Edinburgh. Work by Bobrow and Fraser and by Woods developed and popularized the idea soon thereafter. Woods, especially, became a major contributor with his work at Harvard and at Bolt, Beranek, and Newman, Inc. The following papers were particularly important to development:

- J. Thorne, P. Bratley, and H. Dewar, "The Syntactic Analysis of English by Machine," in *Machine Intelligence 3,* edited by Donald Michie, Edinburgh University Press, 1968.

- Daniel G. Bobrow and Bruce Fraser, "An Augmented State Transition Network Analysis Procedure," *Proceedings of the First International Joint Conference on Artificial Intelligence,* 1969.

- William A. Woods, "Transition Network Grammars for Natural Language Analysis," *Communications of the Association for Computing Machinery,* vol. 13, no. 10, 1970. This paper not only lays out the basic ideas but also discusses some general issues involved in selecting a representation for syntactic knowledge.

7
REPRESENTING KNOWLEDGE IN FRAMES

A representation has been defined to be a set of conventions for describing things. Experience has shown that designing a good representation is often the key to turning hard problems into simple ones, and it is therefore reasonable to work hard on establishing what symbols a representation is to use and how those symbols are to be arranged to produce descriptions of particular things.

We have informally embraced a number of representations many times, particularly while working with natural language. Our purpose now is to go deeper into representation issues, to have a serious relationship, and to ask about the so-called *frame* representation that has been proposed as a unifying generalization of some of the particular representations seen before. To expose the issues, we first describe the conventions of frame representation using examples addressing simple vision and language problems. Then we speculate on how this representation can help with common-sense reasoning and news understanding.

NETWORKS AND FRAMES

Since most scientists somehow want to work at the highest level of abstraction, many have searched for a good general representation suitable for a wide range of problem domains. Unfortunately, creating such a representation is as elusive as it is challenging, and most efforts produce results with severe limitations.

Minsky's Theory of Frames Is a Theory of Rich Symbolic Structures

The situation would be grimmer were it not for a flurry of exciting ideas, all of which are promising, albeit unseasoned champions, now ready for the arena. Here is the essence of the one this chapter focuses on, Minsky's theory of frames, as explained by Minsky himself in 1974:

When one encounters a new situation (or makes a substantial change in one's view of a problem), one selects from memory a structure called a *frame*. This is a remembered framework to be adapted to fit reality by changing details as necessary.

A *frame* is a data-structure for representing a stereotyped situation like being in a certain kind of living room or going to a child's birthday party. Attached to each frame are several kinds of information. Some of this information is about how to use the frame. Some is about what one can expect to happen next. Some is about what to do if these expectations are not confirmed.

We can think of a frame as a network of nodes and relations. The "top levels" of a frame are fixed, and represent things that are always true about the supposed situation. The lower levels have many *terminals* — "slots" that must be filled by specific instances or data. Each terminal can specify conditions its assignments must meet. (The assignments themselves are usually smaller "subframes.") Simple conditions are specified by *markers* that might require a terminal assignment to be a person, an object of sufficient value, or a pointer to a subframe of a certain type. More complex conditions can specify relations among the things assigned to several terminals.

Collections of related frames are linked together into *frame-systems*. The effects of important actions are mirrored by *transformations* between the frames of a system. These are used to make certain kinds of calculations economical, to represent changes of emphasis and attention, and to account for the effectiveness of "imagery."

For visual-scene analysis, the different frames of a system describe the scene from different viewpoints, and the transformations between one frame and another represent the effects of moving from place to place. For nonvisual kinds of frames, the differences between the frames of a system can represent actions, cause-effect relations, or changes in conceptual viewpoint. *Different frames of a system share the same terminals;* this is the critical point that makes it possible to coordinate information gathered from different viewpoints.

Much of the phenomenological power of the theory hinges on the inclusion of expectations and other kinds of presumptions. A *frame's terminals are normally already filled with "default" assignments.* Thus, a frame may contain a great many details whose supposition is not specifically warranted by the situation. These have many uses in representing general information, most likely cases, techniques for bypassing "logic," and ways to make useful new generalizations.

The default assignments are attached loosely to their terminals, so that they can be easily displaced by new items that better fit the current situation. They thus can serve also as "variables" or as special cases for "reasoning by example," or as "textbook cases," and often make the use of logical quantifiers unnecessary.

The frame-systems are linked, in turn, by an *information-retrieval network*. When a proposed frame cannot be made to fit reality — when we cannot find terminal assignments that suitably match its terminal marker conditions — this network provides a replacement frame. These interframe structures make possible other ways to represent knowledge about facts, analogies, and other information useful in understanding.

All of this has a seductive appeal, but much hard work and use in application is required before the power of the theory can be considered certified. The theory, after all, is not a single, easily debated notion. It is an abstract theory of network descriptions, terminals, prerequisite criteria, transformations, defaults, expectations, and information retrieval — in short, frames theory is an armamentorium rather than a weapon. In introducing this armamentorium we will first discuss notation and then follow Minsky's trail, imagining applications bearing on vision and confirming the theory's broad reach through a retrospective look at various language-understanding theories.

Semantic Network Representations Become Frame-like Slot Arrays in Some Situations

A frame surely must contain representations of facts, but what is a fact? Let us agree, at least temporarily, that a fact is a relationship together with a few things the relationship ties together in a meaningful way. Thus the following are facts:

ERIK LOVES MARGARETA

BALL23 HAS-COLOR RED

FIRE HAS-TEMPERATURE HOT

These are simple facts built out of things like people, objects, properties, and phenomena, tied together by relationships with common names like LOVE or manufactured names like HAS-COLOR and HAS-TEMPERATURE. These manufactured, hyphenated relations are used whenever ordinary English requires descriptive constellations of words instead of a single name. Another departure from ordinary English derives from a need to refer concisely to particular things in a fact. If context leaves open the question of which ball is red, an English speaker might sharpen this fact by saying, "The pyramid on the block is red." Inside a computer this pyramid is a particular pyramid, and as such, it would have a particular name, possibly a mnemonic one like PYRAMID23 for programmer convenience.

Of course it is perfectly in order to say that some particular fact is true, stupid, or surprising. A particular fact with an internal name FACT258 can appear in other facts, each perhaps with its own name in turn.

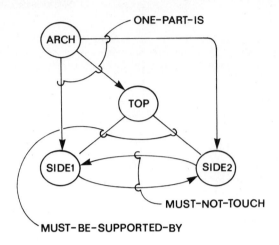

(ARCH ONE-PART-IS SIDE1)
(ARCH ONE-PART-IS SIDE2)
(ARCH ONE-PART-IS TOP)
(TOP MUST-BE-SUPPORTED-BY SIDE1)
(TOP MUST-BE-SUPPORTED-BY SIDE2)
(SIDE1 MUST-NOT-TOUCH SIDE2)
(SIDE2 MUST-NOT-TOUCH SIDE1)

Figure 7-1 Simple networks represent simple concepts more perspicuously than fact lists.

Name	Fact
FACT258	ERIK LOVES MARGARETA
FACT088	FACT258 HAS-AGE MANY-YEARS
FACT034	FACT258 HAS-TRUTH TRUE

There also can be facts about relationships:

LOVES IS-A RELATIONSHIP

IS-A HAS-FREQUENCY OFTEN

Eventually one should understand how such facts can be represented in the data structures offered by symbol manipulation languages. In that context, terms like variable value, property list, s-expression, and associative data base come up and require explanation. That must wait for some understanding of elementary programming, however, and for now we necessarily work from the notion of fact upward toward abstractions, not downward toward implementation options.

In the beginning it is useful to have graphical representations for such facts so as to exploit the visual grouping aid such a representation affords for people. The earlier discussion on learning made heavy use of a representation. Figure 7-1 recalls how a set of facts about an arch translates into a simple graph showing the objects and the relations between them for arches. Note that the use of mnemonic names, for structure parts like SIDE and TOP, is for human use — such names imply facts that would ordinarily be known to a computer explicitly through more relationships.

Although well suited for simple descriptions, the node-and-pointer notation can be an awkward liability in representing the contents of a complicated frame. Converting the nodes and pointers into slots and slot names can help, particularly if there is much to be said about the concept node. Figure 7-2 shows how a network describing the arch concept becomes a more perspicuous array of slots. To some extent the visual organization of nets emphasizes relationships while that of slot arrays emphasizes objects. Which is more appropriate depends on context and switching from one to another can be done on that basis.

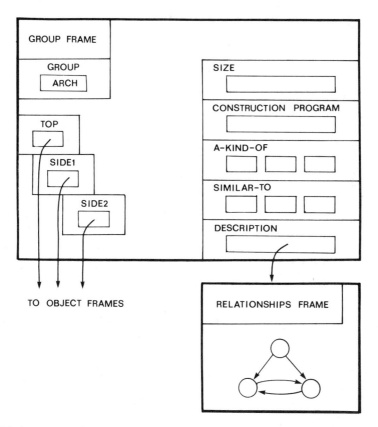

Figure 7-2 As concepts become complicated, network representations give way to frames. Frames for general concepts have slots reserved for various facts of general interest.

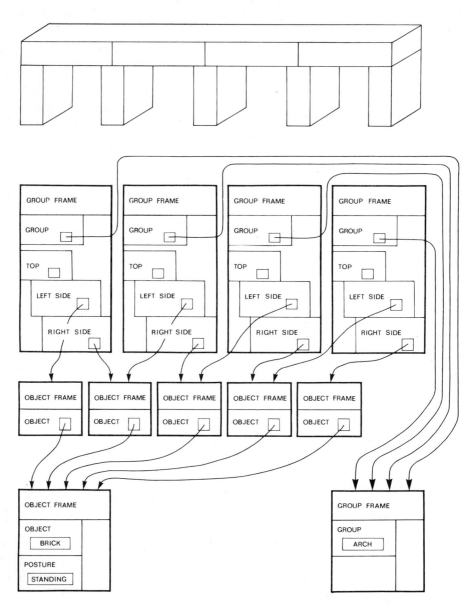

Figure 7-3 Frames may share terminal assignments. Here frames for the arches in an aqueduct share terminal fillers just as the arches share supports.

Arch and Room Frames Illustrate Some Key Ideas in Frame Theory

Note that simple examples on the order of the arch description already allow illustration of many basic frame system notions. The arch frame has slots and terminals, for example. Since some terminals represent objects which could serve simultaneously as parts of other constructions, the possibility of terminal sharing is evident. In figure 7-3 the "aqueduct" is a child's construction which can be viewed as a line of arches which share supports. Note the terminal sharing in the arch frames.

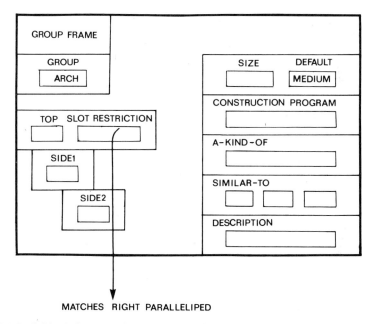

MATCHES RIGHT PARALLELIPED

Figure 7-4 Individual slots may have considerable information attached to them. Here the slot reserved for the top of an arch is restricted to being a right parallelepiped and the size is given as medium unless better information dislodges the default.

The slots may be mere empty holes which may or may not have contents. Alternatively, the slots may have more structure as shown in figure 7-4. There a SIZE slot is shown which contains a default assignment of MEDIUM. There is also a slot which references a restriction criterion.

The need for hierarchy is more pronounced when representing a room in frame-like terms as shown in figure 7-5. The terminals of the room frame are wall and floorplan frames which themselves are broken into terminals representing subdivided territories with their own contents. Any of these can contain a rich variety of slots which carry information ranging from history to purpose.

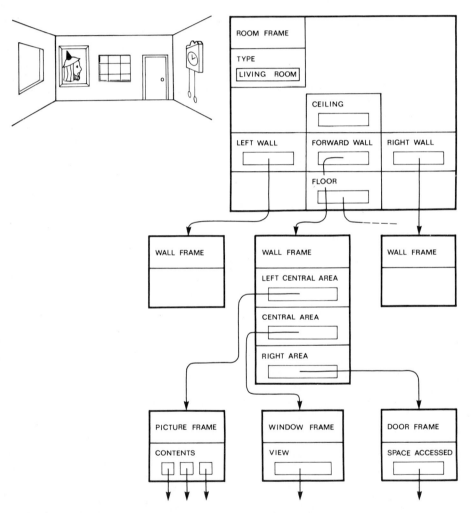

Figure 7-5 Describing a room requires many frames on many levels. Each frame could contain considerable detail.

Information Retrieval Networks Facilitate Identification

Minsky describes several approaches to the problem of hypothesizing new frames when the current frame loses favor. One is to work around in the A-KIND-OF hierarchy searching for related frames with better fit. Another new-hypothesis method uses difference analysis to work through a similarity net in which prominent differences rather than prominent similarities do the grouping.

Probably both the A-KIND-OF networks and the similarity networks should not be thought of as homogeneous structures resembling huge fishing nets. Instead, they should reflect a highly differentiated structure that reflects organized grouping. Minsky alludes to an analogy with the connections of a road map where small local roads provide access to even the obscure villages while larger and less dense arteries bring the local roads within reach of the limited-access superhighways.

Extending the analogy, one can imagine that various cities standing outside the superhighways would be the centers through which all traffic would flow because a given locality would be presumed to be characterized by the qualities of the representative cities. Moving from geography to, say, furniture, one can see that the "localities" in the new space would have names like *chairs, tables,* and *lamps.* Each of these is a broad category and would therefore require multiple city-like reference points. For chairs, there would be particular prototypical stools, arm chairs, reclining chairs, and desk chairs, all linked perhaps to the locality's "capital," namely some generalized notion of flat, horizontal surface of a certain size at a certain height.

The capital for tables would be similar except for different expected sizes and heights. Following the roadmap metaphor, there would be no direct route between things like stool and pedestal. Their physical similarity would be recognized by working through a chain of similarity net differences going through the chair and table capitals.

In all cases the several hypotheses that may be generated when there is a need to change frames should be weighed according to the costs involved in assuming them. Presuming some ability to preserve already accumulated knowledge by transferring invariant terminals from one frame to another, those frames which allow greater transfer should rank high in plausibility.

Transition Networks Use Sentence Fragments to Fill Slots in Simple Frames

So far the examples illustrate frame notions but hardly demonstrate that they are indispensable. Natural language understanding is probably a better place to establish the contribution because there are already well-developed theories that seem like frame systems: on the word-group level, one has Augmented Transition Networks, and on the sentence level, case grammar.

We have seen how Augmented Transition Networks seek out group features as they chew away at the words in a noun group. For noun groups it is easy to

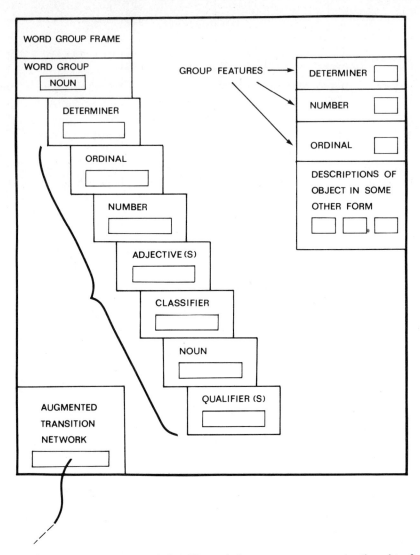

Figure 7-6 The Augmented Transistion Network for noun groups can be thought of as a slot-filling program attached to the noun-group frame.

observe that the feature values can be viewed as the contents of prepared slots. Figure 7-6 shows this for a general noun-group frame.

The ATN is an example of a program which resides in a frame with the purpose of slot filling. The ATN, after all, is there to fill the determiner, the number, and the ordinal slots, among others. (In other frames, a slot-filling procedure certainly could be attached to an individual terminal instead of the frame at large.)

Recall, incidentally, that noun-group frames focus on *objects.* Many sentence frames seem to focus on the *acts* that relate objects and state change together.

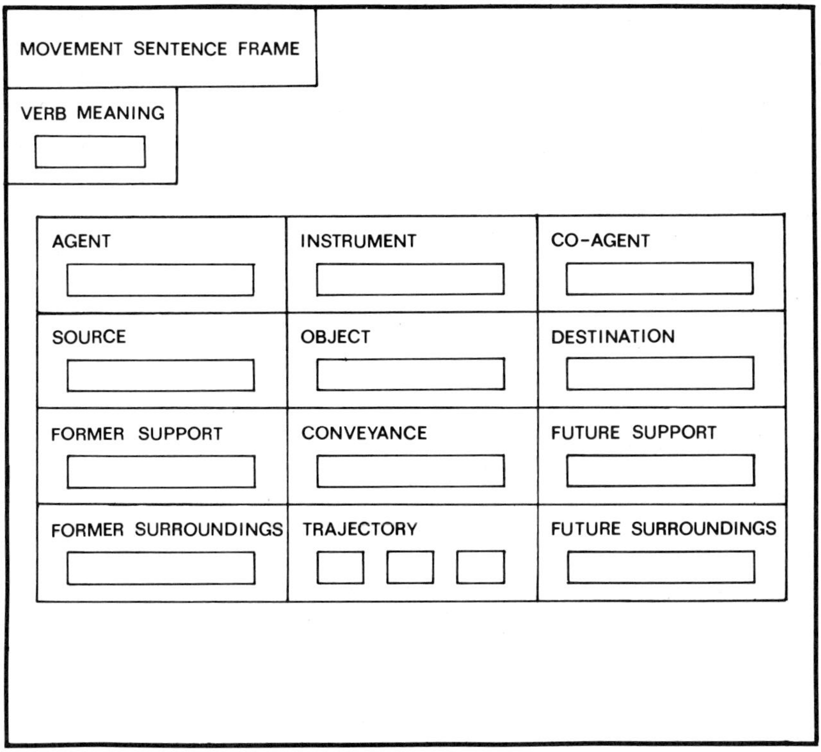

Figure 7-7 The case-grammar view of sentence structure has strong frame-like qualities.

Case Grammar Theory Is a Frame-like Theory of the Sentence

We have already seen that a case-grammar sentence analyzer renders sentences into the verb and the associated objects. We have only to draw attention to the frame-like quality of the case slots to see that case representation fits the frame idea rather well. For a general verb, there is the bare, open frame shown in figure 7-7. More specific verbs have some of the slots filled by tightly bound defaults inasmuch as the fundamental meaning of the verb itself has absorbed case presumptions, a process sometimes called telescoping or incorporation.

Telescoping accounts for an amazing number of superficially distinct verbs. Ogden, a champion of basic English as a world language during the 1930s, argued persuasively that people can get by with a vocabulary of only a thousand words by depending heavily on *come, get, give, go, keep, let, make, put, take, have, say, see, and send.* Apparently most verbs are used as a sort of shorthand for ideas that can be expressed as well by combinations of basic acts together with particle and object-dictated slot constraints. The verb *eat,* for example, has the FUTURE-SURROUNDINGS slot filled by something like EATER'S-BODY. Indeed this default is so firmly expected that an offered replacement is not welcome. One docs not say, "I am eating my sandwich *into my body.*"

COMMON SENSE REASONING AND CONCEPTUAL DEPENDENCY

Having alleged that existing theories of sentence fragment and whole-sentence understanding can be viewed as particular frame theories, it is natural to inquire into the wilderness beneath the surface where one confronts causes, plots, and scenarios. It is here that the problems of natural language shade into problems of common sense reasoning with large libraries of common sense knowledge. There is great challenge here, and undeniably, hard work remains to be done.

Basic Primitives Can Represent Many Complicated Activities

Direct reference to a sentence's cases can answer many questions relevant to the action, but the cases do not supply information about how acts are accomplished or how they are linked by cause-effect relationships. There has been much effort to come to grips with these defects using two key ideas:

■ There should be a library of frames that is rich in defaults for subprocess and cause-effect relationships.

■ There should be a front-line understander charged with reducing all action concepts to simple combinations of a few primitive acts.

Reduction to primitives is advocated for two reasons: first, the size of the knowledge library can be constrained somewhat; and second, canonical reduction is one method whereby paraphrases can be recognized.

Controversy continues. One issue is: Should reduction always go all the way down to the primitive acts? Another is: How many primitive acts should one work with? The collection of basic acts must be small enough to work with, yet large enough to cover most of what can be said. Wilks used 52 primitives in his early work. For the moment we presume a smaller list with the caution that it is for exposition only. This list is based on the work of Schank, another prime mover behind the approach sketched here.

Some acts of the physical world:

MOVE-BODY-PART	MOVE-OBJECT
EXPEL	INGEST
PROPEL	SPEAK

Some acts of perception:

SEE	HEAR
SMELL	FEEL

Some acts of the mental and social worlds:

MOVE-CONCEPT	CONCLUDE
THINK-ABOUT	TRANSFER-POSSESSION

For illustration, let us start with TRANSFER-POSSESSION. *Take* and *give* are words that have TRANSFER-POSSESSION in their semantic definition. Figure 7-8 shows this. Note that *giving* implies TRANSFER-POSSESSION with

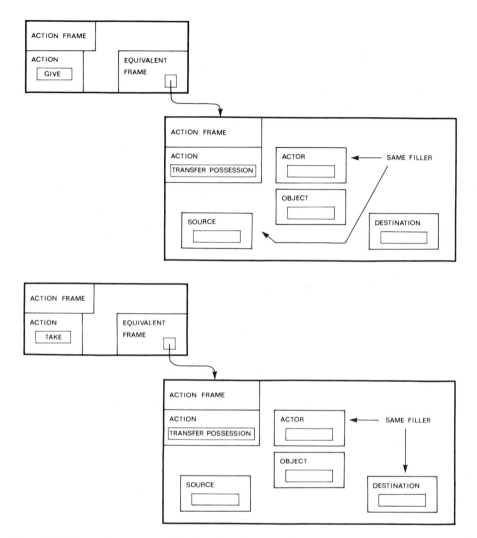

Figure 7-8 Many verbs correspond to simple actions combined with constraints among frame slots. Reducing give and take to the central transfer possession act exposes their similarity.

the same actor and source. *Taking,* in the sense of receiving a gift, is a TRANSFER-POSSESSION as well, but with the same actor and destination. By replacing the surface verb with the primitive act, it is easy to see the similarity.

It is assumed that the reduction of complicated acts and scenarios to combinations of primitive ones can be accomplished when necessary by remembered expectations about frame-slot defaults. Given this ability, a system can identify and generate many paraphrases and elaborations of stated acts.

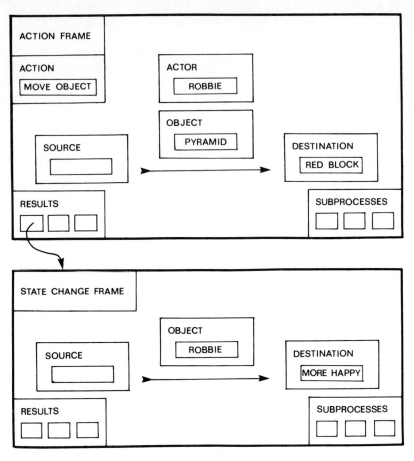

Figure 7-9 Much of the meaning of simple sentences is captured by action frames and state change frames linked together in cause-effect networks. Here putting a pyramid on a red block makes Robbie happier.

Thus the sentence, "Robbie enjoyed putting the pyramid onto a red block," would be understood to mean essentially the same thing as "Moving the pyramid onto a red block made Robbie happy."

Conceptual Dependency Links Deal with Cause-Effect Relationships

Many actor-action units cause important state changes that must be cleanly represented. Consider this again:

Robbie enjoyed putting the pyramid onto a red block.

Evidently the act caused Robbie to be in the state of being happy. Nothing is known about how he felt before he moved the block, but while he was doing it, he was happy. It is convenient to represent such state changes as source-destination pairs connected to the object undergoing the change. Figure 7-9 pictures what happened to Robbie. Note the causation arrow, the one emerging from the RESULTS slot. It means that the actor-action pair causes the state change.

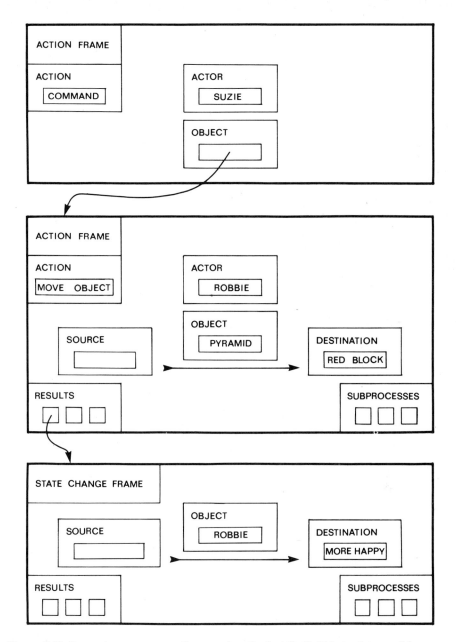

Figure 7-10 One act can cause another as when Suzie tells Robbie to do something.

Actor-action pairs can cause other actor-action pairs as well as pure state changes. This is no more than saying that one act can cause another. This cause-effect relationship is also represented by placing the causation arrow between the two things involved. Suppose, for example, that Robbie had moved a pyramid as a direct result of being commanded to by Suzie. Then the diagram of figure 7-10 is appropriate.

Some sentences at first do not seem amenable to representation in terms of cause-effect linked state change operations because the verbs they contain announce only state changes rather than the acts which cause them. Suppose someone says this:

Robbie comforted Suzie.

Certainly there is a state change because Suzie is less sad than she was (a presupposition of using *comfort* is original sadness). But what exactly did Robbie do? He caused Suzie to be less sad but by what act? Did he talk with her, take her for a walk, give her a stiff drink, or just move the pyramid? There is no way of knowing from the tiny fragment given, so all that can be done is to represent what is known as shown in Figure 7-11. Note the use of the DO default for the act.

Let us look at one more example which shows that state changes and actor-action pairs can interdigitate:

Suzie was gored by the test.

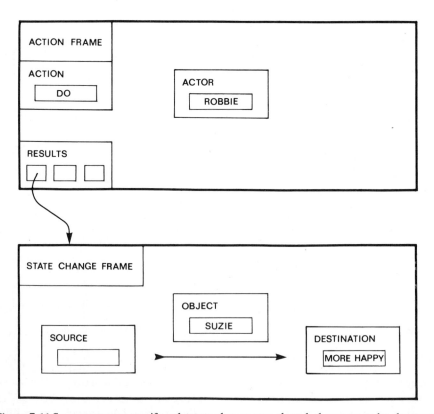

Figure 7-11 Some sentences specify only state change even though they seem to be about acts. Saying Robbie comforted Suzie gives no clue about how Suzie's improved state is achieved.

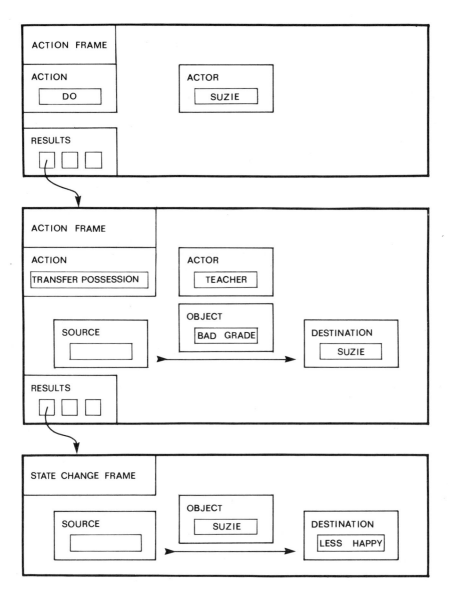

Figure 7-12 Considerable knowledge may be needed to expand some simple-sounding metaphors into an arrangement of primitive acts. The diagram here represents a statement to the effect that Suzie was gored by a test.

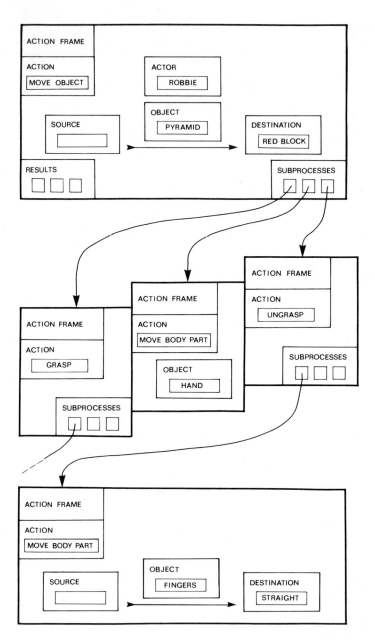

Figure 7-13 Subprocess slots offer another way of linking action frames together. This simple arrangement shows that moving a pyramid is ultimately accomplished by a sequence of body movements.

This is metaphoric language. The test itself presumably did no damage to poor Suzie; it was getting the grade that hurt her. Moreover, no one stuck a horn in her gut, something merely made her feel bad. The real image conveyed, when stripped of the color, is represented in Figure 7-12. Note the use of DO. It is used because it would be hard to guess precisely what Suzie did or perhaps failed to do. Overall, the example demonstrates again that a sentence's verb may promote a state change image rather than an act. We can see that the cause of the state change may very well be different from the occupant of the case analysis' agent case.

Tasks Can Be Viewed as Sequences of Acts and State Changes

If one task is required as part of a sequence which accomplishes another, then the SUBPROCESS slot is used as the origin of the arrow connecting the two. In this way acts reveal their pieces and then the pieces themselves are further dissected. Although in a sense the subprocess relation is a special case of the causes relation, it is prominent enough to grant independence.

Figure 7-13 indicates that grasping and hand moving and ungrasping are subprocesses of putting the ubiquitous pyramid on a red block. Moving the hand employs MOVE-BODY-PART directly, thus bringing the putting action a bit closer to explanation in terms of the primitives which allegedly stand beneath everything else. The reduction is completed by writing out the GRASP and UNGRASP in terms of finger movements using MOVE-BODY-PART.

Note that subtasks are always actor-action pairs.

For another example, suppose that Robbie ate some ice cream. Figure 7-14 shows how the basic act, INGEST, calls to mind a MOVE involving a spoon. The move in turn is effected by way of moving Robbie's hand, a MOVE-BODY-PART operation. Of course there is no way of knowing that Robbie ate the ice cream with a spoon, given only "Robbie ate ice cream." He may have eaten an ice cream cone or drunk a milk shake. Using a spoon is only a default presumption, a general image called up if explanation is wanted and nothing specific to the situation dislodges the default.

Now consider this:

Robbie and Suzie are eating breakfast. Being mischievous, Suzie decides to get up some excitement, so she hits Robbie.

What happens next? Although we cannot be sure, one of the following obvious possibilities may come to mind immediately:

Being aggressive, Robbie slugs her back and starts a fight.
Being shy, Robbie starts to cry.

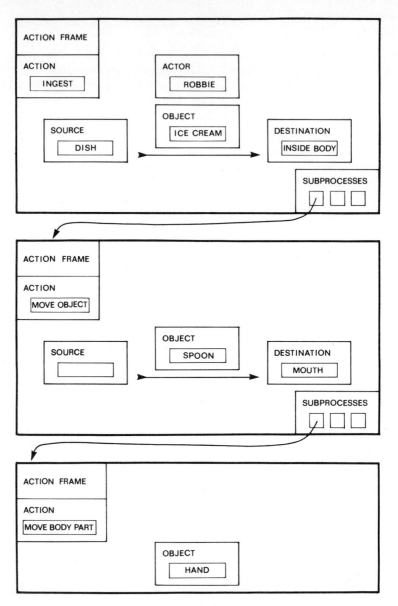

Figure 7-14 In this example, eating ice cream is done by moving a spoon to the mouth. Moving the spoon is done by moving the hand.

Figure 7-15 shows a way of diagramming these two possibilities. Neither is a certainty, both are possible. Such expectations are what understanders imagine in order to have a coherent overall image. Some expectations thus represent common sense knowledge about likely cause-effect relationships of the world. Others concern other types of assumed properties and relationships.

Naturally expectations should be marked as such when used. A chunk of knowledge marked as an expectation should be dislodged whenever specific

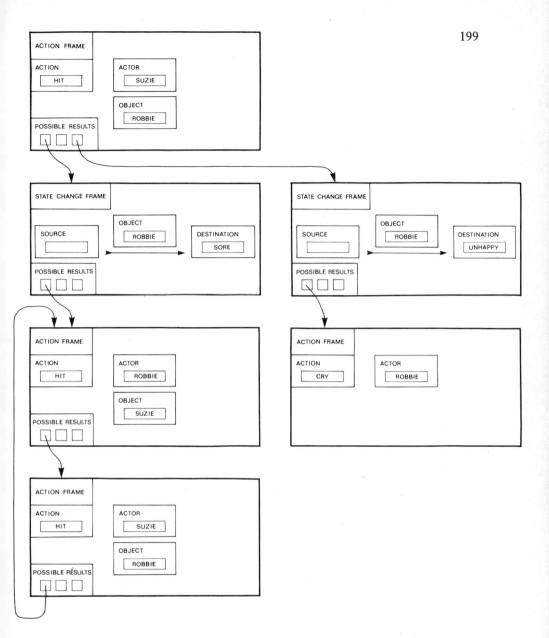

Figure 7-15 Chains of default hypotheses can evoke complete scenarios. Here Susie hits Robbie and either starts a fight or makes him cry. The possible results stored in memory suggest both possibilities.

information is available. Some expectations ought to be harder to dislodge than others. Neither given in the example is particularly strong, and both would succumb to this new information:

Robbie noted nothing because Suzie cannot hit very hard.

NEWS ARTICLES AND CHILDREN'S STORIES

We have moved up from representations of individual noun groups, through simple case representations of sentences, on through cause-effect frames, and now we are ready to address still larger questions of global knowledge and how to use it. We have enough apparatus to assert the following:

■ Simple stories are arrangements of interwoven actor-action frames and state-change frames related by cause-effect relationships.

■ More complicated stories are arrangements of interwoven frames of all sorts related in all sorts of ways.

Understanding News Seems to Involve Frame Finding and Slot Filling

Certain characteristics of news articles seem to make them easier to understand in the sense that they require less deduction. Because transferring information speedily and without taxing the mind is journalism's prime consideration, any characteristics that force application of slow deductive or inductive processes are out. Instead, the skillful news writer relies on frame finding and slot filling to build up comprehension. It is not at all strange, therefore, to find that news stories tend toward the following characteristics:

■ The title of a news story and perhaps the first sentence or two evoke a frame.

The number of frames needed to understand news, even a specialized form of news like the financial section, is a mystery. Compared to understanding children's stories, understanding news may involve simpler reasoning over a larger data base, but there is certainly no guarantee that creating the initial data base is not, in itself, a major obstacle to successful understanding.

■ Subsequent material fills slots in the central frame. The slot-filling process may evoke new frames introducing more open slots.

Once a frame is in hand, the sentences which fill its slots are often sufficiently independent that they can be placed in any order.

■ Knotty pronoun references are avoided, especially when they must be linked across sentences.

Instead of pronouns, a more elaborate form of paraphrase is likely to link the information in a new sentence tightly to its target frame. The nation's legislature may bow as "Congress," or "Capitol Hill," or "Washington's lawmakers," according to fancy. Elsewhere "the chief executive," or "the White House," or "the president," or "Mr. X" may identify the same person.

Some of these differences between stories and news are illustrated by examining the following story fragment:

> *Robbie and Suzie were going to Marvin's birthday party. One of them wanted to buy a kite. "But he already has one," he said, "he will ask you to take it back."*

Unravelling the pronoun references is a real chore, yet somehow it is clear that eventually the following assignments hold:

one	(first instance)	=	Suzie
he	(first instance)	=	Marvin
one	(second instance)	=	kite
he	(second instance)	=	Robbie
he	(third instance)	=	Marvin
you	(third instance)	=	Suzie
it	(fourth instance)	=	kite

Manifestly, working these out requires something more than gender and proximity considerations. Any understanding program would therefore necessarily have sophisticated pronoun-reference machinery in addition to whatever else is required to incorporate the content into a frame of some sort. Rewriting the story in the form of news circumnavigates the pronoun reference problems:

ROBBIE VETOES SUZIE'S GIFT IDEA

Suzie recently announced an intention to buy a kite for Marvin because the young man's birthday party is imminent. Reliable sources disclosed that Robbie objected to the proposed purchase because the birthday boy is known to have a good windy-day toy already.

At once some characteristics of the somewhat spoofy news story version are evident. One is that there are no pronouns, only paraphrases. Another is that causes need not be deduced, they are given explicitly by *because*. Thus simplified, one can imagine how a frame-oriented understander might absorb the information conveyed. Keep in mind that the understander is *imagined*. Having one with the power implied lies in the future.

First, one might suppose that the word *vetoes* in the title would establish action-blocking as the central frame. Any action-blocking frame surely has a slot for the action to be blocked and a reason for blocking it, hence filling these slots becomes an immediate objective of a frame-oriented understander. It is also suggested by the title that the action was thought up by Suzie and that it involved a gift. Knowing these facts, the understander would set up a prerequisite for the action slot to the effect that Suzie must be the actor and it would set up an expectation that a birthday, Christmas, or some other gift-giving occasion must be involved. All of these event frames would indicate that buying a present is a default prerequisite for attendance.

Happily, the action of buying a kite appears in the very first line following the title. Since it is to be an act of Suzie, the prerequisite condition for the action slot of the action-blocking frame is satisfied and the action slot is filled by a buy frame with kite in the item-to-be-bought slot.

Part of the buy frame should be the purpose for buying. The buy frame indicates that having something is a typical purpose. Even with this alone it is possible to propose that the having-of-the-kite cause for buying is related to the having-of-a-gift prerequisite for gift occasions. It is helpful that a kite is known to be ordinarily suitable as a gift via the gift frame.

Confirming the proposed link between kite and gift is immediate as the word *because* specifies a strong connection between buying and a birthday party wherein Marvin is the birthday boy. Of course the understander must know that a purpose link specifying an event can relate to prerequisite conditions for the event.

Next it is learned that there is an objection frame with Robbie as the objector and a buying activity as the act objected to. Since expectations hold that action blocking is a purpose for objecting, and since an action-blocking frame is prominent, it is straightforward for the understander to conclude that the reason to object is to block the action.

Finally comes a statement that some fact causes the objection. Assuming that the elaborate paraphrases, *birthday boy* and *windy-day toy* can be handled, the fact involves an ownership frame containing Marvin and kite. Presumably this explains the objection because the reader believes that everyone knows that it is better in general to have many different toys than many similar ones. Perhaps this is simply a special case of some more general knowledge to the effect that choices among activities is desirable, that activities have prerequisites, that enjoyment is sometimes proportional to the extent to which some prerequisite is satisfied, that having a kite is prerequisite to the kite flying, and that the kite-flying activity is one where satisfaction of the prerequisite is strictly an enablement. This seems like complicated deduction, but it need not be if there is a lot of frame-held knowledge available, for surely the block-action frame would contain expectation slots corresponding to the following causes:

- The action has no purpose.
- The action leads to damage.
- The action leads to useless transfer.

Each of these situations in turn must have a frame. The useless transfer frame would contain these causes:

- The recipient does not like transferred item.
- The recipient has enough of transferred item.

Indeed having enough matches the statement that the kite is already owned. The hypothetical analysis is now complete. By tracing down the expected cause paths just a short distance, the supposed understander has pieced together a network of linked frames which constitutes an understanding of the story.

Filled Frames Help Answer Questions

Note that understanding can be demonstrated by ability to answer questions. This is clear because the following questions and responses would require nothing more than a perusal of the frame system and its surroundings:

Why did Robbie complain?
    Marvin had a kite.

What effect did Robbie have?
  He prevented Suzie from buying a kite.

Why did Suzie want a kite?
  To have it to give away.

Why did she want to give it away?
  She likes Marvin or she wanted to go to his party.

Much Remains to Be Done

Representation seems to be the key to creating computer intelligence. Yet a theory of representation is only now emerging. Many questions remain tantalizingly open:

■ How should matching programs compare frames? It is necessary to deal with situations in which things almost match but do not quite. Perhaps part of the matching knowledge should be contained in the frames themselves.

■ How many frames are needed to handle various target domains like child world, financial world, law world, politics world, and the real world at large?

■ How can new frames be learned through specialization or generalization of old ones? How can analogy relate worlds such that new frames for one can be generated automatically from another?

Although these are hard problems, there is no reason to be pessimistic. Courageous people are at work in this area.

SUMMARY

■ Frame theory is a theory of representation that stresses a rich symbolic fabric woven out of shared terminals, prerequisite conditions, viewpoint transformations, defaults, expectations, and information retrieval ideas.

■ A frame may be a simple collection of objects and relationships pictured as a network or a more complicated arrangement better shown as an array of named slots. The diagrammatic choice influences only the human viewer's focus since computer embodiment is the same either way.

■ Both Augmented Transition Networks and Case Grammars create frame-like structures.

■ Libraries of actions and state changes related by plausible causes help carry natural language theory beyond the bog of the sentence into the mire of common-sense reasoning about everyday situations.

■ Understanding, from the operational point of view of creating a question-answering performance, probably involves the creation of a richly connected set of frames.

■ For getting at frame-finding and slot-filling issues, news stories may prove more direct and illuminating than typically written children's stories. News stories avoid heavy pronoun reference problems through paraphrase and avoid deduction by sticking to slot filling.

REFERENCES

■ Robert Simmons, "Semantic Networks: their Computation and Use for Understanding English Sentences," in *Computer Models of Thought and Language,* edited by Rodger Schank and Kenneth Colby, W. H. Freeman, San Francisco, 1973.

■ Marvin Minsky, "A Framework for Representing Knowledge," in *The Psychology of Computer Vision,* edited by Patrick Henry Winston, McGraw-Hill Book Company, New York, 1975. The paper in which the vocabulary of frames was largely established.

■ Terry Winograd, "Frame Representations and the Declarative/Procedural Controversy," in *Representation and Understanding,* edited by Daniel G. Bobrow and Allan Collins, Academic Press, New York, 1975. An essay which discusses criteria for judging representations. The position of the procedural and declarative extremists are defined and an effort is made at bringing the best features of both points of view toward a frame-like synthesis.

■ Ira P. Goldstein and Seymour A. Papert, "Artificial Intelligence, Language, and the Study of Knowledge," AI-M-337, The Artificial Intelligence Laboratory, Massachusetts Institute of Technology, Cambridge, Massachusetts, 1976. A survey of natural language understanding which argues that frames unify natural language theory.

■ C. K. Ogden, *Basic English: International Second Language,* Harcourt, Brace, and World, New York, 1968. A delightful book which demonstrates that a small vocabulary can convey a lot of information. The purpose was to promote a subset of English in order to solve the international language problem.

■ Yorick A. Wilks, *Grammar, Meaning, and the Machine Analysis of Language,* Routledge and Kegan Paul, London, 1972. A very early piece establishing the importance of semantic primitives. Wilks had working programs in 1967.

■ Roger C. Schank, *Conceptual Information Processing,* North-Holland Publishing Company, New York, 1975. Pioneering work on the epistemology of action. In this summarizing book, Schank argues that a very small handful of primitive acts can represent everything canonically. Schank includes major contributions by Goldman, Rieger, and Riesbeck.

■ Roger C. Schank and Chuck Rieger, "Inference and the Computer Understanding of Natural Language," *Artificial Intelligence,* vol. 5, no. 4, 1974.

■ Chuck Rieger, "The Commonsense Algorithm as a Basis for Computer Models of Human Memory, Inference, Belief, and Contextual Language Comprehension," TR-373, Department of Computer Science, University of Maryland, College Park, Maryland, 1975. A paper which develops a fine structure for causality sufficient to support a symbolic theory. Rieger connects wants, actions, states, state changes, and tendencies using more than 20 varieties of causality.

■ Eugene Charniak, "Toward a Model of Children's Story Comprehension," PhD thesis, AI-TR-266, The Artificial Intelligence Laboratory, Massachusetts Institute of Technology, Cambridge, Massachusetts, 1972. A thesis treating the problem of using world knowledge in understanding children's stories.

■ Steve Rosenberg and Ira Goldstein, personal communication. Source of some of the speculations on and analysis of techniques for news articles.

8
POINTS
OF
VIEW
ON
VISION

The study of computer vision began very early. The problem of seeing and understanding what is seen was to be a testbed for working out deep problem-solving and program-organization issues. Eventually this testbed purpose was served, but only after overcoming many frustrations and solving many unexpected problems. Vision, it was discovered, is very hard. Picking up the gauntlet is a job for hearty people. Goals must be sharply defined and patience must be steadfast.

The purpose of this chapter is to pass around some idea snapshots showing what has been accomplished. There will be examples illustrating facts about light, image array processing, and knowledge structures. We begin with some remarks on related sciences, continue with a reminiscence on the blocks world, and conclude with glimpses of results in the more general world of ordinary objects. The treatment is incomplete, for it would be hard to expand without unleashing temptations that turn chapters into books.

Along the way, some of the topics may seem to take us away from the central core of computer intelligence. Do not think so. To understand how to make a computer see, we must get our hands the whole way around the problem, not just the so-called high level parts of it. The idea that vision is simply a matter of a smart problem solver looking at a few salient image points is not viable.

It is unfortunate that many of the processes to be discussed do not submit to explanation through detailed simulations. We must be content with plausibility arguments and sample results.

■ Vision processing involves considerable computation. Pencil and paper simulation, particularly at the level of images, is unrealistic.

Often we must be content with smelling the cork when we would rather drink the wine.

HERITAGE

People interested in making computers see are privileged to have much previous work from which to go forward. Pattern recognition and physiological psychology, for example, have contributed to today's point of view.

The Technology of Pattern Recognition Solves Different Problems

Pattern recognition systems generally consist of two parts: a feature extractor and a feature evaluator. The features are measurement results on the image to be classified. These measurements, thought of as the coordinates of a point in space, determine identity by their collective proximity to prototypical points.

Young's program, written in the late 1960s, showed that the approach is adequate to divide white blood cells into the standard categories: neutrophils, eosinophils, basophils, lymphocytes, and monocytes. After inventing a family of features, Young took note that each cell type has a territorial claim on the resulting space of features, and determined identity by observing where the features of an unknown land in that space.

Young found that four characteristic features seem good in that the feature values for the separate cell types cluster tightly. This can be readily observed in figure 8-1 where the placement of some sample cells in a two-dimensional feature space is shown. Given first-class, informative features, it is only necessary to pick cluster centers, for then the distance of an unknown cell from each such center is easily determined and compared. The cluster center can be located at the place of the cell judged to be the most beautiful example of its class or, more likely, at a place determined by averaging the feature values of a sample set.

Over the years workers in pattern recognition have worked hard at mathematics because many important problem domains do not have the convenient clustering properties exhibited by the white-blood-cell example. All sorts of complications destroy the straightforward approach: the feature points may not be clustered equally close about each of the class centers; the features may interact with each other producing elliptical rather than circular distributions; or worst of all, the clusters may not look much like the classical Gaussian, bell-shaped arrangement on which much of statistical mathematics depends.

Dealing analytically with such feature spaces has proved difficult, and it is there in the feature-space salt mine that most of the hard work has been. For some classes of problems, the results have been very worthwhile. Today, the practitioner of Pattern Recognition does well when scenes satisfy two criteria:

■ The values exhibited by the characteristic features do not change much over the range of circumstances likely to be encountered.

■ The measurement of the characteristic over the entire image is dominated by the measurement of the characteristic over the object immersed in the image.

These criteria help explain why classifying a single well-framed, flat blood cell is different from deciding if a room has a telephone in it. A robot in an office may

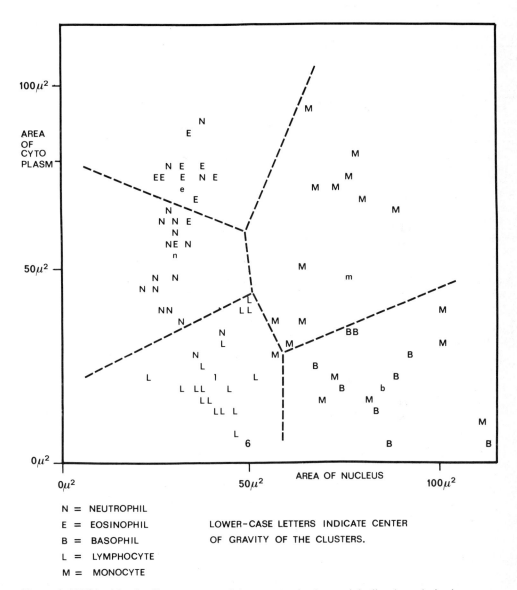

N = NEUTROPHIL

E = EOSINOPHIL   LOWER-CASE LETTERS INDICATE CENTER

B = BASOPHIL   OF GRAVITY OF THE CLUSTERS.

L = LYMPHOCYTE

M = MONOCYTE

Figure 8-1 White blood cells are separated into categories by straight-line boundaries in a simple feature space. More than two features are required for reliable separation. (Diagram courtesy of Dr. Berthold K. P. Horn.)

use color, approximate size, and the vertical coordinate to distinguish among telephones, door knobs, and waste baskets, but a telephone looks different when rotated or seen from different points of view, and from any point of view, a telephone has only minor influence on any globally measured quality. An office robot in a sporting goods store may try to answer a bowling ball!

What is needed, if rooms are to be described and if telephones are to be distinguished from bowling balls, is a theory of vision with much more descriptive machinery. Good description is a constantly recurring theme. Working out sound description procedures for a domain is a necessary prerequisite to the development of real aptitude.

We therefore veer off from the main stream of Pattern Recognition leaving behind the nice mathematics of feature spaces. We carry off only a small legacy of signal filtering and enhancement ideas first applied by Pattern Recognition researchers. Evolutionary descendants of those early image operations seem correct today.

Psychological Research Suggests There Are Computationally Expensive Processing Steps

Before designing a new process, good sense demands looking at existing processes with a view toward copying their features insofar as they are known and appropriate. Since making a seeing computer is no exception, questions should be asked about how people see, for while the physiological psychologists know few secrets, they are the custodians of valuable hints. They know, for example, a great deal about the input-output characteristics of certain retinal and cortical cells through the pioneering work of Barlow, Lettvin and his colleagues, Hubel and Wiesel, and others. By poking electrodes here and there in the neural apparatus, these workers were able to understand the particular stimuli which excite various cell types. Lettvin *et al,* for example, learned that one class of cells in the frog respond wonderfully to small black dots moving across that part of the total field witnessed. These cells are known, affectionately, as bug detectors. They are but one of many cells now catalogued for the frog, the cat, and other animals.

One sobering thing is clear from these physiological studies: the computation power involved is staggering. If much of the evident computation is never used unless attended to by higher-level procedures, then perhaps intelligence can make up for lack of resources. Otherwise computer vision people must hope the electronic miracles in the direction of fast, parallel processors stay on schedule. Thankfully, the technology is progressing very quickly, so that a real-time, flexible visual processor is becoming a serious possibility.

Unfortunately there are many gaps in what is known, and even the now vast literature on the physiological psychology of vision is not a blueprint for building such a processor. Knowing what the primary cells do does not determine how they do it or what they are to do next. Consequently there can be no sensible effort at present to make a computer *simulate* the visual machinery of biological seeing machines. Instead the effort must be, as in dealing with other dimensions of computer intelligence, to make a computer *be* a seeing machine, exploiting hints from all quarters. We must study the issues inherent in the problem because the hardware is too inadequately understood to be copied.

IMAGE ANALYSIS

Picking a domain that is easy enough to handle but rich enough to learn from is tricky. For early vision research the blocks world seemed ideal, just as it was for studying natural language. After all, the object description problem is easy — all the common possibilities are perpendicular projections of triangles, squares, and other simple plane figures. The critical-path subgoal therefore seemed to be problem-solving issues of the sort we now know much about, and creating computer vision, at least for the blocks world, was to be a summer's project. Today that optimism seems foolish. Now we know that the problems are hard and that careful understanding of image processing, constraint exploitation, and knowledge representation are all critically important, even in the innocuous blocks world.

The Blocks World Has Been Studied for a Long Time

Much was learned in the course of building systems for copying blocks structures from samples such as illustrated in figure 8-2. This task, achieved for reasonably general blocks world configurations by Winston, Horn, Binford, and Freuder in December, 1970, consisted of two parts: an image understander, which creates line

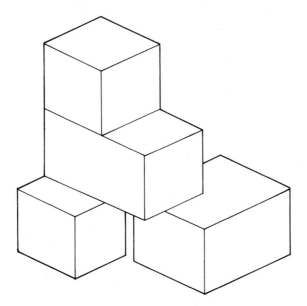

Figure 8-2 The configuration of blocks copied by the Winston-Horn-Binford-Freuder robot in December, 1970.

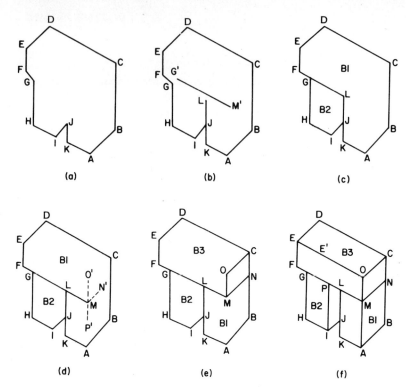

Figure 8-3 Shirai's heterarchical vision system begins analysis by finding the strong background border lines. More difficult interior lines are found by procedures that use knowledge about blocks world images to help track standard intensity profiles. (From *The Psychology of Computer Vision,* by Patrick H. Winston, copyright 1975 by McGraw-Hill Book Company, New York. Used with permission of McGraw-Hill Book Company and Patrick H. Winston.)

drawings, and a scene understander, which uses line drawings. The system looks like a club sandwich with the meat of image analysis and scene analysis nestled between the bread of the image, the line drawing, and the three-dimensional description.

In such systems the image and scene specialists operate quite independently since the only communication is through the drawing. Early on it became clear that more than junction position and connection information should flow upward.

There are two ways to do this. One is to amalgamate the two processing layers; another is to improve the intermediating data base, so far only the representation of a line drawing, a rather narrow channel through which little can flow. Amalgamating layers leads to so-called heterarchical organization and careful attention to control issues. The alternative emphasizes description and converts a plain line drawing into a rich description called a primal sketch. According to one view, the intelligent problem-solving knowledge reaches into even the earliest image-processing functions, altering their behavior on the basis of partial knowledge. The other view holds that problem solving is less useful at the image level than previously believed. Probably both views are good. Both will be explained.

Knowledge-Guided Tracking Produces Blocks World Drawings

Figure 8-3 illustrates the action of Shirai's championship program for finding lines. First it finds the sharply defined background border. Then a basic tracking procedure drives along suspected lines using a profile analyzing module out front like a scout. As figure 8-4 suggests, drift noted in profile analysis supplies correcting feedback.

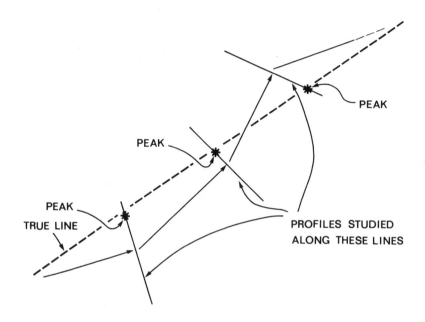

Figure 8-4 Tracking a line. Profiles perpendicular to the direction of track are examined. The observed peaks in these profiles provide direction correcting feedback.

To get the tracker started, Shirai uses heuristic knowledge. Sometimes the knowledge is about the tendency of the blocks world to exhibit parallel lines. Sometimes it is about where to look when lines seem to die out. Sometimes a context expert supplies information about which direction to probe out from junctions. Because such knowledge can be used, the location and direction of faint interior lines can be deduced and verified, using primitives that would prove inadequate otherwise.

Effective though Shirai's program is, it is still not clear that high level knowledge should be brought to bear on image analysis in more general circumstances. The blocks world may be misleading precisely because the giant direct leap from image points to three-dimensional model is possible. It is likely that great strength is needed in layers sandwiched in between if computers are to deal with the real world.

Even Blocks-World Intensity Profiles Need Filtering

Experimentally, the lines that should appear in a drawing of a blocks-world scene correspond to the intensity changes shown in figure 8-5 or some combination of those changes. The *step* is a rise or drop in intensity. The change may be cliff-like or sloped. The *roof* is a change in the rate of intensity change. And the *spike* is a narrow blip.

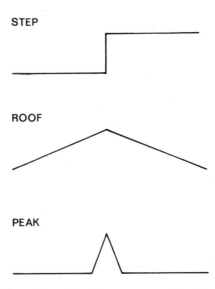

Figure 8-5 The standard intensity profiles. Sharp convex edges should generate sharp steps, but usually generate sloped ones instead. Concave edges produce roofs because the faces involved illuminate one another. Specular reflections produce sharp peaks which are often found combined with other profile types.

In an ideal blocks world, one could look for these characteristic profiles directly, but in practice, corrupting influences force filtering aimed at bringing out genuine changes and suppressing spurious ones.

■   Image input devices do not produce simple clean images. One must understand and account for variations in intensity sensitivity across the image, errors in image coordinate information, electronic noise, light-source hum, and inability to accept wide variations in intensity.

■ Even blocks-world scenes produce complicated images, confusing programs with mutual illumination effects, misleading scratches, finger prints, and dust. One must not approach the blocks world blindly.

One popular filtering operation computes new values from old by adding up several points to the right and subtracting several to the left. This combines averaging with slope detection. Figure 8-6 shows the result when the filter is applied against the standard profiles. Note that the patterns are distinctive. They are easier to pick out in the presence of noise than the unprocessed parent profiles because

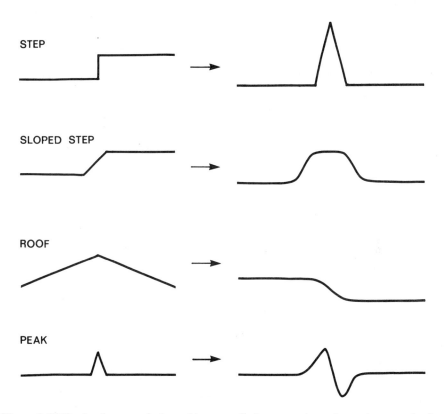

STEP

SLOPED STEP

ROOF

PEAK

Figure 8-6 Filtering by convolution with a so-called step mask produces these results from a step, a sloped step, a roof, and a peak.

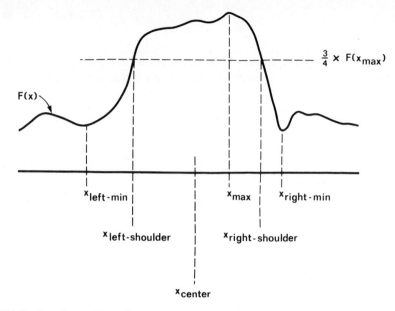

Figure 8-7 Finding the position of an edge in a filtered profile. Values for x_{max}, $x_{left-min}$, and $x_{right-min}$ determine whether an edge is present. If so, x_{center} is presumed to be midway from $x_{left-shoulder}$ to $x_{right-shoulder}$.

of the combined averaging and slope measuring effects. Using filtered profiles Shirai's tracking system detected and located step-type edges with the algorithm illustrated by figure 8-7 and specified as follows:

- Assuming filtered intensity is given by $F(x)$, then find position $x = x_{max}$ where $F(x)$ is maximal. For line tracking the filtering extends only a short distance to either side of the direction of travel.

- Check that $F(x_{max}) > T_{min}$ where T_{min} is a threshold establishing minimum peak height.

- Find the places to the left and right of x_{max} where $F(x)$ is minimal. Let these points be $x_{left-min}$ and $x_{right-min}$.

- First check that $F(x_{max}) - F(x_{left-min}) > T_{difference}$, and then check that $F(x_{max}) - T(x_{right-min}) > T_{difference}$. The peak must stick up prominently from its surround.

- Find the steep slopes on either side of maximum by noting where the filtered intensity function achieves about 3/4 of its maximum height. Let these points be the left and right shoulder positions, $x_{left-shoulder}$ and $x_{right-shoulder}$.

- The line is judged to be midway between the two shoulder points at the point $x = .5 \times (x_{left-shoulder} + x_{right-shoulder})$. The shoulder points determine the alleged line position because sloped-step edges produce mesa-like tops and the peak is easily displaced to any point on the mesa by noise.

People familiar with linear system theory can see that the approach differs from simple matched filtering because more is milked from the filter's output than just the peak height and position. Experiments have shown that richer symbolic descriptions are better able to deal with typical noise phenomena. Other examples are found in an earlier line-finding program jointly authored by Binford and Horn and in a later program by Horn which discovers the precise location of integrated circuit chips in preparation for external wiring connection.

The Real World Requires a Primal Sketch

The most sophisticated blocks-world systems were written with the hope that high-level knowledge could be brought to bear in the front-line image-processing programs. Shirai's line tracker, for example, is guided by evolving results coupled with blocks-world shape assumptions. Line tracking and scene understanding go forward cooperatively together. Still, it is not yet clear that vision systems should avoid strong, independent image processing altogether. It does not seem that knowing a lot can substitute for looking a lot.

Marr argues that vision's problem-solving apparatus should not look at the image at all, but should look at a symbolic interpretation of it, the *primal sketch,* instead.

■   Images become primal sketches through processes that find, describe, and group together image features.

Primal-sketch computation therefore resembles line finding because both processes involve filtering and grouping operations. But creating a primal sketch differs from finding a line drawing because the goal is to pass on a rich symbolic description. Consequently the filtering and grouping techniques must be more sophisticated.

This is a typical feature description computed from image point intensity values:

```
(EDGE (TYPE EXTENDED)
      (ORIENTATION 67.5)
      (FUZZ 3)
      (POSITION 271 314))
```

To create such features, Marr begins with filtering operations that look for steep slopes and for rapid changes in slope. If these filters are applied to the one-dimensional, noise-free profiles shown before in figure 8-5, characteristic forms emerge in which some features persist even when noise enters. One of the filtering operations is like that which Shirai used in line tracking: each point in the output is the difference between the average of a few points to the right and a few to the left. The other filter, the one that looks for rapid change in slope, is more complicated: each new value is formed by adding together the nearest points in the input and subtracting a few points that lie just beyond the central group. People

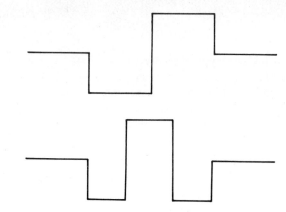

Figure 8-8 Primal sketch filtering amounts to correlation of the observed intensities against these profiles. The first is called an edge mask and the second, a bar mask. The correlations compute approximations to the first and second derivatives.

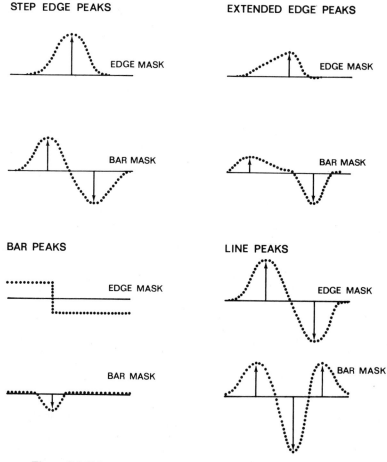

Figure 8-9 Edge types produce characteristic peak combinations.

familiar with linear systems theory know that the filtering operations are convolutions of the image with simple step and bar profiles. Figure 8-8 illustrates.

It is helpful that only the peaks and their positions in the profiles seem to matter. The first peak configuration in figure 8-9 corresponds to the classical step edge. When a rounded boundary edge separates two regions, a negative peak accompanies the basic sloped step and the second configuration occurs. Computation of the primal sketch requires a full catalog of possibilities like these.

The one-dimensional result is extended to two dimensions by the simple expedient of repeating the one-dimensional analysis at eight angles. Each point in the primal sketch is therefore computed from image points arrayed in the pattern shown in figure 8-10. (Using one-dimensional operations at multiple orientations is

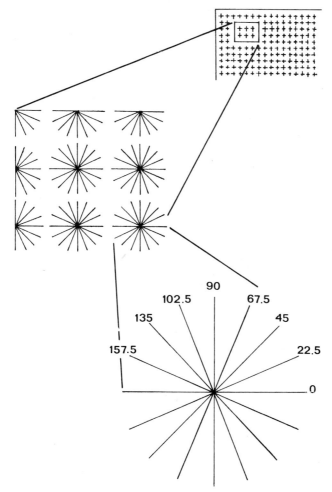

Figure 8-10 To compute the primal sketch, profile rosettes spread out in eight directions from points selected so as to cover the image.

Figure 8-11 The ends of grouped features define places which can be further grouped.

preferred to two-dimensional operations like the gradient or Laplacean for mathematical reasons as well as for inherent simplicity.)

It is already clear that the creation of a primal sketch cannot be cheap. Many people have experimented with less expensive operations on images with the hope of producing good feature information. Today it seems wiser to assume that biological eyes compute like mad for good reasons.

Results from the two basic filtering operations vary according to the number of image points that go into each filtered value. Using both a wide and a narrow version of each filter type may be helpful. Thus four or even more filters may be applied in each direction, not just two. Horrifyingly, each point in the image may therefore generate $4 \times 8 = 32$ filtered profiles. Happily, effects from adjoining orientations are sufficiently decoupled that only four profiles ever need be investigated together.

Once there are features, the next job is grouping. Linking up adjacent points with exact type and orientation match is a sensible first step. The threads so formed can be developed further with less stringent criteria. In the later stages, grouping is done on position alone and quite varied elements can combine to form identifiable groups. Even end points will do as figure 8-11 suggests.

The groups found in the primal sketch of a child's toy bear are shown in figure 8-12. Of course only the position of the features and line fragments is shown. The symbolic description of each contains other information as well.

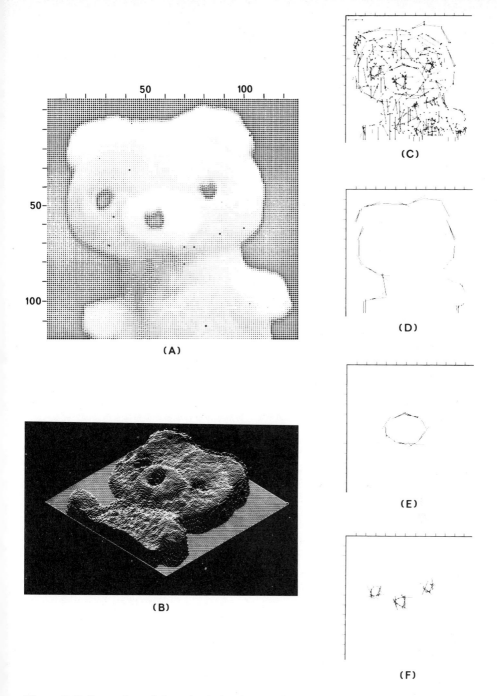

Figure 8-12 Extraction of the primal sketch. Part (a) is the source image. Part (b) is an intensity map. Part (c) shows the segments of the initial primal sketch before much grouping has occurred. Part (d) through part (f) show groups found during the later stages of processing. (From "Early Processing of Visual Information" by David Marr, *Philosophical Transactions of the Royal Society of London,* vol. 275, no. 942, October 19, 1976, copyright 1976 by the Royal Society, London, England. Used with permission of the Royal Society.)

Measurements on the Primal Sketch Seem to Determine Perceived Texture

Once the primal sketch is in hand, small regions in it can be examined for characterizing qualities. Histograms on intensity, line-fragment length, line-fragment orientation, and line-fragment separation are particularly illuminating. One reason is that there is good evidence that perceived texture is closely related to measurements on these histograms. According to this theory, two textures tend to be inseparable if they produce the same histogram features, even though the images differ in other respects. This theory, devised by Marr, successfully predicts that one of the images in figure 8-13 exhibits a distinctive subsquare while the other does not.

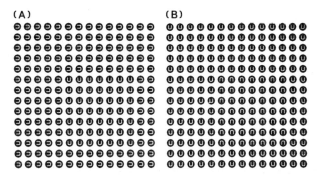

Figure 8-13 Two textures devised by Julesz both contain a square region that differs from the background. The subsquare in the first texture patch stands out while the subsquare in the second does not. Evidently a difference between the orientation histograms of the subsquare and its surroundings are required for separation. (From "Inability of Humans to Discriminate between Visual Textures that Agree in Second-Order Statistics - Revisited" by B. Julesz, E. N. Gilbert, L. A. Shepp, and H. L. Frisch, *Perception,* vol. 2, 1973, copyright 1973 by Pion Limited, London, England. Used with permission of Pion Limited and Dr. Bela Julesz.)

Marr's theory is more satisfying than competing ones because it covers experimental evidence better and because it does not involve the apparatus required to accumulate multi-dimensional histograms on the intensities of *pairs* of image points. Only one-dimensional histograms on computed primal sketch facts are needed.

Certain fish, incidentally, adapt their own appearance to the surrounding environment very well with an adaptation time of only a few seconds. Figure 8-14 demonstrates that they do the imitation well. Evidently the fish measure and match a number of primal sketch texture parameters by adjusting the spots on their backs.

Figure 8-14 Some fish can adjust the spots on their own surface to match the texture of the surrounding ocean bottom. Only a few seconds are required. (Photograph courtesy of Bill Saidel and Dr. Jerome Lettvin.)

Gradient Space Gives Insight into Illumination Constraints

There is curiously little work on the problem of connecting together the tools of computer intelligence with a sound understanding of light. But surely if research is to claim victory over the vision problem, then the physical laws must be understood. *Ad hoc* methods are not good enough. It is not sufficient to try processing techniques in the hope that some can be found that do something useful. Instead, one should realize that images carry a great deal of information about the three-dimensional nature of the corresponding surfaces. To exploit this information, it is important to know how images are formed. Horn has demonstrated this when he showed how to unwind the differential equations of image illumination in a way that allows shape to be recovered from shading gradients for simple reflectivity functions. Later on, working with Marr, Horn generalized a notion conceived by Land and showed that the natural reflectivities in a jumbled array of colored papers can be determined despite complications from uneven illumination. More of this work must be done.

To illustrate the possibilities, we turn to examine certain illumination-dictated constraints. Since some of the necessary mathematical expression may be unfamiliar, we do not go far, but to neglect the subject entirely would be wrong.

Our sample will explain a result developed by Horn. It is simple to state:

■ The orientations of the three surfaces meeting at a trihedral vertex can be determined by the directions of the lines and the observed intensities.

Our path toward this result will be oblique. We first define a two-dimensional transformation of certain vectors which define orientation. We then show that the space defined by the transformation gives insight into the relationship between the faces and edges of a trihedral vertex. Next we consider the relationship between surface orientations and observed brightness, noting that it is possible to draw lines of constant brightness in the newly defined space. And in conclusion we show that constraints from the edges plus constraints from observed intensity are enough to determine surface orientation.

Let us begin. Points in space correspond to coordinate triples, (x, y, z). For our present purpose, it is convenient to think of these triples as the components of a vector, $x\mathbf{i} + y\mathbf{j} + z\mathbf{k}$, drawn to the point from the origin. By taking this point of view, XY space does extended duty since it can display the coordinates of any vectors, not just the position vectors.

When dealing with surfaces, one vector of particular interest is the unit normal, a vector of length one which sticks out of a surface perpendicularly. If the vector $a\mathbf{i} + b\mathbf{j} + c\mathbf{k}$ is a unit normal, then c can be recovered from a and b since the length is one by definition:

$$c = (1 - a^2 - b^2)^{1/2}.$$

Thus the directions of all planes in space are given uniquely by points in XY space lying within the unit circle shown in the first part of figure 8-15.

Now let us define another space, PQ, which will prove particularly useful for displaying the surface normals. Vectors in XYZ space map into PQ according to these formulas:

$$p = -a/c,$$
$$q = -b/c.$$

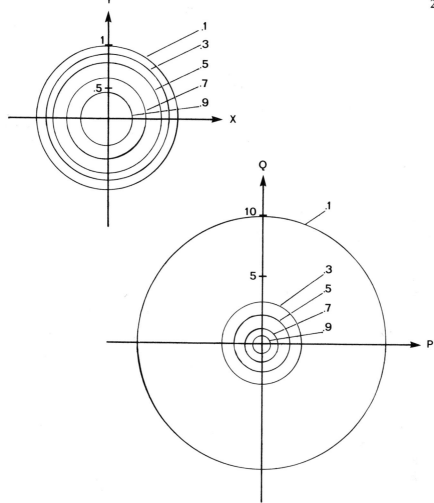

Figure 8-15 All unit normal vectors lie within a unit circle in XY space. There is no such restriction for PQ space. The circles shown are the loci of constant c, the vector component in the **k** direction.

As shown by the second part of figure 8-15, PQ space is much like XY space blown up. The lines of constant c are still circles, but the radii are enlarged such that any point in the whole PQ plane corresponds to a plane at some unique orientation, not just the points in the unit circle. The original vector components can be recovered by these formulas:

$$c = (1 + p^2 + q^2)^{-1/2},$$
$$b = -c \times q,$$
$$a = -c \times p.$$

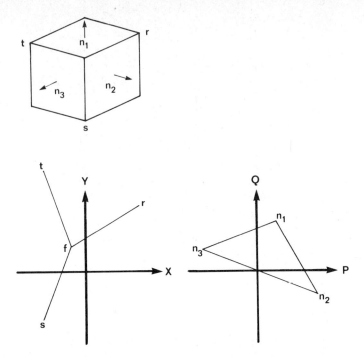

Figure 8-16 A trihedral vertex projects lines into XY space and points into PQ space. The lines in XY space are the orthographic projections of the edges in XYZ space. The points in PQ space represent the gradient vectors for each face. It can be shown that the lines in XY space are perpendicular to lines connecting the gradient points in PQ space. Thus fr is perpendicular to $n_1 n_2$, fs to $n_2 n_3$, and ft to $n_3 n_1$.

PQ space is useful, even though it is isomorphic to XY space, because it brings to the surface a powerful constraint, not previously discernable:

■ The projection in XY space of an edge formed by two planes is perpendicular to a line drawn between those planes' normal vectors in PQ space.

This constraint ties together two planes, the edge formed by their intersection, the images of the planes in PQ space, and the image of the edge in XY space. Figure 8-16 illustrates. The proof, obtained by forming vector cross and dot products, is tedious, but not hard.

When three planes are involved, not just two, the constraint between XY space edge projections and PQ space gradient positions holds for each pair of the three planes involved. Hence the following result:

■ The edges of a fully visible trihedral vertex define a FORK junction in XY space. The faces define a triangle in PQ space. The arms of the FORK are perpendicular to the sides of the triangle.

This is the constraint between edges and surface orientations that we have been seeking. Evidently the edges define a triangle of known shape and orientation but unknown position and size. If the size and position can be determined, we are through, for then the corners of the PQ space triangle give the surface normals of the vertex faces. We look at brightness to find the remaining constraint.

The observed brightness of all planes is fixed by the combination of viewing position, illumination position, surface material, surface position, and surface direction. In general, each possible brightness level corresponds to a family of possible directions which forms a locus of constant brightness in either XY space or PQ space.

To be more specific, suppose the viewer, a light source, and a scene are related by the geometry shown in figure 8-17. Since the scene is presumed to be far away from the light source and the viewer, light falls on all surfaces with equal strength. Consequently, observed brightness depends only on the angle between a surface and the direction of the light.

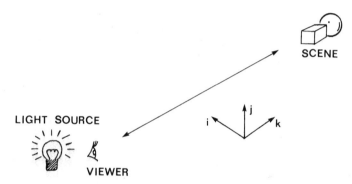

Figure 8-17 When the light source is near the viewer and both are far from the scene, illumination analysis is simplified. For most surfaces the observed brightness is proportional to cos (*i*), where *i* is the incident angle measured with respect to the normal.

■ For most surfaces, the observed intensity varies as the cosine of the incident angle *i* between the surface normal and the light source, being maximum when the surface faces the light squarely. The observed intensity of a sphere dims and goes to zero as the incident light angle goes to 90° and the light just grazes the surface.

■ For some surfaces, the moon's in particular, the observed intensity varies as the ratio of the cosine of *i* and the cosine of the emergent angle, *e,* between the surface normal and the viewer. When the moon is full, *i* and *e* are the equal to each other at all points observed. Consequently cos (*i*) / cos (*e*) is a constant, the observed brightness is constant, there is no dimming at the edges, and the moon looks flat.

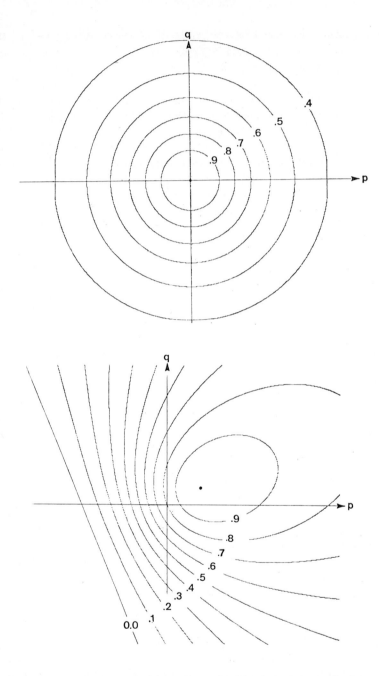

Figure 8-18 Lines of constant brightness for surfaces where brightness is proportional to cos (*i*), where *i* is the incident angle. The numbers labeling the lines are the values of cos (*i*). The first set are for a light source close to the viewer and the second are for a light source separated from the viewer by an angle of 37°.

Let us work with normal surfaces and a light source at the viewer. For this, the cosine, conveniently enough, is given by

$$\cos (i) = c = (1 + p^2 + q^2)^{-1/2}.$$

From this relation, it is clear that keeping $p^2 + q^2$ constant keeps observed brightness constant. Hence the lines of constant brightness in PQ space are circles as shown in the first part of figure 8-18. This is reasonable since holding c constant while varying the other components of a surface's normal vector amounts to spinning the surface around an axis coincident with the direction of the light source.

Of course other arrangements of the viewer, the light source, and the scene yield different isobrightness lines. The second part of figure 8-18 shows the result when the light source is separated from the viewer by an angle of about 37°.

Now we are ready to put things together. We have the shape and orientation of the PQ space triangle defined by the edges of an observed trihedral vertex. We have the observed brightness of the surfaces which correspond to the corners of the triangle. To find surface orientations, one moves and squishes the triangle until the corners lie on isobrightness contours which match the observed brightness values.

Observed brightness also gives surface orientation for curved objects but the development requires the solution of some partial differential equations. The resulting theory supports the conclusion that cosmetics work. Rouge helps darken a too-wide face toward the sides and makes it appear narrower.

SCENE DESCRIPTION

Waltz' work on understanding scenes surprised everyone. Previously it was believed that only a program with a complicated control structure and lots of explicit reasoning power could hope to analyze complicated scenes. Now we know that understanding the constraints the real world imposes at junctions is enough to make things much simpler. A table which contains a list of the few thousand physically possible ways that edges come together and a simple matching program are all that is required. No deep problem-solving effort is required; it is just a matter of executing a very simple constraint-dependent, iterative process that successively throws away incompatible line-arrangement combinations.

With blocks-world line interpretation well in hand, the next problem is object description. There must be a representation to hold the descriptions and a way of building them up from the line drawings of the blocks world and the primal sketches of more general worlds.

Generalized Cylinders Describe Both Planar and Curved Objects

For the blocks world, representation seems simple because blocks and wedges are describable by the coordinates of their vertexes or the surface normals or some other simple expedient. For the real world, however, the description of shape has new dimensions. The problem is difficult, but Binford, with his notion of generalized cylinders, opens a crack for us to widen.

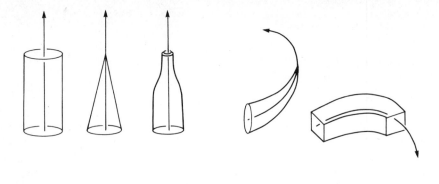

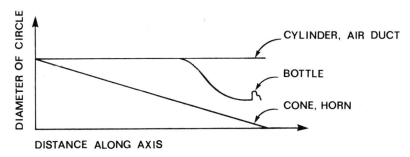

Figure 8-19 The generalized cylinder describes a large class of objects. The simplest generalized cylinders are fixed two-dimensional shapes projected along straight axes. In general the two-dimensional shape need not remain constant and the axis need not be straight. Also, the two-dimensional shape may be arbitrarily complex.

The generalized cylinder idea, like many great ideas, is simple. Think of it as developed in figure 8-19.

- An ordinary cylinder is a circle moved along a line through its center. For a cone, the circle shrinks linearly as it moves. For a bottle, the circle varies in a more complicated way along the axis.

- Generalized cylinders are descriptions that consist of an axis and a two-dimensional shape projected along it. The axis need not be straight and the two-dimensional shape need not be circular. The world of bricks and pyramids is included as a subset since the objects are just straight-axis projections of simple polygons.

Vases Are Simple Generalized Cylinders

Since the two-dimensional projection figure is allowed to vary considerably, a vocabulary is needed to classify the possibilities. Hollerbach has demonstrated such a vocabulary and shown it capable of handling the rich variety of shapes offered by the Greek vases in figure 8-20.

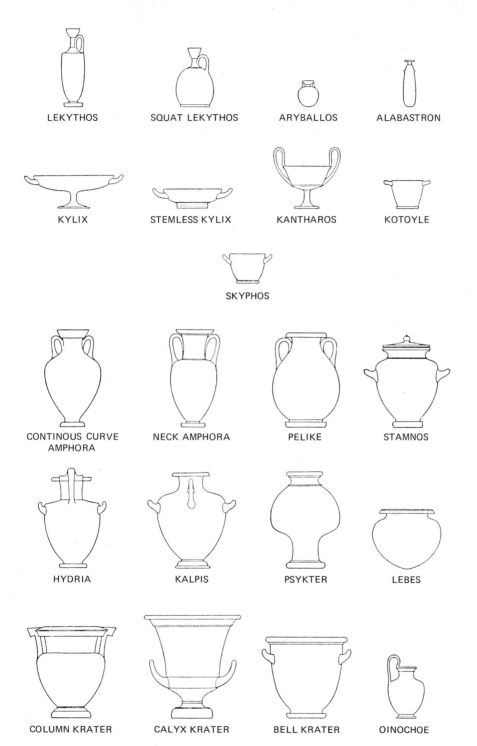

LEKYTHOS SQUAT LEKYTHOS ARYBALLOS ALABASTRON

KYLIX STEMLESS KYLIX KANTHAROS KOTOYLE

SKYPHOS

CONTINOUS CURVE AMPHORA NECK AMPHORA PELIKE STAMNOS

HYDRIA KALPIS PSYKTER LEBES

COLUMN KRATER CALYX KRATER BELL KRATER OINOCHOE

Figure 8-20 Generalized cylinders and an epistemology of axis variations suffice to support procedures which identify the standard Greek vase types of archeological interest.

Altogether, 42 types are recognized:

Liquid-storing	Solid-storing	Pouring-vase	Dispensing-vase
bottle	jar	bowl	pot
flask	neck-amphora	cup	krater
florence flask	continuous-curve	mug	column krater
kjeldahl flask	amphora	pan	bell krater
pitcher	pelike	plate	calyx krater
aryballos	stamnos	cooking pot	psykter
ampulla	urn	cooking pan	lebes
lekythos		ladle	
oinochoe		kotoyle	
bell-mouthed		kantharos	Decorative
oinochoe		kylix	
olpe		skyphos	vase
jug			
alabastron			
hydria			
kalpis			

To do the recognition, Hollerbach's program computes and uses some fraction of the following 105 descriptive terms.

above	convexity	high	neck	slightly
abruptly	curved	high-angle	nonloop	slim
articulation	cylinder	high-shoulder	not-offset	slope
base	deep	horizontal	offset	small
becoming	down	in	open	sphere
bell	end	inverted	orientation	splaying
belly	enormously	junction	out	squat
below	everted	large	ovoid	standard
biconical	extremely	lip	pear	stem
body	flaring	location	pedestal	straight
bottom	flat	loop	pinched-in	strongly
bowl	flat-base	low	rim	tall
brim	foot	low-angle	ring	tallness
broad	gently	low-bellied	round-bottom	top
calyx	globular	lower-shape	segment	up
carinated	gradient	lug	shallow	upper-shape
circular	gradually	middle	short	vertical
concave	greatest-width	minimal	shoulder	very
cone	handles	molded	size	whole
contour	height	mouth	slant	widely
convex	hemisphere	narrow	slight	width

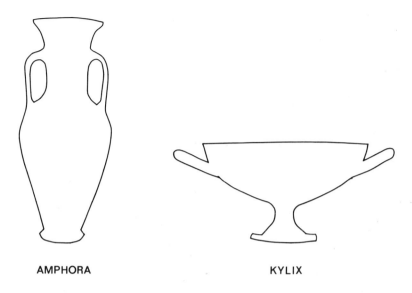

AMPHORA   KYLIX

Figure 8-21 Hollerbach's program successfully describes and identifies an amphora and a kylix.

Description generated for the amphora: type is amphora, used for storing solids — body: tall ovoid, high-shouldered with straight lower profile becoming abruptly rounded — neck: high and broad cylinder, with straight and vertical profile, and offset from the body — lip: rolled — foot: low and narrow molded — handles: two vertical handles from shoulder to neck.

Description generated for the kylix: type is kylix, used for pouring liquids — body: shallow bowl, open-mouthed with convex rounded profile — lip: very low molded — foot: high pedestal, widely splaying with broad stem and narrow base, and offset from the body — handles: two horizontal handles rising at a low angle from the body.

Figure 8-21 gives two examples of vase description using the vocabulary.

Generalized-cylinder theory is now accompanied by theories of amalgamation. Binford and his colleagues have a primitive one for the world at large while Hollerbach has another that focuses mainly on the special case of polygonal cross sections. Figure 8-22 shows Hollerbach's description of a telephone. He sees it as a right wedge truncated at one vertex and notched at the other with two U-shaped parallel protrusions symmetrically seated in the notch cavity.

■   Complicated objects often consist of generalized cylinders stuck together. Often a dominant central cylinder is modified by indentations and protrusions which themselves are cylinders. The result is often like the decompositions found in elementary books on drawing.

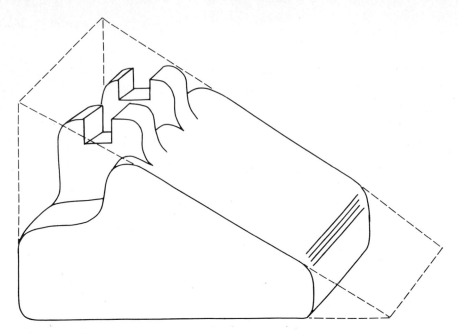

Figure 8-22 Very complex shapes can be described as combinations of simple shapes modified by indentations and protrusions. A telephone is a truncated and notched wedge with U-shaped protrusions set into the notch.

SUMMARY

- Pattern-recognition researchers concentrate on global feature extraction followed by feature space gymnastics. The results often have practical value in solving applied problems.

- There is a huge literature on the physiological psychology of animal vision stretching back to Helmholtz and beyond. The results suggest that animal vision systems use prodigious computation.

- The long-range goal of computer vision research is the creation of programs which describe and understand the visual world. Achieving the goal is difficult. There has been much work, but it is not clear how long the theories will stand.

- Systems in which high-level knowledge reaches down into edge-tracking processes work well in the blocks world. The high-level knowledge supplies good clues about where to look hardest.

- Much computational strength is needed in programs which translate images into symbolic primal sketches. The primal sketch is needed to cope with the additional hazards of working with the vision of real-world objects.

- The first step in forming a primal sketch is filtering the image with bar and edge profiles at many orientations. The resulting peak heights and peak positions are then analyzed and mapped into feature descriptions composed from a few basic descriptors.

- Histograms of primal-sketch properties contain information relevant to texture discrimination. These properties include intensity, edge contrast, edge length, edge orientation, and edge-fragment-separation distance.

- Much of the best vision work explains the constraints the world imposes on images. The best results were obtained by using knowledge about the way the world constrains images. Waltz' work on scenes and Horn's work on extracting shape from shading are representative successes.

- Gradient space is a transformation of real space which brings out constraints among surface orientations, edge orientations, and observed intensities. In the blocks world, many surface orientations can be found by stretching and translating a triangle defined by the edges. In the world of smoothly curved objects, integration of some partial differential equations is required.

- Generalized cylinders are projections of two-dimensional shapes along lines in space. The shapes may vary smoothly along the line. The line may be curved. Generalized cylinders describe a variety of shapes, including those of the blocks world and the Greek-vase world. When several cylinders are allowed to combine, even complicated real-world objects like telephones are within reach.

- Much has been done, but the problems are very hard; much remains to be done, and only hard work will disperse the fog.

REFERENCES

- Richard Duda and Peter Hart, *Pattern Recognition and Scene Analysis,* Wiley, New York, 1973. An excellent introductory text.

- Azriel Rosenfeld, periodic articles in A.C.M. *Computing Surveys* and *Computer Graphics and Image Processing.* Rosenfeld's review articles are the best entry into the literature.

- Ian Theodore Young, "Automated Leukocyte Recognition," PhD thesis, Massachusetts Institute of Technology, Cambridge, Massachusetts, 1969.

- H. B. Barlow, "Summation and Inhibition in the Frog's Retina," *Journal of Physiology,* vol. 119, 1953.

- Jerome Y. Lettvin *et al,* "What the Frog's Eye Tells the Frog's Brain," *Proceedings of the Institute of Radio Engineers,* vol. 47, November, 1959. The classic paper describing the duties of the cells in the frog's retina.

- D. H. Hubel and T. N. Wiesel, "Receptive Fields, Binocular Interaction and Functional Architecture in the Cat's Visual Cortex," *Journal of Physiology,* vol. 160, 1962. The cat's eye exposed.

- Berthold K. P. Horn, "The Binford-Horn Line Finder," AI-M-285, The Artificial Intelligence Laboratory, Massachusetts Institute of Technology, Cambridge, Massachusetts, 1971. Detailed description of a program that finds lines in real images. This is a convincing demonstration that the details to be considered are overwhelming.

- Eugene Freuder, "A Computer System for Visual Recognition Using Active Knowledge," PhD thesis, AI-TR-345, The Artificial Intelligence Laboratory,

Massachusetts Institute of Technology, Cambridge, Massachusetts, 1976. Develops an elaborate theory of heterarchical control for computer vision and other tasks.

■ Patrick Henry Winston, "The M.I.T. Robot," in *Machine Intelligence 7,* edited by Bernard Meltzer and Donald Michie, Edinburgh University Press, Edinburgh, Scotland, 1972. A description of the first system for copying reasonably general blocks-world structures from samples.

■ Yoshiaki Shirai, "Analyzing Intensity Arrays using Knowledge about Scenes," in *The Psychology of Computer Vision,* edited by Patrick Henry Winston, McGraw-Hill Book Company, New York, 1975. A description of the most sophisticated line finder written to date. The system was heterarchical in the sense that high-level knowledge influenced image-level processing.

■ David Marr, "Early Processing of Visual Information," AI-M-340, The Artificial Intelligence Laboratory, Massachusetts Institute of Technology, Cambridge, Massachusetts, 1975. Exciting work developing the primal sketch, how it is formed, and what it can do.

■ B. Julesz, "Experiments in the Visual Perception of Texture," *Scientific American,* vol. 232, April 1975. An article on texture vision offering a theory different from Marr's. Great examples are shown.

■ Berthold K. P. Horn, "Obtaining Shape from Shading Information," in *The Psychology of Computer Vision,* edited by Patrick Henry Winston, McGraw-Hill Book Company, New York, 1975. Horn takes readers on an adventure in applied mathematics to integrate the image-illumination equations, deducing an object's shape thereby.

■ Berthold K. P. Horn, "Determining Lightness from an Image," *Computer Graphics and Image Processing,* Vol. 3, no. 4, December 1974. A theory of how lightness perception (and hence color) can discount slow variations in incident light.

■ David Marr, "The Computation of Lightness by the Primate Retina," *Vision Research,* vol. 14, 1974. A theory of how Horn's lightness theory might be implemented in animal hardware.

■ David Waltz, "Understanding Line Drawings of Scenes with Shadows," in *The Psychology of Computer Vision,* edited by Patrick Henry Winston, McGraw-Hill Book Company, New York, 1975. The definitive paper on the analysis of polyhedral line drawings.

■ Thomas O. Binford, "Visual Perception by Computer," talk given at IFIP Conference, Yugoslavia, 1971. First presentation of the generalized-cylinder approach to object description. The paper was too late to be in the proceedings, but several hundred copies have been distributed privately.

■ John Hollerbach, "Hierarchical Shape Description of Objects by Selection and Modification of Prototypes," AI-TR-346, MS thesis, The Artificial Intelligence Laboratory, Massachusetts Institute of Technology, Cambridge, Massachusetts, 1976. Two theses in one. The first offers a theory of blocks-world descriptions focused on protrusions and indentations; the second, a theory of generalized cylinder description specialized to Greek vases.

■ R. Ohlander, "Analysis of Natural Scenes," PhD thesis, Department of Computer Science, Carnegie-Mellon University, Pittsburgh, Pennsylvania. Separation of regions in a scene based on color. Although simple, the technique works very, very well.

9
KNOWLEDGE ENGINEERING AND TEACHING PEOPLE THINKING

The main purpose of this chapter is to exhibit some representative applications of the ideas that have been developed thereby demonstrating that computer intelligence technology is here now. One application has to do with analyzing mass spectrograms of the sort that organic chemists deal with. Another deals with the analysis and treatment of certain bacterial infections found in the blood.

While looking at programs which solve problems expertly, it is natural to wonder if the ideas and metaphors employed can help make people better problem solvers. The answer may be Yes. People who write intelligent programs often feel that writing smart programs helps the programmer become smarter. There seem to be two reasons for this: first, the person who knows about computer intelligence knows more ways of representing and thinking about knowledge; and second, experience with real implementation accustoms people to the fact that expert-level knowledge can be effectively categorized and listed, even for "nonscientific" activities.

Indeed it seems that even children can profit from knowing programming. Writing a program to guide a mechanical turtle around obstacles can bring the child-programmer to an understanding of concepts like feedback and state at an unusually early age. The chapter proceeds with a look at some of the details.

Finally, for something completely different, we investigate some of the strangely persistent, human-chauvinist charges against the position that computers can become as intelligent as people.

QUESTIONS ABOUT KNOWLEDGE

It would be hard to lay out a design for any expert problem solver, human or computer, without facing basic questions about the knowledge involved.

Understanding these questions along with the generally useful answers creates a kind of knowledge engineering.

What Kind of Knowledge Is Involved?

Does a task require very specialized ideas, or does it succumb to broadly applicable ideas? If broadly applicable ideas work, what are they? What are the most powerful ideas anyway?

How Should the Knowledge Be Represented?

Some knowledge is procedural. Perhaps a set of ideas is best captured by a collection of productions. Other knowledge is factual and belongs somewhere in the spectrum of representational methods extending from simple tables to sophisticated frame systems. Maybe direct, explicit call of each procedure is better. Sometimes whole systems can be powerful metaphors which facilitate problem solution through strong analogical features. Studying them is like studying law school cases.

How Much Knowledge Is Required?

Knowing what kind of knowledge is involved in a task, the next strategic question is How much? Are there forty facts or four hundred or four thousand? Do a dozen basic methods cover most cases? The tendency is to grossly overestimate. There is a one-two-three-infinity phenomenon. After we see that a task is reasonably complicated, we suppose that it is unimaginably complicated. But we have seen how little knowledge is required to do geometric analogy problems, for example, with human-level competence. For that problem, at least, the "infinity" is small.

One reason for asking this question about quantity is the demand for sensible resource allocation among the various knowledge collection chores required. Another is that knowing the size of a problem builds courage, for even if the size is large, knowing bad news is better than suspecting even worse news.

What Exactly Is the Knowledge Needed?

Ultimately, of course, we want the knowledge. In the geometric-analogy task we want the method for determining LEFT and ABOVE; in integral calculus we want the table of basic forms; in electromagnetic theory we want Maxwell's equations and a special-geometry recognizer; and in genetics we need Mendel's laws and the method of computing combinations. Much of learning a subject is collecting such knowledge. Whether this is an interesting puzzle or a frustrating ordeal depends partly on recognizing the equal importance of the *what* and *how much* questions.

Keep in mind that understanding a domain's facts and procedures is not the same as rote memorization. Clear, crisp listing of the knowledge required by a domain is not the same as superficial memorization of formulas. Raw formulas are pieces of compiled knowledge. Like compiled computer programs, memorized formulas give little opportunity for access to the sources, with the natural result being poor response to even slightly unexpected changes. Or, to avoid the computation metaphor, formulas are essences irreversibly distilled from general techniques for summary and speed.

Today's Expert Problem Solvers Are Dangerously Seductive

We are about to see how questions about knowledge are answered in the context of two programs that have achieved expert status in the domains they work in. No one should look at these examples without understanding the following points:

■ Much more is involved than the brief descriptions suggest. Years of team effort have gone into translating the basic strategies into working, useful systems.

■ Success in creating expert problem solvers depends on the cooperation of human experts. Ferreting out what they know and how they work usually requires long, tedious sessions gathering and analyzing introspective information from cooperative people.

■ Production Systems are only one tool. The examples in this chapter are such that simple production-system technology can be exploited, but it is not clear how often this is true. Certainly many limitations can be cited.

ANALYZING MASS SPECTROGRAMS

An organic chemist often wants to know the chemical nature of something newly created in the test tube. The first step, not the one of concern here, is to determine the number of atoms of various kinds in one molecule of the stuff. This is reflected in the chemical formula, $C_8H_{16}O$ being an example describing a chemical used throughout this discussion. The notation indicates that each molecule of the stuff has eight atoms of carbon, sixteen of hydrogen, and one of oxygen.

Once the chemical formula is known, then the chemist can use a sample's mass spectrogram to work out the way the atoms are arranged. This gives the chemical structure. Figure 9-1 shows a typical spectrogram and the structure for $C_8H_{16}O$ consistent with it. Working from formula and spectrogram to a deduced structure like a talented chemist is the purpose of the system we are about to study.

The mass spectrogram is produced as indicated in figure 9-2. The spectrogram machine tortures a sample's molecules by heating them until they break up into charged chunks of various sizes. Then the chunks are sorted by passing them through a magnetic field which deflects the high charge, low weight ones more than the low charge, high weight ones. The deflected chunks then crash into a photographic plate, darkening it in proportion to their number.

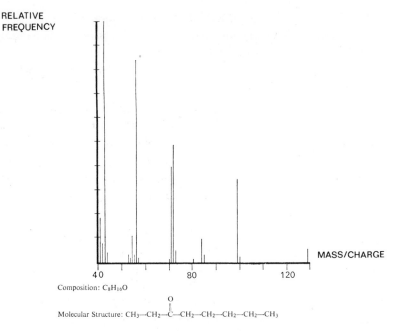

Composition: $C_8H_{16}O$

Molecular Structure: $CH_3—CH_2—\overset{\overset{\displaystyle O}{\|}}{C}—CH_2—CH_2—CH_2—CH_2—CH_3$

Figure 9-1 A sample mass-spectrogram problem. The chemist must use the given chemical formula, $C_8H_{16}O$, together with the spectrogram, to deduce the structural arrangement. (From "Heuristic DENDRAL" by Buchanan, Sutherland, and Feigenbaum, *Machine Intelligence 4,* copyright 1969 by American Elsevier Publishing Company, New York. Used with Permission of Donald Michie, Editor-in-Chief, Machine Intelligence Series, University of Edinburgh, Scotland.)

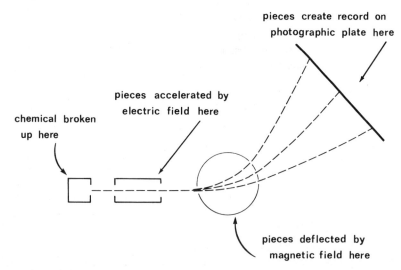

Figure 9-2 The mass spectrometer. First the organic chemical under study is broken up, and then the pieces separated and recorded.

DENDRAL Can Help Chemists Find Chemical Structure

The DENDRAL system works out structures from chemical formulas and mass spectrograms using the following steps:

- The mass spectrogram is used to create lists of required and forbidden substructures.

- The chemical formula is fed to a structure generator capable of generating all possible structures. The structure generator limits its output to things consistent with the lists of required and forbidden substructures.

- The mass spectrogram is predicted for each structure generated.

- The generated mass spectrograms are all compared with the actual experimental spectrogram. The correct structure is the one whose generated spectrogram gives the best match.

One particularly important feature of DENDRAL's structure generator is its ability to shape the output according to lists of necessary and forbidden substructures. Usually the list of necessary substructures is constructed solely from analysis of the mass spectrogram. The forbidden substructure list, however, comes partly from the mass spectrogram and partly from *a priori* chemical knowledge about unstable configurations. The following sulfur fragments, for example, are never found in stable chemicals, and they therefore constitute part of the forbidden substructure list:

S-S-S

O-S

All together the initial forbidden substructure list has about two dozen such items. This initial list by itself provides considerabe constraint. There would be many thousand acyclic, valence-satisfying structures with the formula $C_8H_{16}O$, but of these, only 698 emerge from the structure generator when guided by the initial list of unstable, forbidden substructures.

Analysis of the Experimental Mass Spectrogram Helps Produce Candidate Structures

Even fewer structures are produced, of course, when new members for the lists of required and forbidden structures are found by inspection of the spectrograms for tell-tale peak configurations. The spectrogram shown in figure 9-1, for example, puts N-PROPYL-KETONE3 on the required list because the conditions for the following production are met:

If   there is a high peak at atomic-number/charge point 71,
       there is a high peak at atomic-number/charge point 43,
       there is a high peak at atomic-number/charge point 86,
       and there is any peak at atomic-number/charge point 58,
then there must be an N-PROPYL-KETONE3 substructure.

For any given category of organic chemicals, the keytones or estrogens for example, there are about six to ten such rules. Some make insertions into the list of required substructures, and others add to the forbidden list using the absence of peaks. The net result of the additions recommended by the mass spectrogram reduce the number of structure possibilities for $C_8H_{16}O$ from 698 to a more manageable list of about forty ketone-bearing structures. Thus the information lurking in the mass spectrogram, combined with *a priori* knowledge about stabilities, reduces the number of plausible structures for the example from thousands to tens.

Synthesis of Each Candidate's Mass Spectrogram Helps Select the Best

Next, of course, the answer must be selected from the tens of possibilities since the theory of mass spectrograms inspection evidently is not constraining enough to do the whole job. This is done by another specialist, one which contains another form of expert knowledge, this time about how structures break up in the mass spectrogram machine. Using this specialist, the system can predict a spectrogram for each candidate which then can be judged for similarity to the experimentally derived one.

This mass spectrogram predictor also contains knowledge in production form. The situation-recognition part of each production recognizes the chunk which the production knows about, and the action part specifies what the decomposition products are along with a parameter estimating how much will actually so decompose. In a sense the production system's memory functions like the mass spectrogram's molecular destruction chamber. Altogether about 100 productions have been collected for this purpose so far. Clearly a considerable amount of chemical knowledge is involved.

Having reached the point where a set of structure-spectrogram pairs are in hand, the only remaining problem is the definition of a suitable function for determining how well the synthesized ones match the experimental one. The simplest method, of course, would be measurement of the sum of the squares of the differences in peak heights, the sort of standard engineering measure of signal difference.

The actual DENDRAL matcher is more involved because it is necessary to recognize that some peaks are more significant than others. The procedure used does this by way of the following steps:

- Certain break-up productions mark their products as especially significant.
- If any so-marked significant peak is not in the experimental spectrogram, then the structure which predicted that significant peak is rejected outright.
- The remaining spectrograms are then ranked according to how many of the experimental peaks each accounts for. There are rarely ties.

This procedure usually eliminates all but a few structures which are left ordered. In the $C_8H_{16}O$ example, only one structure survives, namely this one:

$$CH_3\text{-}CH_2\text{-}\overset{\overset{\textstyle O}{\|}}{C}\text{-}CH_2\text{-}CH_2\text{-}CH_2\text{-}CH_2\text{-}CH_3$$

TREATING BACTERIAL INFECTIONS

It is usually necessary to begin antibiotic treatment for bacterial blood infections without knowing exactly which organism is the culprit. Why not simply wait for the laboratory to produce a definitive identification of the infecting organism instead of using partial, imprecise evidence? The answer is that definitive culture evidence accumulates too slowly. For the desperately sick, therapy must begin at once, not two weeks from at once. This leaves two choices: the physician can prescribe so-called broad-spectrum drugs in order to cover all possibilities; or the physician can prescribe better, disease-specific drugs if he can exploit the available evidence as much as possible. Usually a lack of time and experience leads to broad-spectrum treatment. MYCIN is a problem-solving system which can help promote a more disease-specific approach by supplying good advice.

MYCIN Can Help Physicians Diagnose Infections

MYCIN informs itself about particular cases by requesting information about the patient's symptoms, general condition, history, and laboratory results. At each point, the question MYCIN asks is determined by the ongoing analysis of all previous questions. Thus the questions start as if taken from a check list but they vary as evidence builds. Here is a short scenario from a sample session:

■ What is the patient's name?

   John Doe

■ Male or female?

   Male.

■ Age?

   He is 55.

■ Have you obtained positive cultures indicating general type?

   Yes.

■ What type of infection is it?

   Primary Bacteremia.

■ When did symptoms first appear?

   May 5, 1975.

■ Let's call the most recent positive culture CULTURE-1. From what site was CULTURE-1 taken?

From the blood.

■ When?

May 9, 1975.

■ Let's call the first significant organism from this blood culture ORGANISM-1. Do you know the identity of ORGANISM-1?

No.

■ Is ORGANISM-1 a rod or a coccus or something else?

Rod.

■ What is the gram stain of ORGANISM-1?

Gramnegative.

■ Have there been positive cultures from sites which are not associated with infections about which you are seeking advice?

No.

■ Did ORGANISM-1 grow aerobically?

Yes.

■ Did ORGANISM-1 grow anaerobically?

Yes.

■ What is the suspected portal of entry of ORGANISM-1?

The gastrointestinal tract.

.

.

.

When satisfied that it has a reasonably good feel for the situation, MYCIN starts a short line of questions in preparation for recommending a course of treatment:

■ My recommendation will be based on the opinion that the identity of ORGANISM-1 may be 1 Pseudomonas-aeruginosa, 2 Klebsiella-pneumoniae, 3 E. Coli, 4 Bacteroides-fragilis, 5 Enterobacter, or 6 Proteus-non-mirabilis. On a scale of 0 to 4, where higher numbers indicate greater severity, how would you rate the patient's degree of sickness?

3.

■ Does the patient have a clinically significant allergic reaction to any antimicrobial agent?

No.

■ How much does the patient weigh?

70 kilograms.

■   My first recommendation is as follows: In order to cover for items 1, 2, 3, 5, and 6, give Gentamycin using a dose of 119 mg (1.7 mg/kg) q8h IV [or IM] for 10 days. Modify dose in renal failure. And in order to cover for item 4, give Clindamycin using a dose of 595 mg (8.5 mg/kg) q6h IV [or IM] for 14 days. If diarrhea or other gastrointestinal symptoms develop, check for pseudomembranous colitis.

■   Do you wish to see the second choice?

.

.

.

With this kind of help, busy physicians could consider more factors and provide more tailored treatment. Right now an amazing fraction of the population gets a dose of penicillin each year. Of these, some experts believe 90% are unnecessary or inappropriate.

MYCIN Is a Backward-Chaining Deduction System

Some 300 productions constitute MYCIN's pool of knowledge about blood bacterial infections. The following is typical:

> If   the infection type is primary-bacteremia,
>   the suspected entry point is the gastrointestinal tract,
>   and the site of the culture is one of the sterile sites,
> then   there is evidence that the organism is bacteroides.

To use such knowledge, MYCIN works backward. For each of 100 possible diagnoses, MYCIN attempts to work toward primitive facts known from laboratory results and clinical observations.

Backward running is the method of choice if a production system is being used to check out one particular hypothesis. But MYCIN checks every possible hypothesis, so search economy is not the reason involved. Instead, the MYCIN system runs backward so that the questions seem focused. By sticking with the questions that fan out in the implied AND/OR tree beneath a particular hypothesized conclusion, the questions are guaranteed to stick to that hypothesis. A forward-running system can jump around, collecting information relevant first to one hypothesis and then to another, seemingly at random. This sort of behavior irritates people.

MYCIN Computes Certainty Factors

MYCIN works in a domain where deductions are rarely certain. Thus MYCIN developers combined a primitive theory of plausible reasoning with the basic production apparatus. The theory is used to establish a so-called certainty factor for each conclusion in the AND/OR tree, but there are some serious inadequacies in how this is done. Research continues.

Briefly, the theory requires each production description to include what amounts to an attenuation factor which, like the certainty factors, ranges from zero to one. Each production then passes on a number from the hypothesis facts supporting it in the AND/OR tree as follows:

- At AND nodes, the smallest certainty factor on the premise branches is multiplied by the attenuation factor of the production. The product is passed upward. Thus the conclusion can never be stronger than the weakest piece of required supporting evidence.

- At OR nodes, the certainty factors on the branches reinforce one another. With one branch, the overall certainty is the certainty factor associated with that branch. The remaining distance to total certainty is 1 − <certainty factor 1>. Adding a second branch carries the certainty factor over this remaining distance in proportion to the certainty associated with the second branch:

<certainty factor>
= <certainty factor 1>
  + (1 − <certainty factor 1>) × <certainty factor 2>

Thus, the strength of the conclusion increases with the combined strength of the lines of reasoning leading to it. Note that the formula can be written in another way to emphasize symmetry:

<certainty factor>
= <certainty factor 1> + <certainty factor 2>
  − <certainty factor 1> × <certainty factor 2>

Figure 9-3 illustrates how the numbers work their way up a simple AND/OR tree. Note that if the plausibility sinks below some arbitrary threshhold, say .2, then the hypothesis is judged unsupportable and is suppressed.

MYCIN Talks with the Consulting Physician in English

Since MYCIN is intended to help people who are not programming stars, smooth human engineering is an absolute requirement. This has been accomplished in a number of ways, one of which is the inclusion of an English interface. This feature greatly enhances its appeal. No one likes to talk to a computer through a superspecialist.

Fortunately, making the interface was relatively easy because sophisticated natural language processing is not needed to exchange information in MYCIN's world.

The MYCIN System Can Answer a Variety of Questions about Its Knowledge and Behavior

By looking into an historical record of the productions used, MYCIN can answer questions about *why* a fact was used or about *how* a fact was established. Much of this ability stands on the simple, highly constrained format that the production-

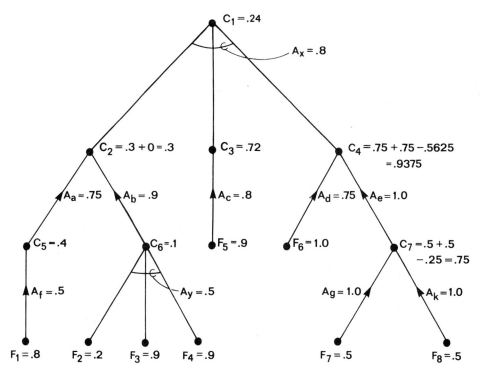

Figure 9-3 MYCIN uses a simple theory of plausible inference to pass certainty factors up the AND/OR tree from the given facts. The Fs are the certainty factors attributed by the user to the facts he supplies, the Cs are the certainty factors computed for each conclusion made, and the As are the "attenuations" that indicate the inherent reliability of the productions. Certainty factors are computed at the AND and OR nodes according to straightforward formulas. The truth of any fact whose certainty factor is computed to be .2 or less is judged unknown and the certainty factor is reset to 0.

system technique imposes on the stored knowedge. To decide how a given fact was concluded, for example, MYCIN reflects on the productions it has used, looking for one that contains the fact in its conclusion set. The required answer is just an enumeration of those productions by name or an enumeration of the facts in the premise set of one of them. Consider this:

■ How do you know that the culture was taken from a sterile source?

RULE001 and RULE022 gave suggestive evidence.

■ How was RULE001 triggered?

It was known that the site is one for which sterility depends on method, the method is one of the recognized ones for the site, and it is not known if care was taken, therefore there is strongly suggestive evidence that the culture was taken from a sterile source.

Answering why a given fact was needed goes the other way, of course. MYCIN looks for a production with the fact in its premise set and reports the facts in the conclusion set.

In addition, there are other recognized questions that deal with knowledge in general rather than specific sessions. The physician can ask questions like these:

■ Do you recommend clindamycin for bacteroides?

Yes, by virtue of RULE060.

■ Is blood a sterile site?

Yes, normally.

■ What are the organisms associated with the gastrointestinal tract?

Enterococcus, Clostridium-gangrene, Bacteroides, Klebisella, Pseudomonas, E. Coli, Enterbacter, and Proteus.

MYCIN Can Assimilate New Knowledge Interactively

MYCIN now has a knowledge-acquisition feature that is a joy to behold. As soon as the physician objects to some conclusion, MYCIN begins to walk with him through the AND/OR tree. This may lead to straightforward modification of some existing rule, but the greater ability to add new rules is there too.

Statistical observations gathered by the system are used to categorize rules according to their typical contents. This helps in acquiring new rules, since once the category of a new rule is known, the MYCIN system uses knowledge about typical contents to extract information from the expert which otherwise might have been overlooked.

TEACHING AND LEARNING POWERFUL IDEAS

Having seen the structure of two computer experts, let us turn to human problem solvers. Here the concern is not so much with how knowledge is embodied, but with what knowledge exists to be embodied.

It is good fortune that some nuggets of knowledge, the *powerful ideas,* are universally useful, appearing over and over in our sciences. Recognizing powerful ideas and recognizing them early is important to intellectual maturity, yet somehow attempts to teach them to children rarely occur, except indirectly through elementary arithmetic. This need not be so. Papert and his associates have demonstrated ways of teaching powerful ideas to even very young children. Let us therefore establish a context for a discussion of them by sketching the route a child might take while working out a project in Papert's education laboratory.

Children Can Teach Mechanical Turtles to Migrate

A child is introduced to a so-called turtle, a small, radio-controlled vehicle that looks like a transparent plastic dome on wheels. The child quickly learns how to control

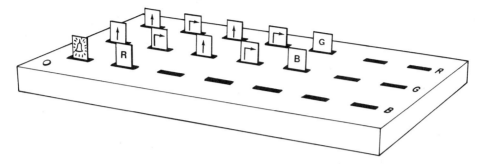

Figure 9-4 Children can write programs using a slot machine. Mnemonically coded cards arranged in rows specify turtle movements. The colored cards cause jumps to the row labeled with the same color. Operational slot machines are four by ten or larger.

the turtle by issuing FORWARD, BACKWARD, RIGHT, and LEFT commands either through a terminal or by arranging mnemonically coded cards in an array of slots as shown in figure 9-4. A square, ten centimeters on a side, is rendered by an eight-instruction sequence:

```
FORWARD 10
RIGHT 90
FORWARD 10
RIGHT 90
FORWARD 10
RIGHT 90
FORWARD 10
RIGHT 90
```

Soon the child writes a program, SQUARE, which enables him to create square turtle paths of any size at will. This merely involves packaging the instructions and using a variable instead of the number 10.

```
TO SQUARE X
1 FORWARD X
2 RIGHT 90
3 FORWARD X
4 RIGHT 90
5 FORWARD X
6 RIGHT 90
7 FORWARD X
8 RIGHT 90
END
```

After this, typing SQUARE 20 causes the turtle to make a 20 centimeter square.

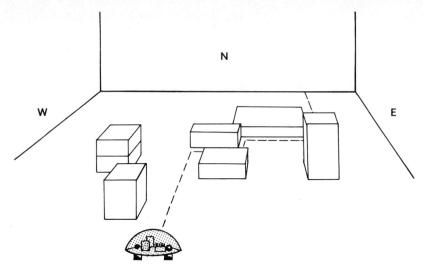

Figure 9-5 Getting to the north wall in spite of obstacles is the turtle migration problem.

A few such experiences prepare a child for the turtle summer migration project. The turtle's goal is to be on the north side of the room illustrated in figure 9-5.

Since obstacles may be in the way, empowering the turtle to crawl all the way around a single object is a sensible subgoal. Once the child has such a program, it can be called on whenever a touch sensor signals collision, and it can be abandoned as soon as the crawling direction is north. Writing this obstacle-handling program is interesting because the turtle must maintain contact constantly with the wall in order to detect the corners. The teacher helps by suggesting an experiment in which the child is blindfolded and told to walk around an obstacle himself. Doing so, it becomes clear that two ideas are involved:

- If there is wall contact, the turtle should turn slightly right. Otherwise friction increases, possibly stopping progress altogether, especially at concave corners.

- If there is no wall contact, the turtle should turn slightly left. Otherwise the turtle would drift away from the obstacle and wander aimlessly off into space, especially at convex corners.

Figure 9-6 shows the locus of a turtle or person using either of these programs. Note that some experiment is needed to determine the heading correction rate. It should be high enough to avoid serious overshoot at the corners, but low enough to keep wall walking smooth. These ideas are captured by a very simple program:

```
TO WALKAROUND
1 FORWARD 1
2 TEST LEFTTOUCH
3 IF TRUE RIGHT 5
4 IF FALSE LEFT 5
5 GO 1
END
```

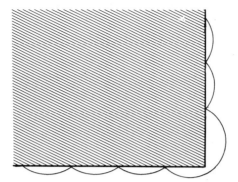

Figure 9-6 Walking around the outside of an obstacle is simple. The turtle turns right if it feels contact with the wall and left otherwise. Some care is needed to select a turn rate for which wall-walking is smooth yet corner turning is tight.

Line 1 causes the turtle to move forward a short distance. Line 2 determines whether the movement brings the turtle into contact with the wall or away from it. Line 3 and line 4 do the appropriate corrective action. Line 5 causes the move-test-react cycle to repeat over and over. Thus the procedure iterates. Another way to achieve the same end is given in this recursive variation:

```
TO WALKAROUND
1 FORWARD 1
2 TEST LEFTTOUCH
3 IF TRUE RIGHT 5
4 IF FALSE LEFT 5
5 WALKAROUND
END
```

As given, **WALKAROUND** is nearly ready for installation in the migration system. It is only necessary to check the direction periodically, quitting when it becomes zero:

```
TO AVOID
1 FORWARD 1
2 TEST LEFTTOUCH
3 IF TRUE RIGHT 5
4 IF FALSE LEFT 5
5 IF HEADING < 10 STOP
6 IF HEADING > 350 STOP
7 GO 1
END
```

This of course assumes that the direction is available through the variable **HEADING**, just as contact was established through **LEFTTOUCH**.

The result is an adequate subroutine that works most of the time. It does succumb to the turtle trap shown in figure 9-7, however. Inside it the turtle mistakenly thinks it has cleared the obstacle when in fact it has only found a place where the concavity permits travel northward. The turtle is doomed. It repeats the mistake over and over. Evidently it is not enough to know only the current orientation. The turtle needs knowledge of the total amount of turn. When the total turn returns to zero, forward motion is resumed, not before, and certainly not every time the HEADING variable approaches zero.

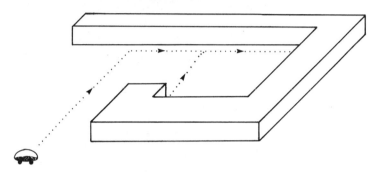

Figure 9-7 The turtle trap. If only heading is known, the turtle falsely believes the obstacle is circumnavigated as soon as the direction of movement is north.

Teaching Turtles to Migrate Helps Children Learn Powerful Ideas

Of course, a child is entranced. By use of turtles and other robotic devices he identifies with projects in a way absolutely foreign to most elementary school subjects. There is something he himself is controlling, quite the reverse of the usual situation for a child. A natural reaction is that the child feels he cannot be learning because he is having too much fun!

But he is learning — he is learning concepts normally thought of as deep or advanced. They are powerful ideas like these:

The ideas of state and state variable. It is hard to imagine a science which does not and could not make good use of the notion of state. Certainly if a science deals with change, it deals with descriptions of situations before, after, and perhaps during the change. Typically the descriptions are in the form of numbers summarizing particular aspects of the situations relevant to understanding or predicting change. These are the state variables. They may be continuous or discrete. Examples are the temperature in a room, the current in a wire, and the location of an object. For the migrating turtle, the orientation and position are state variables.

The idea of input or control variable. If we are to control something, there must be some access to it through an input or control variable. If the situation is simple, there is a straightforward relationship between selection of a control variable value and a resulting change in state. The setting of a thermostat and the resulting room temperature are simply related in the sense that setting the thermostat higher results in higher room temperature. At a more detailed level the simplicity evaporates because of effects from outside temperature, planned or unplanned hysteresis, air currents, and whether the fireplace is going. If there are several state variables to be controlled, one may hope for an equal number of inputs, each of which influences only one state variable value. In turtle geometry, the inputs are the movement and turn commands which independently control changes in the position and orientation state variables. In Newtonian physics an object's state is given by its position and momentum. Regrettably the only control is force, which directly influences momentum and indirectly changes position.

The ideas of subproblem and subgoal. Divide and conquer is the first principle of scientific attack. The problem of breaking a difficult question into tractable pieces is often the only problem. Although this idea was not emphasized, turtle migration requires it because migration is racing north plus obstacle circumnavigation.

The ideas of local-global connection and independence. Complicated systems are understood by first explaining the parts and then understanding the way they fit together. It is lucky if they combine linearly, that is, if the combined behavior is a simple, additive consequence of the independent behavior. On an abstract level, the combination of the AVOID process with others in the migration system is linear because attending to local properties leads smoothly to understanding global phenomena. Science thrives on understanding systems that behave linearly, and struggles with systems that do not.

The idea of feedback. Feedback is everywhere, both in nature and in the artificial. Our bodies rely on it, our economy is subject to it, and our engineers exploit it. Ordinarily the notion of feedback cannot be found in early curricula. It is prominent in turtle migration. There is no other way to circumnavigate the obstacles.

The ideas of iteration and recursion. These two notions are fundamental control ideas. The two forms of the simple WALKAROUND process exhibit them.

The idea of debugging. A first analysis of hard problems is rarely good enough, but if the initial ideas are good, sound ideas, it would be foolhardy to start over. Instead, the weaknesses of the first attempt should be attacked with an orderly debugging procedure. Errors and discrepancies should be welcomed as potentially informative friends rather than be greeted as certain ogres. Both the circumnavigation problem and the turtle trap problem required debugging activity. Things nearly worked, but not quite.

The idea of state-variable extension. If a problem seems intractable, the trouble may be that more knowledge about state may be needed, and increasing the number of state variables or extending the range of the ones in hand may be sensible. Generalizing the orientation state variable was the right step in solving the turtle trap problem.

MYTHS ABOUT THINKING

To know about computer intelligence and like it is to be doomed: a perpetual argument follows the initiated, raising itself up at cocktail parties and other social events. Usually these arguments start off on ground littered with worn-out errors. Let us look at some.

Myth: Computers Can Never...

It hardly matters how the sentence is finished because the standard proof is as weak as it is inevitable. Stripped of obfuscation, it goes like this: "Computers cannot ..., because no one has thought of a way to make them ..." The elusive qualities most frequently proposed by the critics of computer intelligence include learning, introspection, and aesthetic feeling, all of which suggest a certain unfamiliarity with the literature. Programs and ideas described in this book already manifest these abilities to some degree. Their competence certainly leaves much to be explored, but doors are swinging open nevertheless.

Of course to believe in human superiority is a tradition. Once our earth was the center of the universe, now it is an undistinguished planet. Once our creation was direct and divine, now some people believe it is the good luck of the primates. Once our intelligence was unchallenged, yet someday computers may laugh at us and wonder if biological information processors could be really smart. Beware of those who think it can never happen. Their ancestors hassled Galileo and ridiculed Darwin.

Myth: Computers Are Not Intelligent Because They Do not Write like Shakespeare, Compose like Beethoven, or Do Science like Newton

Logic dictates that true demonstration of computer intelligence need not hinge on producing superhuman computer performance. Otherwise we ordinary writers, musicians, and scientists would necessarily and painfully find ourselves among the unintelligent.

Myth: Computers Can Do Only What They Are Programmed to Do

Intelligent computers do not organize themselves out of nothing, so in some uninteresting sense their abilities descend from human programmers. But it is equally true that humans are indebted to the genetic code. Somehow there must be enough innate information processing power to get beyond the threshhold above which learning from the environment takes place. Once humans bring computer intelligence up to this level, computers will no doubt augment their directly programmed gifts by the same means humans do: by being told, by reading, by asking questions, by doing experiments, and by being curious.

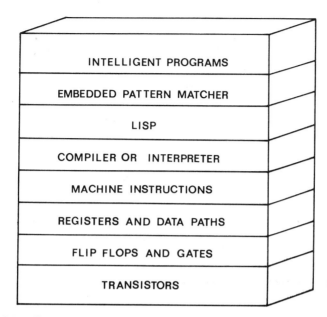

Figure 9-8 Intelligent programs are built on many layers of information processing.

Myth: Software Can Never Equal Brainware Because Transistors Are Different from Neurons

If we look at what has produced computer intelligence so far, we see multiple layers, each of which rests on primitives of the next layer down, forming a hierarchical structure with a great deal interposed between the intelligent program and the transistors which ultimately support it. Figure 9-8 illustrates.

All of the complexity of one level is summarized and distilled down to a few simple atomic notions which are the primitives of the next layer up. But with so much insulation, it cannot possibly be that the detailed nature of the lower levels can matter to what happens above. This argues against the idea that studying neurons can lead to much of an understanding about intelligence. Understanding them beautifully and entirely can no more produce an understanding of intelligence than a complete understanding of transistors can yield insight into how a computer can understand scenes or respond to English. People cannot think if we pluck the neurons out of their brains; but if we study only neurons, we have only a slender chance of getting at intelligence.

Still, some critics argue that computers cannot be intelligent because digital hardware made of silicon can never do what brains made of neurons do. Their position is weakened by the hierarchy argument and the lack of solid knowledge about what the unthinkably tangled neuropil does.

Myth: Probabilistic Machinery Causes Inspiration and Explains Free Will

People love explanations. Even when something defies analysis, default explanations fill the void, allowing uncomfortable puzzles to be settled with a minimum of fuss. Many ancient Greeks supported Socrates' opinion that deep, inexplicable thoughts come from the gods. Today's equivalent to those gods is the erratic, even probabilistic neuron. It is more likely that increased randomness of neural behavior is the problem of the epileptic and the drunk, not the advantage of the brilliant. Powerful computer intelligence will rest on description, representation, problem solving, and other powerful ideas, not on disorder.

Myth: Computers Can Never Appreciate Aesthetics

It is argued that creative arts of various sorts never can be approached scientifically. Beauty must be felt, it cannot be reduced to rules and rational thinking. Even the attempt eviscerates.

Certainly some artists find it difficult to vocalize what they do, but this is not a proof that computers can never create or enjoy a painting, a play, or a symphony. Indeed smart computers will undoubtedly find art a challenge since descriptions and interactions of descriptions must surely be central to understanding why any art form is interesting, moving, pleasing, disquieting, or new.

In any event, if computers do get good at artistic craftsmanship, there may be some question about wherein the art lies. If a person writes a program capable of 10,000 string quartets a day, do those quartets constitute the art? Probably not. Oddly, but inevitably, the art will be in the program.

Myth: Intelligence Can Never Be Understood

Of all the myths, this is perhaps the nearest to truth, but for an unexpected reason. To be intelligent is to be mysterious. "How did he know that?" we say. As long as the origin of an idea is obscure, its invention seems profound, but as soon as the explanation surfaces, we wonder, "Why didn't I think of that, it's trivial!" As soon as a process is dissected, studied, and grasped, the intelligence invariably seems to vanish.

Much the same happens when programs are studied. Vintage performance becomes *vin ordinaire* once details are exposed and limitations are seen. Instead of embracing a system's intelligence, study dilutes it. One must recognize this natural tendency or it leads to a poor attitude.

SUMMARY

■ Answering questions about knowledge is the first step in learning to be an expert at any sort of problem solving. What kind of knowledge is involved? How should it be represented? How much is there? What knowledge specifically? Concepts uncovered to cope with these questions when creating computer problem solvers appear to be good for amplifying human intelligence as well.

■ DENDRAL is a problem-solving system designed to help organic chemists understand mass spectrograms. It uses the spectrograms twice, once to guide a structure generator and once to select the best structure generated. Production rules are used to decide how the spectrogram should specify required and forbidden substructures for the structure generator, and they are used inside the structure generator as well.

■ The MYCIN system also demonstrates problem-solving power that may be able to help physicians understand and treat certain infections. It is basically a backward-running deduction system.

■ People creating computer intelligence and people studying human education have much to say to one another. In particular, teaching children to program helps explain important elements of human thought to them through analogy.

■ Powerful ideas accessible through experiment with simple turtle programs include the notions of state, input, subgoal, feedback, iteration, recursion, and debugging.

■ There are many myths about human and computer intelligence.

REFERENCES

■ B. Buchanan, G. Sutherland, and E. A. Feigenbaum, "Heuristic DENDRAL: A Program for Generating Explanatory Hypotheses in Organic Chemistry," in *Machine Intelligence 4,* American Elsevier, New York, 1969.

■ Randall Davis, Bruce Buchanan, and Edward Shortliffe, "Production Rules as a Representation for a Knowledge-Based Consultation Program," *Artificial Intelligence,* vol. 8, 1977. A good overview of work on the MYCIN program.

■ Richard O. Duda, Peter E. Hart, and Nils J. Nilson, *Subjective Bayesian Methods for Rule-Based Inference Systems,* TR-124, Artificial Intelligence Center, Stanford Research Institute, Menlo Park, California, 1976. A better theory of how to move plausibility estimates through a Production System's chain of reasoning.

■ Peter Hart, "Progress on a Computer Based Consultant," *Advance Papers of the Fourth International Joint Conference on Artificial Intelligence,* available through the M.I.T. Artificial Intelligence Laboratory, Cambridge, Massachusetts, 1975.

■ David Waltz, "Natural Language Access to a Large Data Base: an Engineering Approach," *Advance Papers of the Fourth International Joint Conference on Artificial Intelligence,* available through the M.I.T. Artificial Intelligence Laboratory, Cambridge, Massachusetts, 1975.

■ Seymour Papert and Cynthia Solomon, "Twenty Things to do with a Computer," AI-M-248, The Artificial Intelligence Laboratory, Massachusetts Institute of Technology, Cambridge, Massachusetts, 1971. A famous paper showing how children learn by teaching computers. Language, music, geometry, and physics are typical of the disciplines computers make interesting and fun.

■ Seymour Papert, "Uses of Technology to Enhance Education," AI-M-298, The Artificial Intelligence Laboratory, Massachusetts Institute of Technology, Cambridge, Massachusetts, 1973. Original source of the discussion on turtle migration.

■ Marvin Minsky, "Matter, Mind, and Models," in *Semantic Information Processing*, edited by Marvin Minsky, The M.I.T. Press, Cambridge, Massachusetts, 1968. Minsky argues that free will is a human device required because each person craves explanations for his own behavior but must necessarily obtain explanations using an internal model of himself which is incomplete. Free will is that part of behavior determined by mechanisms which lie outside of those in the model.

■ Joseph Weizenbaum, *Computer Power and Human Reason,* W. H. Freeman, San Francisco, 1976. Weizenbaum argues, in part, that there are areas of human activity that computers should not get involved in no matter how intelligent they may become.

10
UNDERSTANDING PROGRAMMING

The purpose of this brief chapter is to explain why understanding programming is important and why LISP is the language to start with.

THE ROLE OF PROGRAMMING

One must see some examples of intelligent processing developed all the way down to the level of programs if one is to have a deep, as well as a broad, understanding of the issues. Seeing some concepts in program form is *de rigueur* for the most serious students. There is an artificial intelligence without programs but it is a bit thin by comparison. There are many reasons.

Programs Are Testable

Artificial Intelligence is a laboratory science. Theories about intelligence can be verified or denied by experiments with a flexibility and precision previously impossible. If there is a question about the importance of knowing the allowable interpretations for certain junctions in a scene analysis problem, then it is a simple matter to turn off access to the junction table entries for those junctions. It is not a simple matter to ask a person to forget what he knows about them. He does not know what he knows, and even if he did, he could not turn it off.

Programming Has Led to New and Powerful Ideas about Representing Knowledge

Even after one elementary programming course, people often use the metaphors of programming and computing to describe their own thinking:

I don't have any procedures for dealing with that.

Let's reload and start over with a trace.

Those nuts are stuck in a loop.

It is wrong to think of this use of language as merely eccentric and cute. The language of computation is in part the language of process and in part the language of data structures. Its terms and metaphors therefore offer an important contribution to the vocabulary for thinking about thought.

Programmed Implementations Encourage Rigor

For a theory to be manifested in operating programs, it must be exact and fully specified. Hand-waving is not only not allowed, it is not possible.

Working Programs Manifestly Bound the Information-Processing Power Required for the Task Performed

It is dangerous to speculate on human thinking processes and to postulate theories based on operationally sufficient programs. At the very least, however, the operationally sufficient program provides a variety of upper bounds on how much is required to do the task. How much of what? The bound may be in terms of facts known, lines of program used, words of memory required, or other measures which may not strike everyone as completely relevant and meaningful. Yet these bounds are bounds, and until equally rigorous and precise measures of information-processing power are offered, they stand as the only measures that say *something* about inherent task complexity. To be sure, one programmer's code may be half as long as another's, and some languages use more memory than others, but this makes little difference. The general state of our understanding of intelligence makes numbers with large variance quite acceptable.

Programs Can Be Crisp, Exact Specifications of Theories

Occasionally, after seeing what a program can do, someone will ask for a specification of the theory behind it. Often the correct response is that the program *is* the theory.

How can this be? Suppose there is a Utopia in which everyone is a computer programmer. Suppose further that the tax law in this Utopia has become convoluted beyond recognition and certainly beyond calculation by hand. Surely it is inevitable that the Utopian legislature consider funding the development of a program to compute taxes, since private companies have created tax programs in places where hardly anyone knows about programming. But how can any program be certified to perform exactly in accordance with the complicated tax law? The legislators may argue but the answer is clear. Proving a correspondence is unnecessary. The program itself can *be* the tax law!

But can a program be a theory of language comprehension or scene analysis? Certainly. After all, a theory is a description that usefully encompasses some phenomenon. It may be useful in that it summarizes many facts, demonstrates regularity, or provides predictive power. Historically, mathematics has been the fundamental structure in which most theories have been embodied because mathematics can be crisp, precise, and predictive, but certainly programs, if written in a suitably high level, expressive language, can perform the same function. Programs can be crisp descriptions of processes. Their structure can reflect the structure of the problems they are designed for. They have enormous predictive power. And indeed, programming can provide the student of intelligence with the same sort of tool that mathematics provides the student of older sciences.

THE ROLE OF LISP

There has been a kind of tower-of-Babel disaster of computer languages. Fortunately, however, only a few are used in Artificial Intelligence work, and of these LISP is the first among equals.

LISP Is Broadly Used

LISP is like English in human communication in that it is the language that everyone should learn at some stage, and if it should be the first language learned, so much the better. After LISP is understood, other important basic languages for Artificial Intelligence like SAIL and POP-2 are easy by virtue of their analogous forms.

Historically, all contemporary languages for Artificial Intelligence were antedated by IPL, a language developed in the 1950s at Carnegie-Mellon University by Newell, Shaw, and Simon. Having introduced many key ideas, IPL served its purpose with distinction and is now more or less extinct.

LISP Is Easy to Learn

Happily LISP is an easy language to learn, perhaps the easiest. Anyone can learn LISP. At one time LISP was thought to be a difficult language, but that was primarily a side effect of the available documentation. There is no multiplicity of obfuscating syntax rules to learn and a few hours of study is enough to understand some very interesting programs. Previous exposure to some other more common language like FORTRAN or PL/1 is not necessary at all. Indeed such experience can be something of a handicap for there can be a serious danger of developing a bad accent. Those languages do things differently and instruction-by-instruction translation makes for awkward construction.

One reason LISP is easy to learn is that its syntax is extremely simple. Curiously, it became so by accident. John McCarthy, LISP's inventor, originally used a sort of old LISP that is about as hard to read as old English. At one point, however, he wished to use LISP in a context that required both the programs and the data to have the same syntactic form. The resulting form of LISP, which McCarthy intended to use only for developing a piece of mathematics, caught on and quickly became the standard.

SUMMARY

■ Computers play a key role in Artificial Intelligence because they provide a way to make precise, testable theories which are rich in process ingredients. It follows that understanding programs is necessary for complete understanding of Artificial Intelligence.

■ LISP is an outstanding example of the languages used in Artificial Intelligence. It is easy to learn.

REFERENCES

■ John McCarthy, "Recursive Functions of Symbolic Expressions and their Computation by Machine," *Communications of the Association for Computing Machinery,* vol. 3, 1960, and "A Basis for a Mathematical Theory of Computation," in *Proceedings of the Western Joint Computer Conference,* 1961. The original papers on LISP. Of historic interest.

■ John McCarthy *et al, LISP 1.5 Programmer's Manual,* M.I.T. Press, Cambridge, Massachusetts, 1965. An interesting, although quaintly dated commentary on LISP and its early implementation. This book is the source of the misadvised opinion that LISP is hard to learn.

There are a number of LISP textbooks. The following, in particular, may be of interest:

■ C. Weissman, *LISP 1.5 Primer,* Dickenson Publishing Company, Belmont, California, 1967. A very good, but now aging text. It introduces two notions purposely omitted here, namely dotted pairs and EVALQUOTE. We omit the dotted-pair notation because it is a source of great confusion for beginners. We avoid EVALQUOTE because its use is now obsolete.

■ Laurent Siklossy, *Let's Talk LISP,* Prentice-Hall, Englewood Cliffs, New Jersey, 1976. A more recent textbook with many good points.

For other languages of Artificial Intelligence, the following are recommended:

■ J. Feldman *et al,* "Recent Developments in SAIL — An ALGOL-Based Language for Artificial Intelligence," *FJCC Proceedings,* 1972.

■ Allen Newell (editor), *Information Processing Language V Manual,* Prentice-Hall, Englewood Cliffs, New Jersey, 1961. Of historic interest.

■ Carl Hewitt, "Description and Theoretical Analysis (using Schemata) of PLANNER: A Language for Proving Theorems and Manipulating Models in a Robot," PhD thesis, AI-TR-258, The Artificial Intelligence Laboratory, Massachusetts Institute of Technology, Cambridge, Massachusetts, 1972. A long dissertation, as the title suggests, somewhat difficult to penetrate, but important because of the development of demons. Nearly everyone prefers to get at the key ideas through the "MICRO-PLANNER Reference Manual" cited next.

■ Gerald Sussman, Terry Winograd, and Eugene Charniak, "MICRO-PLANNER Reference Manual," AI-M-203A, The Artificial Intelligence Laboratory, Massachusetts Institute of Technology, Cambridge, Massachusetts, 1971. Hewitt's PLANNER rendered easy to understand. PLANNER, however, had a short life. Evolutionary pressure destroyed it in favor of Hewitt's later ACTOR idea and Sussman and McDermott's CONNIVER.

■ R. Reboh and Earl Sacerdoti, "A Preliminary QLISP Manual," SRI Artificial Intelligence Center Technical Note 81, Stanford Research Institute, Menlo Park, California, 1973.

■ R. M. Burstall, J. S. Collins, and R. J. Popplestone, *Programming in POP2,* Edinburgh University Press, Edinburgh, Scotland, 1971.

■ J. M. Davies, "POPLAR: A POP-2 PLANNER," MIP-R-89, School of Artificial Intelligence, University of Edinburgh, Scotland, 1971.

■ Carl Hewitt, "How to Use What You Know," in *Advance Papers of the Fourth International Joint Conference on Artificial Intelligence,* available from The Artificial Intelligence Laboratory, Massachusetts Institute of Technology, Cambridge, Massachusetts. A good introduction to ACTORS.

■ Gerald Sussman and Drew McDermott, "Why Conniving is Better than Planning," AI-M-255A, The Artificial Intelligence Laboratory, Massachusetts Institute of Technology, Cambridge, Massachusetts, 1972. A treatment of PLANNER's defects and the proposal of alternatives in the form of CONNIVER. Substantial arguments are made against automatic backup. Contexts are introduced.

■ D. G. Bobrow and B. Raphael, "New Programming Languages for AI Research," *Association for Computing Machinery Computing Surveys,* vol. 6, no. 3, September 1974. A comparison of the principal programming languages in Artificial Intelligence with control structure discussions.

11
BASIC
LISP
PROGRAMMING

LISP is the language explained here because it is one of the standard vehicles for encoding intelligence-exhibiting processes. Like other languages in its class, LISP is an invaluable aid to process descriptions. Important ideas can be discussed without it, but at some level one hits a brick wall and mystery sets in. We use LISP the way other sciences use differential equations, or a Boolean algebra, because LISP and LISP-like languages are the mathematics of Artificial Intelligence, the precise, unambiguous framework in which theories are ultimately cast. Artificial Intelligence without one of these languages is physics for poets — laudable and useful, but not completely serious.

SYMBOL MANIPULATION

As with other computer languages, the best way to learn LISP is bravely, jumping right into interesting programs. We will therefore look occasionally at code exhibiting mechanisms beyond the readers' current level of complete understanding with a view toward moving as quickly as possible into exciting applications.

To get started, imagine being seated in front of a computer. You begin as if engaging in a conversation, with LISP tossing back "answers" in response to typed input. Suppose, for example, that you would like some help adding numbers. The proper incantation would be

```
(PLUS 3.14 2.71)
```

to which LISP would agreeably respond

```
5.85
```

This is a very simple example of LISP's ability to handle arithmetic. Elementary examples of symbol manipulation are equally straightforward. Suppose, for example, we are interested in keeping track of some facts needed in connection with understanding a children's story about, say, a robot. It might well be important to remember that certain children are friends of the robot. Typically a name is required to denote such a group, and the name FRIENDS will do as well as any other. If Dick and Jane and Sally are friends, this fact could be remembered by typing this line:

```
(SETQ FRIENDS '(DICK JANE SALLY))
```

The single quote mark is something to ignore for now. The SETQ associates FRIENDS with (DICK JANE SALLY) so that typing FRIENDS now causes the list of friends to be typed in response:

```
FRIENDS
  (DICK JANE SALLY)
```

There could be a similar list established for enemies:

```
(SETQ ENEMIES '(TROLL GRINCH GHOST))
```

But because friends and enemies tend to be dynamic categories in children's worlds, it is often necessary to change a particular individual's category. The ghost ceases to be an enemy and becomes a friend after typing two lines like this:

```
(SETQ ENEMIES (DELETE 'GHOST ENEMIES))
(SETQ FRIENDS (CONS 'GHOST FRIENDS))
```

The first line changes the remembered list of enemies to what it was minus the entry GHOST. The second line would be simpler if CONS were replaced by something more mnemonic like ADD, but we are stuck with historical convention. In any event FRIENDS and ENEMIES have been changed such that we now get properly altered responses:

```
ENEMIES
  (TROLL GRINCH)
FRIENDS
  (GHOST DICK JANE SALLY)
```

Later we will see how to write a program that does the same job. In particular we will understand how the following creates a program named NEWFRIEND for changing a person from enemy into friend:

```
(DEFINE (NEWFRIEND NAME)
        (SETQ ENEMIES (DELETE NAME ENEMIES))
        (SETQ FRIENDS (CONS NAME FRIENDS)))
```

With NEWFRIEND, the previous elevation of GHOST can be achieved more simply by typing only

```
(NEWFRIEND 'GHOST)
```

LISP Programs and Data Are Constructed out of S-Expressions

We already should make note of some important points. First, requests to LISP are always surrounded by a left and right parenthesis. We call the result a list and speak of its elements. In our very first example, the list (PLUS 3.14 2.71) has three elements, PLUS, 3.14, and 2.71.

Note the peculiar location of the function PLUS, standing strangely before the two things to be added rather than between them as in ordinary arithmetic notation. Uniformity dictates this choice. In LISP the function to be performed is always given first, followed then by the things that the function is to work with, the arguments. Thus 3.14 and 2.71 are the arguments given to the function PLUS.

Let us look at more examples of this so called prefix notation. We will stick to arithmetic for the moment since that domain is initially more comfortable than symbol manipulation. LISP's responses are indented in order to keep things straight.

```
(DIFFERENCE 3.14 2.71)
  .43
(TIMES 9 3)
  27
(QUOTIENT 9 3)
  3
(MAX 2 4 3)
  4
(MIN 2 4 3)
  2
(ADD1 6)
  7
(SUB1 6)
  5
(SQRT 4)
  2
(EXPT 2 3)
  8
(MINUS 8)
  -8
```

Of about forty common functions in LISP, about half are highly mnemonic arithmetic operations like these. Note that MAX selects the largest of the numbers given as arguments. As with MAX, PLUS and TIMES can be asked to work on more than two arguments. There is never any confusion because the end of the argument sequence is signaled clearly by the right parenthesis. SQRT of course takes the square root. ADD1, SUB1, SQRT, and MINUS all deal with a single argument.

Now consider the expression

```
(PLUS (TIMES 2 2) (QUOTIENT 2 2))
```

If we think of this as directions for something to do, it is easy to see that the subexpression (TIMES 2 2) evaluates to 4, (QUOTIENT 2 2) evaluates to 1, and these results fed in turn to PLUS gives 5 as the result. But if the whole expression is viewed as a kind of list, then we see that PLUS is the first element, the entire expression (TIMES 2 2) is the second element, and (QUOTIENT 2 2) is the third. Thus lists themselves can be elements of other lists. Said another way, we permit lists in which individual elements are lists themselves.

Things like PLUS and 3.14 which have obvious meaning, as well as things like FOO, B27, and 123XYZ, are called atoms. Both atoms and lists are often called s-expressions, s being short for symbolic.

CAR and CDR Take Lists Apart

Examples from arithmetic are simple, but arithmetic does not expose the talent of LISP for manipulating s-expressions. Suppose we have an s-expression like (FAST COMPUTERS ARE NICE). We might like to chip off the first element leaving (COMPUTERS ARE NICE), or we might like to insert a new first element producing something like (BIG FAST COMPUTERS ARE NICE). It is time to look at such manipulations starting with basic techniques for dissecting lists. In particular we must understand the functions CAR, CDR, APPEND, and CONS. A regrettable historical convention has left three of these four key functions terribly nonmnemonic — their meaning simply has to be memorized.

Some examples will help explain how the basic CAR, CDR, APPEND, and CONS functions work. Do not worry about the single quote marks that appear. They will be explained very soon.

To work. CAR returns the first element in a list:

```
(CAR '(FAST COMPUTERS ARE NICE))
  FAST
(CAR '(A B C))
  A
(CAR '((A  B) C))
  (A B)
```

Note in the last example that the argument given to CAR was the two-element list ((A B) C). The first element is itself a list, (A B), and being the first element of the argument, (A B) is returned by CAR.

CDR does the complementary thing. It accepts a list and returns what remains after the first element is removed.

```
(CDR '(FAST COMPUTERS ARE NICE))
  (COMPUTERS ARE NICE)
(CDR '(A B C))
  (B C)
(CDR '((A B) C))
  (C)
```

Evaluation Is Often Purposely Inhibited by Quoting

Now it is time to understand those single quote marks that have been appearing. We will use the fact that CAR and CDR operations can be nested together just like the arithmetic functions. To pick out the second element of some list, the first thing to use is CDR and the second is CAR. Thus if we want the second element of (A B C), it might seem reasonable to write this:

```
(CAR (CDR (A B C)))
```

There is a problem, however. We want CDR to take (A B C) and give back (B C). Then CAR would certainly return B, the second element in the original list. But how is LISP to know where the specification of what to do leaves off and the data to be manipulated begins? Looking at the embedded list

```
(A B C)
```

LISP might legitimately think that A is some sort of function, perhaps one defined by the user. On the other hand

```
(CDR (A B C))
```

is certainly a list, and the first element is surely CDR. Thus

```
(CAR (CDR (A B C)))
```

could well result in an answer of CDR!

The question is how far down into an s-expression to go with the evaluation process. LISP needs help in making this decision. The user specifies where to stop evaluation by supplying an evaluation-inhibiting signal in the form of a single quote character, '.

Thus

```
(CAR (CDR '(A B C)))
```

returns B because the quote mark prevents LISP from wading in and thinking of

```
(A B C)
```

as an s-expression in which A is a function to be applied to B and C. Instead, (A B C) is given to CDR which then hands (B C) to CAR resulting finally in just plain B.

Moving the quote mark changes the result. If we type (CAR '(CDR (A B C))), then LISP does not try to take the CDR of anything but simply gives the s-expression (CDR (A B C)) to CAR as a list to work on, resulting in CDR since CDR is the first element.

Leaving out the quote mark altogether would result in an effort to use A as a function. There is no function supplied by LISP and if none had been defined by the user, LISP would choke and report an undefined function error.

■ It is important to know that the scope of the quoting mechanism is exactly the immediately following s-expression. A quote in front of a list prevents any attempt at evaluating the list as if it specified something to do.

■ There is no "unquote" mechanism. That is, there is no way of turning on the evaluation process somewhere down inside of a quoted list.

Composing CARs and CDRs Makes Programming Easier

When many CARs and CDRs are needed to pick some item out of a nested spot inside an s-expression, it is usually convenient to substitute a composite function of the form C-R, C--R, C---R, or C----R. Each — is either an A, signifying CAR, or D, signifying CDR. Thus (CADR '(A B C)) is completely equivalent to (CAR (CDR '(A B C))).

APPEND and CONS Construct Lists

While CAR and CDR take things apart, APPEND and CONS put them together. APPEND strings together the elements of all lists supplied as arguments:

```
(APPEND '(A B) '(C D))
  (A B C D)
```

Note the need for the quote marks to protect A and C from being treated as functions to be applied. Be sure to understand that APPEND combines the elements of the lists supplied on the top level only:

```
(APPEND '((A) (B)) '((C) (D)))
```

yields

```
((A) (B) (C) (D))
```

not

```
(A B C D)
```

CONS is a sort of complement to CAR. That is, rather than chipping off the first element of a list, it takes a list and inserts a new first element. Let us adopt a convention by which the words between angle brackets are taken as descriptions of what should appear in the position occupied. Then the CONS function can be described as follows:

```
(CONS <new first element> <some list> )
```

Thus we have

```
(CONS 'A '(B C))
  (A B C)
```

Now if we type (CONS '(A B) '(C D)), then the result is ((A B) C D) in which the list (A B) has become the first element of a list which was just (C D) before.

ATOMS \ PROPERTIES	VALUE	FATHER	PURPOSE	BADWORD
VITAMIN	B12			
PLUS			ARITHMETIC	NIL
DAMN				T
ATOM				
BAR	(THIS IS A LIST)		DRINKING	
LEIF		ERIK		
T	T			
NIL	NIL			

Figure 11-1 Atoms and their properties form a table of property values. In the example, ERIK is the value of the FATHER property of the atom LEIF. The VALUE property is a special case.

Note how CONS and APPEND differ:

```
(CONS '(A B) '(C D))
   ((A B) C D)
(APPEND '(A B) '(C D))
   (A B C D)
```

Atoms Have Values

So far we have seen how symbolic structures can be taken apart and put together by evaluating lists which begin with CAR, CDR, APPEND, and CONS. We have also seen how arithmetic can be done by evaluating lists which begin with PLUS, DIFFERENCE, and other similar functions. Indeed it seems like LISP's goal is always to evaluate something and return a value. This is true for atoms as well as lists. Suppose we type a plain atom and wait for LISP to respond:

X

On seeing X, LISP tries to return a value for it, just as it would if some s-expression like (PLUS 3 4) were typed. But for an atom, the value is something looked up in a table rather than the result of some computation as when dealing with lists.

Imagine a table with atom names along one axis and property names along another. See figure 11-1. The value is simply one of the properties that atom can have. It is somewhat special in that it is the result that the atom yields up when evaluated.

■   T and NIL are special atoms in that their values are preset to T and NIL. That is, the value of T is T and the value of NIL is NIL.

■   All numbers are also special in the same way. The value of a number is the same number.

Other property names and values are left to the imagination of the user. An example is the FATHER property. We note from the table that the value of the FATHER property of the atom LEIF is ERIK. Note that the value of a property can be any s-expression. The PARENTS property of LEIF could be a list of two atoms, each naming one of LEIF's parents. Functions for assigning property values and retrieving them will be described later. Right now it is sufficient to remember that the value property of an atom is just a special case of a more general notion.

Note, incidentally, that the word *value* is being used in two senses: first, we talk of the value of some particular property of some particular atom; and second, we talk of the special property whose name is *value*. Thus it is not a joke to talk of the value of the value property, although generally one just calls this the value.

In the special case of a value property the value is established by a special function, SET. It causes the value of its second argument to become the value property of the first argument. Typing (SET 'L '(A B)) results in a value of (A B) for the expression. But more importantly, there is a side effect because (A B) is attached to L as the value property. If we now type L, we see that (A B) comes back:

L
   (A B)

Thus the expression (SET <arg1> <arg2>) is executed mainly for the side effect of value assignment to the atom <arg1>.

Now since the value of L is established to be (A B), L can be used in working through some examples of the basic list manipulating functions. These illustrate that LISP seeks out the value of atoms not only when they are typed in by themselves, but also when the atoms appear as arguments to functions. The errors shown occur because a function is given an atom when it expects a list.

L
   (A B)
'L
   L
(CAR L)
   A
(CAR 'L)
   ERROR
(CDR L)
   (B)

```
(CDR 'L)
  ERROR
(APPEND 'L L)
  ERROR
(APPEND L L)
  (A B A B)
(CONS 'L L)
  (L A B)
(CONS L L)
  ((A B) A B)
(SET 'A 'B)
  B
(SET 'B 'C)
  C
A
  B
B
  C
(EVAL A)
  C
```

Note how the function EVAL explicitly calls for another round of evaluation. The atom A is first evaluated because it is the unquoted argument to a function. The result is then evaluated because the function is EVAL. EVAL causes whatever the value is to be evaluated!

A Predicate Is a Function Whose Value Is T or NIL

Our next job is to understand a collection of functions called predicates. A predicate is a function whose value is limited to be one of two special atoms, T or NIL. These values of T and NIL correspond to the conversational notions of true and false.

```
(SET 'L '(A B))
  (A B)
(ATOM L)
  NIL
(ATOM 'L)
  T
(ATOM '(A B))
  NIL
(EQUAL L L)
  T
(EQUAL L 'L)
  NIL
(EQUAL L '(A B))
  T
```

NOT returns T only if its argument is NIL. NULL checks to see if its argument
is an empty list.

```
(NOT NIL)
  T
(NOT T)
  NIL
(NOT L)
  NIL
(NOT 'L)
  NIL
(NULL '())
  T
(NULL '(A B C))
  NIL
```

MEMBER returns T only if the first argument is an element of the following
list. It is not enough for the first argument to be buried somewhere in the second
argument: it must be a top-level element.

```
(MEMBER 'A '(A B))
  T
(MEMBER 'A L)
  T
(MEMBER 'A '((A B) (C D)))
  NIL
```

For some further examples, let us first establish values for X as well as L. It
is convenient to introduce the function SETQ which is like SET except that SETQ
makes no attempt to evaluate the first argument. This makes SETQ a sort of idiom
because generally all arguments are evaluatd before a function goes to work. SETQ
is much more popular than SET.

```
(SETQ L '(A B))
  (A B)
(SETQ X 4)
  4
```

Often multiple applications of SETQ are run together. The odd numbered arguments
are not evaluated but the even ones are, as would be expected. Thus one SETQ can
do the work of the two above:

```
(SETQ L '(A B) X 4)
  4
```

Now using the values established for L and X, we have the following:

```
(NUMBERP X)
  T
(NUMBERP 'X)
  NIL
```

```
(NUMBERP L)
   NIL
(NUMBERP 'L)
   NIL
(GREATERP X 2)
   T
(LESSP X 2)
   NIL
(ZEROP X)
   NIL
(EQUAL X 4)
   T
```

Note that several predicates end in *P,* a mnemonic for *p*redicate. The predicate ATOM is an unfortunate exception that would tend to suggest that LIST is a predicate too. It is not. LIST is a function which surrounds its arguments by parentheses, thus making a new list more deeply nested by one set of parentheses than any of its arguments:

```
(SETQ L '(A B))
   (A B)
(LIST '(A B))
   ((A B))
(LIST L)
   ((A B))
(LIST L L)
   ((A B) (A B))
(APPEND L L)
   (A B A B)
(APPEND (LIST L) (LIST L))
   ((A B) (A B))
(MEMBER L L)
   NIL
(MEMBER L (LIST L))
   T
(MEMBER L (LIST L L))
   T
```

Predicates Help COND Select a Value among Alternatives

The predicates are most often used to determine which of several possible paths a program should follow. The actual path or branch taken is most often determined by predicates in conjunction with the branching function COND, and COND is therefore an extremely common function. Regrettably, it has a somewhat peculiar syntax. The function name COND is followed by some number of lists, each of which contains a test and something to return if the test works out. Thus the general syntax is as follows:

```
(COND <listl>
      <list2>
         .
      .)
```

Each list is called a clause. Breaking the clause syntax up into more detail, we have this:

```
(COND ( <a test> ... <a result> )
      ( <a test> ... <a result> )
         .
         .
         .
      ( <a test> ... <a result> ))
```

One of the evaluated result elements will be the value of the entire COND. The idea is to cruise through the lists looking only at the first elements until one is found whose value is *not* NIL. Then everything else in the winning list is evaluated and the last thing evaluated is returned as the value of the COND. Evidently any expressions standing between the first and the last elements in a COND list must be there only for side effects since they certainly cannot influence the value of the COND.

There are two special cases:

■   If no winning list is found, COND returns NIL.

■   If the winning list consists of only one element, then the value of that element itself is returned. Said another way, the test and result elements may be the same.

It may seem strange, incidentally, that T is not strictly required to trigger a clause, and anything other than NIL will do. This is a desirable feature because it allows test functions whose outcomes are not limited to T and NIL values as predicates are. There will be many examples later.

While on the subject of strange things, one particular one deserves special attention:

■   The empty list, ( ), and NIL are equivalent in all respects. For example, they satisfy the equal predicate: (EQUAL NIL '( )) returns T.

Some say the reason this was originally arranged has to do with the instruction set of the ancient 709 computer. Others believe the identity was always known to be a programming convenience. No one seems to know for sure. In any case, the first element in a COND clause is frequently a variable whose value is a list that may be empty. If the list is empty, it does not trigger the COND clause since it acts like NIL. On the other side, occasional bugs derive from the fact that (ATOM '( )) is T.

PROGRAMMING IN LISP

We now have some ingredients. Let us see how they can be combined into new functions using the function DEFINE. It has the following syntax:

```
(DEFINE <form> <process description>)
```

As before, the angle brackets delineate descriptions of things. (The descriptions may denote atoms, lists, or even fragments as appropriate.) DEFINE does not evaluate its arguments. It just looks at them and establishes a function definition as a side effect. The value returned is the function name, but this is of little consequence.

DEFINE Creates New Functions

Using DEFINE, a primitive POWER function limited to powers of 0, 1, and 2 is created as follows:

```
(DEFINE (POWER M N)
        (COND ((EQUAL N 0) 1)
              ((EQUAL N 1) M)
              ((EQUAL N 2) (TIMES M M))))
   POWER
```

Once defined, POWER is easy to use:

```
(POWER 3 0)
  1
(POWER 3 1)
  3
(POWER 3 2)
  9
```

Note how the part of the definition indicated by <form> shows what the function looks like when used. It gives the name of the function and indicates the number of arguments involved. Importantly, it also shows how the arguments are to be used by the function. Without displaying the variable names somewhere in the definition in the order they are to be given to the function, there would be no way of deciding if (POWER 3 2) means 3^2 or 2^3 since there is no way of knowing if we want

$$M — 3 \qquad \text{or} \qquad M \diagdown 3$$
$$N — 2 \qquad\qquad\qquad N \diagup 2$$

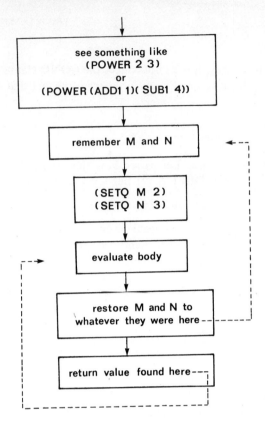

Figure 11-2 When entering a function, variables in the form part of the definition receive assignments which are used in the evaluation of the body. Variable values are restored to previous values when leaving.

What actually goes on when we use POWER is as if the action shown in figure 11-2 were happening.

Variables May Be Free or Bound

This process of assigning values to variables on entering a function is called LAMBDA binding for historical reasons.

Look at this nonsense function to be sure you have the idea:

```
(DEFINE (NONSENSE X)
        (SETQ X (SQRT X))
        (SETQ Y X))
   NONSENSE
(SETQ X 4)
   4
(SETQ Y 4)
   4
```

```
(NONSENSE 9)
   3
Y
   3
X
   4
```

The value of Y was permanently altered while that of X was not. Temporarily X was changed — it became 9 on entry to NONSENSE, and then 3 by virtue of the SETQ. The difference lies in the fact that X is assigned on entry and restored on exit, because it appears in the <form> part of the function definition. We say that X is bound with respect to NONSENSE while Y is free in the same context. It makes no sense to speak of a variable as bound or free unless we also specify with respect to what function the variable is free or bound.

Recursion Allows Functions to Use Themselves

We are ready to follow the history of variables in more complicated situations where the stored history may contain many remembered values for a single variable. This happens when a function solves problems by repeatedly simplifying them slightly and starting off fresh on the simplified forms. For example, to calculate the Nth power of some number, M, it is sufficient to do the job for the N-1th power because this result multiplied by M is the desired result for the Nth power. Definitions which describe a process partly in terms of fresh starts on simpler arguments are called recursive definitions. Let us look at a recursive POWER function expressed in LISP:

```
(DEFINE (POWER M N)
        (COND ((ZEROP N) 1)
              ((TIMES M (POWER M (SUB1 N)))))))
```

Using figure 11-3, we can easily follow the history of M and N as LISP evaluates (POWER 2 3). The convention used to show how the recursion works is a tree where the branches under a node represent fresh entries to the function as required by the computation at the parent node. Each entry is listed with its order in the sequence of entries to the function. Downward portions of the flow of control show the argument or arguments carried down while upward portions indicate the value returned.

Having seen recursion at work on a simple numerical problem, look at a recursive function that counts the atoms other than NIL in some given s-expression:

```
(DEFINE (COUNTATOMS S)
        (COND ((NULL S) 0)
              ((ATOM S) 1)
              (T (PLUS (COUNTATOMS (CAR S))
                       (COUNTATOMS (CDR S)))))))
```

The first line announces that the function COUNTATOMS of one argument, S, is about to be defined. The first two clauses of the COND enumerate the very

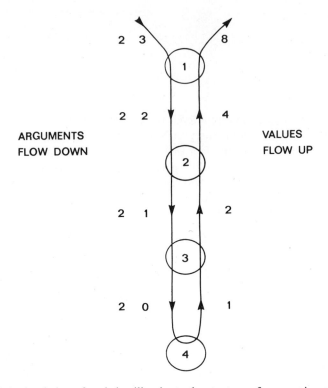

Figure 11-3 A simulation often helps illuminate the strategy of a recursive program. Here each copy of the POWER function reduces the value of N by one and passes it on until N is reduced to zero. The arrows show how control moves from one numbered application of POWER to another. Arguments are shown on the downward pointing arrows; values returned, on the upward.

simplest cases returning 0 for empty lists and 1 for atoms. The third clause handles other situations by converting big problems into smaller ones. Lists are broken up using CAR and CDR and COUNTATOMS is applied to both resulting fragments. Since every atom in the list is either in the CAR or the CDR, every atom gets counted. The PLUS combines the results together. Eventually, after perhaps many, many applications of itself, COUNTATOMS reduces the hard cases to something that either the first or the second COND clause can handle.

At this point it is helpful to see how COUNTATOMS can take an s-expression apart and reduce it successively to the simple cases. As shown in figure 11-4, the particular expression whose atoms are to be counted is (TIMES X (SQRT 4)). Note that the data expression itself is in the form of an expression one might think of executing for a value. Here then is an example of a program, COUNTATOMS, examining some other piece of program and performing a computation on it.

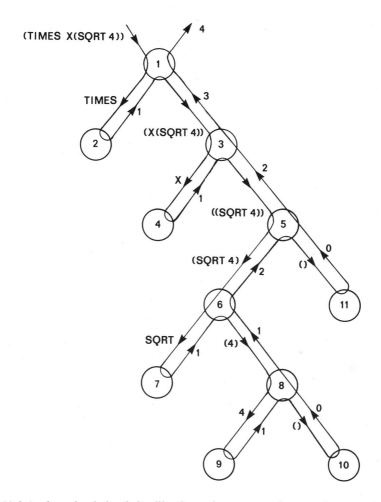

Figure 11-4 Again a simulation helps illuminate the strategy of a recursive program. Here the s-expression (TIMES X (SQRT 4)) is broken up into its constituent pieces by the function COUNTATOMS. The arrows show how control moves from one numbered application of the function to another. Arguments are shown on the downward pointing arrows; values returned, on the upward.

At each stage the argument to COUNTATOMS gets broken into two smaller pieces. Once the answers for both pieces are at hand, the PLUS adds the results together and returns the value to a higher-level place further up the tree.

Note that the T in COUNTATOMS insures that the last clause will be triggered if the others are not. A T is often seen in the last clause of a COND where it clearly establishes that the evaluation will not run off the end. The T is not really necessary, however, since the same values would result were it left out.

```
(DEFINE (COUNTATOMS S)
        (COND ((NULL S) 0)
              ((ATOM S) 1)
              ((PLUS (COUNTATOMS (CAR S))
                     (COUNTATOMS (CDR S))))))
```

This works because COND triggers on anything but NIL, not just T. PLUS can never produce a NIL, and the clause therefore triggers for sure just as if the T were there. Since the clause has only one element, that element is both first and last and provides both the test and the value returned.

Using a T is better programming practice because it clearly signals the fact that the programmer expects the last clause to be used when all else fails. Using a T clearly indicates that there can be no falling through the COND completely with the default value of NIL.

Dealing with Lists of Arguments Often Calls for MAPCAR and APPLY

A somewhat more elegant way to define programs like COUNTATOMS is through the functions MAPCAR and APPLY, two new functions which are very useful and very special in the way they handle their arguments.

MAPCAR is used when the same operation is to be performed on a whole list of things. Suppose for example that it is useful to add one to each number in a list of numbers. Then from

```
(1  2  3)
```

we would want

```
(2  3  4)
```

To accomplish such transformations with MAPCAR, one supplies the name of the operation together with a list of things to be handed one after the other to the operation.

```
(MAPCAR 'ADD1        ;function to work with
        '(1 2 3))    ;arguments to be fed to the function
   (2 3 4)
```

There is no restriction to functions of one variable, but if the function is a function of more than one variable, there must be a corresponding number of lists of things to feed the function. MAPCAR works something like an assembly machine, taking one element from each list of arguments and assembling them together for the function:

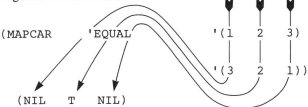

Consider now a common error which shows why the function APPLY is necessary. Suppose we want to add up a list of numbers, L.

```
(SETQ L '(4 7 2))
  (4 7 2)
```

Do we want to evaluate (PLUS L)? No! This is wrong because PLUS is expecting arguments which are numbers. But here PLUS is given one argument which is a *list* of numbers rather than an actual number. PLUS can only gag and choke, not knowing what to do with the unexpected argument form. It is as if we tried to evaluate (PLUS '(4 7 2)) instead of (PLUS 4 7 2).

To make PLUS work, we must use APPLY, which takes two arguments, a function name and a list, and arranges to have the function act on the elements in the list as if they appeared as proper arguments. Thus

```
(APPLY 'PLUS L)
  13
```

is a special case of the general form:

```
(APPLY <function description>
       <list of arguments>)
```

Now using APPLY and MAPCAR we can work up a more elegant way of counting atoms:

```
(DEFINE (COUNTATOMS S)
        (COND ((NULL S) 0)
              ((ATOM S) 1)
              (T (APPLY 'PLUS (MAPCAR 'COUNTATOMS S)))))
```

As suggested by the first two COND clauses, simple cases are handled as before. And once again, the objective is to reduce the more complex expressions to the simple ones. Only now MAPCAR is used to simplify s-expressions rather than CAR and CDR. This version of COUNTATOMS takes advantage of MAPCAR's talent in going after every element of a list with a specified function, in this case a recursive application of COUNTATOMS itself.

Now assuming for a moment that the function works, we see that the MAPCAR comes back with a list of numbers which must be added together. This is why

APPLY appears. PLUS wants numbers, not a list of numbers. APPLY does the appropriate interfacing and hands the list of numbers to PLUS as if each element in the list were itself an argument to PLUS.

Simulating COUNTATOMS is easier to follow than before since recursion is less deep and complicated. See figure 11-5.

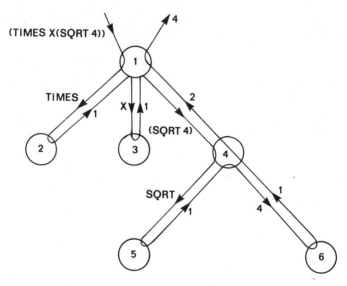

Figure 11-5 A version of COUNTATOMS using MAPCAR instead of CARs and CDRs exhibits less recursion. There are only six entries on three levels rather than eleven on six.

Now it is easy to modify COUNTATOMS to do other things. For example, to determine the depth of an s-expression, the following simple modifications to COUNTATOMS are all that is necessary: change the name to DEPTH, change the empty list and atom results, change PLUS to MAX, and insert ADD1. These changes yield DEPTH:

```
(DEFINE (DEPTH S)
        (COND ((NULL S) 1)
              ((ATOM S) 0)
              (T (ADD1 (APPLY 'MAX (MAPCAR 'DEPTH S)))))))
```

Figure 11-6 shows how DEPTH works on the same expression previously used to illustrate COUNTATOMS. Again at each branching, we see how MAPCAR splits up an expression into simpler elements to be worked on.

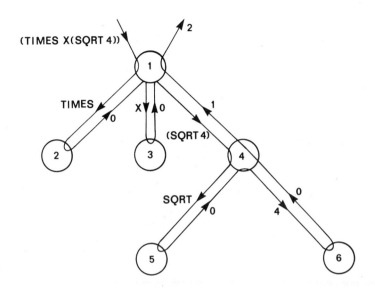

Figure 11-6 The recursion pattern for DEPTH is the same as the one for COUNTATOMS.

Local Definitions Are Handled Using LAMBDA

To introduce our next function, consider the problem of checking which elements in a list L are numbers between two limits named HIGH and LOW. One way would be to define TEST using GREATERP, a predicate which accepts any number of numerical arguments and returns T if those arguments appear in descending order:

```
(DEFINE (TEST N) (GREATERP HIGH N LOW))
```

Then we can write

```
(SETQ L '(4 7 2))
   (4 7 2)
(SETQ HIGH 7)
   7
(SETQ LOW 3)
   3
(MAPCAR 'TEST L)
   (T NIL NIL)
```

This is a little painful. Passing over a list with a simple procedure should not require going off somewhere to define a function. Why not make the programmer's intention more transparent by laying out the procedure at the spot where it is to be used.

```
(MAPCAR (DEFINE (TEST N) (GREATERP HIGH N LOW)) L)
```

DEFINE works because MAPCAR wants a function name and the value of DEFINE is the name of the function defined. But to avoid the proliferation of useless names, the name can be dropped if it is used only here! In this event, the lack of a function name is signaled by using something different from DEFINE to define the procedure. For historical reasons this new function defining "function" uses the name *LAMBDA*. The correct way to use a local definition would therefore follow the form of this example:

```
(MAPCAR '(LAMBDA (N) (GREATERP HIGH N LOW)) L)
```

■ No one would actually use DEFINE in a MAPCAR anyway since such a practice would be hopelessly inefficient — all the trouble of setting up a function with the inevitable overhead would happen each time the section of program is used. The DEFINE was used here only as a way of introducing LAMBDA-style definitions.

A longer but perhaps more informative name for locally defining functions would be DEFINE-ANONYMOUS. We will stick to LAMBDA for historical compatibility, but if confusion ever sets in, a good heuristic for understanding LAMBDA is to translate it to DEFINE-ANONYMOUS.

Note that LAMBDA definitions require a quote to suppress evaluation. Thus MAPCAR does not get a function name; instead it has a function description to deal with. No matter. MAPCAR can handle either a function name or a function description.

LAMBDA is sometimes used to interface functions to argument lists. The following example involves a function which determines how many times the atom X is to be found in the expression S. (Symbolic-mathematics systems make use of such a function to determine if an s-expression represents a constant.)

```
(DEFINE (PRESENCE X S)
        (COND ((EQUAL X S) 1)
              ((NULL S) 0)
              ((ATOM S) 0)
              (T (APPLY 'PLUS
                        (MAPCAR '(LAMBDA (E) (PRESENCE X E))
                                S))))))
```

Here we need LAMBDA to match PRESENCE, a function of two variables, to one list of MAPCAR arguments! Using 'PRESENCE in place of the LAMBDA definition illustrates a common error. Since PRESENCE expects two arguments and since there is only one list, S, to supply arguments, such a program is doomed.

The Interpreter Helps Explain How LISP Works

What exactly does LISP do with an expression that is typed in? What, that is, does the evaluation of an expression look like when splayed out into flow-chart form?

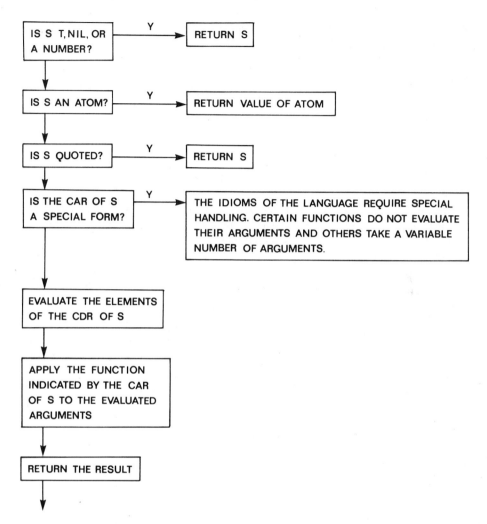

Figure 11-7 The EVAL function, core of the LISP interpreter.

The flowchart in figure 11-7 describes what happens in effect. Keep in mind that it may not be how things actually happen on the implementation level.

SUMMARY

- CAR, CDR, CONS, and APPEND are the basic symbol-manipulating functions. SET and SETQ are the basic assignment functions.

■ The quoting convention is needed to mark the point where LISP's evaluation process is to stop.

■ Predicates work with COND to direct the flow of control.

■ DEFINE allows users to create their own procedures. In LISP, functions can use themselves in their own definition. By definition LISP is therefore a recursive language.

REFERENCES

There are definitive manuals for the principal LISP dialects. The following are particularly noteworthy:

■ David A. Moon, *MACLISP Reference Manual,* Project MAC, Massachusetts Institute of Technology, Cambridge, Massachusetts, 1974. MACLISP differs from the LISP used in this book only in the syntax of the function defining function. MACLISP uses

```
(DEFUN <function name>
        (<argl> ... <argn>)
        <process description>)
```

where this book uses

```
(DEFINE (<function name> <argl> ... <argn>)
        <process description>)
```

■ Warren Teitelman, *INTERLISP Reference Manual,* available from Xerox Palo Alto Research Center, Palo Alto, California, or Bolt, Beranek, and Newman, Cambridge, Massachusetts, 1974.

12

THE

BLOCKS

WORLD

So far the programming examples have been a single function or perhaps a small collection of cooperating functions. Here we turn to a system of programs with the purpose of learning about some points of good programming style and practice. The task of the system is to create plans by which various blocks-world commands can be carried out. Typically the commands involve picking up an object or putting one object on another.

PLANNING MOTION SEQUENCES

In the course of moving things, it is often necessary to move obstructions out of the way and to make sure every object is properly supported at all times. It is assumed that the hand can grasp only objects which do not support anything. Furthermore, all objects rest on only one support.

The plan is created by either of two functions:

```
(PICK-UP <object name>)
```

```
(PUT-ON <object name> <support name>)
```

The plan has the form of a list of instructions for a physical arm or a simulated one. It is a series of MOVETO, GRASP, and UNGRASP instructions like the following one created for the situation in figure 12-1 in response to the command (PUT-ON B C):

```
((MOVETO 1 1 4)
 (GRASP A)
 (MOVETO 1 5 2)
 (UNGRASP A)
 (MOVETO 1 1 2)
 (GRASP B)
 (MOVETO 7 1 2)
 (UNGRASP B))
```

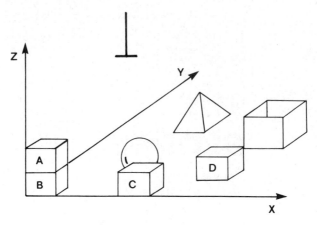

Figure 12-1 The robot's world.

The possible objects are blocks, boxes, pyramids, and balls. Each particular object is represented by an atom that carries a lot of information in the form of property-value pairs. All of these pairs constitute the atom's so-called property list. This is a typical property list for a block:

Property values for block B:

```
SUPPORTED-BY        TABLE
DIRECTLY-SUPPORTS   (A)
PLACE               (1 1 0)
SIZE                (2 2 2)
TYPE                BLOCK
COLOR               RED
```

The SIZE property of blocks is given as width, depth, and height. The SIZE property of pyramids and balls is given by the dimensions of circumscribing blocks as shown in figure 12-2.

Figure 12-2 To simplify position planning, the robot treats spheres and pyramids as if they were circumscribed by blocks.

For the hand, we have something like this:

Property values for the hand:

```
GRASPING                    NIL
POSITION                    (2 5 7)
```

GET and PUTPROP Are the Masters of Property Lists

To retrieve property values, GET is used:

```
(GET 'HAND 'GRASPING)
  NIL
(GET 'HAND 'POSITION)
  (2 5 7)
```

To place or replace a property value, the complementary function, PUTPROP, does the job:

```
(PUTPROP 'HAND 'A 'GRASPING)
  A
(PUTPROP 'HAND '(1 1 4) 'POSITION)
  (1 1 4)
```

Note that the value returned by PUTPROP is the same as the value it attaches to the atom given as the first argument. It is also good to know that GET returns NIL if no property with the given name exists yet.

PROG Creates Variables and Supports Iteration

PROG is a very popular function in the blocks-world system, partly because it creates new variables and partly because it provides one way to write procedures that loop, or said more elegantly, that iterate.

The syntax for PROG is easier to explain through an immediate example rather than through discussion. Here, therefore, is one way to write a factorial function:

```
(DEFINE (FACTORIAL N)
        (PROG (RESULT)
              (SETQ RESULT 1)
              LOOP
              (COND ((ZEROP N) (RETURN RESULT)))
              (SETQ RESULT (TIMES RESULT N))
              (SETQ N (SUB1 N))
              (GO LOOP)))
```

Several things must be explained. Keep in mind that the objective is to multiply n times n-1 times n-2 and so on down to 1. This will be accomplished by passing repeatedly through the code just after LOOP.

■ The arguments to a PROG are mostly s-expressions which are evaluated one after the other. If control runs off the end of a PROG, then NIL is returned, just as with COND.

■ The first position in a PROG is always occupied by a list of variables which are all bound on entering the PROG and restored to old values on exit. Each is given an initial value of NIL automatically.

■ Whenever the function RETURN is reached when evaluating a PROG, the PROG is terminated immediately. The value of the terminated PROG is the value of the argument to the RETURN that stopped the PROG.

■ Any atom appearing as an argument to a PROG is considered to be a position marker. These atoms mark places to which control is transferred by GO functions. (GO <tag>) transfers control to the marker named <tag>.

It is clear then that the factorial function works by looping through the tag named LOOP until the variable N is counted down to zero. Each time through the loop, RESULT is changed through multiplication with N. The COND tests for the stop condition, N = 0, and executes a RETURN when the test succeeds. RESULT starts with a value of NIL as all PROG variables do, but is set to 1 before the loop is entered.

Current trends are away from the use of GO functions because they tend to make programs hard to follow and hence hard to debug. The alternative is the DO function now available in some versions of LISP. Regrettably not all LISPs have a DO function built in, although it is easy enough to write one using PROG.

The Blocks-World System Requires Some Number-Crunching Functions

Shortly we will look at the code for the plan creating system. First we list some auxiliary functions for which program definitions will not be given:

■ GET-POSSIBLE-SUPPORT: A function which looks at the size and place properties of all objects to determine if there is an object lying directly under the position of a given object.

■ FIND-SPACE: A function which tries to find a place for a given object on a given support. It works by trying CLEARP at a series of places selected at random on the top of the support. After ten tries, without success, FIND-SPACE gives up and returns NIL. FIND-SPACE always returns NIL immediately when the object involved is a pyramid or ball.

■ TOPCENTER: A function which determines where to place the hand given a block to touch and the block's position.

■ REPORT: A debugging function which prints its argument and then stops, allowing the user to examine variable values.

The Blocks-World System's Procedures Are Relatively Transparent

The plan itself is manufactured using the functions given in the network shown in figure 12-3 along with those listed above. The solid arrows represent function calls which always happen. Dotted line arrows represent function calls which may or may

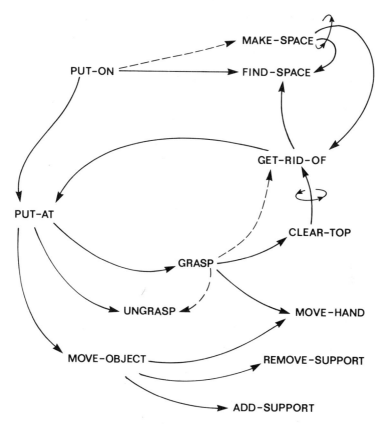

Figure 12-3 The robot's planning program uses many short goal-oriented procedures. PUT-ON means put one block on another. PUT-AT means put a block at a specified location. PUT-AT is used both to accomplish the main goal and to help clear away obstacles on the block to be moved and the target block. MAKE-SPACE is more powerful than FIND-SPACE because it will move things if no room is available otherwise. REMOVE-SUPPORT and ADD-SUPPORT are auxiliary functions that do bookkeeping. ADD-SUPPORT refuses to act if the supporting object is a ball or pyramid.

not happen depending on the state of the blocks world. Now let us examine these functions in the network in some detail.

The goal of PUT-ON is to place one object on another. On entry, it checks if both objects are the same. If they are, the REPORT debugging function is executed, printing an illuminating message. Normally this does not happen, and the first COND has no effect. The real work is done by finding a place and then putting the object at that place. If FIND-SPACE cannot locate a suitable place, then

MAKE-SPACE is given a chance. We shall see that MAKE-SPACE is more powerful than FIND-SPACE because it can clear away obstructions to make room.

```
(DEFINE (PUT-ON OBJECT SUPPORT)
  (PROG (PLACE)
        (COND ((EQUAL OBJECT SUPPORT)
                 (REPORT '(   PUT-ON -- CANNOT PUT
                              SOMETHING ON ITSELF))))
        (COND ((SETQ PLACE (FIND-SPACE SUPPORT OBJECT)))
              ((SETQ PLACE (MAKE-SPACE SUPPORT OBJECT)))
              ((REPORT '(   PUT-ON -- NO PLACE
                            FOR THE OBJECT))))
        (PUT-AT OBJECT PLACE)
        (RETURN T)))
```

Note that PUT-ON must certainly accomplish its purpose through side effects since it always returns T as its value. As with most of the procedures in the system, the value returned is ignored by the higher-level calling procedure.

PUT-AT differs from PUT-ON in that its second argument is a specific point in space rather than the name of an object. This is accomplished straightforwardly by three of the last four lines of the program which call GRASP, MOVE-OBJECT, and UNGRASP.

Before these programs are called, however, an introductory COND checks for errors. It must be the case that CLEARP believes there is room for the object and that GET-POSSIBLE-SUPPORT finds something underneath the proposed target place.

```
(DEFINE (PUT-AT OBJECT PLACE)
  (PROG ()
        (COND ((AND (CLEARP PLACE OBJECT)
                    (GET-POSSIBLE-SUPPORT PLACE)))
              ((REPORT '(   PUT-AT -- CANNOT FIND SPACE
                            FOR OR SUPPORT FOR THE OBJECT))))
        (GRASP OBJECT)
        (MOVE-OBJECT PLACE)
        (UNGRASP OBJECT)
        (RETURN T)))
```

Note that AND is used to combine (CLEARP PLACE OBJECT) and (GET-POSSIBLE-SUPPORT PLACE) into one COND clause trigger. This is possible even though GET-POSSIBLE-SUPPORT is not a predicate returning either T or NIL. Evidently AND, like COND, behaves a bit asymmetrically with respect to T and NIL.

■   AND evaluates its arguments from left to right. If a NIL is encountered, NIL is returned immediately and any remaining arguments are ignored. Otherwise AND returns the value of its last argument.

In other words, anything other than NIL behaves like T as far as logical considerations are concerned. This is a great feature. An OR behaves similarly:

■ OR evaluates its arguments from left to right. If something other than NIL is encountered, it is returned immediately and any remaining arguments are ignored. Otherwise OR returns NIL.

Moving on, one might be surprised at GRASP's complexity, but GRASP has many responsibilities.

■ First it checks if the object to be grasped is already held, in which case there is an immediate return.

■ Next, the property list of the object is examined to see if the property DIRECTLY-SUPPORTS indicates that the top is free to be grasped by the hand. If it is not, a call is made to CLEAR-TOP. If CLEAR-TOP refuses to win, then an error is signaled through the REPORT message.

■ Finally it may be that the hand is currently grasping something else which of course must be dispensed with. UNGRASP will do the job if the object is supported underneath by some other object. GET-RID-OF is required otherwise.

After all of these tests are done and responses are made, then GRASP makes a note that the hand is grasping the object by appropriately modifying the GRASP property of HAND. Then GRASP passes off its responsibility to MOVE-HAND, which moves the hand into position over the object to be grasped. Finally an addition is made to the plan by using CONS to add an element reflecting the grasping action. We shall see that the only other functions which can add to the plan are UNGRASP and MOVE-HAND.

```
(DEFINE (GRASP OBJECT)
  (PROG (KRUFT)
    (COND ((EQUAL OBJECT (GET 'HAND 'GRASPING))
           (RETURN T)))
    (COND ((NOT (GET OBJECT 'DIRECTLY-SUPPORTS)))
          ((CLEAR-TOP OBJECT))
          ((REPORT '(  GRASP -- TOP OF OBJECT
                       CANNOT BE CLEARED))))
    (COND ((SETQ KRUFT (GET 'HAND 'GRASPING))
           (COND ((UNGRASP KRUFT)) ((GET-RID-OF KRUFT)))))
    (MOVE-HAND (TOPCENTER (GET OBJECT 'PLACE) OBJECT))
    (PUTPROP 'HAND OBJECT 'GRASPING)
    (SETQ PLAN (CONS (LIST 'GRASP OBJECT) PLAN))
    (RETURN T)))
```

Once an object has been grasped, PUT-AT uses MOVE-OBJECT to get it into position. MOVE-OBJECT, like grasp, does an initial test to see if its job is done. Usually it is not and MOVE-OBJECT must go on to changing the place property of the object and to updating the hand information (by calling MOVE-HAND). REMOVE-SUPPORT and ADD-SUPPORT take care of keeping the SUPPORTED-BY properties up to date.

```
(DEFINE (MOVE-OBJECT NEWPLACE)
  (PROG (OBJECT OLDPLACE)
        (COND ((EQUAL (GET 'HAND 'POSITION) NEWPLACE)
               (RETURN T)))
        (COND ((NOT (SETQ OBJECT (GET 'HAND 'GRASPING)))
               (REPORT '(   MOVE-OBJECT -- NOT
                            GRASPING ANYTHING))))
        (REMOVE-SUPPORT OBJECT)
        (MOVE-HAND (TOPCENTER NEWPLACE OBJECT))
        (PUTPROP OBJECT NEWPLACE 'PLACE)
        (ADD-SUPPORT OBJECT NEWPLACE)
        (RETURN T)))
```

MOVE-HAND changes the place of the hand and adds to the plan.

```
(DEFINE (MOVE-HAND POSITION)
  (PROG ()
        (COND ((EQUAL (GET 'HAND 'POSITION) POSITION)
               (RETURN T)))
        (PUTPROP 'HAND POSITION 'POSITION)
        (SETQ PLAN (CONS (LIST 'MOVETO POSITION) PLAN))
        (RETURN T)))
```

UNGRASP, like GRASP, tests on entry to see if its goal is already accomplished. It does this simply by checking to see if the hand is not grasping anything. Next it proceeds to let go by modifying the same GRASPING property it just checked and by adding to PLAN's value. Note however that these changes happen only if UNGRASP is sure there is a support. If the SUPPORTED-BY property has a NIL value, then UNGRASP returns NIL.

```
(DEFINE (UNGRASP OBJECT)
  (PROG ()
    (COND ((NOT (EQUAL OBJECT (GET 'HAND 'GRASPING)))
           (RETURN T))
          ((GET OBJECT 'SUPPORTED-BY)
           (PUTPROP 'HAND NIL 'GRASPING)
           (SETQ PLAN (CONS (LIST 'UNGRASP OBJECT) PLAN))
           (RETURN T))
          (T NIL))))
```

GET-RID-OF is very simple. It puts an object on the table by finding a place for it and moving it to that place. Note the use of PUT-AT. This completes a loop in the network of functions, giving the system thoroughly recursive behavior.

```
(DEFINE (GET-RID-OF OBJECT)
        (PROG (PLACE)
              (SETQ PLACE (FIND-SPACE 'TABLE OBJECT))
              (PUT-AT OBJECT PLACE)
              (RETURN T)))
```

Now we turn to CLEAR-TOP. Its purpose is to remove all the objects directly supported by something the hand is supposed to grasp. This is done by using a GO function which causes looping until each object found under the DIRECTLY-SUPPORTS property is placed on the table by GET-RID-OF.

```
(DEFINE (CLEAR-TOP OBJECT)
  (PROG (OBSTRUCTION POSSIBILITIES)
        (SETQ POSSIBILITIES (GET OBJECT 'DIRECTLY-SUPPORTS))
        LOOP
        (COND (POSSIBILITIES (SETQ OBSTRUCTION
                                     (CAR POSSIBILITIES))
                             (GET-RID-OF OBSTRUCTION)
                             (SETQ POSSIBILITIES
                                     (CDR POSSIBILITIES))
                             (GO LOOP))
              ((RETURN T)))))
```

REMOVE-SUPPORT involves two tests useful while debugging, but otherwise just changes the support relationships that existed at the old place. REMOVE-SUPPORT uses the function DELETE that removes elements from lists. The first argument given to DELETE is the element to be removed and the second is the list the element is to be removed from.

```
(DEFINE (REMOVE-SUPPORT OBJECT)
  (PROG (SUPPORT)
        (COND ((GET OBJECT 'DIRECTLY-SUPPORTS)
               (REPORT '(   REMOVE-SUPPORT -- CANNOT
                            MOVE A SUPPORTING OBJECT)))
              ((NOT (GET OBJECT 'SUPPORTED-BY))
               (REPORT '(   REMOVE-SUPPORT -- OBJECT
                            WAS ALREADY UNSUPPORTED))))
        (PUTPROP (SETQ SUPPORT (GET OBJECT 'SUPPORTED-BY))
                 (DELETE OBJECT
                         (GET SUPPORT 'DIRECTLY-SUPPORTS))
                 'DIRECTLY-SUPPORTS)
        (PUTPROP OBJECT NIL 'SUPPORTED-BY)
        (RETURN T)))
```

ADD-SUPPORT is more complicated. Its purpose is to put in new support relationships corresponding to the new position of the object just moved. It refuses to do this, however, if there is no object in a position to do some supporting or if the object proposed as a support fails to be either the table or a block. Pyramids and balls will not do. Failure to make supported-by changes causes REPORT to stop further action.

```
(DEFINE (ADD-SUPPORT OBJECT PLACE)
  (PROG (SUPPORT)
        (COND ((SETQ SUPPORT (GET-POSSIBLE-SUPPORT PLACE)))
              ((REPORT '(   ADD-SUPPORT -- THERE IS
                            NO POTENTIAL SUPPORT)))))
        (COND ((OR (EQUAL SUPPORT 'TABLE)
                   (EQUAL (GET SUPPORT 'TYPE) 'BLOCK))
               (PUTPROP SUPPORT
                        (CONS OBJECT
                              (GET SUPPORT
                                   'DIRECTLY-SUPPORTS))
                        'DIRECTLY-SUPPORTS)
               (PUTPROP OBJECT SUPPORT 'SUPPORTED-BY)
               (RETURN T))
              ((REPORT '(   ADD-SUPPORT -- THERE IS
                            NO SUPPORT FOR OBJECT)))))))
```

MAKE-SPACE is nothing more than a repeated appeal to GET-RID-OF to clear away space for a new object. The loop containing GET-RID-OF returns just as soon as enough clutter has been cleared away to make room enough for FIND-SPACE to succeed.

```
(DEFINE (MAKE-SPACE SURFACE OBJECT)
  (PROG (SPACE CLUTTER POSSIBILITIES)
    (SETQ POSSIBILITIES (GET SURFACE 'DIRECTLY-SUPPORTS))
    TAG
    (COND (POSSIBILITIES (SETQ CLUTTER
                               (CAR POSSIBILITIES)))
          ((REPORT '(   MAKE-SPACE -- NO SPACE BUT NO
                        CLUTTER EITHER))))
    (GET-RID-OF CLUTTER)
    (COND ((SETQ SPACE (FIND-SPACE SURFACE OBJECT))
           (RETURN SPACE))
          (T (SETQ POSSIBILITIES (CDR POSSIBILITIES))
             (GO TAG)))))
```

PRINT and READ Help Functions Communicate with Users

Before leaving the basic blocks world, let us dissect the debugging function, REPORT. There are two reasons. The first is to draw attention to the very important practice of peppering programs with debugging aids. The second is to introduce two very useful functions, PRINT and READ. Without PRINT, the only way a user can learn about what a LISP function is doing is by waiting for a value to appear. Without READ, the only way a function can get information is through its arguments and global variables. PRINT and READ therefore open the door to much more communication. Happily, both are very simple.

PRINT evaluates its single argument, prints it, and returns T as its value. Thus the following function will print out all the numbers until something drops dead:

```
(DEFINE (BORE-ME)
        (PROG (N)
              (SETQ N 0)
              LOOP
              (PRINT N)
              (SETQ N (ADD1 N))
              (GO LOOP)))
   BORE-ME
(BORE-ME)
   0
   1
   2
   3
   .
   .
   .
```

PRINT always returns T as its value:

```
(PRINT 'EXAMPLE)
   EXAMPLE
   T
```

When (READ) is encountered, **LISP** stops and waits for the user to type an s-expression. That s-expression, without evaluation, becomes the value of (READ). Using **READ** by itself therefore causes total inactivity until the user types something to be read:

```
(READ)EXAMPLE
   EXAMPLE
```

PRINT and **READ** enable **REPORT** to be defined:

```
(DEFINE (REPORT MESSAGE)
        (PROG (INPUT)
              (PRINT MESSAGE)
              LOOP
              (SETQ INPUT (READ))
              (COND ((AND (NOT (ATOM INPUT))
                          (EQUAL (CAR INPUT) 'REPORT))
                     (RETURN (EVAL (CADR INPUT))))
                    (T (PRINT (EVAL INPUT))))
              (GO LOOP)))
   REPORT
```

When encountered, **REPORT** prints its argument and then goes into a loop. Each time through, the user types an expression and the value is printed. To escape from the loop, the user need only type (REPORT <any s-expression>). Then **REPORT** will return the value of the s-expression as its value and things will go on as usual.

Debugging functions tend to be system-specific and much more elaborate than the simple REPORT given here. One reason is that there must be some way of catching errors encountered while evaluating the result of READ before they destroy the context REPORT is trying to examine.

The Blocks-World System has Some Heterarchical Flavor

Some languages make such a big deal out of procedure interaction that having one procedure call on another one is a major event. The connections among procedures written in such languages tend to resemble the example of figure 12-4 where one sees one major procedure with a few subprocedures shallowly arrayed under it. This is like totalitarianism.

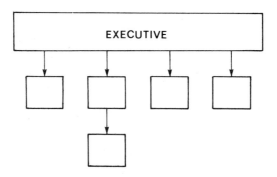

Figure 12-4 Most programming languages encourage shallow system organization with little subprocedure depth.

In other languages, the notion of subprocedure is so intimately involved with the language's fundamental structure that essentially everything is best thought of as a subprocedure call. A deep hierarchy of subroutine arrangements is very natural. Symbol-manipulation languages are usually like that, producing connections among procedures like those suggested back in figure 12-3. Superior procedures accept tasks and hand them to subordinate procedures. Along the way the original task is perhaps simplified a bit or at least is divided up. When all of the subordinates are through, the superior passes the results upward, perhaps adding a bit of embellishment. This is like a bureaucracy.

Since the late 1960s, new programming concepts have promoted movement away from both the totalitarian and the bureaucratic style. The resulting systems often look like democratic communities of cooperating experts. The term *heterarchy* refers to this style of programming. The following ideas are involved, some of which are just ordinary rules of good programming practice:

- Executive control should be distributed.

- Procedures should be built around goals.

- Procedures should presume as little as possible about the situation in effect when they are called.

- Advice, suggestion, and complaint should pass freely among the procedures.

- A system should have facilities for making tentative conclusions.

- A system should contain sufficient knowledge of itself to debug some of its own errors.

In general, heterarchy makes more adaptable programs while hierarchy makes more efficient ones in contexts where adaptability is not required.

The blocks-world system is not a fantastic example of heterarchy in action since it lacks explicit knowledge of itself and it lacks a sexy flow of advice, suggestion, complaint, remark, and criticism. Nevertheless, in some respects the system exhibits elements of good programming practice that border on heterarchy. Here is why:

- Executive control is distributed throughout the system. The modules interact like a community of experts. Graphically the system looks more like a network of procedures rather than an executive with subroutines, each called in an orderly, immutable sequence. Procedures are connected to others via potential control-transfer links which are used according to the context, the context being jointly determined by the system and the problem undergoing analysis.

- The system is goal oriented. Procedures at all levels are fairly short and associated with some definite goal. Goals are satisfied by invoking a small number of subgoals for other procedures to handle or by directly calling a few primitives.

- The procedures themselves contain the necessary machinery to set up conditions that are required before they do their jobs. This is done through specifications lying near the beginning of each procedure. Typically simple references to the data base insure that the world is in a proper state to go ahead, but if not, the appropriate introductory procedures are called.

Simulation Is Straightforward

At this point it is helpful to walk through and simulate the actions that follow from an effort to place block B on block C given the situation in figure 12-1. Both the procedures themselves and the control connections shown in figure 12-3 are helpful. The diagram below gives the result. The superior-inferior relationships between procedures are indicated by indentation showing who calls whom. Time order is given by the vertical arrangement.

```
PUT-ON
    PUT-AT
        GRASP
            CLEAR-TOP
                GET-RID-OF
                    PUT-AT
                        GRASP
                            MOVE-HAND
                        MOVE-OBJECT
                            REMOVE-SUPPORT
                            ADD-SUPPORT
                            MOVE-HAND
                        UNGRASP
            MOVE-HAND
        MOVE-OBJECT
            REMOVE-SUPPORT
            ADD-SUPPORT
            MOVE-HAND
        UNGRASP
```

LISP systems invariably offer tracing functions for debugging which automatically generate diagrams like this.

Blocks-World Problems Are Good Tests for Planning Ideas

The system as described offers interesting behavior in spite of its simplicity. There are many problems far beyond its reach, however, and some blocks-world problems are even hard enough to seriously strain advanced problem-solving strategies.

Simultaneous achievement of multiple goals is one of the popular hard problems. Figure 12-5 provides a simple illustration. Block A is to be on block B, *and* block B is to be on block C. If these goals are attacked in the order given, the first step of a simple-minded system would be to place A on B. But then to get B on C, it is necessary to take A off of B, thus undoing the first step. A close analysis of the simultaneous goals and their subgoals is required to understand and avoid the mistake.

This analysis can be approached in many ways and something of a contest has developed for the best solution. The principal direct result of the contest is a family of new ideas about planning. One other result is a richer vocabulary for talking about goals, bugs, and plans. It seems likely that this will have far-reaching usefulness for computer programming in general. One day phrases like "prerequisite subgoal clobbers brother goal result" may become part of everyday language for people who know about computers.

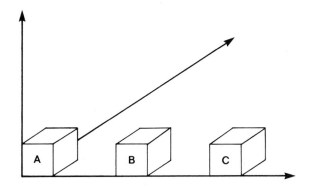

Figure 12-5 The problem here is to put A on B and B on C. If the two parts are attacked in the wrong order, work will be wasted.

ANSWERING QUESTIONS ABOUT GOALS

The plan is only a list of sequential instructions for a real or simulated hand. It does not offer much insight into how and why those instructions were given. If *how* and *why* questions are likely to come up, then it is useful for the system itself to have access to a tree structure, similar to a debugging trace, showing the locus of the system as it moves from one program to another. Since the system is organized around programs which each work toward an identifiable goal, it is easy for the system to answer many questions about its own behavior by looking into the tree structure and performing a sort of introspection.

Figure 12-6 shows why this is so. It is another representation of the goal tree. Each node represents an instance in which the named program was invoked. A node branches out into other nodes for the programs called to help out.

The Blocks-World System Can Introspect to a Degree

The question, "Why did you put A on the table?" is correctly answered by finding (PUT-ON A <position with $z = 0$>) in the goal tree, looking up to the next higher node, and answering that the action was performed in order to get rid of A. "Why did you do that?" then requires one more step up the tree, producing a remark about clearing off B. Repeating the question eventually gets to an answer involving the need to put B on C and repeating again leads to the universal top-level response, "Because you told me to."

Questions about *how* go the other way. "How did you put B on C?" causes a response of, "I put it at (7 1 2)." Repeating causes recitation of the goals listed directly under (PUT-AT B (7 1 2)), namely, "First I grasped B; then I moved B; finally I let go of B."

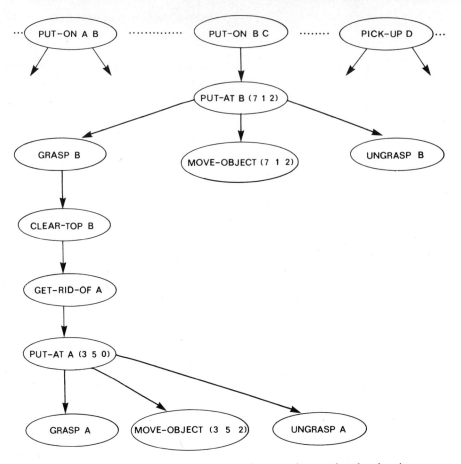

Figure 12-6 Answering how, why, and when questions requires tracing the planning program as it builds its goal trees. In general, moving one level down handles questions about how; one level up, why; and all the way to the top, when.

Questions about *when* can be handled also. The trick is to trace up the tree from the node asked about all the way to the node at the top, which represents the originating command. Thus "When did you grasp A?" can be answered, "While I was putting B on C." If the question refers to a top-level node, then of course no upward tracing is possible and it is necessary to nail down the time by reference to the next top-level command or the one done just before. "When did you put B on C?" might well be answered, "After I put A on B and before I picked up D." The following summarizes:

■ *Why* questions are answered by either moving one step up the goal tree and describing the goal found there or by saying, "Because you told me to."

■ *How* questions are answered by either enumerating the goals found one step down in the goal tree or by saying, "I just did it!"

■ *When* questions are answered by either reference to a top level goal or by reference to adjacent top level goals in the recorded history.

Thus it is clear that a tree of program calls is a key element in answering *how,* *why,* and *when* questions related to accomplished actions. How can such a tree be constructed? One way is to build some slight extra machinery into some of the programs in the existing blocks-world system. So far all of the action is focused on creating the plan — the NIL and T values returned by the functions are mostly ignored. The values are therefore more or less available for the job of creating a system-accessible goal tree. Instead of NIL and T, let us arrange certain of the programs to return NIL on failure, and subgoal information on success instead of just T.

Remembering Function Calls Creates a Useful History

More precisely, the idea is to use nesting in list structure to reflect goal-subgoal relationships. The fact that function F called functions X, Y, and Z is represented by a list with F and its arguments in first position and descriptions of the action at and below X, Y, and Z in the subsequent positions. Clearly the description of the action resulting from the call to, say, X, will involve a list with X and its arguments in first position with subsequent positions occupied by descriptions of activity associated which X itself called. Thus the representation scheme is a recursive one.

PUT-AT, for example, does essentially three things via the three programs, GRASP, MOVE-OBJECT, and UNGRASP. PUT-AT should therefore return something like the following:

```
((PUT-AT <name of object> <name of support>)
 <result of call to GRASP>
 <result of call to MOVE-OBJECT>
 <result of call to UNGRASP>)
```

Transparently, this is done by adding variables G1, G2, and G3 to the PROG variables, setting one to the result of each call, and using instances of LIST to construct the proper structure:

```
(SETQ G1 <result of call to GRASP>)
(SETQ G2 <result of call to MOVE-OBJECT>)
(SETQ G3 <result of call to UNGRASP>)
(RETURN (LIST (LIST 'PUT-AT OBJECT SUPPORT) G1 G2 G3))
```

Each result indicated is created in a similar way ordinarily and will therefore be some list itself. Thus the overall result in complicated cases will be a deeply nested structure in which each level of nesting corresponds to a level in the goal tree. Nesting terminates at functions which make no interesting calls to other programs. UNGRASP, for example, returns just a simple

```
((UNGRASP <name of object>))
```

The necessary code for this is

```
(RETURN (LIST (LIST 'UNGRASP OBJECT)))
```

Now PUT-AT and UNGRASP look like this:

```
(DEFINE (PUT-AT OBJECT PLACE)
  (PROG (G1 G2 G3)
    (COND ((AND (CLEARP PLACE OBJECT)
                (GET-POSSIBLE-SUPPORT PLACE)))
          ((REPORT '(   PUT-AT -- CANNOT FIND SPACE
                     FOR OR SUPPORT FOR THE OBJECT))))
    (SETQ G1 (GRASP OBJECT))
    (SETQ G2 (MOVE-OBJECT PLACE))
    (SETQ G3 (UNGRASP OBJECT))
    (RETURN (LIST (LIST 'PUT-AT OBJECT PLACE) G1 G2 G3))))
(DEFINE (UNGRASP OBJECT)
  (PROG ()
    (COND ((NOT (EQUAL OBJECT (GET 'HAND 'GRASPING)))
           (RETURN NIL))
          ((GET OBJECT 'SUPPORTED-BY)
           (PUTPROP 'HAND NIL 'GRASPING)
           (SETQ PLAN (CONS (LIST 'UNGRASP OBJECT) PLAN))
           (RETURN (LIST (LIST 'UNGRASP OBJECT))))
          (T NIL))))
```

Some interesting problems come up in connection with GET-RID-OF and MAKE-SPACE, which involve loops, and with GRASP, which may or may not call CLEAR-TOP. Once these are solved, the revised system not only will create a plan and make it the value of PLAN, but also will build a trace of the goal history as the overall value of the top-level function. The list structure below is equivalent to the goal locus given before in figure 12-6.

```
((PUT-ON B C)
 ((PUT-AT B (7 1 2))
  ((GRASP B)
   ((CLEAR-TOP B)
    ((GET-RID-OF A)
     ((PUT-AT A (3 5 0))
      ((GRASP A)
       ((MOVE-HAND (1 1 4))))
      ((MOVE-OBJECT (3 5 2))
       ((MOVE-HAND (3 5 2))))
      ((UNGRASP A)))))
   ((MOVE-HAND (1 1 2))))
  ((MOVE-OBJECT (7 1 4))
   ((MOVE-HAND (7 1 4))))
  ((UNGRASP B))))
```

GETTING PROGRAMS FROM DATA

Many processes can be applied to a variety of arguments with the details of the process depending strongly on the type of the particular things involved. Addition and multiplication, for example, are defined differently for numbers, complex numbers, matrixes, and many other mathematical entities. Similarly, and perhaps

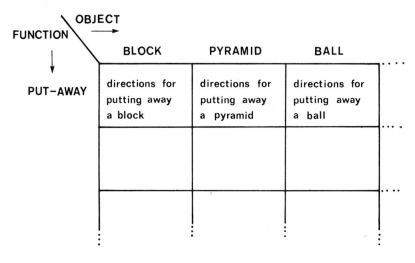

Figure 12-7 Things to do and things to do to them form a table. In some circumstances it is better to record the table vertically, putting function information on the property lists of the data types, rather than horizontally, putting object type information into functions.

more familiarly, a person's personal greet, arrange-to-see, and buy-present procedures no doubt depend on whether the operatee involved is a relative, an ordinary friend, a romantic friend, a professor, or a robot.

Functions and Object Types Form a Table

Still another example, easy to develop in Robbie's blocks-world context, concerns putting the blocks away. Assume that Robbie has a toy box for each type of block: box BLOCKS is for rectangular blocks; box PYRAMIDS is for pyramids; and box BALLS is for balls. The function PUT-AWAY is to take some block as its argument and put it in the right box. Thus (PUT-AWAY 'A) should arrange for execution of (PUT-ON 'A 'BLOCKS). Conceptually PUT-AWAY and its possible argument types form part of a table as shown in figure 12-7.

The program embodiment of the table can be done in many ways. The simplest, and perhaps the worst, is to concatenate the name of the operation and the name of the object type for each viable combination making a new function for each pair. One would then have PUT-AWAY-BLOCK, PUT-AWAY-PYRAMID, and PUT-AWAY-BALL.

One reason this solution is bad is that the programmer must know the type of thing that the argument is when he writes the program. This is usually inconvenient and may be impossible. It is better to ask the programmed function to figure out the type later while it is running.

An obvious improvement is to have the general PUT-AWAY function defer to special-purpose functions. For this to work, each possible object must reveal its type through a TYPE property on its property list. Then the particular special-purpose function selected depends on the result of examining the argument's TYPE property:

```
(DEFINE (PUT-AWAY OBJECT)
        (COND ((EQUAL 'BLOCK (GET OBJECT 'TYPE))
               (PUT-AWAY-BLOCK OBJECT))
              ((EQUAL 'PYRAMID (GET OBJECT 'TYPE))
               (PUT-AWAY-PYRAMID OBJECT))
              ((EQUAL 'BALL (GET OBJECT 'TYPE))
               (PUT-AWAY-BALL OBJECT)))))
```

Arguments May Supply Their Own Procedures

Another, better solution considerably changes the way the general program is connected to the special purpose ones. The special purpose function names are not reached by checking object types in the COND clause. Instead, the special purpose function names are accessed through the property lists of the type names. The type BLOCK, for example, has a property named PUT-AWAY-FUNCTION. The general PUT-AWAY function can therefore decide that some object, say A, should be put away using PUT-AWAY-BLOCK through the following steps:

■ Object A has a TYPE property.

■ The value of the TYPE property is BLOCK.

■ BLOCK has a PUT-AWAY-FUNCTION property.

■ The value of the property is PUT-AWAY-BLOCK.

FUNCALL Enables Function Names or Descriptions to Be Computed

This can be implemented many ways, one of which uses FUNCALL. The FUNCALL function uses its first argument to compute a function name or LAMBDA description and then applies the result to the other arguments. Thus the following are equivalent:

```
(PUT-AWAY-BLOCK 'A)
```

```
(FUNCALL 'PUT-AWAY-BLOCK 'A)
```

But the FUNCALL form generalizes to allow the following which have the same result as well:

```
(FUNCALL (GET 'BLOCK 'PUT-AWAY-FUNCTION) 'A)
```

```
(FUNCALL (GET (GET 'A 'TYPE) 'PUT-AWAY-FUNCTION) 'A)
```

Thus PUT-AWAY can be defined as follows:

```
(DEFINE (PUT-AWAY OBJECT)
        (FUNCALL (GET (GET OBJECT 'TYPE)
                      'PUT-AWAY-FUNCTION)
                 OBJECT))
```

Importantly, the general idea works as well if LAMBDA definitions are placed in the PUT-AWAY-FUNCTION property slots rather than function names! There is no need to form function names for the special-purpose functions unless they are referenced more than once and storage efficiency is of interest. Thus the following arrange for equivalent results when PUT-AWAY is used on a block:

Method 1:
```
(DEFINE (PUT-AWAY-BLOCK OBJECT) (PUT-ON OBJECT 'BLOCKS))
(DEFINE (PUT-AWAY-PYRAMID OBJECT) (PUT-ON OBJECT 'PYRAMIDS))
(DEFINE (PUT-AWAY-BALL OBJECT) (PUT-ON OBJECT 'BALLS))
(PUTPROP 'BLOCK 'PUT-AWAY-BLOCK 'PUT-AWAY-FUNCTION)
(PUTPROP 'PYRAMID 'PUT-AWAY-PYRAMID 'PUT-AWAY-FUNCTION)
(PUTPROP 'BALL 'PUT-AWAY-BALL 'PUT-AWAY-FUNCTION)
```

Method 2:
```
(PUTPROP 'BLOCK
         '(LAMBDA (OBJECT) (PUT-ON OBJECT 'BLOCKS))
         'PUT-AWAY-FUNCTION)
(PUTPROP 'PYRAMID
         '(LAMBDA (OBJECT) (PUT-ON OBJECT 'PYRAMIDS))
         'PUT-AWAY-FUNCTION)
(PUTPROP 'BALL
         '(LAMBDA (OBJECT) (PUT-ON OBJECT 'BALLS))
         'PUT-AWAY-FUNCTION)
```

Using one method, the function body is right there under the PUT-AWAY-FUNCTION property. In the other, it is found one step removed through an intervening function name.

One speaks of the general program dispatching to a special-purpose function name or LAMBDA description on the basis of the argument type observed. Conceptually this happens as if there were a table with general things to do on one axis, argument types on the other, and special purpose functions in the cells. This abstract table is called a dispatch table when it is used to access data-dependent functions through TYPE properties.

Data-Driven Programming Is Becoming Popular

Note that the two major alternatives amount to recording the dispatch table either horizontally, by stuffing type information into general-purpose functions, or vertically by stuffing procedural information into the types' property lists. Keeping the information in the body of general-purpose functions requires program surgery whenever additions are to be made. Keeping it on property lists requires additions to the data base instead. Which is better depends on details of circumstance. Sandewall and others have argued lucidly that both techniques should be in the tool bag.

The data-driven style of programming has been promoted through a number of very successful programs using it. Sussman and Stallman have one for electronic circuit analysis, and Sandewall has one for storing and retrieving information from data bases.

SUMMARY

- Property lists in general can be helpful repositories of information, reflecting knowledge about objects, their properties, and their relationships. Most of the classical great programs relied either heavily or exclusively on property lists.

- By adhering to some rules of good programming practice, intricate looking, interesting tasks can be planned by a system that is both capable and simple. Among these rules are maxims specifying short, goal-oriented procedures, distributed executive responsibility, and introductions to the procedures that check the state of the world. The question of whether distributed executive responsibility is good causes arguments.

- *How, why,* and *when* questions often can be answered by reference to a remembered tree containing goal-subgoal relationships. Such trees are conveniently represented as nested list structure.

- Type-specific functions in the form of LAMBDA expressions can be stored on the property lists of type-describing atoms. These functions can be fetched later when an argument of the given type appears. This facilitates data-driven programming, a style of programming in which the boundary line between programs and data becomes even more blurred than usual. Data-driven programming is particularly appropriate if the types of objects involved in a system are difficult to circumscribe when system building begins.

REFERENCES

- Terry Winograd, *Understanding Natural Language,* PhD thesis, Academic Press, 1972. A synopsis is available in *Computer Models of Thought and Language,* edited by Rodger Schank and Kenneth Colby, W. H. Freeman, San Francisco, 1973. The blocks program given here is an adaptation of programs appearing in support of Terry Winograd's system for understanding text. In the original version, the programs were written in MICROPLANNER, a variant of Hewitt's PLANNER. The first reprogramming was a translation into CONNIVER. The second put them into ordinary LISP. It is generally agreed that both steps improved transparency! Curiously, the MICROPLANNER version was once used to support the usefulness of the MICROPLANNER language. In fact, the heterarchical style encouraged by MICROPLANNER syntax was extremely beneficial, but not the language *per se.*

- Erik Sandewall, "Ideas About Management of LISP Data Bases," *Advance Papers of the Fourth International Joint Conference on Artificial Intelligence,* available through the M.I.T. Artificial Intelligence Laboratory, Cambridge, Massachusetts, 1975. Description of an application of data-driven programming.

■ Erik Sandewall, "Some Observations on Conceptual Programming," in *Machine Intelligence 8,* edited by E. W. Elcock and D. Michie, John Wylie, 1976. A good discussion of the issues involved in data-driven programming.

The next several references are particularly recommended as entry points into the literature on blocks-world debugging and planning ideas:

■ Gerald Sussman, *A Computer Model of Skill Acquisition,* PhD thesis, American Elsevier, 1975.

■ Earl Sacerdoti, "The Nonlinear Nature of Plans," *Advance Papers of the Fourth International Joint Conference on Artificial Intelligence,* available through the M.I.T. Artificial Intelligence Laboratory, Cambridge, Massachusetts, 1975.

■ Carl Hewitt, "How To Use What You Know," *Advance Papers of the Fourth International Joint Conference on Artificial Intelligence,* available through the M.I.T. Artificial Intelligence Laboratory, Cambridge, Massachusetts, 1975.

13
THE
GAMES
WORLD

The principal objective of this chapter is to show how programs are developed by showing all of the steps leading toward a working alpha-beta program. This particular example is used because it proves to be an interesting and entertaining example of symbol manipulation in LISP. Keep in mind that there is more to game playing than search, however.

IMPLEMENTING MINIMAX SEARCH

To begin with, it is certainly clear that a game tree can be straightforwardly represented as a list structure. Each node is represented as a list whose elements are representations of the nodes below. Figure 13-1 shows how this works.

Basic Minimaxing Is Easy to Implement

Now recall how minimax works. Applying the minimax rules for determining the best move for the player at the top means alternately finding the maximum and the minimum of situation scores working from the bottom of the tree to the top.

It is easy to write a function which very nearly performs this service, namely BIGGEST.

```
(DEFINE (BIGGEST S)
        (COND ((ATOM S) S)
              ((APPLY 'MAX (MAPCAR 'BIGGEST S)))))
```

If this function is applied to the list representation of the game tree we are using as an example, it ends up returning the biggest number in the s-expression, namely 9, since at each level in the recursion it returns the biggest of the numbers it is given.

SMALLEST, defined in the obvious way as the complement of BIGGEST, does the wrong thing as well. Curiously the two can be modified slightly and combined to do just what we want:

311

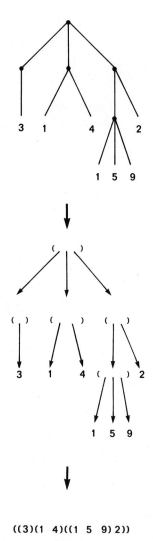

((3)(1 4)((1 5 9) 2))

Figure 13-1 Game trees are easily represented as s-expressions.

```
(DEFINE (BIGGEST1 S)
        (COND ((ATOM S) S)
              ((APPLY 'MAX (MAPCAR 'SMALLEST1 S))))))
(DEFINE (SMALLEST1 S)
        (COND ((ATOM S) S)
              ((APPLY 'MIN (MAPCAR 'BIGGEST1 S))))))
```

BIGGEST and SMALLEST are to evolve through a sequence of versions until the behavior is just right. The changes reflect those made by a programmer working from the simple basic program toward one that eventually embraces alpha-beta pruning. BIGGEST1 and SMALLEST1 are the first in the sequence.

As with BIGGEST, BIGGEST1 uses MAX to come up with the largest element returned by the MAPCAR. But now the MAPCAR uses SMALLEST1. Evidently MAX works on the results obtained by applying SMALLEST1 to each element of BIGGEST1's argument, S. SMALLEST1 in turn uses MIN on the results of applying BIGGEST1 to each element of its argument. Thus we have the required alternation between maximizing and minimizing at each level. At the top, the result is the score found at the bottom of the path through the tree which follows the choice most favorable to the player with the move at each node.

Move Generation and Minimaxing Can Be Intertwined

Returning the expected score using a completed tree is all well and good, but the game tree must be generated somehow. This could be done by an entirely separate program as a first step, but it is better to anticipate the introduction of alpha-beta pruning by combining move generation and minimaxing.

It is not necessary, thankfully, to get into the details of how static evaluation and plausible move generation might work for a particular game. Instead we presume a function called STATIC-VALUE which takes a board as an argument and returns an opinion of its strength in the form of a single number. We further presume a move generator, PLAUSIBLE-MOVES, which accepts a board representation and returns a list of new board representations achievable in one move. In general this list of new situations may be empty if PLAUSIBLE-MOVES finds a situation discouraging, but for the moment, we presume that the plausible move generator produces at least one candidate.

Now the tree can be generated on the fly. The argument passed to BIGGEST2 is a single board representation instead of a complete tree. This single board is expanded down inside BIGGEST2 by PLAUSIBLE-MOVES. Note that the recursion (and the move generation) stop when the function QUIET thinks the board situation is settled enough for a good static evaluation to be performed.

```
(DEFINE (BIGGEST2 BOARD)
        (COND ((QUIET BOARD) (STATIC-VALUE BOARD))
              ((APPLY 'MAX
                      (MAPCAR 'SMALLEST2
                              (PLAUSIBLE-MOVES BOARD))))))
```

Since SMALLEST2 is just like BIGGEST2 with the obvious swap of BIGGEST2 for SMALLEST2 and MIN for MAX, it is omitted and its descendants will be omitted as well, all to save space.

ADDING ALPHA-BETA PRUNING

So far our program has been simple. Alpha-beta complicates it quite a bit, but generalization toward an alpha-beta capability will be done in several steps.

Alpha-Beta Introduces Some Complications

First of all, it is clear that the MAPCAR in BIGGEST3 must go because SMALLEST3 may or may not be used on all the board positions in the list returned by PLAUSIBLE-MOVES. It depends on the values returned by SMALLEST3 as it works down the list. The whole purpose of the alpha-beta technique depends on the ability to avoid looking at avoidable parts of the tree or, indeed, even generating those parts.

Using a PROG is one way to replace the MAPCAR by introducing an explicit loop:

```
(DEFINE (BIGGEST3 BOARD)
  (COND
    ((QUIET BOARD) (STATIC-VALUE BOARD))
    ((APPLY 'MAX
      (PROG (BOARD-LIST NEXT-BOARD NEW-LIST)
            (SETQ BOARD-LIST (PLAUSIBLE-MOVES BOARD))
       START(COND ((NULL BOARD-LIST)
                    (RETURN (REVERSE NEW-LIST))))
            (SETQ NEXT-BOARD (CAR BOARD-LIST))
            (SETQ NEW-LIST (CONS (SMALLEST3 NEXT-BOARD)
                                 NEW-LIST))
            (SETQ BOARD-LIST (CDR BOARD-LIST))
            (GO START))))))
```

As before, recursion stops when QUIET says stop. Otherwise the call to SMALLEST3, down inside the PROG, pushes the tree further down. The key variable introduced by the PROG is BOARD-LIST, which begins its life assigned to all the immediate descendants of BOARD found by PLAUSIBLE-MOVES. Each time through the loop, BOARD-LIST is shortened, until the repeat test located just after the tag START discovers that BOARD-LIST is completely drained. Then the iteration is terminated, causing the return of whatever NEW-LIST has become. NEW-LIST, it is clear, expands as BOARD-LIST contracts. Each time through the iteration, the front element of BOARD-LIST is fed through NEXT-BOARD to SMALLEST3 with the resulting value then grafted on to the front of NEW-LIST.

Assuming that SMALLEST3 returns a number as in previous versions, NEW-LIST
will be a list of numbers. The PROG returns this list when complete, and MAX
selects the largest number from the list to be the value of BIGGEST3.

To summarize, board positions are passed down and expanded by way of
PLAUSIBLE-MOVES; lists of numbers are passed back up and contracted by way
of minimaxing back and forth between BIGGEST3 and SMALLEST3. This is just
as it was before, except that the trip down the list of moves produced by
PLAUSIBLE-MOVES is done by explicit looping in a PROG rather than by the
implicit looping effected previously by MAPCARs. The change is demanded
because of the need to terminate the investigation of the list early by right of
alpha-beta cutoff.

Onward. We know that alpha-beta cutoff depends on comparisons of newly
computed subtree values with established minimum or maximum standards. The
next version expands a bit in preparation for these comparisons. The standards are
given to BIGGEST4 through input variables named ALPHA and BETA, naturally
enough.

```
(DEFINE (BIGGEST4 BOARD ALPHA BETA)
   (COND
      ((QUIET BOARD) (STATIC-VALUE BOARD))
      ((APPLY 'MAX
              (PROG (BOARD-LIST NEXT-BOARD NEW-VALUE NEW-LIST)
                    (SETQ BOARD-LIST (PLAUSIBLE-MOVES BOARD))
               START(COND ((NULL BOARD-LIST)
                           (RETURN (REVERSE NEW-LIST))))
                    (SETQ NEXT-BOARD (CAR BOARD-LIST))
                    (SETQ NEW-VALUE
                          (SMALLEST4 NEXT-BOARD ALPHA BETA))
                    (SETQ NEW-LIST (CONS NEW-VALUE NEW-LIST))
                    (SETQ BOARD-LIST (CDR BOARD-LIST))
                    (GO START))))))
```

NEW-VALUE is a new variable on which now hangs the value coming up from
below via SMALLEST4. Nothing new happens yet; the changes are only
anticipatory.

As it stands now, ALPHA and BETA are available but nowhere set and
nowhere used. First, to prepare to use them, the MAX function is drawn into the
PROG so that some as yet uninstalled test can stop the iteration and cause the value
of the PROG to be the value of BIGGEST5 rather than a list of candidate values
to be then compared by MAX. BIGGEST-VALUE is the variable returned, not
NEW-LIST as before. Somewhat wastefully, updated values are determined each
time around the loop, not just after the last time around.

```
(DEFINE (BIGGEST5 BOARD ALPHA BETA)
  (COND
    ((QUIET BOARD) (STATIC-VALUE BOARD))
    ((PROG (BOARD-LIST NEXT-BOARD NEW-VALUE
             NEW-LIST BIGGEST-VALUE)
           (SETQ BOARD-LIST (PLAUSIBLE-MOVES BOARD))
     START(COND ((NULL BOARD-LIST) (RETURN BIGGEST-VALUE)))
           (SETQ NEXT-BOARD (CAR BOARD-LIST))
           (SETQ NEW-VALUE
                 (SMALLEST5 NEXT-BOARD ALPHA BETA))
           (SETQ NEW-LIST (CONS NEW-VALUE NEW-LIST))
           (SETQ BIGGEST-VALUE (APPLY 'MAX NEW-LIST))
           (SETQ BOARD-LIST (CDR BOARD-LIST))
           (GO START)))))
```

Now the next step introduces some action. The biggest value found so far from subtrees is compared against BETA.

```
(DEFINE (BIGGEST6 BOARD ALPHA BETA)
  (COND
    ((QUIET BOARD) (STATIC-VALUE BOARD))
    ((PROG (BOARD-LIST NEXT-BOARD NEW-VALUE
             NEW-LIST BIGGEST-VALUE)
           (SETQ BOARD-LIST (PLAUSIBLE-MOVES BOARD))
     START(COND ((NULL BOARD-LIST) (RETURN BIGGEST-VALUE)))
           (SETQ NEXT-BOARD (CAR BOARD-LIST))
           (SETQ NEW-VALUE
                 (SMALLEST6 NEXT-BOARD ALPHA BETA))
           (SETQ NEW-LIST (CONS NEW-VALUE NEW-LIST))
           (SETQ BIGGEST-VALUE (APPLY 'MAX NEW-LIST))
           (COND ((GREATERP BIGGEST-VALUE BETA)
                  (PRINT 'BETA-CUTOFF)
                  (RETURN BIGGEST-VALUE)))
           (SETQ BOARD-LIST (CDR BOARD-LIST))
           (GO START)))))
```

If the biggest value found is greater than the value of BETA, then it is demonstrated that further study of the plausible moves below the situation represented by BOARD is fruitless. Why? Because BIGGEST6 is called by a minimizing instance of SMALLEST6 exploring moves of which one is already known to lead to a score of BETA. If the minimizing SMALLEST6 standing just above several instances of BIGGEST6 knows that the board situation given to one particular BIGGEST6 can be played to a score worse for it than BETA, then it is foolish to study that particular situation further. Cutoff occurs, and the biggest value found so far, the one that demonstrates that the move is a bad choice, is returned.

Alpha and Beta Values Flow up and down the Tree

Now that the use of ALPHA and BETA is in hand, attention must be given to setting them at the correct values. This is tricky. First of all BIGGEST7, which *uses* the BETA value from above, will be the function that *sets* the ALPHA value to be used below. This is true because an instance of SMALLEST7 exploring an alternative descendant from BOARD will want to quit if it sees that its situation leads to a score that is worse than one BIGGEST7 already knows is achievable. But the best score known to BIGGEST7 is the larger of the ALPHA value coming down through the argument list and the biggest value for NEW-VALUE found so far. Said another way, the ALPHA to pass on is either the one received or the biggest NEW-VALUE seen. This means that BIGGEST-VALUE and NEW-LIST can be eliminated by appropriately resetting ALPHA each time around the loop.

```
(DEFINE (BIGGEST7 BOARD ALPHA BETA)
  (COND ((QUIET BOARD) (STATIC-VALUE BOARD))
        ((PROG (BOARD-LIST NEXT-BOARD NEW-VALUE)
               (SETQ BOARD-LIST (PLAUSIBLE-MOVES BOARD))
          START(COND ((NULL BOARD-LIST) (RETURN ALPHA)))
               (SETQ NEXT-BOARD (CAR BOARD-LIST))
               (SETQ NEW-VALUE
                   (SMALLEST7 NEXT-BOARD ALPHA BETA))
               (SETQ ALPHA (MAX NEW-VALUE ALPHA))
               (COND ((OR (GREATERP ALPHA BETA)
                          (EQUAL ALPHA BETA))
                      (PRINT 'BETA-CUTOFF)
                      (RETURN ALPHA)))
               (SETQ BOARD-LIST (CDR BOARD-LIST))
               (GO START)))))
```

The alpha-beta procedure now works fine, the value returned by the top-level function application is correct, and no more of the tree is explored than necessary. One defect, however, is that there is no way of knowing which move is correct! Keeping track of which moves in the plausible-move lists lie on the minimax line of play was forgotten. The next collection of changes prepares to solve this problem by introducing MOVE-NUMBER, a variable which is incremented each time around the PROG loop.

```
(DEFINE (BIGGEST8 BOARD ALPHA BETA)
  (COND
    ((QUIET BOARD) (STATIC-VALUE BOARD))
    ((PROG (BOARD-LIST MOVE-NUMBER NEXT-BOARD NEW-VALUE)
           (SETQ BOARD-LIST (PLAUSIBLE-MOVES BOARD))
           (SETQ MOVE-NUMBER 1.)
      START(COND ((NULL BOARD-LIST) (RETURN ALPHA)))
           (SETQ NEXT-BOARD (CAR BOARD-LIST))
           (SETQ NEW-VALUE
               (SMALLEST8 NEXT-BOARD ALPHA BETA))
           (COND ((GREATERP NEW-VALUE ALPHA)
                  (SETQ ALPHA NEW-VALUE)))
           (COND ((OR (GREATERP ALPHA BETA)
                      (EQUAL ALPHA BETA))
                  (PRINT 'BETA-CUTOFF)
                  (RETURN ALPHA)))
           (SETQ BOARD-LIST (CDR BOARD-LIST))
           (SETQ MOVE-NUMBER (ADD1 MOVE-NUMBER))
           (GO START)))))
```

Now the PROG looping mechanism contains a loop number named MOVE-NUMBER signifying which element of the plausible-move list it is working on, and moreover, the moves which produce new maximum scores are easy to single out inasmuch as they cause ALPHA to be reset. These new additions will be used to produce a description of the minimax line of play because in the next version, BIGGEST9 constructs a list of move numbers which specify the correct sequence. The list begins at the bottom of the tree as NIL, since below the bottom node there are no moves.

Moving back from the bottom, it is only necessary to add on the value of MOVE-NUMBER deemed the winner at each level. The only problem is that the list of correct moves cannot be passed upward as the values for BIGGEST9 and SMALLEST9 since they already serve to pass minimax values. The solution, although awkward, is to combine both the minimax value and the path into a single, two-element list which then is the value returned.

```
(DEFINE (BIGGEST9 BOARD ALPHA BETA)
  (COND
    ((QUIET BOARD) (LIST (STATIC-VALUE BOARD) NIL))
    ((PROG (BOARD-LIST MOVE-NUMBER NEXT-BOARD NEW-VALUE
            MOVE-LIST RESULT)
           (SETQ BOARD-LIST (PLAUSIBLE-MOVES BOARD))
           (SETQ MOVE-NUMBER 1.)
           (SETQ RESULT (LIST ALPHA NIL))
     START(COND ((NULL BOARD-LIST) (RETURN RESULT)))
           (SETQ NEXT-BOARD (CAR BOARD-LIST))
           (SETQ NEW-VALUE (SMALLEST9 NEXT-BOARD ALPHA BETA)
            MOVE-LIST (CADR NEW-VALUE)
            NEW-VALUE (CAR NEW-VALUE))
           (COND ((GREATERP NEW-VALUE ALPHA)
                  (SETQ ALPHA NEW-VALUE)
                  (SETQ RESULT (LIST NEW-VALUE
                                     (CONS MOVE-NUMBER
                                           MOVE-LIST)))))
           (COND ((OR (GREATERP ALPHA BETA)
                      (EQUAL ALPHA BETA))
                  (PRINT 'BETA-CUTOFF)
                  (RETURN RESULT)))
           (SETQ BOARD-LIST (CDR BOARD-LIST))
           (SETQ MOVE-NUMBER (ADD1 MOVE-NUMBER))
           (GO START)))))
```

At the bottom of the recursion, QUIET's success leads to a returned value consisting of the static evaluation together with an empty path list. Working upward, a more complicated SETQ is needed to set the values for NEW-VALUE and MOVE-LIST, since those values must be unpacked from the two-element lists returned from below. RESULT consists of the minimax value, NEW-VALUE, together with MOVE-LIST augmented by MOVE-NUMBER. It may be reset many times before being returned. Note that return results either when alpha-beta comparison demands it or the plausible-move list is empty. Of course RESULT must be initialized just in case no NEW-VALUE is bigger than the initial ALPHA. Should this happen, the ALPHA value in RESULT insures that the path will not be used and the NIL path list is therefore never inspected.

The next changes do nothing more than dress things up a bit by adding a depth-counting variable and a print function. QUIET might well use DEPTH to help decide if further branching would be appropriate.

```
(DEFINE (BIGGEST10 BOARD ALPHA BETA DEPTH)
  (COND
    ((QUIET BOARD) (LIST (STATIC-VALUE BOARD) NIL))
    ((PROG (BOARD-LIST MOVE-NUMBER NEXT-BOARD NEW-VALUE
            MOVE-LIST RESULT)
          (SETQ BOARD-LIST (PLAUSIBLE-MOVES BOARD))
          (SETQ MOVE-NUMBER 1.)
          (SETQ RESULT (LIST ALPHA NIL))
     START(COND ((NULL BOARD-LIST) (RETURN RESULT)))
          (SETQ NEXT-BOARD (CAR BOARD-LIST))
          (SETQ NEW-VALUE (SMALLEST10 NEXT-BOARD
                                      ALPHA
                                      BETA
                                      (ADD1 DEPTH)))
             MOVE-LIST (CADR NEW-VALUE)
             NEW-VALUE (CAR NEW-VALUE))
          (COND ((GREATERP NEW-VALUE ALPHA)
                 (SETQ ALPHA NEW-VALUE)
                 (SETQ RESULT (LIST NEW-VALUE
                                    (CONS MOVE-NUMBER
                                          MOVE-LIST)))))
          (COND ((OR (GREATERP ALPHA BETA)
                     (EQUAL ALPHA BETA))
                 (PRINT-MESSAGE 'BETA BOARD-LIST DEPTH)
                 (RETURN RESULT)))
          (SETQ BOARD-LIST (CDR BOARD-LIST))
          (SETQ MOVE-NUMBER (ADD1 MOVE-NUMBER))
          (GO START)))))
```

At this point things are well in hand, but a close look shows that the program stumbles if PLAUSIBLE-MOVES happens to return an empty list. This is easy to fix by testing for the empty list and returning the static value of the current board if it ever occurs. The test is done in BIGGEST11 in combination with the quiescence test. Both tests are done now inside the scope of the PROG so that BOARD-LIST can be set at the same time.

```
(DEFINE (BIGGEST11 BOARD ALPHA BETA DEPTH)
  (PROG (BOARD-LIST MOVE-NUMBER NEXT-BOARD NEW-VALUE
         MOVE-LIST RESULT)
        (COND ((OR (QUIET BOARD)
                   (NOT (SETQ BOARD-LIST
                              (PLAUSIBLE-MOVES BOARD))))
               (RETURN (LIST (STATIC-VALUE BOARD) NIL))))
        (SETQ MOVE-NUMBER 1.)
        (SETQ RESULT (LIST ALPHA NIL))
        START
        (COND ((NULL BOARD-LIST) (RETURN RESULT)))
        (SETQ NEXT-BOARD (CAR BOARD-LIST))
        (SETQ NEW-VALUE
              (SMALLEST11 NEXT-BOARD
                          ALPHA
                          BETA
                          (ADD1 DEPTH))
              MOVE-LIST
              (CADR NEW-VALUE)
              NEW-VALUE
              (CAR NEW-VALUE))
        (COND ((GREATERP NEW-VALUE ALPHA)
               (SETQ ALPHA NEW-VALUE)
               (SETQ RESULT
                     (LIST NEW-VALUE
                           (CONS MOVE-NUMBER
                                 MOVE-LIST)))))
        (COND ((OR (GREATERP ALPHA BETA)
                   (EQUAL ALPHA BETA))
               (PRINT-MESSAGE 'BETA BOARD-LIST DEPTH)
               (RETURN RESULT)))
        (SETQ BOARD-LIST (CDR BOARD-LIST))
        (SETQ MOVE-NUMBER (ADD1 MOVE-NUMBER))
        (GO START)))
```

One Function Can Serve Both Players

Finally, advantage can be taken of the symmetry between BIGGEST11 and
SMALLEST11 to combine them both into a single function, MINIMAX. This is
done by arranging for **MINIMAX** to negate and swap ALPHA and BETA during
the downward recursion and to negate the sign of the scores on the way up
unwinding the recursion. The combination recognizes that the minimizer and
maximizer are using the same strategy but have opposite definitions of the direction
of goodness.

```
(DEFINE (MINIMAX BOARD ALPHA BETA DEPTH)
  (PROG (BOARD-LIST MOVE-NUMBER NEXT-BOARD NEW-VALUE
         MOVE-LIST RESULT)
        (COND ((OR (QUIET BOARD)
                   (NOT (SETQ BOARD-LIST
                              (PLAUSIBLE-MOVES BOARD))))
               (RETURN (LIST (NEW-STATIC-VALUE BOARD
                                               DEPTH)
                             NIL))))
        (SETQ MOVE-NUMBER 1.)
        (SETQ RESULT (LIST ALPHA NIL))
```

```
      START
      (COND ((NULL BOARD-LIST) (RETURN RESULT)))
      (SETQ NEXT-BOARD (CAR BOARD-LIST))
      (SETQ NEW-VALUE
            (MINIMAX NEXT-BOARD
                     (MINUS BETA)
                     (MINUS ALPHA)
                     (ADD1 DEPTH))
            MOVE-LIST
            (CADR NEW-VALUE)
            NEW-VALUE
            (MINUS (CAR NEW-VALUE)))
      (COND ((GREATERP NEW-VALUE ALPHA)
             (SETQ ALPHA NEW-VALUE)
             (SETQ RESULT
                   (LIST NEW-VALUE
                         (CONS MOVE-NUMBER
                               MOVE-LIST)))))
      (COND ((OR (GREATERP ALPHA BETA)
                 (EQUAL ALPHA BETA))
             (PRINT-MESSAGE 'MINIMAX
                            BOARD-LIST
                            DEPTH)
             (RETURN RESULT)))
      (SETQ BOARD-LIST (CDR BOARD-LIST))
      (SETQ MOVE-NUMBER (ADD1 MOVE-NUMBER))
      (GO START)))
```

STATIC-VALUE has become NEW-STATIC-VALUE with an extra argument so that the static evaluator can look at the situation from the proper point of view.

When applied to the earlier sample tree, represented by the LISP list as

```
((3) (1 4) ((1 5 9) 2))
```

MINIMAX would yield the following:

```
MINIMAX TRIMS AWAY 1
BRANCH LEVEL = 1
MINIMAX TRIMS AWAY 0
BRANCH LEVEL = 1
(3 (1 1))
```

For the much more complicated tree represented by

```
(((8 7 3) (9 1 6) (2 4 1))
 ((1 3 5) (3 9 2) (6 5 2))
 ((1 2 3) (9 7 2) (1 6 4)))
```

we have

```
MINIMAX TRIMS AWAY 2
BRANCH LEVEL = 2
MINIMAX TRIMS AWAY 1
BRANCH LEVEL = 2
MINIMAX TRIMS AWAY 2
BRANCH LEVEL = 2
MINIMAX TRIMS AWAY 2
BRANCH LEVEL = 1

(5 (2 1 3))
```

The function **PRINT-MESSAGE** requires some new primitive functions for its definition. The details follow for those who must know, but be warned that input-output functions tend to be highly implementation specific when one goes beyond **READ** and **PRINT**.

```
(DEFINE (PRINT-MESSAGE M B D)
        (PROG NIL
              (TERPRI)(TERPRI)
              (PRINC M)
              (PRINC '/ TRIMS/ AWAY/ )
              (PRINC (LENGTH (CDR B)))
              (TERPRI)
              (PRINC 'BRANCH/ LEVEL/ =/ )(PRINC D)))
```

TERPRI causes a carriage return. PRINC prints an atom, but unlike PRINT, it neither precedes it with a carriage return nor follows it with a space. The / characters destroy the ability of the following spaces to separate atoms. Thus the odd character string / TRIMS/ AWAY/ is printed as if it were one atom, but with spaces before, after, and inside.

SUMMARY

■ Basic minimaxing is easy to implement. Two symmetrical functions alternately find the minimum and maximum static values as returned from the bottom of the tree.

■ Adding alpha-beta pruning is harder because it is tricky to cause the alpha and beta values to be created, modified, and used.

■ The development of a complicated program should be done incrementally with each step introducing only a small amount of extension.

REFERENCES

References on the ALPHA-BETA algorithm and other search techniques are given in Chapter 4.

14
SYMBOLIC
PATTERN
MATCHING

Pattern matching is the process of comparing symbolic expressions to see if one is similar to another. The purpose of this chapter is to develop some pattern-matching functions and to look at examples which show that a matching capability can be a key element in making otherwise large, complicated efforts reachable. Consider, for example, the DOCTOR program, one of the most famous of all toy programs. It is capable of engaging in dialogue like the following:

```
(I DO NOT LIKE COMPUTERS)
   (DO MACHINES FRIGHTEN YOU)
(NOT LIKE MY MOTHER)
   (TELL ME MORE ABOUT YOUR FAMILY)
(YES)
   (PLEASE DO NOT BE SO SHORT WITH ME)
(I AM WORRIED ABOUT FOOD)
   (HOW LONG HAVE YOU BEEN WORRIED ABOUT FOOD)
```

One might think that writing such a program would be a big undertaking. However, the computer's appearance of understanding is derived only from a clever use of key words rather than from genuine analysis and appreciation of what is said. Pattern-matching functions reduce things like the basic DOCTOR program to a few lines of code.

BASIC PATTERN MATCHING

Although LISP itself has no pattern matching built in, it is easy to write pattern-matching functions in LISP. Hence, we say that LISP is a good implementation language for pattern matchers. Many of the matching sublanguages that have been embedded in LISP exhibit the sort of features developed here.

Matching Involves Comparison of Similar S-Expressions

Let us begin by thinking in terms of *pattern* lists and *fact* lists. Often fact lists will be used to represent true statements about some real or supposed world. For the moment, both patterns and facts will be restricted to be lists of atoms. Patterns, however, can contain certain special atoms not allowed in facts, the single character atoms, ? and *, for example.

```
Facts:            (THIS IS A FACT)
                  (COLOR APPLE RED)
                  (SUPPORTS TABLE BLOCK12)
Patterns:         (THIS * PATTERN)
                  (COLOR ? RED)
                  (SUPPORTS TABLE BLOCK12)
```

Soon we will develop a function named MATCH that will compare one pattern and one fact. This function will be used heavily to illustrate matching function implementation and use. First, however, let us see what basic things MATCH is to look for.

When a pattern containing no special atoms is compared to a fact, the two match only if they are exactly the same, with each corresponding position occupied by the same atom. If we match the pattern (COLOR APPLE RED) against the identical fact (COLOR APPLE RED), the match will of course succeed:

```
(MATCH '(COLOR APPLE RED) '(COLOR APPLE RED))
  T
```

But matching (COLOR APPLE RED) against (COLOR APPLE GREEN) loses:

```
(MATCH '(COLOR APPLE RED) '(COLOR APPLE GREEN))
  NIL
```

The special atom ? has the privilege of matching any atom. This greatly expands the usefulness of MATCH:

```
(MATCH '(COLOR APPLE ?) '(COLOR APPLE GREEN))
  T
(MATCH '(COLOR ? RED) '(COLOR APPLE RED))
  T
```

The * similarly expands the flexibility of MATCH by matching *one or more* atoms. Patterns with a * can match against facts that have more atoms in them than the pattern:

```
(MATCH '(* MOTHER *) '(MY MOTHER DISTURBS ME))
  T
```

Now let us see how to implement MATCH. We adopt a strategy of moving down both the pattern and the fact, atom by atom, making sure that the pattern atom and the fact atom match in every position. Translated into LISP terms, we create a function which checks the first elements of two lists, and if satisfied, moves on by calling itself recursively on the CDR of the lists:

```
(DEFINE (MATCH P D)
        (COND ((AND (NULL P) (NULL D)) T)
              ((EQUAL (CAR P) (CAR D))
               (MATCH (CDR P) (CDR D)))))
```

The first clause in the COND checks for when the end of the lists is reached, thus terminating the recursion. Now since we want to proceed not only if the pattern atom and fact atom are the same but also if the pattern atom is a question mark, we generalize slightly:

```
(DEFINE (MATCH P D)
        (COND ((AND (NULL P) (NULL D)) T)
              ((OR (EQUAL (CAR P) '?)
                   (EQUAL (CAR P) (CAR D)))
               (MATCH (CDR P) (CDR D)))))
```

But we must also be sure to check for the case where one of the two lists is shorter than the other — otherwise MATCH would drive itself off the end of the shorter list if the shorter list matched the beginning of the longer list.

```
(DEFINE (MATCH P D)
        (COND ((AND (NULL P) (NULL D)) T)
              ((OR (NULL P) (NULL D)) NIL)
              ((OR (EQUAL (CAR P) '?)
                   (EQUAL (CAR P) (CAR D)))
               (MATCH (CDR P) (CDR D)))))
```

Suppose we try some examples.

```
(MATCH '(COLOR ? RED) '(COLOR APPLE RED))
```

We get a T as the ultimate result as indicated in figure 14-1. But if we were to try

```
(MATCH '(COLOR ORANGE RED) '(COLOR APPLE RED))
```

we would get a NIL result as shown in figure 14-2.

Now to greatly expand the power of our matching function, we incorporate a feature by which a * will match against *one or more* atoms. This is a tentative version:

```
(DEFINE (MATCH P D)
        (COND ((AND (NULL P) (NULL D)) T)
              ((OR (NULL P) (NULL D)) NIL)
              ((OR (EQUAL (CAR P) '?)
                   (EQUAL (CAR P) (CAR D)))
               (MATCH (CDR P) (CDR D)))
              ((EQUAL (CAR P) '*)
               (COND ((MATCH (CDR P) D))
                     ((MATCH (CDR P) (CDR D)))
                     ((MATCH P (CDR D)))))))
```

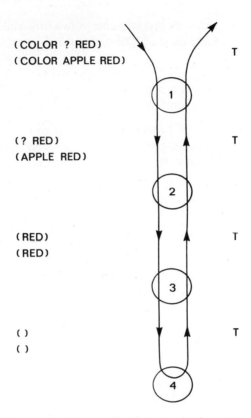

(COLOR ? RED)   T
(COLOR APPLE RED)

(? RED)   T
(APPLE RED)

(RED)   T
(RED)

( )   T
( )

Figure 14-1 MATCH recurses as long as the first atom in the pattern is a ? or is the same as the first atom in the fact. On reaching the end of the pattern and the fact simultaneously, T is returned by the lowest level and passes up to the top.

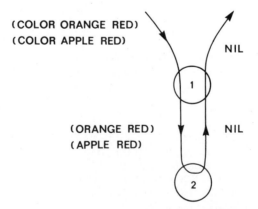

(COLOR ORANGE RED)   NIL
(COLOR APPLE RED)

(ORANGE RED)   NIL
(APPLE RED)

Figure 14-2 As soon as MATCH recurses to a pattern and fact which do not agree in the first position, NIL is returned by the lowest level and passes up to the top.

The *-keyed COND clause in this tentative version initiates recursive calls to MATCH to see if one of three possibilities works out: the * matches nothing, in which case we chip it off and work on the rest of the pattern; the * matches one atom, in which case we chip off both the * and the atom it matches; or the * matches two or more atoms, in which we work forward in the recursive spirit by retaining the * in the pattern while discarding the first of the atoms it matches before recursing.

The second term in the *-keyed COND is really redundant if the * is to match any number of atoms including none. It can be purged and MATCH will still work. For then MATCH chops off the * and matches the remainder of P with the untouched D or keeps the * and moves over one atom of the data, on the presumption that it is one of the atoms matching the *. Probably a simulation would help clarify how the recursion works under these circumstances. See figure 14-3.

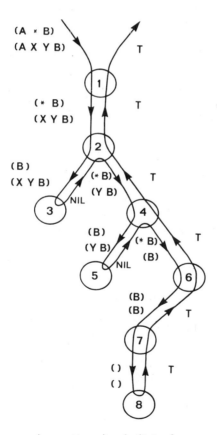

Figure 14-3 When a * appears in a pattern, it substitutes for any number of fact items. To handle *, MATCH deletes either it or the first item in the fact at every level. Deleting the * is tried before absorbing another fact item by retaining it.

Alternatively the first clause of the COND can be dropped rather than the second. Then the * would be forced to match at least one atom as originally specified.

Simultaneous Assignment Adds Expressive Power to Matching Operations

The next dimension of improvement lies in generalizing MATCH so that it assigns values if match is successful. Atoms that begin with > and * act as ? and * for matching purposes, but if match succeeds, their *value* is set to whatever they matched. The > variables are to come out with atomic values while the * variables come out with values that are lists of the atoms matched. The > notation used here is intended to suggest shoving values *into* the variables which are prefixed by the >. Designers of matching languages are often quite baroque in their selection of syntax.

```
(MATCH '(PLUS >A >B) '(PLUS 2 3))
  T
A
  2
B
  3
(MATCH '(*L MOTHER *R) '(MY MOTHER DISTURBS ME))
   T
L
  (MY)
R
  (DISTURBS ME)
```

The > match and assign feature can be implemented by using two new functions, ATOMCAR and ATOMCDR, and adding a clause to the COND in which ATOMCAR peels off the first character in the atom for inspection. Note the use of SET to assign the pattern variable's value to the item it matches in the data.

```
((AND (EQUAL (ATOMCAR P) '>) (MATCH (CDR P) (CDR D)))
 (SET (ATOMCDR P) (CAR D))
 T)
```

Thus we first see if the pattern atom begins with a > and if the rest of the match succeeds. If so we do the indicated variable assignment and pass on a T to the next level up.

In fact, most LISP systems do not have ATOMCAR and ATOMCDR, but often something like EXPLODE and IMPLODE instead. EXPLODE appears in code in order to break up an atom into a list of its constituent characters, each appearing as a single character atom:

```
(EXPLODE 'ATOM)
  (A T O M)
(EXPLODE 'X)
  (X)
```

IMPLODE performs the complementary operation of running a list of atoms together into a single atom:

```
(IMPLODE '(A B A N D C))
   ABANDC
```

ATOMCAR and ATOMCDR are easy to define using EXPLODE and IMPLODE:

```
(DEFINE (ATOMCAR X)
        (CAR (EXPLODE X)))
(DEFINE (ATOMCDR X)
        (IMPLODE (CDR (EXPLODE X))))
```

■ This implementation of the simultaneous assignment feature suffers from inefficiency because the EXPLODE and IMPLODE operations happen very often. It would clearly be faster to use a more awkward syntax where the atom >XYZ is represented as the list, (> XYZ). Instead of writing

```
(MATCH '(PLUS >A >B) '(PLUS 2 3))
```

one would write

```
(MATCH '(PLUS (> A) (> B)) '(PLUS 2 3))
```

■ The best of both alternatives can be had in advanced LISP systems which permit characters to be declared to have certain special properties when moving from a file or a keyboard into active central memory. Then it can be arranged that atoms beginning with the > are converted to two-element lists beginning with > once and for all. The user sees only nice syntax, but internally, LISP exploits the ugly, efficient syntax.

The * variables are handled in the same spirit, this time setting their values to a list of the atoms matched by using the following:

```
((EQUAL (ATOMCAR (CAR P)) '*)
 (COND ((MATCH (CDR P) (CDR D))
        (SET (ATOMCDR (CAR P)) (LIST (CAR D)))
        T)
       ((MATCH P (CDR D))
        (SET (ATOMCDR (CAR P))
             (CONS (CAR D) (EVAL (ATOMCDR (CAR P)))))
        T)))
```

Note that no assignment takes place and no SETs are executed until all recursion has happened and it is definitely known that the match has succeeded. Then as T values return through higher and higher levels, the relevant SETs are executed and proceed to build the appropriate list. The process begins with the expression:

```
(SET (ATOMCDR (CAR P)) (LIST (CAR D)))
```

This begins the construction of the list at the point where the * is matched finally against the last atom it represents and is no longer carried forward in the recursion.

Then, as unwinding proceeds through levels where the * was retained to match atoms further down the list, we find the expression:

```
(SET (ATOMCDR (CAR P))
     (CONS (CAR D) (EVAL (ATOMCDR (CAR P)))))
```

The EVAL obtains the list of atoms seen so far using (ATOMCDR (CAR P)), the CONS adds the atom matched at the current level, and the SET causes the augmented list to become the new value of the * variable. And so it goes until all atoms matched are in the list.

Look carefully at this example.

```
(MATCH '(A *L B) '(A X Y B))
```

Figure 14-4 shows that *L should match with X and Y, assigning L to (X Y) in the process.

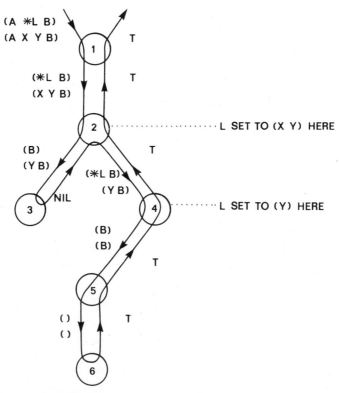

Figure 14-4 Variables prefaced by * substitute for any number of fact items. Successful matching leads to setting the * variables to the fact items they account for.

Restrictions Limit What a Pattern Variable Can Match

Another improvement may be made if we wish neither to specify a particular atom in a position nor to permit any atom at all. Rather we demand a member of some class of atoms like the numbers or the atoms of a particular length or the atoms with a particular property on their property list. For these purposes we introduce the restriction feature. To use it, one substitutes a descriptive list into the pattern where previously only atoms were expected. The list has the form:

```
(RESTRICT <either ? or a > variable>
          <a predicate>
             .
             .
          .)
```

The idea is that the corresponding position in the fact must be occupied by an atom which satisfies all of the one or more predicates listed in the restriction. Thus, we might define a predicate that has the value T only on atoms of four letters:

```
(DEFINE (4LETTERP A) (EQUAL (LENGTH (EXPLODE A)) 4))
```

Such a predicate could then be used in a restriction package to limit the class of acceptable atoms in the corresponding fact position to those of four letters. The restriction package would have the form:

```
(RESTRICT ? 4LETTERP)
```

and could be used as in the following example, where we use >V instead of using a ? to allow a look at what the package matches.

```
(MATCH '(* (RESTRICT >V 4LETTERP) *)
       '(THE HOUSE IS BLUE AND WHITE))
   T
```

V now has the value BLUE.

Restrictions can be implemented for the ? as follows:

```
((AND (NOT (ATOM (CAR P)))
      (EQUAL (CAAR P) 'RESTRICT)
      (EQUAL (CADAR P) '?)
      (APPLY 'AND
             (MAPCAR '(LAMBDA (PRED)
                               (FUNCALL PRED (CAR D)))
                     (CDDAR P))))
 (MATCH (CDR P) (CDR D)))
```

Once the appropriate tests are made to determine that a restriction package is present, the atom in the fact is supplied to the predicates in the restriction through the MAPCAR. The AND tests afterward to see if all predicates involved returned Ts, and if so, the entire COND test is successful and recursion takes place through this item. Of course a similar feature could be added for *-type variables.

A definition for **MATCH** follows which includes everything other than restricted * variables which are omitted merely to keep the size of the program smaller:

```
(DEFINE (MATCH P D)
  (COND
    ((AND (NULL P) (NULL D)) T)
    ((OR (NULL P) (NULL D)) NIL)
    ((AND (NOT (ATOM (CAR P)))
          (EQUAL (CAAR P) 'RESTRICT)
          (EQUAL (CADAR P) '?)
          (APPLY 'AND
                 (MAPCAR '(LAMBDA (PRED)
                                  (FUNCALL PRED (CAR D)))
                         (CDDAR P))))
     (MATCH (CDR P) (CDR D)))
    ((AND (NOT (ATOM (CAR P)))
          (EQUAL (CAAR P) 'RESTRICT)
          (EQUAL (ATOMCAR (CADAR P)) '>)
          (APPLY 'AND
                 (MAPCAR '(LAMBDA (PRED)
                                  (FUNCALL PRED (CAR D)))
                         (CDDAR P)))
          (MATCH (CDR P) (CDR D)))
     (SET (ATOMCDR (CADAR P)) (CAR D))
     T)
    ((OR (EQUAL (CAR P) '?) (EQUAL (CAR P) (CAR D)))
     (MATCH (CDR P) (CDR D)))
    ((AND (ATOM (CAR P))
          (EQUAL (ATOMCAR (CAR P)) '>)
          (MATCH (CDR P) (CDR D)))
     (SET (ATOMCDR (CAR P)) (CAR D))
     T)
    ((EQUAL (CAR P) '*)
     (COND ((MATCH (CDR P) (CDR D))) ((MATCH P (CDR D)))))
    ((AND (ATOM (CAR P))(EQUAL (ATOMCAR (CAR P)) '*))
     (COND ((MATCH (CDR P) (CDR D))
            (SET (ATOMCDR (CAR P)) (LIST (CAR D)))
            T)
           ((MATCH P (CDR D))
            (SET (ATOMCDR (CAR P))
                 (CONS (CAR D) (EVAL (ATOMCDR (CAR P)))))
            T)))))
```

There are, incidentally, other things of value in a matcher. For one thing, it is often useful to get values out of pattern variables as well as in. This is illustrated by the following which uses a < syntax to demand that the fact element must correspond to the values of the data element, not the data element itself.

```
(MATCH '(>THIS)
       '(A))
  T
(MATCH '(<THIS)
       '(A))
  T
(MATCH '(<THIS)
       '(B))
  NIL
```

With this addition the > and < characters form a nicely mnemonic and complementary pair. One means *shove* a value into the variable *after* match; the other means *pull* a value out *before* match.

In subsequent chapters > and < variable features are required while the * features are not.

Many Matching Problems Remain

The matcher just described is a simple one because it focuses on matching one list of atoms against another. Moreover, no such thing as close match is involved — the matcher either succeeds or fails. Dealing with networks or frames or other larger knowledge chunks may be much harder since the following possibilities arise:

- The matcher must deal with more general data structures. There is flexibility in how parts may correspond.
- The matcher is to report how the match scores on a scale ranging from not at all through poor and good all the way to perfect. Perhaps there should be a summary description of the match.

Building in these capabilities can be very hard. The literature offers very little guidance.

THE SIMULATED PSYCHIATRIST

With just what we have so far, it is easy to write a simple version of a program which seems to interact with persons at a terminal much like the way one type of psychiatrist interacts with a patient on the couch. The program, DOCTOR, is just a loop through a COND which contains tests for key words and phrases, together with appropriate responses.

```
(DEFINE (DOCTOR)
        (PROG (L MOTHER S)
              (PRINT '(SPEAK UP!))
              LOOP
              (SETQ S (READ))
              (COND ((MATCH '(I AM WORRIED *L) S)
                     (PRINT (APPEND '(HOW LONG
                                          HAVE
                                          YOU
                                          BEEN
                                          WORRIED)
                                    L)))
                    ((MATCH '(* MOTHER *) S)
                     (SETQ MOTHER T)
                     (PRINT '(TELL ME
                                   MORE
                                   ABOUT
                                   YOUR
                                   FAMILY)))
                    ((MATCH '(* COMPUTERS *) S)
                     (PRINT '(DO MACHINES FRIGHTEN YOU)))
                    ((OR (MATCH '(NO) S) (MATCH '(YES) S))
                     (PRINT '(PLEASE DO
                                     NOT
                                     BE
                                     SO
                                     SHORT
                                     WITH
                                     ME)))
                    ((MATCH '(* (RESTRICT ? BADWORD) *) S)
                     (PRINT '(PLEASE DO
                                     NOT
                                     USE
                                     WORDS
                                     LIKE
                                     THAT)))
                    (MOTHER (SETQ MOTHER NIL)
                            (PRINT '(EARLIER YOU
                                             SPOKE
                                             OF
                                             YOUR
                                             MOTHER)))
                    (T (PRINT '(I AM SORRY OUR TIME IS UP))
                       (RETURN 'GOODBY)))
              (GO LOOP)))
```

Note that READ and PRINT establish communication with the user. Note also that if a sentence containing MOTHER is encountered, the variable MOTHER is set to T. Then later on if nothing else in the conditional is triggered, the response of EARLIER YOU TALKED OF YOUR MOTHER seems very judicious.

The Doctor Program Can Seem to Understand

The program could and has been elaborated greatly with large scripts, but even our simple version can carry out a dialogue for a few steps:

```
(SPEAK UP)
   (I AM WORRIED ABOUT THE WEATHER)
(HOW LONG HAVE YOU BEEN WORRIED ABOUT THE WEATHER)
   (SINCE MY MOTHER PASSED AWAY)
(TELL ME MORE ABOUT YOUR FAMILY)
   (THEY ARE ALL INTO COMPUTERS)
(DO MACHINES FRIGHTEN YOU)
   (NO)
(PLEASE DO NOT BE SO SHORT WITH ME)
   (I AM SORRY)
(EARLIER YOU TALKED OF YOUR MOTHER)
```

Further improvement can be had through little functions that replace instances of MY by YOUR in the matched patterns, so that something like:

```
(I AM WORRIED ABOUT MY HEALTH)
```

might give

```
(YOU SAY YOU ARE WORRIED ABOUT YOUR HEALTH)
```

The Doctor Program Is Stupid

It is important to note that the DOCTOR program has no real understanding of the user. It builds no model of the problems it seems to discuss, but depends instead on superficial key-word observations.

THE ALGEBRA STUDENT

It is now relatively easy to understand the operation of a set of programs found at the heart of Bobrow's system for working high-school algebra problems. The principal programs are as indicated in figure 14-5.

■ In step 1, compound English sentences are broken up by SEPARATE into the so-called kernel sentences, each of which corresponds to exactly one equation.

■ In step 2, each kernel sentence is converted into an equation in LISP form using the TRANSLATE program.

■ In step 3, the equations are solved by SOLVE, a program that we will not explore here.

■ In step 4, the answer is reported or more information is requested by ANSWER, a program much like the DOCTOR program in the sense that there are some standard answer formats with empty slots ready to receive information from SOLVE.

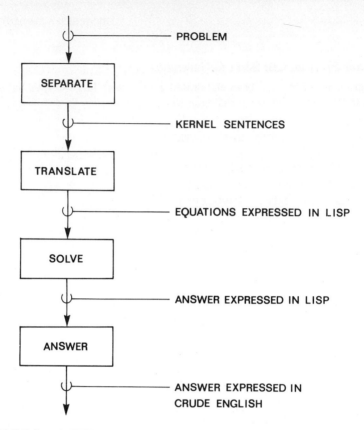

Figure 14-5 Bobrow's STUDENT is a program which solves high-school algebra problems stated in simple English. The strategy is to translate descriptions in English into simultaneous equations, a special case of translation from a communication language into a problem-oriented language.

Working Word Problems Requires Little Other Than English-to-Prefix Conversion

To get a better feel for the function of these procedures, consider a simple example, given first as it would appear in a textbook:

> *If the number of customers Tom gets is twice the square of 20 percent of the number of ads he runs, and the number of ads he runs is 45, what is the number of customers he gets?*

Translated into a form suitable for attack, we have this:

```
(IF THE NUMBER OF CUSTOMERS TOM GETS IS TWICE THE SQUARE OF
20 PERCENT OF THE NUMBER OF ADS HE RUNS C AND THE NUMBER OF
ADS HE RUNS IS 45 C WHAT IS THE NUMBER OF CUSTOMERS HE GETS
Q)
```

The whole problem has become a long list and normal English punctuation marks have been replaced by C, P, and Q. Punctuation replacement is required partly because the comma and period have special, albeit now obsolete meaning in LISP. The question mark has also been replaced in order to avoid problems of conflict with the ? symbol recognized by MATCH.

The list as shown is certainly a compound sentence and must be broken down by SEPARATE into pieces which correspond to equations. SEPARATE yields the following result:

```
((THE NUMBER OF CUSTOMERS TOM GETS IS TWICE THE
  SQUARE OF 20 PERCENT OF THE NUMBER OF ADS HE RUNS)
 (THE NUMBER OF ADS HE RUNS IS 45)
 (UNKNOWN IS THE NUMBER OF CUSTOMERS HE GETS))
```

Now that each element of the list generated by SEPARATE clearly specifies an equation, TRANSLATE can operate on them to produce these:

```
((EQUAL (THE NUMBER OF CUSTOMERS TOM GETS)
        (TIMES 2.
               (EXPT (TIMES 0.2
                            (THE NUMBER OF ADS HE RUNS))
                     2.)))
 (EQUAL (THE NUMBER OF ADS HE RUNS) 45)
 (EQUAL (UNKNOWN) (THE NUMBER OF CUSTOMERS HE GETS)))
```

Note that lists have the odd role of acting as algebraic variables in the resulting expressions. The particular set of equations from the sample problem requires some extra work because the pronoun HE must be matched against TOM, but otherwise no problems are evident. When SOLVE does its duty, the result is:

```
(EQUAL (THE NUMBER OF CUSTOMERS HE GETS) 162)
```

ANSWER can then report:

```
(THE NUMBER OF CUSTOMERS HE GETS IS 162 P)
```

Compound Sentences Are First Translated into Kernels

So far we have the overall strategy of the system in hand. To understand the details, first consider SEPARATE, the program for preparing problems for translation. It does its job by searching for key word and punctuation combinations, segmenting according to what is found, and passing the pieces on for further separation. When the input shows no signs of being compound, recursion stops and the resulting kernel sentences are assembled together by applications of APPEND as the recursion is unwound.

```
(DEFINE (SEPARATE S)
  (PROG (R L W)
        (RETURN (COND ((MATCH '(IF *L
                                   C
                                   (RESTRICT >W QWORD)
                                   *R)
                              S)
                       (APPEND (SEPARATE L)
                               (SEPARATE (CONS W R))))
                      ((MATCH '(*L C AND *R) S)
                       (APPEND (SEPARATE L) (SEPARATE R)))
                      ((MATCH '((RESTRICT >W QWORD) *R Q) S)
                       (SEPARATE (CONS 'UNKNOWN R)))
                      ((MATCH '(*L P *R) S)
                       (APPEND (SEPARATE L) (SEPARATE R)))
                      (T (LIST S))))))
```

Note that the situations recognized arc thc following:

> IF ... C <question word> ...
>
> ... C AND ...
>
> ... P ...
>
> ... <question word> ... Q

English to Prefix Translation Converts Kernels into Equations

TRANSLATE converts English sentences representing algebraic relationships into LISP expressions reflecting the same constraints. On inspection, it is clear that the basic strategy is the same as for **SEPARATE**, but some of the details have changed.

```
(DEFINE (TRANSLATE E)
  (PROG (V L R)
    (RETURN
      (COND
        ((MATCH '(*L IS *R) E)
         (LIST 'EQUAL (TRANSLATE L) (TRANSLATE R)))
        ((MATCH '(THE DIFFERENCE BETWEEN *L AND *R) E)
         (LIST 'DIFFERENCE (TRANSLATE L) (TRANSLATE R)))
        ((MATCH '(THE SUM OF *L AND *R) E)
         (LIST 'PLUS (TRANSLATE L) (TRANSLATE R)))
        ((MATCH '((RESTRICT >V NUMBERP) PERCENT *R) E)
         (TRANSLATE (APPEND (LIST (QUOTIENT V 100.0)) R)))
        ((MATCH '(*L TIMES *R) E)
         (LIST 'TIMES (TRANSLATE L) (TRANSLATE R)))
        ((MATCH '(TWICE *R) E)
         (LIST 'TIMES 2. (TRANSLATE R)))
        ((MATCH '((RESTRICT >V NUMBERP) OF *R) E)
         (LIST 'TIMES V (TRANSLATE R)))
        ((MATCH '(THE SQUARE OF *R) E)
         (LIST 'EXPT (TRANSLATE R) 2.))
```

```
((MATCH '(*L SQUARED) E)
 (LIST 'EXPT (TRANSLATE L) 2.))
((MATCH '((RESTRICT >V NUMBERP)) E) V)
(E)))))
```

The principal difference between **SEPARATE** and **TRANSLATE** is that **SEPARATE** has less to do during the unwinding phase. **SEPARATE** and **TRANSLATE** both have the following basic structure:

```
(DEFINE (<function name> <variable>)
        (PROG (<prog variables>)
              (RETURN (COND <clauses containing recursive
                            calls to the function and
                            directions for assembling
                            a result>))))
```

In TRANSLATE, note that there is liberal use of the RESTRICT facility. This is necessary because determining whether some words are used as operators requires an examination of their context. For example, the presence of a preceding fraction is a strong clue that *of* is being used as a multiplication operator rather than as a preposition. This usage allows proper translation of

```
.8 OF THE ...
```

but does not try to similarly interpret

```
BOX OF APPLES
```

Recursion is terminated whenever no operators are found in the list handed to the function as an argument. If the list just contains a single number, the number is returned. Otherwise the list is returned as is, unaltered.

When applied to the sentences from a word problem, a set of equations is produced which SOLVE uses to answer the question. Figure 14-6 illustrates how one of the sample kernel sentences from the example is split up and reassembled in the course of TRANSLATE's reflections.

The Notion of Translation Is Extremely Important

The algebra-word-problem system deserves no accolades for its syntactic prowess. Both SEPARATE and TRANSLATE are hopelessly ignorant of noun group and sentence structure. Nevertheless the system is important inasmuch as it demonstrated the utility of translating English descriptions into other descriptions suited for immediate problem solution. For algebra problems, the language of equations is the appropriate target. For blocks-world robot discourse, the language of programs serves and English is better translated into function calls or data-base searches. Because it focused on description translation, Bobrow's program was the beginning of an intellectual tradition that attempts to face the semantics of language.

(THE NUMBER OF CUSTOMERS TOM GETS IS TWICE THE SQUARE
OF 20. PERCENT OF THE NUMBER OF ADS HE RUNS)

(EQUAL (THE NUMBER OF CUSTOMERS TOM GETS)
    (TIMES 2. (EXPT (TIMES 0.2 (THE NUMBER OF ADS HE RUNS)) 2.)))

(THE NUMBER OF CUSTOMERS TOM GETS)

(THE NUMBER OF CUSTOMERS TOM GETS)

(TWICE THE SQUARE OF 20. PERCENT OF THE NUMBER OF ADS HE RUNS)

(TIMES 2. (EXPT (TIMES 0.2 (THE NUMBER OF ADS HE RUNS)) 2.))

(THE SQUARE OF 20. PERCENT OF THE NUMBER OF ADS HE RUNS)

(EXPT (TIMES 0.2 (THE NUMBER OF ADS HE RUNS)) 2.)

(20. PERCENT OF THE NUMBER OF ADS HE RUNS)

(TIMES 0.2 (THE NUMBER OF ADS HE RUNS))

(0.2 OF THE NUMBER OF ADS HE RUNS)

(TIMES 0.2 (THE NUMBER OF ADS HE RUNS))

(THE NUMBER OF ADS HE RUNS)

(THE NUMBER OF ADS HE RUNS)

Figure 14-6 After compound sentences are broken into their constituent parts, translation begins. The translation specialist recurses into a sentence by matching it against a library of standard patterns. An algebraic equation is built up when the recursion unwinds.

SUMMARY

■ Pattern matching is found frequently at the heart of good systems. One reason for the popularity of LISP lies in its power as a language for implementing pattern-matching functions.

■ Matching functions exhibit some combination of features beyond the ability to handle basic equivalence. Among the very useful are provisions for simultaneous matching and variable assignment and for matching with restrictions.

■ While the DOCTOR program must be considered strictly a toy, it nevertheless shows how a powerful matching function can simplify programming. The fundamental principle is that psychiatrist-like responses can be selected by examining the patient's sentences for key words and combinations of key words.

■ The algebra word problem system, STUDENT, is on the main evolutionary path of work in natural-language understanding because it demonstrates the power of description translation. It consists of programs for four activities, SEPARATE, TRANSLATE, SOLVE, and ANSWER. The first two convert problem input into a set of algebraic equations expressed in LISP. Both are simple, straightforward programming exercises.

REFERENCES

■ Joseph Weizenbaum, "ELIZA — A Computer Program for the Study of Natural Language Communication between Man and Machine," *Communications of the Association for Computing Machinery,* vol. 9, no. 1, January 1965. The original DOCTOR was a program written for the interpretive system called ELIZA. ELIZA itself was written in MAD, an ALGOL like language, augmented by the list processor SLIP. Other ELIZA scripts enabled ELIZA to accumulate some knowledge about what was being talked about, to make some inferences, and to do some computations in the domain of discourse. (See Weizenbaum's paper "Contextual Understanding by Computers," Communications of the Association for Computing Machinery, vol. 10, no. 8, August 1967.) The interesting thing about the DOCTOR script is that it illustrates how little machinery is required to create the *illusion* of understanding. One should keep in mind that the ELIZA system was written to explore what were then new ideas in pattern matching and symbol manipulation. It was not thought of as a crucial step toward computer understanding of natural language. Weizenbaum himself feels that DOCTOR was largely a joke that, unfortunatly, some people took too seriously.

■ Daniel G. Bobrow, "Natural Language Input for a Computer Problem-Solving System," in *Semantic Information Processing,* edited by Marvin Minsky, The M.I.T. Press, Cambridge, Massachusetts, 1968. This is one of the great classics of early Artificial Intelligence. It is possible to see the program as a precurser to much subsequent natural-language work since the theme of translation from English description to problem-solving description is strong. Bobrow's matching language, METEOR, strongly resembles the one developed here.

■   A. P. Ambler, H. G. Barrow, C. M. Brown, R. M. Burstall and R. J. Popplestone, "A Versatile System for Computer Controlled Assembly," *Artificial Intelligence,* vol. 6, no. 2, 1975. This paper describes work on network matching in the course of discussing assembly issues. The network matching is not at all limited to that context, however.

15

IMPLEMENTING
EMBEDDED
LANGUAGES

This chapter has three purposes. The first is to show how LISP can be used to implement other languages via translation processes. The second is to gain a second look at the Augmented Transition Networks and Production Systems notions by using them in language-implementation examples. And the third is to better understand how LISP itself operates by sketching out a LISP definition in LISP.

A compiler and two interpreters will be involved. Take note that the word *compiler* is used in a general sense meaning a translator from one language into another, somehow more convenient one. This is different from the more restricted sense of the word which implies that the translation is into some computer's basic instruction set.

COMPILING AUGMENTED TRANSITION NETWORKS INTO LISP PROGRAMS

The purpose here is to show how Augmented Transition Networks can be translated from graphs into LISP. Deepening the inquest into matching and natural-language understanding is one purpose with illuminating the symbol manipulation involved in compiling special-purpose languages being an additional goal.

Recall that a transition network is a formalism designed to capture the regularities of natural-language syntax.

■ Any given network consists of nodes linked by arcs labeled with abbreviated names for word classes like noun, verb, adjective, preposition, determiner, and the like. Analysis of a word sequence is accomplished in the course of driving a path through the network, taking the word classes as instructions for what arcs to take. Legitimate sequences lead to so-called terminal states.

343

■ Several smaller networks may be linked together into one larger system through a convention by which some arcs correspond to successful traversal of a network rather than just the consumption of one word. For example, a noun group network has a preposition group arc and a preposition group has a noun group arc, thus giving a recursive flavor to the formalism.

■ There may be more action taking place on the arcs than just recognition of word classes and movement down a sentence. The transition network is said to be augmented if it is permitted to make notes as arcs are traversed and to refer to those notes. One might, for example, make a note that a noun group is surely singular in moving over the determiner arc with the word *a*. A later test could check that conclusion when the noun is encountered.

Sometimes a combination of state and next word is encountered which allows more than one exit to another state, some of which may lead to a reasonable interpretation with others going toward dead ends. A full-capability ATN should have some way of coping with this branching. Usually depth-first search through automatic backup is specified on the ground of relative simplicity.

Warning: the automatic backup feature of the standard ATN formalism is *not* to be implemented. There are two reasons for omitting backup. First, there is considerable doubt about the wisdom of depth-first search and stronger alternatives are under development. And second, omitting the search permits even greater simplicity, albeit with a loss of power.

Satisfying an Augmented Transition Network Constitutes a Kind of Match

From a certain point of view, an augmented transition network is a generalized pattern of the sort seen already. The changes are considerable however:

■ In ATN "matches," any word feature can be tested, not just the word itself.

■ In ATN "patterns," subpatterns can be specified by reference to allied networks. These references can be recursive.

■ In ATN "execution," progress can be guided by dynamic changes in mode dictated by setting and examining registers.

Making LISP from Augmented Transition Networks Is Easy

Translating basic transition network process descriptions into program form is straightforward, but one must choose among a number of ways to do things. The development given here was chosen for relative transparency rather than for speed or size considerations. Note that since no backup is allowed, no alternatives from the same state can be considered once an arc is traversed.

Each state in the transition net to be copied will have an associated PROG tag in the program form. Assume for now that S is a variable whose value is a list of words remaining to be analyzed and W is a variable whose value is the current word, the one that is the CAR of S. Then the following program fragment would look for a determiner followed by any number of adjectives followed by a noun.

```
   .
   .
   .
S1 (COND ((MEMBER 'DET (GET W 'FEATURES))
          (SETQ W (CAR (SETQ S (CDR S))))
          (GO S2))
         (T (RETURN NIL)))
S2 (COND ((MEMBER 'ADJ (GET W 'FEATURES))
          (SETQ W (CAR (SETQ S (CDR S))))
          (GO S2))
         ((MEMBER 'NOUN (GET W 'FEATURES))
          (SETQ W (CAR (SETQ S (CDR S))))
          (RETURN T))
         (T (RETURN NIL)))
   .
   .
   .
```

From this it is clear that the classification type of a word appears on the property list of the word under the property name FEATURES. Other features such as SING, for singular, or IMP, for imperative verb, may appear on the same list with the type feature.

Getting to the features, adding new features, and changing the values for S and W as arcs are traversed are such common activities that the temptation to define simple functions to do these chores is overwhelming. We succumb to this temptation here, but will resist in general so as to avoid a need to remember the particulars of too many subordinate bookkeeping functions.

```
(DEFINE (GOBBLE)
        (COND (S (SETQ S (CDR S)) (SETQ W (CAR S)))
              (T (SETQ W NIL))))

(DEFINE (GETF W) (GET W 'FEATURES))
(DEFINE (PUTF W NF)
        (COND ((NULL NF))
              ((ATOM NF)
               (PUTPROP W
                        (CONS NF
                              (DELETE NF (GET W 'FEATURES)))
                        'FEATURES))
              ((PUTPROP W
                        (UNION NF (GET W 'FEATURES))
                        'FEATURES))))
```

Note that GOBBLE checks S to be sure it does not CDR off the end of a list. PUTF uses a test to avoid duplicating entries. It can handle the addition of either a feature or a list of features. With these new functions, the original program fragment can be rewritten:

```
     .
     .
     .
S1 (COND ((MEMBER 'DET (GETF W))
          (GOBBLE)
          (GO S2))
         (T (RETURN NIL)))
S2 (COND ((MEMBER 'ADJ (GETF W)) (GOBBLE) (GO S2))
         ((MEMBER 'NOUN (GETF W)) (GOBBLE) (RETURN T))
         (T (RETURN NIL)))
     .
     .
     .
```

Now it is time to see what the fragment is imbedded in. It is assumed that several objectives are to be met by the instructions that set things up and provide for return:

■ There are to be specialists for the various group types. NOUNG is the noun group specialist.

■ A new atom is created for each newly discovered word group. NOUNG3 would be a typical name for a noun group. This new atom can have a FEATURES property for holding information about the corresponding group.

■ The relationship between any noun group and the higher-level group of which it is a part must be remembered. This is accomplished by passing the name of the higher-level group to the specialist program as an argument and by using PUTPROP to create and modify appropriate PARENT and OFFSPRING properties if everything works out.

■ A group may be optionally initialized by installing features through a non-NIL value for the FEATURES argument of the specialist.

■ If the search for a group fails somewhere, then the S and W variables must be restored to their values on entry.

The following framework accomplishes these objectives by way of entry and exit instructions. Note that (RETURN T) and (RETURN NIL) instructions in the previous fragment are to be replaced by (GO WIN) and (GO LOSE).

```
(DEFINE (NOUNG PARENT FEATURES)
        (PROG (NODE HOLD)
              (SETQ HOLD S W (CAR S) NODE (GENNAME 'NOUNG))
              (PUTF NODE FEATURES)
         S1
                   .
                   .
                   .

         WIN  (PUTPROP NODE PARENT 'PARENT)
              (PUTPROP PARENT
                        (CONS NODE (GET PARENT 'OFFSPRING))
                        'OFFSPRING)
              (RETURN NODE)
         LOSE (SETQ S HOLD W NIL)
              (RETURN NIL)))
```

GENNAME generates a unique new atom each time it is evaluated. When the value of the argument of GENNAME is NOUNG as above, then the new atom is of the form NOUNGn where the number n increases by one each time the function is used with NOUNG as the value of its argument. GENNAME is not a standard LISP function, but it can be defined in terms of EXPLODE and IMPLODE.

So far, so good. After making provision for further feature transferring and for prepositional groups following the noun, we then have the following:

```
(DEFINE (NOUNG PARENT FEATURES)
        (PROG (NODE HOLD)
              (SETQ HOLD S W (CAR S) NODE (GENNAME 'NOUNG))
              (PUTF NODE FEATURES)
         S1   (COND ((MEMBER 'DET (GETF W))
                     (PUTF NODE (GETF W))
                     (GOBBLE)
                     (GO S2))
                    (T (GO LOSE)))
         S2   (COND ((MEMBER 'ADJ (GETF W)) (GOBBLE) (GO S2))
                    ((MEMBER 'NOUN (GETF W))
                     (PUTF NODE (GETF W))
                     (GOBBLE)
                     (GO S3))
                    (T (GO LOSE)))
         S3   (COND ((PREPG NODE NIL) (GO S3)) (T (GO WIN)))
         WIN  (PUTPROP NODE PARENT 'PARENT)
              (PUTPROP PARENT
                        (CONS NODE (GET PARENT 'OFFSPRING))
                        'OFFSPRING)
              (RETURN NODE)
         LOSE (SETQ S HOLD W NIL)
              (RETURN NIL)))
```

This program becomes more simple and hence more transparent if a word specialist assumes the duty of testing words and doing bookkeeping when expected ones are identified. The new variable, LAST-CREATED, gets a value inside the word specialist. The value is the node created for the word.

```
(DEFINE (NOUNG PARENT FEATURES)
        (PROG (NODE HOLD)
              (SETQ HOLD S W (CAR S) NODE (GENNAME 'NOUNG))
              (PUTF NODE FEATURES)
         S1   (COND ((WORD NODE '(PROPERNOUN)) (GO WIN))
                    ((WORD NODE '(DET))
                     (PUTF NODE (GETF LAST-CREATED))
                     (GO S2))
                    (T (GO LOSE)))
         S2   (COND ((WORD NODE '(ADJ)) (GO S2))
                    ((WORD NODE '(NOUN))
                     (PUTF NODE (GETF LAST-CREATED))
                     (GO S3))
                    (T (GO LOSE)))
         S3   (COND ((PREPG NODE NIL) (GO S3))
                    (T (GO WIN)))
         WIN  (PUTPROP NODE PARENT 'PARENT)
              (PUTPROP PARENT
                       (CONS NODE (GET PARENT 'OFFSPRING))
                       'OFFSPRING)
              (SETQ LAST-CREATED NODE)
              (RETURN NODE)
         LOSE (SETQ S HOLD W NIL)
              (RETURN NIL)))
```

Note that LAST-CREATED is given a new value as NOUNG concludes its work. Thus LAST-CREATED, by convention, always holds on to the last node created. Note also that the new version of NOUNG handles proper nouns. The word-group specialist which has appeared is defined as follows:

```
(DEFINE (WORD PARENT FEATURES)
        (PROG (NODE HOLD)
              (SETQ HOLD S W (CAR S) NODE (GENNAME 'WORD))
              (PUTF NODE FEATURES)
         S1   (COND ((EQUAL (LENGTH (INTERSECT (GETF W)
                                               (GETF NODE)))
                            (LENGTH (GETF NODE)))
                     (PUTF NODE (GETF W))
                     (PUTPROP NODE W 'WORD)
                     (GOBBLE)
                     (GO WIN))
                    (T (GO LOSE)))
```

```
WIN     (PUTPROP NODE PARENT 'PARENT)
        (PUTPROP PARENT
                    (CONS NODE (GET PARENT 'OFFSPRING))
                    'OFFSPRING)
        (SETQ LAST-CREATED NODE)
        (RETURN NODE)
LOSE    (SETQ S HOLD W NIL)
        (RETURN NIL)))
```

Since the word specialist creates nodes for the words it encounters, an initial value of (THE PYRAMID ON A RED BLOCK) for S produces quite a number of nodes when (NOUNG 'CLAUSE NIL) is evaluated:

NOUNG1:	PARENT	CLAUSE
	FEATURES	(NOUN SING DET)
	OFFSPRING	(PREPG1 WORD4 WORD2)
WORD2:	PARENT	NOUNG1
	WORD	THE
	FEATURES	(DET)
WORD4:	PARENT	NOUNG1
	WORD	PYRAMID
	FEATURES	(SING NOUN)
PREPG1:	PARENT	NOUNG1
	OFFSPRING	(NOUNG2 WORD5)
WORD5:	PARENT	PREPG1
	WORD	ON
	FEATURES	(PARTICLE PREP)
NOUNG2:	PARENT	PREPG1
	FEATURES	(NOUN DET SING)
	OFFSPRING	(WORD10 WORD8 WORD7)
WORD7:	PARENT	NOUNG2
	WORD	A
	FEATURES	(SING DET)
WORD8:	PARENT	NOUNG2
	WORD	RED
	FEATURES	(ADJ)
WORD10:	PARENT	NOUNG2
	WORD	BLOCK
	FEATURES	(SING NOUN)

The tree structure of the nodes is given by figure 15-1.

LISP Translations of ATN Networks Can Be Compiled from Transparent Specifications

Since translating ATN graphs into LISP programs is straightforward but tedious, the job should really be done by a program. Developing such a translation program is at hand. The result will be a compiler.

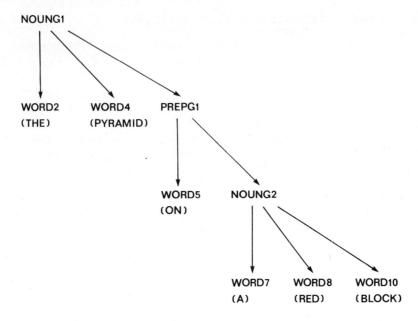

Figure 15-1 Augmented Transition Networks create trees in addition to finding features and filling slots. The structure given is for the noun group "the pyramid on a red block."

■ A compiler is a program which translates procedure descriptions from one language into another.

First there must be a source language for the ATNs that is suitable for typing yet sufficiently like the graphical form that very little work need be done to produce descriptions in it. To a large extent the details are a matter of taste and invention. The following basic syntax for a one-exit state is therefore only one of many possibilities:

```
(<state name> (IF <test>  ➤  <new state>))
```

The test can be any LISP form. The arrow is intended to stir up the transition image. More transitions simply add more arrow-containing state-change descriptions. If transition is to be accompanied by side effects, those side-effects are specified by a LISP form following the suggestive atom AFTER:

```
(<state name> (IF <test>
               ➤ <new state>
               AFTER <side effects>))
```

Thus the entire noun group and word specialist definitions could be written as follows:

```
(ABSORB NOUNG
        (S1 (IF (WORD NODE '(PROPERNOUN)) > WIN)
            (IF (WORD NODE '(DET))
                >
                S2
                AFTER
                (PUTF NODE (GETF LAST-CREATED))))
         (S2 (IF (WORD NODE '(ADJ)) > S2)
             (IF (WORD NODE '(NOUN))
                 >
                 S3
                 AFTER
                 (PUTF NODE (GETF LAST-CREATED))))
          (S3 (IF (PREPG NODE NIL) > S3) (IF T > WIN)))
(ABSORB WORD
        (S1 (IF (EQUAL (LENGTH (INTERSECT (GETF W)
                                          (GETF NODE)))
                       (LENGTH (GETF NODE)))
                >
                WIN
                AFTER
                (PUTF NODE (GETF W))
                (PUTPROP NODE W 'WORD)
                (GOBBLE))))
```

Now the problem is creating **ABSORB**, a **LISP** function which converts the new perspicuous description into the old one **LISP** understands directly. Thankfully the job involves nothing more than the symbol-manipulating flair so characteristic of LISP.

First, of course, each transition specifying parcel must be ripped apart and reassembled into a COND clause. Then the several clauses for each state must be amalgamated into a single COND structure. Naturally, CARs, CDRs, CONSs, and APPENDs abound.

Assuming that CLAUSE has an assignment corresponding to one of the transition specifications, then the following identifications hold:

```
(CADR CLAUSE)        <test>
(CADDDR CLAUSE)      <new state>
(CDDDDDR CLAUSE)     <side effects>
```

Figure 15-2 shows how these pieces go into a COND clause. The construction can be done by this fragment:

```
(APPEND (LIST (CADR CLAUSE))
        (COND ((CDDDDR CLAUSE) (CDR (CDDDDR CLAUSE))))
        (LIST (LIST 'GO (CADDDR CLAUSE))))
```

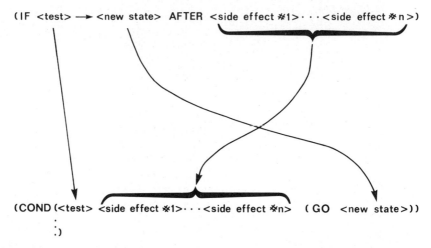

Figure 15-2 Augmented Transition Networks are compiled from a language with tailored syntax into equivalent LISP expressions by reassembling the pieces involved. The translation shown takes an arc description into a COND clause. There is heavy use of LISP's symbol manipulation talent.

The menagerie of functions is needed to create the proper final list structure. Writing it of course is a job which demands interactive debugging — no one gets it right the first time.

Note that the buried test simply checks if side-effect descriptions are present and returns them if they are. If not, a NIL is returned which disappears when the APPEND is executed.

The COND clauses for a particular state are assembled together by a MAPCAR and LAMBDA combination operating on the list of transition specifications found in the value of the variable STATE, assumed to contain the complete description package.

```
(MAPCAR '(LAMBDA (CLAUSE)
                 (APPEND (LIST (CADR CLAUSE))
                         (COND ((CDDDDR CLAUSE)
                                (CDR (CDDDDR CLAUSE))))
                         (LIST (LIST 'GO (CADDDR CLAUSE)))))
        (CDR STATE))
```

Once this is understood, then the required COND structure and all its clauses can be assembled by the following instructions:

```
(LIST (CAR STATE)
  (CONS 'COND
    (APPEND
      (MAPCAR
        '(LAMBDA (CLAUSE)
                (APPEND (LIST (CADR CLAUSE))
                        (COND ((CDDDDR CLAUSE)
                               (CDR (CDDDDR CLAUSE))))
                        (LIST (LIST 'GO (CADDDR CLAUSE)))))
        (CDR STATE))
      '((T (GO LOSE))))))
```

The grafting of (T (GO LOSE)) onto the end of the clause list allows the user to omit this implied default from his state transition descriptions. The atom COND is affixed to the other end, of course, and the whole package is then preceded by the state name as ferreted out by (CAR STATE).

The entire middle portion of the target LISP program is created by repeating the prescribed COND manufacture for each state specified by the body of the ATN description. Handling the repetition by a MAPCAR and LAMBDA arrangement yields the following somewhat complicated looking result:

```
(SETQ MIDDLE
  (APPLY 'APPEND
    (MAPCAR
      '(LAMBDA (STATE)
        (LIST (CAR STATE)
          (CONS 'COND
            (APPEND
              (MAPCAR
                '(LAMBDA (CLAUSE)
                  (APPEND (LIST (CADR CLAUSE))
                          (COND ((CDDDDR CLAUSE)
                                 (CDR (CDDDDR CLAUSE))))
                          (LIST (LIST 'GO (CADDDR CLAUSE)))))
                (CDR STATE))
              '((T (GO LOSE)))))))
      BODY)))
```

Thankfully the entire translation is nearly complete because the middle portion of the target program is the only part which is very sensitive to the description given. In fact, the end portion is always the same and appears simply as a giant quoted list:

```
(SETQ END
      '(WIN (PUTPROP NODE PARENT 'PARENT)
            (PUTPROP PARENT
                     (CONS NODE (GET PARENT 'OFFSPRING))
                     'OFFSPRING)
            (SETQ LAST-CREATED NODE)
            (RETURN NODE)
            LOSE
            (SETQ S HOLD W NIL)
            (RETURN NIL)))
```

The beginning is only a little more complicated. The quoted general form must be modified to get the name of the program into proper position inside the GENNAME function. The function SUBST can do the modification because it substitutes its first argument for all instances of its second argument that appear inside its third argument:

```
(SETQ BEGINNING
      (SUBST (LIST 'QUOTE NAME)
             'REPLACE
             '(PROG (NODE HOLD)
                    (SETQ HOLD
                          S
                          W
                          (CAR S)
                          NODE
                          (GENNAME REPLACE))
                    (PUTF NODE FEATURES))))
```

Having the beginning, middle, and end, the total program description is easy to get:

```
(SETQ PROGRAM (APPEND BEGINNING MIDDLE END))
```

The value of **PROGRAM** is exactly the ordinary **LISP** form of the LISP program desired. To actually effect the definition, the newly created LISP program must be combined with a name and argument list, placed together inside a **DEFINE** form, and evaluated:

```
(RETURN (EVAL (LIST 'DEFINE
                    (LIST NAME 'PARENT 'FEATURES)
                    PROGRAM)))
```

Almost everything is in place now. It remains only to discuss how the variables **NAME** and **BODY** come to have the values necessary to make everything work. The simplest way is to define **ABSORB** as a function of two arguments:

```
(DEFINE (ABSORB NAME BODY) . . .)
```

While acceptable, this demands the annoyance of quoting each argument when given:

```
(ABSORB 'NOUNG '((S1 (IF . . .) . . .). . .))
```

Fexprs Are Functions Which Do Not Evaluate Their Arguments

Since ABSORB always wants to manipulate its arguments without prior evaluation, it would be nice to avoid the constant quoting. But since ordinary user-defined functions always evaluate their arguments, evidently something new is needed. There must be a way to order DEFINE to create functions which are *not* ordinary. Here is how it is done:

```
(DEFINE FEXPR (<function name> <single argument>) <body>)
```

The inserted FEXPR is the signal to DEFINE that orders special treatment. The resulting function is called a FEXPR which distinguishes it from the ordinary functions, often called EXPRs. It is regrettable that these names have only obscure mnemonic content.

The special treatment is limited to the handling of arguments. First FEXPRs never evaluate any of their arguments. Second, all arguments that appear in a FEXPR application, however many, are formed into a list which then becomes the value of the single atom that appears with the FEXPR's name when defined. An example will make this clear. Suppose DEMONSTRATE is defined as a FEXPR:

```
(DEFINE FEXPR (DEMONSTRATE ARG) (PRINT ARG) (LENGTH ARG))
```

Now suppose DEMONSTRATE is used as follows:

```
(DEMONSTRATE THIS FUNCTION)
```

No attempt is made to evaluate either THIS or FUNCTION. Instead the list (THIS FUNCTION) becomes the value of ARG. The PRINT therefore causes (THIS FUNCTION) to be printed, while the LENGTH causes 2 to be returned as the function's value:

```
(DEMONSTRATE THIS FUNCTION)
  (THIS FUNCTION)
  2
```

Now ABSORB, the ATN compiler function, can be defined as a FEXPR without the quoting of arguments. With this our development is complete. Listing the total result shows why ABSORB has been introduced in pieces.

```
(DEFINE FEXPR (ABSORB DESCRIPTION)
 (PROG (NAME BODY PROGRAM BEGINNING MIDDLE END)
  (SETQ NAME (CAR DESCRIPTION) BODY (CDR DESCRIPTION))
  (SETQ BEGINNING
        (SUBST (LIST 'QUOTE NAME)
               'REPLACE
               '(PROG (NODE HOLD)
                      (SETQ HOLD
                            S
                            W
                            (CAR S)
                            NODE
                            (GENNAME REPLACE))
                      (PUTF NODE FEATURES))))
  (SETQ MIDDLE
   (APPLY 'APPEND
    (MAPCAR '(LAMBDA (STATE)
              (LIST (CAR STATE)
               (CONS 'COND
                (APPEND
                 (MAPCAR '(LAMBDA (CLAUSE)
                   (APPEND (LIST (CADR CLAUSE))
                           (COND ((CDDDDR CLAUSE)
                                  (CDR (CDDDDR CLAUSE))))
                           (LIST (LIST 'GO (CADDDR CLAUSE)))))
                  (CDR STATE))
                 '((T (GO LOSE))))))))
            BODY)))
  (SETQ END
        '(WIN (PUTPROP NODE PARENT 'PARENT)
              (PUTPROP PARENT
                       (CONS NODE (GET PARENT 'OFFSPRING))
                       'OFFSPRING)
              (SETQ LAST-CREATED NODE)
              (RETURN NODE)
              LOSE
              (SETQ S HOLD W NIL)
              (RETURN NIL)))
  (SETQ PROGRAM (APPEND BEGINNING MIDDLE END))
  (RETURN (EVAL (LIST 'DEFINE
                      (LIST NAME 'PARENT 'FEATURES)
                      PROGRAM)))))
```

Of course many improvements and extensions suggest themselves. Error-handling, reporting, and debugging features, for example, are missing. Indeed all of the implementation examples in this chapter are defective in that they ignore those important topics.

Compilers Are Usually Major Undertakings

In the ATN example LISP is both the compiler's implementation language and the compilation's target language. Creating the compiler was straightforward because both compiling and working with word strings are symbol-manipulating tasks for which LISP is eminently suited. Often compilers translate from source languages into assembler-level languages to achieve high running speed. Working with such compilers is much harder, especially if the compiler itself must be written in an assembler language, again for reasons of speed.

INTERPRETING PRODUCTION SYSTEMS

Now that the parentheses of LISP-like notation is familiar, it is possible to look at a simple production system in some detail. The first step is to describe a set of elementary productions capable of doing something. The second is to develop a notation for elementary productions. The third is to develop a set of LISP functions that understands the notation well enough to do what the productions prescribe.

Robbie Moves Some Furniture Using Productions

For an example, let us explore how Robbie could handle the problem of moving a bit of Aunt Agatha's furniture from place to place. The goals posed will appear in short-term memory with something like the following form:

```
STM: (PUT-AT TABLE XYZ)
        ---
        ---
        ---
        ---
        ---
        ---
```

An outline of each production's purpose may help the study of the detailed descriptions that follow:

P1 converts a request to put an object on some support into a command to put the object at a particular position in space.

P2 expands a goal to put an object at a position into grasp goals and remembered target locations.

P3 helps to forget invalidated support relations.

P4 moves the object-bearing hand and ungrasps it when motion is complete.

P5 moves the object-free hand to a specified object and grasps it.

P6 directs that obstacles be put out of the way on the floor.

P7 interacts with the world to identify obstacles.

For expository simplicity, these are examined in an order different from the necessary long-term-memory arrangement.

The first one to think about is the one that converts PUT-AT goals into combinations of GRASP goals and remembered target locations. Like all the productions, it must be built out of the basic primitives, the write, notice, mark, and communicate operations:

```
PRODUCTION P2:
If stm contains          (PUT-AT >OBJECT >NEWPLACE)
Then            mark     the first item in STM
                shove    (TARGET <OBJECT <NEWPLACE)
                shove    (GRASP <OBJECT)
```

The names beginning with the symbol > are to successfully match anything whatever and the thing matched against is remembered. These remembered identifications are later recalled when the same names are used with the complementary symbol < appearing as a prefix.

Following the execution of P2, STM has the following contents:

```
STM: (GRASP TABLE)
     (TARGET TABLE XYZ)
     (MARKED (PUT-AT TABLE XYZ))
     ---
     ---
     ---
     ---
```

Note that parentheses group items together, facilitating structuring conventions. The (PUT-AT TABLE XYZ) item is marked by combining it with the symbol MARKED. This insures that production P2 cannot lock up the system by triggering on the same short-term-memory combination endlessly.

The next production triggers only if an object is to be grasped which is known to be free of supported clutter. Note that STM must contain two specified items before this production can be activated. *When a production has several items to be matched against STM, the items must appear in STM in the same order as in the production, but they need not be consecutive.*

```
PRODUCTION P5:
If STM contains          (GRASP >OBJECT)
                         (<OBJECT SUPPORTS NOTHING)
Then            mark     the first item in STM
                shove    (MOVE <OBJECT)
                send     (MOVE-HAND (TOP OF <OBJECT))
                send     (GRASP <OBJECT)
```

The *send* commands communicate with a manipulator system and a vision system which are presumed to accomplish simple primitive acts. The communication can go both ways as illustrated by the next production which queries the vision system about what a given piece of furniture supports:

```
PRODUCTION P7:
If STM contains          (GRASP >OBJECT)
Then               send  (WHAT IS ON <OBJECT)
                   receive
                   notice  (GRASP <OBJECT)
```

The *receive* action accepts answers from the vision system of the form (TABLE SUPPORTS NOTHING) or (TABLE SUPPORTS LAMP). If nothing is supported, STM will contain the items necessary to trigger P5. Note that P5 must appear before P7, for the item demanded by P7 is a subset of those demanded by P5. If P7 were first, P5 could never be activated.

Following activation of P7, assuming the table was free, the STM contains the following:

```
STM: (GRASP TABLE)
     (TABLE SUPPORTS NOTHING)
     (TARGET TABLE XYZ)
     (MARKED (PUT-AT TABLE XYZ))
     ---
     ---
     ---
```

The (GRASP TABLE) item is in front by direct result of the notice action used in P7. This determines that P5's conditions are satisfied, immediately producing the following:

```
COMMANDS:      MOVE-HAND (TOP OF TABLE)
               GRASP TABLE
STM: (MOVE TABLE)
     (MARKED (GRASP TABLE))
     (TABLE SUPPORTS NOTHING)
     (TARGET TABLE XYZ)
     (MARKED (PUT-AT TABLE XYZ))
     ---
     ---
```

The next production waits for the MOVE TABLE item:

```
PRODUCTION P4:
If STM contains          (MOVE >OBJECT)
Then               mark   the first item in STM
                   notice (TARGET <OBJECT >NEWPLACE)
                   send   (MOVE-HAND <NEWPLACE)
                   send   (UNGRASP)
```

This causes two more manipulation commands:

```
COMMANDS:      MOVE-HAND XYZ
               UNGRASP
```

STM is also altered:

```
STM:  (TARGET TABLE XYZ)
      (MARKED (MOVE TABLE))
      (MARKED (GRASP TABLE))
      (TABLE SUPPORTS NOTHING)
      (MARKED (PUT-AT TABLE XYZ))
      ---
      ---
```

This concludes the action. If the table supported something, say a lamp, things would have been more complicated. Assuming that Robbie, being a bit shaky, always prefers to clear off all furniture before moving it, then clearing must happen first. Production P6 would have responded to the need to clear off the table:

```
PRODUCTION P6:
If STM contains       (GRASP >OBJECT)
                      (<OBJECT SUPPORTS >OBSTRUCTION)

Then          shove   (PUT-ON <OBSTRUCTION FLOOR)
```

Production P1 would convert this into a new PUT-AT goal:

```
PRODUCTION P1:
If STM contains       (PUT-ON >OBJECT >SUPPORT)
Then          mark    the first item in STM
              shove   (PUT-AT <OBJECT (SPACE ON <SUPPORT))
```

One final production is needed because moving clutter invalidates the support relations that were reported. P3 does this:

```
PRODUCTION P3:
If STM contains       (MOVE >OBJECT)
                      (>SUPPORT SUPPORTS <OBJECT)

Then          mark    (<SUPPORT SUPPORTS <OBJECT)
```

Now the complete system of seven productions could handle a table with a lamp on it were there enough short-term memory. There is not enough, however. The target position for the table drops off the end unless short-term memory is extended to 11 items. Extending allows the sequence shown in figure 15-3. (See pp. 362–363.)

English-like Productions Are Easily Converted into a Convenient Notation

Creating a transparent syntax for ATNs was clearly a good idea. Similarly, it is clear that the same effort for production systems permits something like the following syntax:

```
((<production name> <pattern> → <list of actions>) . . .)
```

This formula for situation-action combinations enables Robbie's furniture-moving system to be written concisely as shown below. The symbol ✶✶ represents the first item in STM.

```
(P1 ((PUT-ON >OBJECT >SUPPORT))
    ➤
    ((MARK ✶✶)
     (SHOVE (PUT-AT <OBJECT (SPACE ON <SUPPORT)))))
(P2 ((PUT-AT >OBJECT >NEWPLACE))
    ➤
    ((MARK ✶✶)
     (SHOVE (TARGET <OBJECT <NEWPLACE))
     (SHOVE (GRASP <OBJECT))))
(P3 ((MOVE >OBJECT) (>SUPPORT SUPPORTS <OBJECT))
    ➤
    ((MARK (<SUPPORT SUPPORTS <OBJECT))))
(P4 ((MOVE >OBJECT))
    ➤
    ((MARK ✶✶)
     (NOTICE (TARGET <OBJECT >NEWPLACE))
     (SEND (MOVE-HAND <NEWPLACE))
     (SEND (UNGRASP))))
(P5 ((GRASP >OBJECT) (<OBJECT SUPPORTS NOTHING))
    ➤
    ((MARK ✶✶)
     (SHOVE (MOVE <OBJECT))
     (SEND (MOVE-HAND (TOP OF <OBJECT)))
     (SEND (GRASP <OBJECT))))
(P6 ((GRASP >OBJECT) (<OBJECT SUPPORTS >OBSTRUCTION))
    ➤
    ((SHOVE (PUT-ON <OBSTRUCTION FLOOR))))
(P7 ((GRASP >OBJECT))
    ➤
    ((SEND (WHAT IS ON <OBJECT))
     (RECEIVE)
     (NOTICE (GRASP <OBJECT))))
```

These productions could be compiled into the clauses of a COND once and for all, just as the transitions of an ATN were. Alternatively they can be retained in their user form permanently and translated only as they are needed by an interpreter.

■ An interpreter is a program that effects the processes described in a user language by interleaving program examination and process performance steps.

(GRASP TABLE)
(TARGET TABLE XYZ)
(MARK (PUT-AT TABLE XYZ))
NIL
NIL
NIL
NIL
NIL
NIL
NIL
NIL
NIL
NIL
NIL

>>> (WHAT IS ON TABLE)

(GRASP TABLE)
(TABLE SUPPORTS LAMP)
(TARGET TABLE XYZ)
(MARK (PUT-AT TABLE XYZ))
NIL
NIL
NIL
NIL
NIL
NIL
NIL
NIL
NIL
NIL

(PUT-ON LAMP FLOOR)
(GRASP TABLE)
(TABLE SUPPORTS LAMP)
(TARGET TABLE XYZ)
(MARK (PUT-AT TABLE XYZ))
NIL
NIL
NIL
NIL
NIL
NIL
NIL
NIL
NIL

(PUT-AT LAMP (SPACE ON FLOOR))
(MARK (PUT-ON LAMP FLOOR))
(GRASP TABLE)
(TABLE SUPPORTS LAMP)
(TARGET TABLE XYZ)
(MARK (PUT-AT TABLE XYZ))
NIL
NIL
NIL
NIL
NIL
NIL
NIL
NIL

(GRASP LAMP)
(TARGET LAMP (SPACE ON FLOOR))
(MARK (PUT-AT LAMP (SPACE ON FLOOR)))
(MARK (PUT-ON LAMP FLOOR))
(GRASP TABLE)
(TABLE SUPPORTS LAMP)
(TARGET TABLE XYZ)
(MARK (PUT-AT TABLE XYZ))
NIL
NIL
NIL
NIL
NIL
NIL

>>> (WHAT IS ON LAMP)

(GRASP LAMP)
(LAMP SUPPORTS NOTHING)
(TARGET LAMP (SPACE ON FLOOR))
(MARK (PUT-AT LAMP (SPACE ON FLOOR)))
(MARK (PUT-ON LAMP FLOOR))
(GRASP TABLE)
(TABLE SUPPORTS LAMP)
(TARGET TABLE XYZ)
(MARK (PUT-AT TABLE XYZ))
NIL
NIL
NIL
NIL
NIL

>>> (MOVE-HAND (TOP OF LAMP))

>>> (GRASP LAMP)

(MOVE LAMP)
(MARK (GRASP LAMP))
(LAMP SUPPORTS NOTHING)
(TARGET LAMP (SPACE ON FLOOR))
(MARK (PUT-AT LAMP (SPACE ON FLOOR)))
(MARK (PUT-ON LAMP FLOOR))
(GRASP TABLE)
(TABLE SUPPORTS LAMP)
(TARGET TABLE XYZ)
(MARK (PUT-AT TABLE XYZ))
NIL
NIL
NIL
NIL

(MARK (TABLE SUPPORTS LAMP))
(MOVE LAMP)
(MARK (GRASP LAMP))
(LAMP SUPPORTS NOTHING)
(TARGET LAMP (SPACE ON FLOOR))
(MARK (PUT-AT LAMP (SPACE ON FLOOR)))
(MARK (PUT-ON LAMP FLOOR))
(GRASP TABLE)
(TARGET TABLE XYZ)
(MARK (PUT-AT TABLE XYZ))
NIL
NIL
NIL
NIL

      >>> (MOVE-HAND (SPACE ON FLOOR))

      >>> (UNGRASP)

(TARGET LAMP (SPACE ON FLOOR))
(MARK (MOVE LAMP))
(MARK (TABLE SUPPORTS LAMP))
(MARK (GRASP LAMP))
(LAMP SUPPORTS NOTHING)
(MARK (PUT-AT LAMP (SPACE ON FLOOR)))
(MARK (PUT-ON LAMP FLOOR))
(GRASP TABLE)
(TARGET TABLE XYZ)
(MARK (PUT-AT TABLE XYZ))
NIL
NIL
NIL
NIL

      >>> (WHAT IS ON TABLE)

(GRASP TABLE)
(TABLE SUPPORTS NOTHING)
(TARGET LAMP (SPACE ON FLOOR))
(MARK (MOVE LAMP))
(MARK (TABLE SUPPORTS LAMP))
(MARK (GRASP LAMP))
(LAMP SUPPORTS NOTHING)
(MARK (PUT-AT LAMP (SPACE ON FLOOR)))
(MARK (PUT-ON LAMP FLOOR))
(TARGET TABLE XYZ)
(MARK (PUT-AT TABLE XYZ))
NIL
NIL
NIL

      >>> (MOVE-HAND (TOP OF TABLE))

      >>> (GRASP TABLE)

(MOVE TABLE)
(MARK (GRASP TABLE))
(TABLE SUPPORTS NOTHING)
(TARGET LAMP (SPACE ON FLOOR))
(MARK (MOVE LAMP))
(MARK (TABLE SUPPORTS LAMP))
(MARK (GRASP LAMP))
(LAMP SUPPORTS NOTHING)
(MARK (PUT-AT LAMP (SPACE ON FLOOR)))
(MARK (PUT-ON LAMP FLOOR))
(TARGET TABLE XYZ)
(MARK (PUT-AT TABLE XYZ))
NIL
NIL

      >>> (MOVE-HAND XYZ)

      >>> (UNGRASP)

(TARGET TABLE XYZ)
(MARK (MOVE TABLE))
(MARK (GRASP TABLE))
(TABLE SUPPORTS NOTHING)
(TARGET LAMP (SPACE ON FLOOR))
(MARK (MOVE LAMP))
(MARK (TABLE SUPPORTS LAMP))
(MARK (GRASP LAMP))
(LAMP SUPPORTS NOTHING)
(MARK (PUT-AT LAMP (SPACE ON FLOOR)))
(MARK (PUT-ON LAMP FLOOR))
(MARK (PUT-AT TABLE XYZ))
NIL
NIL

Figure 15-3 A Production System solves the problem of moving a table. Short-term memory originally contains (PUT-AT TABLE XYZ). Subsequently the contents of short-term memory changes as shown. NIL indicates empty slots. Communications to sensory and motor devices are indicated by >>>.

A Production-System Interpreter Is Simple

Figure 15-4 gives the structure of a production-system interpreter. Each cycle consists of two parts: a search through the production list to find the first one with a pattern matching short-term memory followed by execution of the directions specified by the matching production's action list. All of this is handled by USE-PRODUCTION:

```
(DEFINE (USE-PRODUCTION)
  (PROG (PRODUCTIONS NEXT NAME PATTERN ACTIONS)
        (SETQ PRODUCTIONS LTM)
   TAG  (COND ((NULL PRODUCTIONS) (RETURN NIL)))
        (SETQ NEXT (CAR PRODUCTIONS))
        (SETQ NAME (CAR NEXT))
        (SETQ PATTERN (CADR NEXT))
        (SETQ ACTIONS (CADDDR NEXT))
        (COND ((MATCH-STM PATTERN)
               (PERFORM-ACTION ACTIONS)
               (RETURN T)))
        (SETQ PRODUCTIONS (CDR PRODUCTIONS))
        (GO TAG)))
```

Manifestly USE-PRODUCTION merely slithers down the list of productions until MATCH-STM finds one it likes, whereupon PERFORM-ACTION does its duty. Of these two subordinates, PERFORM-ACTION is the simpler, requiring mostly a loop through a big COND which performs each action specified by the elements of the list ACTION-LIST. The possibilities are SHOVE, NOTICE, MARK, SEND, and RECEIVE. Anything not found to be one of these is simply shoved onto short-term memory:

```
(DEFINE (PERFORM-ACTION ACTION-LIST)
  (PROG (ACTION FUNCTION)
   NEXT (COND ((NULL ACTION-LIST) (RETURN T)))
        (SETQ ACTION (CAR ACTION-LIST))
        (SETQ ACTION (SUBSTITUTE-VARIABLES ACTION))
        (COND ((ATOM ACTION) (SETQ STM (SHOVE ACTION STM)))
              ((EQUAL (SETQ FUNCTION (CAR ACTION))
                      'SHOVE)
               (SETQ STM (SHOVE (CADR ACTION) STM)))
              ((EQUAL FUNCTION 'NOTICE)
               (MATCH-STM (CDR ACTION)))
              ((EQUAL FUNCTION 'MARK)
               (SETQ STM
                     (CONS ACTION
                           (DELETE (CADR ACTION) STM 1))))
              ((EQUAL FUNCTION 'SEND)
               (PRINT-MESSAGE (CADR ACTION)))
              ((EQUAL FUNCTION 'RECEIVE)
               (SETQ STM (SHOVE (READ) STM)))
              (T (SETQ STM (SHOVE ACTION STM))))
        (SETQ ACTION-LIST (CDR ACTION-LIST))
        (GO NEXT)))
```

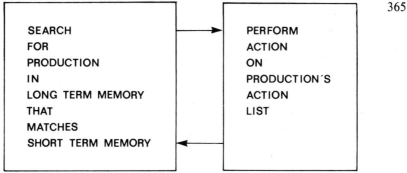

Figure 15-4 Production Systems can be interpreted by shuttling back and forth between fetch and execution specialists.

The SHOVE operation is handled by an auxiliary function. All other action commands are executed directly.

```
(DEFINE (SHOVE NEW-ITEM LIST)
        (CONS NEW-ITEM (REVERSE (CDR (REVERSE LIST)))))
```

The matching initiated by **MATCH-STM** is considerably hairier inasmuch as several auxiliary functions are involved:

```
(DEFINE (MATCH-STM PATTERN)
  (PROG (NOTICED-THINGS)
    (COND ((MATCH1 PATTERN STM)
           (PULL-TO-FRONT-OF-STM (REVERSE NOTICED-THINGS))
           (RETURN T)))))

(DEFINE (PULL-TO-FRONT-OF-STM ELEMENTS)
        (MAPCAR '(LAMBDA (X) (SETQ STM (DELETE X STM 1.)))
                ELEMENTS)
        (SETQ STM (APPEND ELEMENTS STM)))

(DEFINE (MATCH1 P D)
  (COND ((NULL P) T)
        ((NULL D) NIL)
        ((MATCH2 (CAR P) (CAR D))
         (SETQ NOTICED-THINGS (CONS (CAR D) NOTICED-THINGS))
         (MATCH1 (CDR P) (CDR D)))
        ((MATCH1 P (CDR D)))))

(DEFINE (MATCH2 P D)
        (COND ((NULL P) T)
              ((NULL D) NIL)
              ((ATOM P)
               (COND ((OR (EQUAL P D) (EQUAL P '?)))
                     ((EQUAL (ATOMCAR P) '>)
                      (SET (ATOMCDR P) D)
                      T)
                     ((EQUAL (ATOMCAR P) '<)
                      (EQUAL (EVAL (ATOMCDR P)) D))))
              ((AND (NOT (ATOM P)) (NOT (ATOM D)))
               (AND (MATCH2 (CAR P) (CAR D))
                    (MATCH2 (CDR P) (CDR D))))))
```

Looking through these, it is clear that the following responsibilities hold:

MATCH-STM is a simple executive which arranges for matched items to migrate to the front of STM whenever there is a successful match.

PULL-TO-FROM-OF-STM merely effects the migration.

MATCH1 keeps one finger on the pattern and one on STM, marching down both as appropriate. The details of recursion provide that extraneous STM items are skipped. The STM items that do match are recorded for later use.

MATCH2 compares one item with another and deals with all matching options. The ? symbol matches everything. Variables beginning with $>$ match everything as well with assignment being a side effect. The $<$ variables make use of those assignments because such variables are replaced by their values before being checked for match. Nested item structures are handled by recursion. The peculiar termination conditions allow for successful match if the complete pattern is merely the front of a longer STM item.

It is convenient to make use of the variable assignments made during matching later in the action part of the cycle. This is handled in PERFORM-ACTION by using the function SUBSTITUTE-VARIABLES:

```
(DEFINE (SUBSTITUTE-VARIABLES S)
        (COND ((ATOM S)
               (COND ((EQUAL (ATOMCAR S) '<)
                      (EVAL (ATOMCDR S)))
                     ((EQUAL S '**) (CAR STM))
                     (T S)))
              (T (MAPCAR 'SUBSTITUTE-VARIABLES S))))
```

Note that SUBSTITUTE-VARIABLES introduces another special symbol possibility, **, which stands for the item currently first in STM.

Finally, there is only the simple function RUN which repeats the USE-PRODUCTION cycle.

```
(DEFINE (RUN STM LTM)
        (PROG ()
         NEXT (COND ((USE-PRODUCTION)
                     (GO NEXT))))))
```

Three simple auxiliary functions are used in various places:

```
(DEFINE (ATOMCAR X) (CAR (EXPLODE X)))
```

```
(DEFINE (ATOMCDR X) (IMPLODE (CDR (EXPLODE X))))
```

```
(DEFINE (PRINT-MESSAGE M)
        (TERPRI)
        (TERPRI)
        (PRINC '/ / / / >>>/ )
        (PRINC M)
        (TERPRI))
```

LISP IN LISP

What we have just done may certainly be thought of as an *implementation* of a production language interpreter, but from another point of view, it is also a precise *description* of how such a language works. We now go on to do the same thing again for a primitive symbol manipulation language. Let us call this language MICRO as it will be a sort of super-primitive micro-LISP.

A Simple Symbol-Manipulation Language Can Be Interpreted by a Small Number of LISP Functions

The first question, of course, must be the selection of an appropriate language in which to implement MICRO. It clearly must be a language well suited to moving around in the list structures out of which symbol manipulation programs are made. The strange yet suspected truth is that LISP itself is a good language for our present purpose.

To keep things straight, let us begin with some naming conventions.

- All functions in MICRO are prefaced by M-. Thus M-CAR, M-CDR, M-CONS, M-EQUAL and M-ATOM are the MICRO analogs to CAR, CDR, CONS, EQUAL and ATOM in LISP.
- All LISP-defined functions needed to implement MICRO are prefaced by MICRO-. Thus MICRO-EVAL, MICRO-APPLY, and MICRO-DEFINE are all critical functions defined in LISP in order to interpret MICRO expressions.

The key functions are MICRO-EVAL and MICRO-APPLY. All of the work could, in fact, be stuffed into MICRO-EVAL and MICRO-APPLY, but this is not done because having auxiliary functions keeps the system simpler and more readable. MICRO-EVAL and MICRO-APPLY divide the work of program interpretation as follows:

- MICRO-EVAL accepts programs in the form of s-expressions. If the given s-expression is an atom, its value is returned. Otherwise MICRO-EVAL checks for the special forms M-QUOTE and M-COND, and if neither are involved, it arranges for the standard depth-first, left-to-right order of execution.
- MICRO-APPLY recognizes and executes the primitive functions M-CAR, M-CDR, M-CONS, M-ATOM, and M-EQUAL. MICRO-APPLY fetches definitions for all functions encountered other than the five primitives. MICRO-APPLY also keeps variable values straight as M-LAMBDA expressions are entered and exited.

Here is MICRO-EVAL:

```
(DEFINE (MICRO-EVAL S ALIST)
  (COND ((NULL S) NIL)
        ((ATOM S)
         (COND ((EQUAL S T) T)
               ((EQUAL S NIL) NIL)
               (T (CADR (ASSOC S ALIST)))))
        ((EQUAL (CAR S) 'M-QUOTE) (CADR S))
        ((EQUAL (CAR S) 'M-COND)
         (MICRO-EVALCOND (CDR S) ALIST))
        (T (MICRO-APPLY (CAR S)
                        (MAPCAR '(LAMBDA (X)
                                         (MICRO-EVAL X
                                                     ALIST))
                                (CDR S))
                        ALIST))))
```

Observe that variables and variable values are kept on the alist, short for *association list,* as pairs. Consider an alist with the following value:

```
((VASE CROCK) (SENTENCE (THIS IS A VASE)) . . .)
```

It indicates that the value of SENTENCE is the list (THIS IS A VASE) and the value of VASE is CROCK. The values are obtained when needed by a combination of a new function ASSOC helped with a CADR.

■ ASSOC uses its first argument as a key and looks for that key in the alist supplied as the second argument. In operation, ASSOC cruises down the alist until it finds a list element whose CAR is the key. The value of the ASSOC is the entire element so discovered, key and all, or NIL if the key is never found.

The test for M-QUOTE is needed because MICRO needs some equivalent to the single quote device of LISP. M-QUOTE is the answer because unlike other functions, it refuses to evaluate its argument, thus protecting expressions in the same way LISP's single quote does. Indeed LISP's real handling of the single quote mark is very closely related:

■ When LISP code is read from a file into central memory, single-quote marks are translated into applications of the function QUOTE. This is necessary because the LISP interpreter requires all programs and data to be expressed strictly and uniformly in s-expression form. The single-quote device does not fit into the s-expression definition although it makes programs clearer and learning easier. LISP is therefore buffered from text prepared by programmers by a program which, among other things, effects the following translation:

```
'<s-expression>  ➤  (QUOTE <s-expression>)
```

Returning to MICRO-EVAL, note that ordinarily all arguments are evaluated and the function, evaluated arguments, and current alist are all three handed over to MICRO-APPLY:

```
(DEFINE (MICRO-APPLY FUNCTION ARGS ALIST)
  (COND ((ATOM FUNCTION)
         (COND ((EQUAL FUNCTION 'M-CAR) (CAAR ARGS))
               ((EQUAL FUNCTION 'M-CDR) (CDAR ARGS))
               ((EQUAL FUNCTION 'M-CONS)
                (CONS (CAR ARGS) (CADR ARGS)))
               ((EQUAL FUNCTION 'M-ATOM) (ATOM (CAR ARGS)))
               ((EQUAL FUNCTION 'M-EQUAL)
                (EQUAL (CAR ARGS) (CADR ARGS)))
               (T (MICRO-APPLY (GET FUNCTION 'M-EXPR)
                               ARGS
                               ALIST))))
        ((EQUAL (CAR FUNCTION) 'M-LAMBDA)
         (MICRO-EVAL (CADDR FUNCTION)
                     (APPEND (MICRO-PAIR (CADR FUNCTION)
                                         ARGS)
                             ALIST)))))
```

Shortly it will be clear that evaluating m-lambda expressions is the key to everything. Note that they get into MICRO-EVAL in this form:

```
((M-LAMBDA <list of variables> <body>)
 <list of unevaluated arguments>)
```

Such expressions are handed over to MICRO-APPLY with MICRO-APPLY's variables assigned:

```
Value of FUNCTION:      (M-LAMBDA <list of variables> <body>)
Value of ARGS:          <list of evaluated arguments>
```

To deal with these, MICRO-APPLY makes a list of pairs of variables and arguments, sticks that list on to the alist, and then hands the body of the m-lambda expression right back to MICRO-EVAL with the new, augmented value for the alist. MICRO-APPLY destroys m-lambda expressions, creating material for MICRO-EVAL out of their pieces.

Defined functions receive similar treatment because in this implementation, function definitions are stored under the property M-EXPR in the form of m-lambda expressions. Thus m-lambda expressions of MICRO, which may have seemed like an annoyance at first, are what all function applications look like on their way to being evaluated. When an atom name stands in function position rather than a m-lambda expression, it is there only as a stand-in for the m-lambda expression hidden away on its property list.

Two auxiliary functions are used, one of which handles the special syntax of M-COND and one which pairs variables with values:

```
(DEFINE (MICRO-PAIR L1 L2)
        (COND ((OR (NULL L1) (NULL L2)) NIL)
              (T (CONS (LIST (CAR L1) (CAR L2))
                       (MICRO-PAIR (CDR L1) (CDR L2)))))))
(DEFINE (MICRO-EVALCOND CLAUSES ALIST)
        (COND ((NULL CLAUSES) NIL)
              ((MICRO-EVAL (CAAR CLAUSES) ALIST)
               (MICRO-EVAL (CADAR CLAUSES) ALIST))
              (T (MICRO-EVALCOND (CDR CLAUSES) ALIST))))
```

Note that this definition of **MICRO-EVALCOND** permits M-CONDs to have only clauses with two elements, as in some early LISP systems.

There remains the execution of the five **MICRO** primitives. As the definition of **MICRO-APPLY** indicates, they are directly simulated by equivalent LISP functions working on the list of arguments attached to the atom ARGS.

Placing function definitions on property lists is the duty of **MICRO-DEFINE**, a function which converts function definitions in the accustomed style into m-lambda forms:

```
(DEFINE FEXPR
        (MICRO-DEFINE X)
        (PUTPROP (CAAR X)
                 (LIST 'M-LAMBDA (CDAR X) (CADR X))
                 'M-EXPR)
        (CAAR X))
```

This concludes the basic development of **MICRO**. From here, more and more power could be developed by bootstrapping using **MICRO**'s own function-defining mechanism. **M-NULL AND M-APPEND**, for example, can be defined in terms of the primitives:

```
(MICRO-DEFINE (M-NULL L) (M-EQUAL L (M-QUOTE ())))
(MICRO-DEFINE (M-APPEND L1 L2)
             (M-COND ((M-NULL L1) L2)
                     (T (M-CONS (M-CAR L1)
                                (M-APPEND (M-CDR L1) L2)))))
```

Indeed **MICRO** could be brought up to LISP's level through such additions together with some strengthening of the interpreter, principally extension to handle numbers, PROG forms, and FEXPR type function definitions.

LISP Is Best Defined in LISP

It was fraudulent to say that MICRO is LISP-like because MICRO is really LISP in disguise. By dropping the M- and MICRO- prefixes in the interpreter definition, it is clear that MICRO is LISP!

It may seem weird, almost incestuous to define LISP in terms of itself this way, but keep in mind that programs describe processes. Since LISP evaluation is a process and since LISP itself is a clear, transparent language, the LISP evaluation process might just as well be described by a program in LISP!

■ Defining how LISP works using LISP as a tool is very like the way a dictionary defines words in terms of other, presumably simpler words. Our reduction of LISP is toward a known number of core functions whose definitions are primitives.

That this could be done using only the simple functions described by the given LISP programs is suggestive, for it means that a primitive, slow LISP can be created by implementing only the given functions in another language using the LISP descriptions as a guide. Demonstrating this is not the main point, however. So far we have been casual, almost slipshod in explaining what really happens when a function is defined or used. It has been said that function descriptions are somehow stored, somehow retrieved, and somehow applied to arguments which are themselves ordinarily evaluated in left to right order. We have made this description more precise in MICRO with a view toward showing how LISP works at a deeper level.

In doing this, we see in some detail what LISP actually does when encountering user-defined functions. LISP actually does go to the property list for m-lambda definitions.

Fancy Control Structures Usually Start out as Basic LISP Interpreters

Inserting a layer of interpretation is the first step toward implementing very fancy control structures. An interpreter interposed between the standard LISP evaluation procedure and a user's program provides the programming language surgeon with a place to make incisions. He need not tamper with the offered version of a LISP interpreter which is usually rendered obscure by virtue of implementation in assembly-level programs. Instead, he can frolic at will in the more exposed LISP-level implementation. He can invent new control structures because the stuff of which control structures are built are available in a relatively transparent, easy to use form. This is the way many very-high-level languages are first implemented and tested. There is usually a severe price to pay, however. The extra layer of interpretation generally brings along a ghastly reduction of program speed.

SUMMARY

■ Compiling is that process by which algorithms are translated from one language into another. Usually the source language is more convenient for writing and the destination language is better for running. The compiler example developed produces a new LISP program for every ATN specification supplied.

■ Interpretation is that process by which algorithms are executed by continual inspection of user programs written to describe them. The interpreter example implements production systems by following the encoded productions. Those productions are retained intact throughout execution.

■ As a general rule, interpreters are easier to create and work with than compilers. Debugging is easier because the source program is retained.

■ The essentials of a LISP interpreter can be described by a LISP program. Only a few LISP functions are needed to describe the basic operating principles.

■ Creating a LISP-like interpreter in LISP is often a first step toward implementing advanced new languages with more sophisticated control-structure possibilities.

REFERENCES

■ John McCarthy, "Recursive Functions of Symbolic Expressions," *Communications of the Association for Computing Machinery,* vol. 3, 1960, and "A Basis for a Mathematical Theory of Computation," in *Proceedings of the Western Joint Computer Conference,* 1961. The classic papers in which McCarthy introduced the LISP language. The relationship between LISP and the lambda calculus is discussed.

■ S. W. Galley and Greg Pfister, "The MDL Language," Laboratory of Computer Science, Massachusetts Institute of Techonology, Cambridge, Massachusetts, 1975. FEXPRs were introduced in order to have more control over how a function's arguments are handled. These days the FEXPR solution is seen to be in danger of extinction. The MDL language, LISP-like in many respects, introduced some new conventions which seem very flexible and highly desirable. It allows a specification by which individual arguments may or may not be evaluated, may or may not be present, may or may not have default values if not present, and so on. LISP systems will likely use the MDL conventions eventually.

16
DATA
BASES
AND
DEMONS

Problem solvers need facts. Pattern-oriented data bases offer one way of storing, forgetting, and retrieving them. Our purpose now is to expose the essential ideas by building parts of such a data-base system. The development will be very sketchy, for there are too many ideas to sample for a more thorough accounting. The matching functions previously developed will be used. Efficiency will continue to be sacrificed for simplicity.

BIBLE WORLD

Here are some sample facts from the initial world of Adam and Eve:

```
(ADAM LOCATED-AT PARADISE)
(EVE LOCATED-AT PARADISE)
(HUMAN ADAM)
(HUMAN EVE)
(SINNER EVE)
```

The collected facts constitute the data base. As figure 16-1 suggests, there are three things to do in connection with these facts. To get facts in and out, the functions ADD and REMOVE must be defined:

```
(REMOVE '(ADAM LOCATED-AT PARADISE))

(ADD '(ADAM LOCATED-AT OUTER-DARKNESS))
```

ADD and REMOVE Modify the Data Base

There are many ways to structure the data base and implement ADD and REMOVE. The simplest idea is to put the facts together in a list and make that list the value of some atom. Let us use the atom DATA for its mnemonic value. ADD puts a new fact into the data base by adding it to the front of the list that

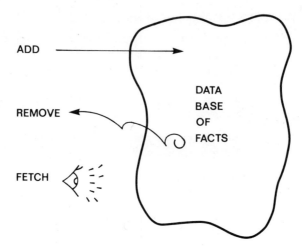

Figure 16-1 Storing information in associative data bases is an alternative to using atom properties and values. Typically the data base items are lists of atoms, but general s-expressions are possible. Basic functions insert, delete, and search.

is the value of **DATA**. First, however, **ADD** checks to see if the new fact is already present or else duplications appear:

```
(DEFINE (ADD NEWFACT)
        (COND ((MEMBER NEWFACT DATA) NIL)
              (T (SETQ DATA (CONS NEWFACT DATA)) NEWFACT)))
```

The function returns **NIL** if the new fact is already present and otherwise the new fact itself. This is a detail — since **ADD** is used for its data base effect, not for its value, the choice is somewhat arbitrary. It does seem good to avoid returning the new value of **DATA** because it could easily choke a terminal or other output device.

The function **REMOVE** is simpler. This version uses a simple application of the system-supplied function, **DELETE**, and arranges for the fact to be returned if it was in the data.

```
(DEFINE (REMOVE OLDFACT)
        (COND ((MEMBER OLDFACT DATA)
               (SETQ DATA (DELETE OLDFACT DATA))
               OLDFACT)))
```

FETCH and TRY-NEXT Find Instances of Patterns

What about looking for facts which match a pattern? Suppose we want to see if there are people in the data base. FETCH is the function that decides:

```
(FETCH '(HUMAN ?))
```

Before we can write FETCH, we must decide on what it should do if instances of the pattern are present. Returning the first instance found and assigning the pattern variables accordingly is one easy solution. The MATCH function, installed in a suitable loop, can compare the pattern against successive data items and assign variables:

```
(DEFINE (FETCH PATTERN)
        (PROG (ITEMS)
              (SETQ ITEMS DATA)
              LOOP
              (COND ((NULL ITEMS) (RETURN NIL))
                    ((MATCH PATTERN (CAR ITEMS))
                     (RETURN (CAR ITEMS))))
              (SETQ ITEMS (CDR ITEMS))
              (GO LOOP)))
```

This FETCH is simple and clean. Unfortunately it is worthless whenever it is necessary to collect all the data items that match the pattern. Using this FETCH, only the first item that matches the pattern is accessible.

Returning a list of all matches is the obvious correction. Then each element in the returned list can be used according to the taste of the program that does the FETCH. Under these circumstances, FETCH should do no pattern-variable assignment since it has no way of knowing which of the matching data items should supply the instantiations. The new FETCH therefore uses TEST, a function which does not alter variable values:

```
(DEFINE (FETCH PATTERN)
  (PROG (ITEMS RESULT)
        (SETQ ITEMS DATA RESULT NIL)
        LOOP
        (COND ((NULL ITEMS) (RETURN RESULT))
              ((TEST PATTERN (CAR ITEMS))
               (SETQ RESULT (CONS (CAR ITEMS) RESULT))))
        (SETQ ITEMS (CDR ITEMS))
        (GO LOOP)))
```

TEST is obtained from the old MATCH by scratching the assignment feature and replacing it with a curious alternative:

```
(DEFINE (MATCH P D)
  (COND ((AND (NULL P) (NULL D)) T)
        ((OR (NULL P) (NULL D)) NIL)
        ((OR (EQUAL (CAR P) (CAR D)) (EQUAL (CAR P) '?))
         (MATCH (CDR P) (CDR D)))
        ((EQUAL (ATOMCAR (CAR P)) '>)
         (SET (ATOMCDR (CAR P)) (CAR D))
         (MATCH (CDR P) (CDR D)))
        ((EQUAL (ATOMCAR (CAR P)) '<)
         (MATCH (CONS (EVAL (ATOMCDR (CAR P))) (CDR P)) D))))
(DEFINE (TEST P D)
        (PROG (ALIST DISCOVERY)
              (RETURN (TESTAUX P D))))
(DEFINE (TESTAUX P D)
  (COND ((AND (NULL P) (NULL D)) T)
        ((OR (NULL P) (NULL D)) NIL)
        ((OR (EQUAL (CAR P) (CAR D)) (EQUAL (CAR P) '?))
         (TESTAUX (CDR P) (CDR D)))
        ((EQUAL (ATOMCAR (CAR P)) '>)
         (SETQ ALIST (CONS (LIST (ATOMCDR (CAR P)) (CAR D))
                           ALIST))
         (TESTAUX (CDR P) (CDR D)))
        ((EQUAL (ATOMCAR (CAR P)) '<)
         (TESTAUX (CONS (COND ((SETQ DISCOVERY
                                     (ASSOC (ATOMCDR (CAR P))
                                            ALIST))
                               (CADR DISCOVERY))
                              (T (EVAL (ATOMCDR (CAR P)))))
                        (CDR P))
                  D))))
```

Simply throwing out (SET (ATOMCDR (CAR P)) (CAR D) would be a poor solution because it disallows patterns like (>X <X) for which assignments fixed early are used later. On the other hand, keeping the program intact is forbidden by the demand that variables emerge from matching unaltered.

The solution, of course, is to maintain a temporary, separate list of assignments, leaving the variable values alone. This is done by creating an alist, an idea reminiscent of the technique introduced in connection with the LISP interpreter. Whenever a > variable is encountered, that variable and its matching data item are listed together and stashed in the alist. Then when the < variables demand replacement by values, the alist is consulted. The ordinary value is used only if the alist refuses to help because there is no prior use of a corresponding > variable in the pattern.

The variable DISCOVERY holds the result of the alist search. The CADR function, after all, cannot be used on the result directly because that would risk doing

CADR on NIL. An alternative version, perhaps more elegant, uses a lambda variable rather than a PROG variable to avoid recomputation of the search:

```
(DEFINE (TEST P D) (TESTAUX P D NIL))
(DEFINE (TESTAUX P D ALIST)
  (COND
    ((AND (NULL P) (NULL D)) T)
    ((OR (NULL P) (NULL D)) NIL)
    ((OR (EQUAL (CAR P) (CAR D)) (EQUAL (CAR P) '?))
     (TESTAUX (CDR P) (CDR D) ALIST))
    ((EQUAL (ATOMCAR (CAR P)) '>)
     (TESTAUX (CDR P)
              (CDR D)
              (CONS (LIST (ATOMCDR (CAR P)) (CAR D))
                    ALIST)))
    ((EQUAL (ATOMCAR (CAR P)) '<)
     (TESTAUX (CONS ((LAMBDA (DISCOVERY)
                             (COND (DISCOVERY (CADR
                                              DISCOVERY))
                                   (T (EVAL (ATOMCDR (CAR
                                              P)))))))
                    (ASSOC (ATOMCDR (CAR P)) ALIST))
              (CDR P))
              D
              ALIST))))
```

In a separate refinement, the alist is passed about as a TESTAUX variable allowing the PROG in TEST to be dropped entirely. Whether the result is better is mostly a matter of taste, although the new approach would yield different results if the matcher were extended to handle recursive patterns.

Using the new version of FETCH, the following result obtains in Bible world:

```
(FETCH '(HUMAN ?))
  ((HUMAN ADAM) (HUMAN EVE))
```

For many purposes, this would be satisfactory enough, but one further improvement simplifies computations that move through the list of discovered matches one by one, assigning the pattern variables and doing something for each. Printing the name of each human in Bible world is a simple, albeit dull example, for which the results of (FETCH '(HUMAN >X)) must get to (PRINT X) through assignments for X.

Sussman and McDermott's CONNIVER language has a good way to arrange for successive assignment. The function TRY-NEXT does the job in cooperation with a slightly modified FETCH. The FETCH conjures up a list of possibilities which ordinarily become the value of some variable through a SETQ operation. Here is an example:

```
(SETQ PEOPLE (FETCH '(HUMAN >P)))
```

TRY-NEXT then works on the possibilities through the atom. Each time TRY-NEXT is applied, it causes a new assignment until all possibilities are exhausted. This is the way to print the names of all humans:

```
.
.
.
(SETQ PEOPLE (FETCH '(HUMAN >P)))
LOOP
(TRY-NEXT 'PEOPLE)
(PRINT P)
(GO LOOP)
.
.
.
```

How do FETCH and TRY-NEXT work? Since assignment is to be done by TRY-NEXT, it must somehow get hold of the pattern that was supplied to FETCH. This is easy to arrange; FETCH merely tacks the pattern onto the front of the list that it returns so that TRY-NEXT can look at it when dealing with the list of matches. Very little modification is necessary:

```
(DEFINE (FETCH PATTERN)
  (PROG (ITEMS RESULT)
        (SETQ ITEMS DATA RESULT NIL)
        LOOP
        (COND ((NULL ITEMS) (RETURN (CONS PATTERN RESULT)))
              ((TEST PATTERN (CAR ITEMS))
               (SETQ RESULT (CONS (CAR ITEMS) RESULT))))
        (SETQ ITEMS (CDR ITEMS))
        (GO LOOP)))
```

Now (FETCH '(HUMAN >P)) returns

```
((HUMAN >P)
 (HUMAN ADAM)
 (HUMAN EVE))
```

When TRY-NEXT is applied to such a list, it must assign pattern variables as directed by the first data item in the list and then remove that data item so that the next one is used when TRY-NEXT is next applied. Consider this version:

```
(DEFINE (TRY-NEXT POSSIBILITIES)
        (PROG (ELEMENTS)
              (SETQ ELEMENTS (EVAL POSSIBILITIES))
              (COND ((NULL (CDR ELEMENTS)) (RETURN NIL)))
              (ASSIGN (CAR ELEMENTS) (CADR ELEMENTS))
              (SET POSSIBILITIES
                   (CONS (CAR ELEMENTS) (CDDR ELEMENTS)))
              (RETURN T)))
```

Why EVAL and SET? Remember that TRY-NEXT must modify the value of the atom fed to it. But to do that, the guts of TRY-NEXT must have access to the atom itself, not just its value. Consequently, the argument appears in TRY-NEXT quoted by convention; then the *value* of TRY-NEXT's atom POSSIBILITIES is the atom whose value is to be changed; and to get at that value, a second evaluation cycle must be invoked and therefore EVAL must be used. A few lines later, SET is used instead of SETQ, again because the atom supplied to TRY-NEXT is the value of POSSIBILITIES, not POSSIBILITIES itself.

Note that ASSIGN performs the desired variable assignment. Like TEST, it, too, is similar to the old variable-assigning MATCH:

```
(DEFINE (ASSIGN P D)
        (COND ((AND (NULL P) (NULL D)) T)
              ((OR (NULL P) (NULL D)) 'ERROR)
              ((EQUAL (ATOMCAR (CAR P)) '>)
               (SET (ATOMCDR (CAR P)) (CAR D))
               (ASSIGN (CDR P) (CDR D)))
              (T (ASSIGN (CDR P) (CDR D))))))
```

Data Base Changes Can Trigger Demons

Suppose Eve eats the apple number A27182. Then the following ADDs and REMOVEs are appropriate:

```
(REMOVE '(A27182 IS-A APPLE))
(REMOVE '(ADAM LOCATED-AT PARADISE))
(ADD '(ADAM LOCATED-AT OUTER-DARKNESS))
(REMOVE '(EVE LOCATED-AT PARADISE))
(ADD '(EVE LOCATED-AT OUTER-DARKNESS))
```

The first REMOVE is the important change. The rest is really bookkeeping and could be put in a subroutine with a gain in modularity and a reduction in distraction. Demons are useful for this purpose. Demons are subroutines called automatically by specified data-base additions and removals. As suggested by figure 16-2, they keep watch over what goes in and what comes out and activate themselves when something goes by that they like. Activation requires successful match between a data item and a pattern associated with a demon. The demon BAD-NEWS is defined with a pattern that will match apple removals:

```
(DEFINE-DEMON BAD-NEWS
              IF-REMOVED
              (? IS-A APPLE)
              (REMOVE '(ADAM LOCATED-AT PARADISE))
              (ADD '(ADAM LOCATED-AT OUTER-DARKNESS))
              (REMOVE '(EVE LOCATED-AT PARADISE))
              (ADD '(EVE LOCATED-AT OUTER-DARKNESS)))
```

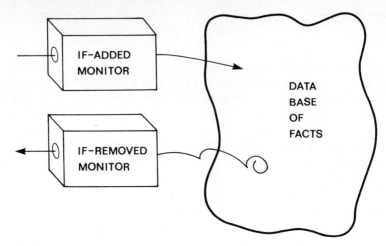

Figure 16-2 Demons watch the traffic into and out of a data base. An if-added demon triggers whenever an insertion matches a pattern specified when the demon was defined. An if-removed demon triggers on deletions.

BAD-NEWS is the demon's name, IF-REMOVED is the demon's type, and (? IS-A APPLE) is the triggering pattern. Since the pattern certainly matches (A27182 IS-A APPLE), the demon is activated when that item is deleted from the data base. Thus a remove operation causes two other REMOVEs and two ADDs by way of the demon. Of course the REMOVEs and ADDs in the demon can also cause their own if-removed or if-added demon activations. Annoying demon loops are possible.

Demons Are Useful

Here are two reasons for using demons:

■ Demons add knowledge to a system without specification of where it will be used. There is no need to work over a system when a new demon becomes available. Like competent assistants, they do not need to be told when to act. They are called up when some situation occurs, not because some program references them. This is particularly important when systems are to be jointly authored by many contributors.

■ Demons encapsulate bookkeeping operations that otherwise litter programs. Systems with demons can be rewritten without them by carefully inserting tests and subsequent actions at those places where demons might be activated. Such systems are longer and generally less readable. By contrast, demons remove bookkeeping details from center stage. They keep watch over what is happening and do their job unobtrusively as circumstances dictate. Programs become more readable because they list only the important actions with demons handling the clutter and keeping it out of sight.

Many programming languages now provide demon-like facilities in that procedures can be activated by specified additions to, deletions from, and searches over a data base of facts.

DEFINE-DEMON Enters Demons into the Data Base

Our purpose now is to implement if-added and if-removed methods. Some orientation may be helpful:

- We want to implement a system dealing with Adam and Eve which exercises data base functions.
- We have implemented ADD, REMOVE, FETCH, and TRY-NEXT.
- Now we are implementing DEFINE-DEMON so that if-added and if-needed demons can be defined.

The strategy involves modifying ADD and REMOVE and adding demon-triggering information to the data base. For BAD-NEWS the new data-base item is as follows:

```
(BAD-NEWS IF-REMOVED (? IS-A APPLE))
```

The general form follows the BAD-NEWS model, combining the name, type, and pattern of the demon. To make use of such entries, ADD and REMOVE are augmented to search for them. Successful search calls for execution of the associated function.

```
(DEFINE (REMOVE OLDFACT)
  (PROG (DEMON DEMONS)
        (COND ((NOT (MEMBER (SETQ OLDFACT
                                  (SUBSTITUTE OLDFACT))
                            DATA))
               (RETURN NIL)))
        (SETQ DATA (DELETE OLDFACT DATA))
        (SETQ DEMONS
              (FETCH (LIST '>DEMON 'IF-REMOVED OLDFACT)))
        LOOP
        (COND ((NOT (TRY-NEXT 'DEMONS)) (RETURN OLDFACT)))
        (FUNCALL DEMON)
        (GO LOOP)))
```

Note that REMOVE has been generalized slightly to allow < variables by using SUBSTITUTE:

```
(DEFINE (SUBSTITUTE P)
        (COND ((NULL P) NIL)
              ((EQUAL (ATOMCAR (CAR P)) '<)
               (CONS (EVAL (ATOMCDR (CAR P)))
                     (SUBSTITUTE (CDR P))))
              ((CONS (CAR P) (SUBSTITUTE (CDR P)))))))
```

If the removed fact is (A27182 IS-A APPLE) then certainly the pattern supplied to the FETCH is

```
(>DEMON IF-REMOVED (A27182 IS-A APPLE))
```

which will match the pattern inserted when BAD-NEWS was defined:

```
(BAD-NEWS IF-REMOVED (? IS-A APPLE))
```

Note, however, that success requires generalization of the function TEST used by FETCH, for now ? is allowed on the data side of the match as well as on the pattern side. Moreover both the pattern and the data are no longer restricted to atoms but have elements that are themselves lists. Hence the needed new TEST function should be recursive in order to accept and work with the more general pattern and data items.

If the pattern created in the ADD matches a data item, then a function name eventually is bound to the atom DEMON and is executed. Note that the function is expected to have no arguments. This is no surprise since the implicit call through a pattern offers no route through which arguments could be passed.

Evidently the job of DEFINE-DEMON must have two parts: first it must put the proper association of function name, demon type, and pattern into the data base; and second, it must actually arrange the definition of the function that occupies the function slot in the association. It is correct to suppose that a combination of CARs, CDRs, CONs, APPENDs, and EVALs can accomplish these purposes.

Seeing

```
(DEFINE-DEMON <name>
              <IF-ADDED or IF-REMOVED>
              <pattern>
              <body>)
```

should cause a definition to be made as if (DEFINE (<name>) <body>) were seen instead.

Since the arguments are not to be evaluated, manifestly DEFINE-DEMON must be a FEXPR. Let DEFINITION be its argument:

```
(DEFINE FEXPR (DEFINE-DEMON DEFINITION) . . .)
```

Now looking at DEFINE-DEMON's syntax, it is clear that the proper pieces for an ordinary function definition can be fished out of DEFINITION:

```
<function name>          (CAR DEFINITION)
<body>                   (CDDDR DEFINITION)
```

Thus the definition effect of DEFINE-DEMON is handled by putting these elements together along with the atom DEFINE and evaluating the result:

```
(APPLY 'DEFINE (CONS (LIST (CAR DEFINITION))
                     (CDDDR DEFINITION)))
```

Similarly the proper demon item for the data base uses a selection of DEFINITION's elements:

```
<function name>        (CAR DEFINITION)
<demon type>           (CADR DEFINITION)
<pattern>              (CADDR DEFINITION)
```

The data-base item is therefore properly manufactured by this:

```
(LIST (CAR DEFINITION)
      (CADR DEFINITION)
      (CADDR DEFINITION))
```

Thus to define DEFINE-DEMON, we have this:

```
(DEFINE FEXPR
        (DEFINE-DEMON DEFINITION)
        (ADD (LIST (CAR DEFINITION)
                   (CADR DEFINITION)
                   (CADDR DEFINITION)))
        (APPLY 'DEFINE
               (CONS (LIST (CAR DEFINITION))
                     (CDDDR DEFINITION))))
```

All of this is easier to keep straight if one remembers that two distinct definition operations are under discussion. The first is that of defining DEFINE-DEMON, which is a FEXPR. Next is the use of DEFINE-DEMON which involves creating and executing a second defining operation. This second defining operation creates particular demons, which are ordinary EXPRs.

Demons Can Be Added and Removed

Sometimes a method may be only temporarily relevant. For this reason, it is a happy thing that demons can be added and removed. DEFINE-DEMON handled additions. REMOVEs are done as in this BAD-NEWS example:

```
(DEFINE-DEMON BAD-NEWS
  IF-REMOVED
  (? IS-A APPLE)
  (PROG (TYPE PATTERN)
        (REMOVE '(ADAM LOCATED-AT PARADISE))
        (ADD '(ADAM LOCATED-AT OUTER-DARKNESS))
        (REMOVE '(EVE LOCATED-AT PARADISE))
        (ADD '(EVE LOCATED-AT OUTER-DARKNESS))
        (SETQ P (FETCH '(BAD-NEWS >TYPE >PATTERN)))
        (TRY-NEXT 'P)
        (REMOVE '(BAD-NEWS <TYPE <PATTERN))))
```

Methods are activated by the data base functions only while in the data base. There is, after all, no point in watching for apple eating after the fall.

If-Needed Demons Are Triggered by FETCH and TRY-NEXT Activity

In an advanced system, FETCH and TRY-NEXT also can initiate function calls to perform certain actions when dealing with the data base. Before the triggering operation was removing or adding; now it is searching.

■ FETCH demons are most commonly used to retrieve data items that are implied by the facts but that are not really present.

Suppose someone wants a list of fallible beings. To now execute (FETCH '(FALLIBLE >VICTIM)) serves no purpose because there are no such items explicitly in the data base. But surely all humans are fallible, and it makes sense to list them. A fetch demon does the job; its use requires several new ideas:

```
(DEFINE-DEMON HUMAN-FACT-1
              IF-NEEDED
              (FALLIBLE ◂F)
              (PROG (PEOPLE)
                    (SETQ PEOPLE (FETCH '(HUMAN >F)))
                    LOOP
                    (COND ((NOT (TRY-NEXT 'PEOPLE)) (ADIEU)))
                    (RECORD-INSTANCE)
                    (GO LOOP)))
```

The syntax of the method pattern will be explained in a moment. For now, note that the loop starts off by making PEOPLE a possibilities list. PEOPLE is shortened and the new function RECORD-INSTANCE is executed on each trip through the test section of the loop. When no more possibilities remain, the loop is complete, the test succeeds, and the function ADIEU causes return from the method.

Since the details are complicated, it is best to walk through the example looking for fallible beings:

■ The FETCH in (SETQ EXAMPLE (FETCH '(FALLIBLE >VICTIM))) can find no data items but it does locate a method. The value of EXAMPLE is:
```
((FALLIBLE >VICTIM)
 (METHOD (HUMAN-FACT-1 IF-NEEDED (FALLIBLE ◂F))))
```
Since the elements of all possibilities lists now can be methods as well as items, the markers METHOD and ITEM are needed to keep things straight. Of course FETCH and TRY-NEXT must be modified to handle this change in syntax for items as well as the generalization for methods.

■ TRY-NEXT therefore encounters a method the first time it sees the value of the atom EXAMPLE.

■ Inside HUMAN-FACT-1, now activated, another FETCH creates a possibilites list assigned to PEOPLE:
```
((HUMAN >F) (ITEM (HUMAN ADAM)) (ITEM (HUMAN EVE)))
```

■ Each time the loop repeats, RECORD-INSTANCE adds the method pattern, (FALLIBLE ∧F), to an invisible internal list after ∧F is replaced with F's current value. The new ∧ prefix is used only in if-needed patterns. It indicates that values are to move up out of the method to the FETCH that calls it. The loop repeats once for each PEOPLE possibilities list instance until all are exhausted. The internal record therefore has one element for each human on the PEOPLE list:

```
((ITEM (FALLIBLE EVE)) (ITEM (FALLIBLE ADAM)))
```

■ Terminating the loop leads to ADIEU. This special kind of return splices the internal list generated by RECORD-INSTANCE into the higher level possibilities list used by the instance of TRY-NEXT that caused the method to be used. Since TRY-NEXT was working on EXAMPLE when HUMAN-FACT-1 was called, EXAMPLE is changed. The HUMAN-FACT-1 method is consumed, being replaced by the list of items it generated:

```
((FALLIBLE >VICTIM) (ITEM (FALLIBLE EVE))
                    (ITEM (FALLIBLE ADAM)))
```

■ Finally, TRY-NEXT, realizing that it encountered a method, not an item, looks at the new possibilities list as if the long detour had not occurred. This consumes the first of the two new items and assigns EVE to VICTIM.

In summary, the method call is transparent. TRY-NEXT acts as if everything comes directly from the data base. The following would print EVE and then ADAM:

```
(SETQ EXAMPLE (FETCH '(FALLIBLE >VICTIM)))
(PROG ()
     LOOP
     (COND ((NOT (TRY-NEXT 'EXAMPLE)) (RETURN NIL)))
     (PRINT VICTIM)
     (GO LOOP))
```

Thus the RECORD-INSTANCE function appearing in IF-NEEDED methods place data-like items on a list which eventually gets spliced into the possibilities list that contained the IF-NEEDED method. RECORD-INSTANCE constructs each item it places by instantiating the IF-NEEDED pattern. Whew!

Demons Handle the Fall

Let us combine what we have into a system that watches for the appearance of the devil, picks a fallible sinner, gets rid of the apple, and moves Adam and Eve. The devil-watching demon is the only thing remaining to be written:

```
(DEFINE-DEMON DEVIL-WATCHER
  IF-ADDED
  (DEVIL LOCATED-AT PARADISE)
  (PROG (PEOPLE APPLES VICTIM)
       (SETQ PEOPLE
             (FETCH '(FALLIBLE >VICTIM))
             APPLES
             (FETCH '(>A IS-A APPLE)))
       (COND ((NOT (TRY-NEXT 'APPLES)) (RETURN 'DONE)))
       LOOP
       (COND ((NOT (TRY-NEXT 'PEOPLE)) (RETURN 'DONE)))
       (COND ((PRESENT '(SINNER <VICTIM))
             (REMOVE '(<A IS-A APPLE))
             (RETURN 'DONE)))
       (GO LOOP)))
```

The loop terminates as soon as an instantiation of VICTIM passes the sinner test, (PRESENT '(SINNER <VICTIM)). As suggested by its name, the function PRESENT searches the data base, as does FETCH, but only to see if there is *any* instance of the pattern. It returns either T or NIL.

Remember that the removal of the apple triggers the BAD-NEWS demon that takes care of the LOCATED-AT items for ADAM and EVE. Thus doing what is started by (ADD '(DEVIL LOCATED-AT PARADISE)) does everything.

FETCH and TRY-NEXT Are Flexible

Some problem-solving experts like the way FETCH works with TRY-NEXT because the possibilities list is exposed, ready to be modified if the function using it so desires. Methods and items can be rearranged and undesired ones can be exorcized between TRY-NEXT applications. In CONNIVER the possibilities list is even accessible from inside IF-NEEDED methods as the value of the free variable POSSIBILITIES. Thus both the caller and called have complete modification authority. Many languages do not allow this; for them a decision to use if-needed methods is a commitment — there is no way to pause and look over the field before going on.

MULTIPLE WORLDS

Sometimes a problem encourages development of several alternative approaches. Typically one attack is pushed forward until it sours. Temporarily abandoned, it may be reactivated if other sorties into the problem become relatively worse. Meanwhile most facts about the world remain unchanged even though some are undoubtedly added and deleted in connection with the active lines of thought. It is therefore necessary to maintain several nearly identical world models and to provide some way to switch the target of the data base functions from one to another.

Multiple Contexts Facilitate Problem-Solving Knowledge Probes

Suppose, for example, that Adam wants to check out some new places to live. He might imagine himself in those places by establishing a world model for each. Most facts about life will be the same independent of the world. For the sake of efficiency each world model set up should refer to a central collection of these facts rather than to a privately held copy of them.

Figure 16-3 shows abstractly what is needed. Most facts are stored only in the data base at the top, the initial data base. Each supplement is a record of additions

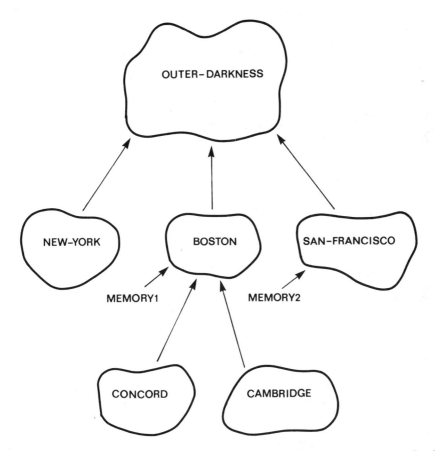

Figure 16-3 Data bases can be arranged into trees for greater storage economy. In this example, New York has all of the properties of Outer Darkness except for specific differences noted in the New York node. Concord is like Outer Darkness as amended by information in the Boston node and in the Concord node. A fact can be present in the Outer Darkness data base, absent from the Boston one, and present again in Concord or Cambridge.

or removals. The entry to the data base is ordinarily through one of these supplements. The chain of links from the entry supplement all the way to the initial data base determines the set of supplementary additions and removals that is honored.

What must be done at the s-expression level to implement such a data base of linked multiple contexts? Before, DATA's value was a list of all data base items; now there must be several connected lists, one for each collection of items. DATA becomes a list of lists; each element corresponds to a supplement.

New slots are created by the function PUSH-CONTEXT. Suppose DATA's value indicates a two context chain:

```
((<items in supplement>) (<items in initial data base>))
```

Then executing (SETQ DATA (PUSH-CONTEXT DATA)) gives the following new value to DATA:

```
(() (<items in supplement>) (<items in initial data base>))
```

Naturally a new slot starts out empty.

POP-CONTEXT does the opposite; it is used to reset the DATA pointer to the next place up the chain. If there is some possible need to return to a state in effect just prior to a POP-CONTEXT, clearly some variable must be set to preserve the contents of the data base at that point. This does it:

```
(SETQ SAVE DATA)
```

```
(SETQ DATA (POP-CONTEXT DATA))
```

Later on a simple (SETQ DATA SAVE) restores.

Let us pause to summarize.

■   The value of DATA is a list of subcontexts.

■   New, initially empty subcontexts are sprouted by the function PUSH-CONTEXT.

■   Old states are saved explicitly by setting atoms to the existing value of the atom DATA.

■   Old states are restored either by setting DATA to saved values or by using POP-CONTEXTs if the state to be restored is somewhere up the linkage chain from the current context.

Adding Contexts Requires Work

Naturally implementing multiple contexts requires major surgery to ADD, REMOVE, and FETCH. FETCH must look for matching items not only in the first supplement in the chain but also in each subcontext up the access path. Removing things also creates problems. Any item removed should vanish for FETCHs operating through the value of DATA in effect when the item was removed, but if the context is reset by POP-CONTEXT, FETCH must get the item. It is removed only with respect to access paths going *through* the entry subcontext, not for others.

One way to handle the problem involves prefacing each item in the data base with either +, if it is an addition, or a −, if a removal. Then REMOVE would actually delete an item only if it appears in the entry subcontext. Otherwise it would insert it with a − symbol indicating local removal.

Follow this sequence to see how this works:

```
DATA
     (())
(ADD '(ADAM LOCATED-AT PARADISE))
     (((+ ADAM LOCATED-AT PARADISE)))
(SETQ DATA (PUSH-CONTEXT DATA))
     (()
      ((+ ADAM LOCATED-AT PARADISE)))
(REMOVE '(ADAM LOCATED-AT PARADISE))
     (((- ADAM LOCATED-AT PARADISE))
      ((+ ADAM LOCATED-AT PARADISE)))
(ADD '(ADAM LOCATED-AT NEW-YORK))
     (((+ ADAM LOCATED-AT NEW-YORK)
       (- ADAM LOCATED-AT PARADISE))
      ((+ ADAM LOCATED-AT PARADISE)))
(REMOVE '(ADAM LOCATED-AT NEW-YORK))
     (((- ADAM LOCATED-AT PARADISE))
      ((+ ADAM LOCATED-AT PARADISE)))
(ADD '(ADAM LOCATED-AT BOSTON))
     (((+ ADAM LOCATED-AT BOSTON)
       (- ADAM LOCATED-AT PARADISE))
      ((+ ADAM LOCATED-AT PARADISE)))
(SETQ MEMORY1 DATA)
(SETQ DATA (POP-CONTEXT DATA))
     (((+ ADAM LOCATED-AT PARADISE)))
(SETQ DATA (PUSH-CONTEXT DATA))
     (()
      ((+ ADAM LOCATED-AT PARADISE)))
(REMOVE '(ADAM LOCATED-AT PARADISE))
     (((- ADAM LOCATED-AT PARADISE))
      ((+ ADAM LOCATED-AT PARADISE)))
(ADD '(ADAM LOCATED-AT SAN-FRANCISCO)
     (((+ADAM LOCATED-AT
                SAN-FRANCISCO)
       (- ADAM LOCATED-AT PARADISE))
      ((+ ADAM LOCATED-AT PARADISE)))
(SETQ MEMORY2 DATA)
(SETQ DATA MEMORY1)
     (((+ ADAM LOCATED-AT BOSTON)
       (- ADAM LOCATED-AT PARADISE))
      ((+ ADAM LOCATED-AT PARADISE)))
```

The various contexts deal only with the evolution of Adam's location. Evidently Adam is casting about looking for a good spot to settle down. He tries New York and rejects it immediately. Boston does not look good either, but apparently it is worth remembering. San Francisco is next, but it is not perfect either. It is remembered while Boston gets a second look.

In examining the Boston area further, contexts might be sprouted for Concord and Cambridge using two independent PUSH-CONTEXT applications on MEMORY1. This would correspond to the context structure shown abstractly before.

The Implementation Is Grossly Inefficient

There has been no particular effort to present fast programs at the level of either LISP programming techniques or algorithm selection. Instead simple exposition was the first consideration. Consequently the programs run like molasses. Certainly replacing the matcher with one that uses reader macros rather than ATOMCAR and ATOMCDR would help a lot because it is bad to use expensive operations on atom names.

It is also *very* bad to maintain the data base in the form of a list. When a data-base list becomes large, sweeping all the way through it for a fetch becomes very expensive. Various new forms of traditional computer science hash tables help considerably. Efficiency remains a problem, however, and research continues.

PROCEDURALISTS AND DECLARATIVISTS

In normal systems some knowledge is contained in programs and some in declarative knowledge structures. It is tempting to suppose that for any particular purpose the choice should be obvious. Knowledge about how to do things is procedural; all else is the fodder that procedures feed on. There is often room for argument, however, and from time to time the procedural-declarative feud comes to the surface, for there are some who favor putting as much as possible into procedures while others prefer to think in terms of very simple programs operating on large data bases.

People Argue about Whether Knowledge Should Be in Programs or in Data Bases

Just for fun, let us look at an imagined, yet somehow representative conversation:

Declarativist: You might as well burn a fact as try to store it as a piece of programmed procedure. I can understand facts, but once facts disappear into programs, they're gone. No one can find them. Proceduralists simply cannot contest the *transparency* of a set of unprofaned facts.

Proceduralist: *Au Contraire!* You just don't know how to program. You'll love it once I teach you how. Besides, if you try to tell me that storing knowledge about how to do something doesn't demand representation as a program, I'll know you're crazy.

Declarativist: No one taught you that divide and understand is the key principle of science. I'll suffer a bit with my way of keeping knowledge about processes because my way allows extensibility. Your programmer friends can't do anything without complicated and unpredicted interactions screwing up everything. I know about the debugging problem and what it costs. You would be better off sticking to minimal programs operating on big data bases where every fact stands by itself.

Proceduralist: Bah! You're right about dividing and understanding. Nearly decomposable systems are the stuff the world is made of, and I agree that the best way to approach most problems is by studying the pieces independently with the hope that their behavior doesn't change much when we put them together. But at some point you have to face life. There are interactions, and what we have done is make it possible to control and exploit those very interactions you want to ignore. True, the vast freedom of programming languages does need some bridling. But don't forget that Structured Programming has taken hold. Barricades are built in front of the pitfalls by insisting that programmers think in terms of the goals their programs are to accomplish and by insisting that programs use only the three allowed fasteners for making big ones out of little ones, namely the SEQUENCE, the IF-THEN-ELSE combination, and some sort of REPEAT-UNTIL mechanism.

Referee: Let's not get too technical! I'm not sure we all understand those references yet.

Declarativist: Well I do, and I admit that Structured Programming has done some good, but its gains are offset in your fancy new programming theories, Heterarchy for example.

Proceduralist: Not at all. There is no collision because there are two levels involved. Heterarchy is like the dogma of a religion, with Structured Programming being the handbook dictating the details of ceremony. Heterarchy demands richness of the spirit; Structured Programming dictates cleanliness of the body. On one hand there are semantic questions of *what* should pass between modules; on the other, syntactic rules of form for *how*.

Declarativist: Oh well, I have heard, for example, that programs may wake up and act more or less randomly.

Proceduralist: Now you must be talking about the demon idea. They are not random at all, they simply watch for opportunities to apply their special expertise. They are *very* goal oriented, fitting right in with your concession that goal-oriented programming is a good thing. Besides, if you are really obsessed by the so-called problem of interprocess control, you can work with a production system, where after all, all the communication goes through the short term memory where even you should be able to watch it.

Declarativist: Be serious. I have friends who write production systems and they bleed all over me about unpredictable interactions....

Proceduralist: You didn't listen. Those unpredictable interactions are fortunate, not disastrous. How do you expect to get inspiration into a system?

Referee: Come, let's not wander around so. You are both getting a little emotional.

Declarativist: If he is so smart, let's see him represent *2* as a program.

Proceduralist: Hah! I've got you. *Two* is a program. If you write $2 + 3$ you are really sending the 2 and 3 programs a message they jointly understand through interprocess messages. The result is 5, by the way.

Referee: That seems an extreme view,...

Proceduralist: You are supposed to be neutral!

Referee: ...but in any event, perhaps you two could make your views more concrete by saying something about some specific quantum of knowledge, say for example, the fact that all humans are fallible.

Declarativist: Yes, well I would just have the fact recorded more or less as you stated it, without prejudicing its use by getting it all tangled up in a procedure.

Proceduralist: That advantage turns against you. By professing to defer the decision about how the fact is to be used, you actually forfeit any possibility of deciding. You cannot tell your system which of four ways the fact should be used.

Referee: Four ways?

Proceduralist: Yes. First it may be desirable to note that an entity is fallible if ever it is found to be human. Alternatively, if I want to show that something is fallible, trying to show that it is human may be a good way. These are the antecedent and consequent choices that my declarativist colleague does not, indeed cannot distinguish. Then of course, there are parallel possibilities taken from the negations: if something is shown not fallible, I can deduce and record that it is not human; if desired to show something is not human, showing it is not fallible may be sensible.

Declarativist: How can that be efficient? You will have to store my simple fact four ways!

Proceduralist: It only costs four bits to cover all possible combinations. That's nothing these days.

The Proceduralists and the Declarativists Secretly Agree

And so these discussions go, sometimes becoming heated. Curiously, though, in the pure form, both extremist postures are rather closer to each other than each is to the middle ground. Those myriad programs that the proceduralist creates out of former data items are *still* data with respect to the computer that acts in accordance with them. And on the other side, the nonproceduralist, who is forced to bury procedural advice in the apparently factual data base, creates camouflaged sequences which his uniform reasoning procedure interprets as slavishly as if they were consciously written programs. The whole thing makes for good conversation because it is easy to switch sides!

SUMMARY

■ A basic associative data base requires functions for adding, removing, and fetching data items. Matching is used by these functions.

■ To make use of fetched items, the combination of FETCH and TRY-NEXT is particularly convenient. FETCH finds items and TRY-NEXT instantiates them.

■ Demons add considerable power to an associative data-base system. If-added demons watch additions to the data base, and if-removed demons watch removals.

■ Demons can be implemented by data-base additions containing their name, type, and triggering pattern.

■ If-needed demons are fetched along with data items by FETCH. They are executed when encountered on a possibilities list by TRY-NEXT. Execution generally finds new possibilities which are inserted in front of the other possibilities remaining.

■ Multiple contexts permit easy switching from world to world in pursuing problem-solving hypotheses. Using incremental contexts in a tree structure saves considerable copying since only differences need be recorded to make a new context from an old, similar one.

■ Making associative data bases efficient is a hard problem. There are some answers, but more are needed.

■ There are arguments for and against the procedural and declarative positions on how knowledge should be stored. In most situations, the best plan is to face the problems in a bipartisan way drawing on talents from both sides of the aisle.

REFERENCES

■ Drew V. McDermott and Gerald J. Sussman, "The CONNIVER Reference Manual," AI-M-259A, The Artificial Intelligence Laboratory, Massachusetts Institute of Technology, Cambridge, Massachusetts, 1974. Many of the advanced data-base structures described in this chapter are styled after features of the CONNIVER language. Their implementation is quite different, in general, for reasons of efficiency.

■ Drew V. McDermott, "Very Large PLANNER-type Data Bases," AI-M-339, The Artificial Intelligence Laboratory, Massachusetts Institute of Technology, Cambridge, Massachusetts, 1975. An insightful investigation into how large assertion-oriented data bases can be made efficient. The paper explains CONNIVER's fetch function which first uses one giant hash table to find all matching items and then examines the context membership indicators carried by each. Of course this is an inversion of the simple, inefficient scheme given in this chapter which looks in contexts for matching items.

17
PROBLEMS
TO
THINK
ABOUT

FOR CHAPTER 2

Problem 2-1

The problem in figure 17-2-1 once appeared on an examination given to determine if the examinee could be expected to become a computer programmer. What is the correct answer? Would the analogy program get it right?

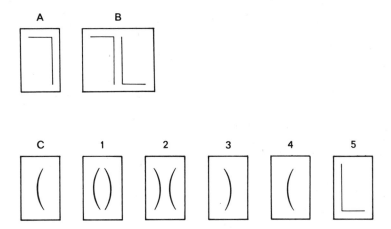

Figure 17-2-1

Problem 2-2

Criticize the following statements: (a) Since a program can now do analogy problems, it makes no sense to use them on human intelligence tests. (b) If one is to construct answers to an analogy test according to some model of the person who designed the test, then one should pay particular attention to the designer's description, description comparison, and comparision of description comparison conventions. (c) The analogy program's intelligence, if any, is inside the description apparatus since the matching and match comparison processes can be described as straightforward rule-like behavior.

Problem 2-3

What parts of the analogy program would need replacement in order to handle the three-dimensional analogy problem in figure 17-2-3? What are the best and the second-best answers?

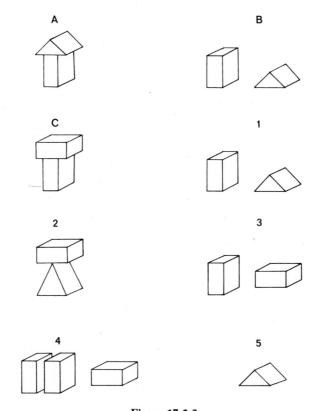

A   B

C   1

2   3

4   5

Figure 17-2-3

Problem 2-4

Write out the rule descriptions in detail to show why the analogy program wrongly selects answer 1 in the problem given in figure 17-2-4.

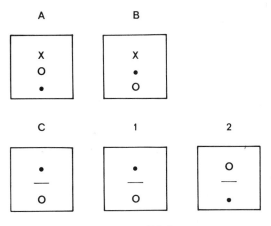

Figure 17-2-4

Problem 2-5 (by Irene Grief and Mark Lavin)

The learning program can modify its models in response to EXAMPLES and NEAR-MISSES. Such modifications are primarily changes in properties of subobjects, and relationships among subobjects; like the analogy program, the learning program has difficulty matching scenes with differing numbers of objects. To address this problem, we introduce a new descriptive device, the GROUP. A group can represent two or more objects in a scene which have similar properties and similar relationships to objects in the scene. Figure 17-2-5-1 illustrates an example of a TABLE, along with its network description. That description may be written out as something like this: A TABLE is composed of a TOP (a LYING BRICK) which is supported by a GROUP of LEGS (STANDING BRICKS). As the figure illustrates, an important feature of the GROUP idea is the presence of a node which represents a typical member of the group. Attached to this node are the properties and relations shared by all group members.

With this in mind, we want to present a series of samples to the learning program so that it can develop a model of SCAFFOLD, defined to be a lying BRICK supported by a group of OBJECTS. We will assume that the following primitive descriptors are being used by the learning program:

STANDING	ONE-PART-IS
LYING	IS-A-KIND-OF
BRICK	IS-SUPPORTED-BY
WEDGE	HAS-PROPERTY-OF
OBJECT	A-TYPICAL-MEMBER-IS
GROUP	

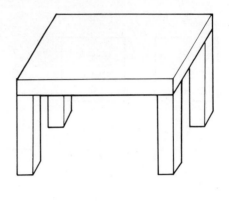

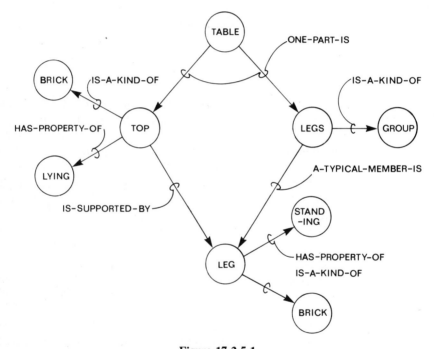

Figure 17-2-5-1

Figure 17-2-5-2 illustrates a number of sample scenes. Assume that the scene at the top is first shown to the program as a positive EXAMPLE of a SCAFFOLD. Your task is to choose a sequence of further samples (both SCAFFOLDs and NEAR-MISSes) to teach the Learning Program that a SCAFFOLD is a lying BRICK supported by a group of OBJECTs. You should try to use as few samples as possible. Indicate the sequence of samples, and briefly describe how each one changes the description.

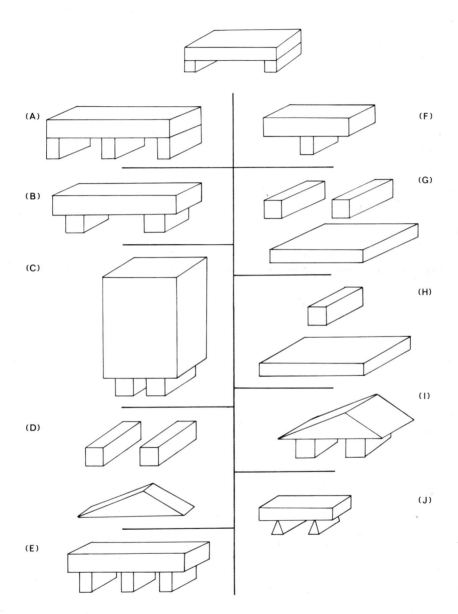

Figure 17-2-5-2

FOR CHAPTER 3

Problem 3-1

Decide if the objects in figure 17-3-1 can be labeled using the Huffman-Clowes label set. Justify your answer.

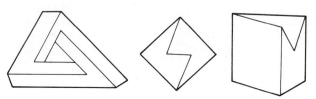

Figure 17-3-2

Problem 3-2

Suppose a robot lives in a world of polyhedra known to have no concave edges. How should the Huffman-Clowes theory be modified by this robot to detect impossible objects in his world? What are the realizable vertexes? Label the objects in figure 17-3-2 using these new labels.

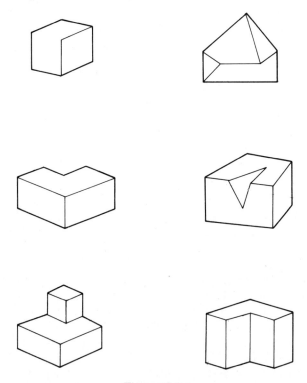

Figure 17-3-1

Problem 3-3 (by Mark Lavin)

The original purpose of Huffman-Clowes labeling was to determine if an object is physically realizable by determining if any consistent labeling exists for that object. However, there may be more than one consistent labeling for some objects.

Part 1. Finish labeling figure 17-3-3 indicating all possible combinations of labels which are consistent with the Huffman-Clowes rules.

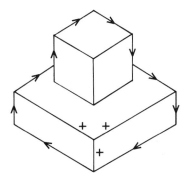

Figure 17-3-3

Part 2. Argue that several consistent labelings must be possible for the given scene by explaining how each could be physically possible.

Part 3. Suppose an intelligent robot is faced with the given scene and has to decide which labeling is correct. What other sources of information could aid in that decision.

Problem 3-4 (by Mark Lavin)

This question deals with the kind of networks used in Chapter 3 to illustrate the various line labels used by Huffman and Waltz. These networks can be generalized to show nonhierarchical relationships among classes of objects; to do this requires introducing some new constructs such as those shown in figure 17-3-4-1 through figure 17-3-4-4. The PARTITION, shown in figure 17-3-4-1 (and introduced in Chapter 3) divides a class into mutually exclusive, collectively exhaustive subclasses. The ALTERNATIVE, shown in figure 17-3-4-2, basically allows a class to be partitioned in a number of different ways. Figure 17-3-4-2 also shows how a class can be identified with a property like FEMALE. Figure 17-3-4-3 and figure 17-3-4-4 show INTERSECTION and UNION constructs, which have their usual set-theory interpretations. Finally, figure 17-3-4-5 illustrates the social structure of a primitive society, using all four of the constructs. The network may be paraphrased like this: "People are divided into ADULTS and CHILDREN or into MALES and FEMALES. BOYS are MALE CHILDREN, WARRIORS are ADULT MALES, and both FEMALES and/or CHILDREN are DEPENDENTS."

Figure 17-3-4-1

Figure 17-3-4-2

Figure 17-3-4-3

Figure 17-3-4-4

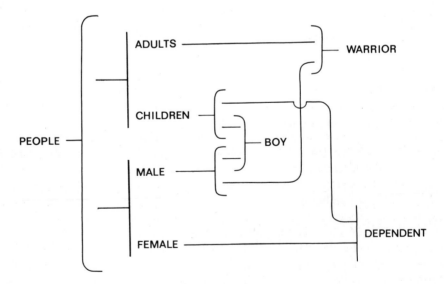

Figure 17-3-4-5

Part 1. Using the constructs introduced above, create a network illustrating the classes and subclasses of the Moon, described as follows:

■ There are only three kinds of things on the moon: moon people, rocks, and cheese.

■ Moon people are docile and consequently never give commands. They do ask questions and state facts.

■ When they state a fact, it may be either a lie or the truth.

■ Rocks are thought of as heavy or light and as shiny or dull.

■ Rocks which are heavy and dull may be either enormous or gargantuan.

■ Only cheese can be sharp. It does not make sense to talk about sharp rocks or sharp moon people.

■ Shiny rocks and cheese are items of commerce and therefore are graded as either rare or common.

Part 2. Describe how the network illustrated in figure 17-3-4-5 indicates that the phrase "boy warrior" is contradictory.

Part 3. Discovering contradictions like the one above may have value in understanding language. Devise a labeling scheme similar to that of Huffman which can detect such contradictions.

Problem 3-5

Identify the case of all noun groups appearing in the following:

Cinderella went to the ball by coach. The Fairy Godmother had made the coach for her out of a pumpkin. During the evening, Cinderella danced with the Prince. She flew down the steps at midnight. The Prince found her with a glass slipper. She went from misery to happiness ever after.

Problem 3-6

Understanding the case identity of the noun groups involved in the previous problem enables answers to some simple, direct questions:

When did Cinderella dance?

Where did Cinderella go?

Other questions are beyond this sort of analysis because they involve questions of cause. Something more than case analysis and something more than the information explicitly given is needed for these questions:

Why did the Prince look for Cinderella?

How did the Prince look for Cinderella?

What is the nature of the background knowledge required by such systems?

Problem 3-7

Case grammar focuses on knowledge conveyed at the level of simple sentences dealing especially with how the objects specified by noun groups relate to the action conveyed by the verb. Speculate on whether there could be a similar grammar relating people to plots. Use some classic plots like that of King Lear or Cinderella to illustrate your conclusions.

FOR CHAPTER 4

Problem 4-1

Explore the game tree in figure 17-4-1 using the alpha-beta technique. Assume the top level is a maximizing level. Indicate all nodes where static evaluation must occur. Indicate the winning terminal node. Repeat, working from right to left through the tree, rather than from left to right. Repeat, assuming the top level is a minimizing level.

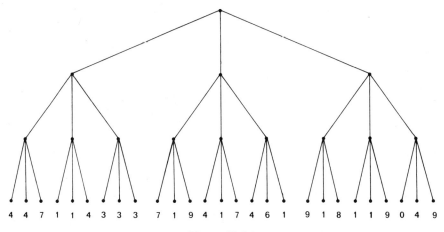

Figure 17-4-1

Problem 4-2

In qualitative terms, how should a better static evaluator, a better plausible move generator, and a more competent opponent affect the balance between depth and breadth of search.

Problem 4-3

Assume that you conspire with an opponent to fix a game. You agree to some secret signals which allow you to tell him exactly how to move. The objective is to beat him as badly as possible. How effective is the alpha-beta technique under these conditions? Thoroughly justify your answer. Is hill climbing a good metaphor for describing what is now happening? Why?

Problem 4-4

Criticize the following statements: (a) The alpha-beta theorem demonstrates that on the average no more than approximately $2b^{n/2} - 1$ terminals need be examined in trees of even depth. (b) Given a plausible move generator that always perfectly orders the moves, the alpha-beta technique gives optimal tree pruning, and only a fool would not use it. (c) The alpha-beta technique can prevent spectacular moves such as queen sacrifices leading to checkmate in chess.

FOR CHAPTER 5

Problem 5-1

Consider the problem faced by a farmer in getting a fox, a goose, and some corn across a river. The farmer can take at most one passenger in addition to himself and must keep in mind the attitudes of foxes toward geese and geese toward corn. Represent the problem as a set of states defining all possible arrangements of the objects involved. Show how the boat trip operator links states. Note if all states are accessible.

Problem 5-2

Using GPS ideas, describe the essentials of a program that would convert scenes consisting of spare parts into scenes consisting of desired configurations. Explain how your program would work on the problem in figure 17-5-2:

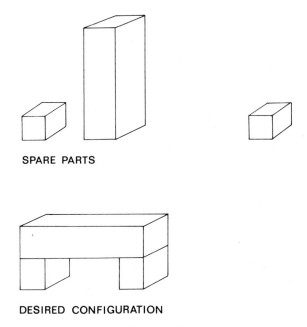

SPARE PARTS

DESIRED CONFIGURATION

Figure 17-5-2

Problem 5-3

Show how the problem of getting a farmer, fox, goose, and some grain across a river can be cast in terms of GPS.

Problem 5-4

Show how the problem of getting Robbie to Aunt Agatha's can be cast in terms of situation-action rules. What generalizations to the basic production system features given would be needed to reduce the situation-action rules to productions operating with a short-term memory?

Problem 5-5

Show how tic-tac-toe can be played using situation-action pairs that resemble productions. Each production-like rule is to be represented as shown in the sample in figure 17-5-5. Do not write down more than one member of rule families generated by rotating or reflecting a pattern.

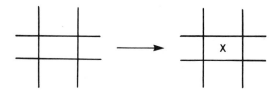

Figure 17-5-5

Problem 5-6

It is often said that cooking is a taxing experience from the point of view of keeping several activities going on simultaneously and synchronously. Would production system models be useful in this context? Try writing a production system for a bread recipe.

Problem 5-7

Triangle tables were shown to be useful as a way of cutting the ends off of an existing operator sequence in order to use it on a new problem. An interesting refinement enables some useless operators to be spliced out of the middle of the remaining sequence. Explain.

FOR CHAPTER 6

Problem 6-1

What natural-sounding English fragments correspond to the following objects:

```
FIND ALL X SUCH THAT
      ?X IS-A BRICK
      THERE ARE = 0 Y SUCH THAT
            ?X SUPPORTS ?Y
            ?Y IS-BIGGER-THAN ?X
FIND ALL Y SUCH THAT
      ?X IS-A ROBOT
      ?Y IS-A SCREWDRIVER
      ?X DESTROYED ?X WITH ?Y
```

Problem 6-2

What English fragment would generate the following:

```
FIND ALL X SUCH THAT
      ?X IS-A BRICK
      ?X HAS-COLOR RED
      ?P1 IS-A PYRAMID
      ?P2 IS-A PYRAMID
      THERE ARE = 0 P SUCH THAT
            P IS-A PYRAMID
            EITHER
                  ?P IS-BIGGER-THAN ?P1
                  ?P2 IS-BIGGER-THAN ?P
      ?P1 IS-BIGGER-THAN ?X
      ?X IS-BIGGER-THAN ?P2
```

Problem 6-3

Write a program-like fragment for "anything red which is either a block or an unsupported pyramid."

Problem 6-4

Woods illustrates the augmented transition network idea at the clause level using the simplified structure shown in figure 17-6-4. Using blocks-world topics, list some sentences illustrating various paths through the network.

Note that an augmented transition network is a useful representation for the structure of noun groups in part because the word order in a noun group is relatively constant. The order of word groups within a clause is more flexible, however, and clause networks tend to be very complicated. Indeed many argue that the augmented transition network is inappropriate at the clause level.

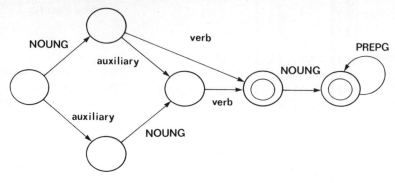

Figure 17-6-4

Problem 6-5

The blocks-world system created a great deal of continuing debate about whether other worlds might be as accessible yet more useful for applications. The following sentences seem excitingly analogous, for example:

Put a pyramid on the biggest red cube.

Book a seat on the last 747 flight.

Part 1. Speculate on the difficulty of handling the following worlds: the world of airline reservations, the world of questions about the weather, and the world of the yellow pages. Use sample sentences in your arguments.

Part 2. List several well-constrained domains that seem much like the blocks world. Illustrate with sample sentences.

FOR CHAPTER 7

Problem 7-1

Schank and others have noted that acts of the mental world involve a movement of facts analogous to the movement of objects in the physical world. The difference is that the places involved are places like LONG-TERM-MEMORY and the CONCEPTUAL-PROCESSOR and the movements are MOVE-CONCEPT operations rather than MOVE-OBJECT.

Part 1. Draw diagrams representing the concepts behind the following sentences:

Robbie recalled the fact.

Robbie learned the fact.

Robbie forgot the fact.

Robbie told Suzie the fact.

Be sure to include the physical acts involved in the last sentence.

Part 2. In the mental world, the object of THINK-ABOUT is a concept or a set of concepts. Whenever THINK-ABOUT appears, there is an explicit or implied MOVE-CONCEPT subprocess with the CONCEPTUAL-PROCESSOR in the DESTINATION slot. Speculate on how the act CONCLUDE must relate to these other two mental acts.

Problem 7-2

This problem illustrates how frames can be useful in organizing knowledge for comparisons. Specifically, it proposes a way of comparing people with a view toward deciding if they would enjoy dating one another.

Part 1. Create a frame structure for information about individual people. The slots are to hold information about physical, intellectual, and emotional characteristics.

Part 2. Discuss how two people frames might be compared to reach conclusions such as, "John and Mary are very different physically, but seem compatible intellectually."

Part 3. Repeat the development using slots relevant to comparing politicians from various points of view. Repeat for countries.

Problem 7-3

Provide a frame-based analysis of the following newspaper story:

THE PRESIDENT BLOCKS ARMS DEAL

The Secretary of State recently announced an intention to rush military aid to Lilliputia in order to participate in a border clash. Reliable sources disclosed that the White House thwarted the proposed deal because the tiny nation is known to have sufficient defensive capability.

Problem 7-4

Recognition and generation of paraphrases is one alleged reason for translating all acts into aggregates containing only a few primitives. We know, for example, that these two sentences translate into the same structure:

Robbie comforted Suzie.

Robbie did something which caused Suzie to become happy.

One program written by Schank and his colleagues can *recognize* that the two such sentences say much the same thing; another program can generate the second sentence, given the first.

Part 1. What sort of paraphrases would be generated for the following sentences:

Robbie insulted Suzie.

Robbie killed a fly.

Robbie opened the door.

Robbie walked to town.

Robbie yelled at the villain.

Robbie hurled a stone into the stream.

Part 2. Would it be significantly more difficult to generate the paraphrases in another language?

Problem 7-5

The purpose of this problem is to think about the problem of maintaining a schedule using the notion of frames to organize relevent knowledge. Assume that the schedule is for busy Professor Mumble.

Part 1. Mumble will certainly spend part of his time lecturing, seeing students, doing research, writing proposals, entertaining visitors, and eating lunch. A program to organize these activities into a sensible schedule will certainly want to know a lot about them. Propose a set of slots for a general committment frame that would be capable of capturing the salient features of any proposed schedule item of the types suggested.

Part 2. Lecturing differs from the other activities in that the time slot must surely hold a tightly bound default. It is reasonable to suppose that the other activities could also have defaults, some of which would conform to Mumble's habits rather than some set of expectations for professors in general. Presumably a scheduling program curious about some fact relevant to scheduling Mumble's students looks first at Mumble's student appointment frame and then, if unsatisfied, looks at the more general student appointment frame. Work out a set of general frames for the activities mentioned and then work out a set for some weird professor, real or imagined.

Part 3. When schedules are sparse, the scheduling program has an easy task, operating by moving forward in time until a satisfactory time slot is found in the calendar it maintains. When schedules get crowded or the constraints on allocated times become serious, then conflicts emerge, compromises must be made, and occasionally, some things left undone. Discuss the issues involved in resolving a conflict between two activities vying for the same spot. Illustrate using filled-in frames for two events of your choosing.

FOR CHAPTER 8

Problem 8-1

Using the Pattern Recognition approach, outline a system for differentiating among a dozen common members of some familiar class such as the birds, flowers, fruits, or insects. Would your system degrade gracefully as the number of types to be recognized increases?

Problem 8-2

Secure a basketball or other sphere and examine it in a room illuminated by a single small light source. Compare with the full moon. Explain the difference, assuming that the moon's shape does not change.

Problem 8-3

Treatises on makeup often suggest using facial rouge to compensate for excessively round or narrow shapes. Explain why this makes sense using an argument based on lines of constant brightness in gradient space. Should people with round faces use dark or light rouge?

FOR CHAPTER 9

Problem 9-1

Robbie wishes to analyze a fruitcake he has just discovered. A friend suggests that he break it up with a hammer and pass the detritus through a series of sieves. This leads him to believe that his friend has been reading the computer intelligence literature. Why?

Problem 9-2

Select some hard-core mathematical science like Newtonian mechanics, electromagnetic theory, or electronic circuit theory and discuss it from the point of view of these questions:

What kind of knowledge is involved?

How should the knowledge be represented?

How much knowledge is required?

What exactly is the knowledge needed?

Problem 9-3

Repeat the previous exercise for some less mathematical discipline like economics, sociology, or music. Compare.

Problem 9-4

Argue about the possibility of powerful computer intelligence with some friends. Keep statistics on the arguments used. Switch sides often to keep the conversation fluid.

FOR CHAPTER 11

Problem 11-1

Evaluate the following s-expressions:

```
(TIMES 2
       (PLUS 3
             (QUOTIENT 4
                       (DIFFERENCE 5
                                   (ADD1 6)))))
(MINUS 6)
(MINUS -6)
(MINUS (SUB1 6))
(LENGTH '(A B C))
(LENGTH '((A B) (C D)))
(PLUS 2 2)
'(PLUS 2 2)
(EVAL (PLUS 2 2))
(EVAL '(PLUS 2 2))
```

Problem 11-2

Evaluate the following s-expressions.

```
(CAR (CDR (CAR '((A B C)))))
(CONS (CAR '(A B C)))
(CDR '((A B C)))
(APPEND (CAR '((A B C) (E F G)))
        (CDR '(W X Y Z)))
(LIST T NIL)
(CONS T NIL)
```

Problem 11-3

Evaluate the following s-expressions:

```
(MEMBER '(PLUS 2 2) '(1 2 3 4))
(MEMBER (PLUS 2 2) '(1 2 3 4))
(MEMBER (PLUS 2 2) '((1 2)(3 4)))
```

```
(LIST T
      'T
      (NULL '())
      (NOT NIL)
      (ZEROP (SUB1 (LENGTH (LIST T))))
      (ATOM (CAR (APPEND (CONS T NIL) NIL))))
(AND (NUMBERP '(A B))
      (GREATERP 3 4 1)
      (LESSP 2 7 1)
      (EQUAL (SETQ X 1) 'X)
      (EQUAL (SETQ X 1) X))
```

Suppose POWER is defined as follows:

```
(DEFINE (POWER M N)
        (COND ((ZEROP N) 1)
              (T (TIMES M (POWER M (SUB1 N)))))))
```

What will happen if the POWER function is given a negative number as an exponent? Generalize the POWER function so that it can properly handle negative exponents.

Problem 11-4

Modify the POWER function to produce a recursive version of the function FACTORIAL that computes the number

$$n! = n \times (n\text{-}1) \times (n\text{-}2) \times ... \times 1$$

Problem 11-5

The Fibonacci numbers are defined to be

$$f(1) = 1$$
$$f(2) = 1$$
$$f(n) = f(n\text{-}1) + f(n\text{-}2)$$

Write a simple LISP function to compute these numbers recursively.

Problem 11-6

Suppose BIGGEST is defined as follows:

```
(DEFINE (BIGGEST S)
        (COND ((ATOM S) S)
              (T (APPLY 'MAX
                        (MAPCAR 'BIGGEST S)))))
```

Modify BIGGEST so as to define a new function SUMUP which adds together all the numbers in an s-expression in which all the atoms are numbers.

Problem 11-7

The Towers-of-Hanoi problem is as follows: given a stack of graduated disks at A, transfer them to B, but move only one disk at a time (the top one in any stack) and never place a larger disk on a smaller one. Figure 17-11-7 illustrates.

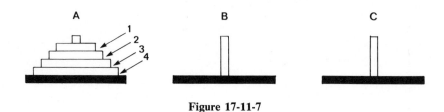

Figure 17-11-7

Part 1. Write a LISP procedure that is the solution to this puzzle for any number of disks. First, of course, you need a suitable representation for this problem. Let A, B, and C be global variables corresponding to the three stacks, the value of each being a list of the disks currently in the stack at that point, ordered from top to bottom. To start with, the value of A is something like (1 2 3 4), while B and C have the value NIL. Your procedure will manipulate this data base just as you would move the actual disks around by hand. Your procedure is to be called MOVE. It should have 4 inputs: N, FROM, TO, and SPARE. Its side effect will be to transfer the top N disks from the stack named FROM to the stack named TO using the stack named SPARE. MOVE's value is irrelevant. For example, (MOVE 'A 'B 'C) should result in solution to the problem above. Here is a big hint: think of how you might move all but the bottom-most disk out of the way so that it can be transferred properly.

Part 2. Let a "move" be the action of transferring a single disk from one stack to another. How many moves are required in your solution for N rings?

FOR CHAPTER 12

Problem 12-1

Some changes to the basic blocks manipulation functions were suggested which would enable the system to create an historical trace of its behavior in the form of a possibly deeply nested s-expression. Referring to the sample history given, write functions DID, HOW, WHY, and WHEN which would perform as suggested by the following:

DID has one argument which looks like a blocks-world function application. It returns T if the argument is present in the historical trace. Thus executing (DID '(GET-RID-OF A)) returns T and (DID '(GET-RID-OF B)) returns NIL.

HOW also looks for its argument in the historical trace, and if it is found, the subgoals, if any, are returned. Thus (HOW '(GET-RID-OF A)) is to return ((PUT-AT A (3 5 0))) and (HOW '(PUT-AT A (3 5 0))) is to return ((GRASP A) (MOVE-OBJECT (3 5 2)) (UNGRASP A)) The atom NIL is to be returned if no match is found and the atom ? is to be returned if there are no subgoals, as in (HOW '(GRASP A)).

Similarly, WHY has one argument, looks for it in the history, and returns the supergoal. Thus (WHY '(GET-RID-OF A)) is to return (CLEARTOP B). The special cases are handled as in HOW.

WHEN is to return the top level goal in the history if the argument is found. Thus (WHEN '(GET-RID-OF A)) returns (PUT-ON B C). NIL is returned if the argument is not found.

Problem 12-2

To implement the history-remembering feature, all blocks-manipulation functions whose subgoals are of possible interest must be modified to return a value which reflects the subgoal history. For functions like PUT-AT and UNGRASP, this was easy since the values they return have no use otherwise. The returned value of MAKE-SPACE, however, already bears the coordinates of the position discovered. Needing more than one returned value is a frequent problem.

Modify the basic MAKE-SPACE and PUT-ON so that the required communication between them is packed into one value by MAKE-SPACE and unpacked by PUT-ON.

Problem 12-3

The modifications suggested for the blocks manipulation system are oriented toward answering questions about past goals. Suppose, however, that the system is to handle questions posed about potential activities such as How would you clear off a block? One way to approach such questions would be via experiments that would produce traces which could be inspected. Another would be to have new programs which look at the programs in the blocks system with a view toward understanding them. Creating such program-understanding programs is a difficult research topic since the problem of program understanding is hard even for people. The following is only intended to provide a hint at what sort of things need to be done.

Part 1. Write a function that has a single s-expression as its argument and returns a list of all atoms in that s-expression which appear in function position.

Part 2. Modify the function written in part 1 so that only the functions of the blocks-world system end up in the list returned. This new function enables the emerging program-understanding program to say that a given function may make use of a function in the list returned. Operating on the definition of CLEAR-TOP, it should therefore return (GET-RID-OF).

Part 3. It would be nice if a program understander would make a special note of subprocedures which appear inside loops. Modify the function written in part 2 so that a list of two sublists is returned. The second sublist is a list of all blocks-world functions found within the scope of DO functions. The first sublist is a list of all blocks-world functions found elsewhere. If CLEAR-TOP had been written with a DO rather than a tag and GO, this new function would return (( ) (GET-RID-OF)) and the understander would properly reply that CLEAR-TOP works by using GET-RID-OF repeatedly. Extending this ability to handle loops formed by tags and GOs is clearly much harder since it is much harder to work out what such loops include. This is consistent with the fact that programs constructed according to the rules of Structured Programming are easier to read. Structured Programming proscribes loops using GO; only DO loops are allowed.

Part 4. Modify the function written in part 2 in another way so that two sublists are again returned, the first being a list of blocks-world functions which are always called and the second being a list of functions which are sometimes called.

A generalization would attempt to say something intelligent about the conditions under which the sometimes-called functions are actually called. For using GET-RID-OF in CLEAR-TOP, the answer should say something about doing it as long as there is something on the object. Getting this idea from the appearance of the program is hard. For one thing the program understander needs to know or guess that the value of POSSIBILITIES is a list of things even though that fact is not explicit in the program. In such circumstances, comments placed for the benefit of human readers help the humans a lot. Comments placed for the benefit of program-understanding programs should do as much for them.

Problem 12-4

So far we have not inquired about how a physical manipulation system would handle the MOVETO commands that appear in the plan. In Winograd's original system, MOVETOs were done in three steps: first the hand was raised to some standard height known to be above everything; then the hand was moved to the XY coordinates as specified by the argument to MOVETO; then finally the hand was dropped down to the proper height above the table. Obstacle avoidance therefore followed from the expedient of raising the hand high before moving horizontally. If the blocks-manipulation system were connected to a real physical robot arm and hand, there would have to be some way of communicating such motions desired to the motor-control devices. These motor-control devices would then do their best to accomplish their assigned tasks.

Assume that at some point the programmer in charge of the LISP system, the programmer in charge of the computer's operating system, and the designer of the arm-control hardware all get together and work out some conventions. Several new functions are added to LISP. SETX is one of these. Executing (SETX <position>) causes the x position information to move into a register inside the arm controller. Feedback mechanisms in the controller constantly monitor arm position and apply corrective forces that move the arm toward the target specified by the value in the register. SETY and SETZ work analogously, placing their arguments in two other registers inside the controller.

Three other new functions, GETDX, GETDY, and GETDZ handle communications going the other way. Executing (GETDX) returns the difference measured by the arm controller between where the x register says the arm should be and where it actually is.

Finally, WAIT is a function which evaluates its argument over and over again until it is nonNIL.

Part 1. Define SORT-OF-EQUAL which evaluates to NIL unless the absolute value of the difference between its first argument and its second argument is less than its third argument.

Part 2. Define DO-MOVE such that (DO-MOVE <X Y Z>) causes the hand to go straight up to $z = 100$, move to the new x and y specified, and then drop to the final z position. Assume that as soon as one motion is within .1 unit of its target, the next can begin.

Part 3. Since measurement errors are always present in mechanical systems, position-oriented controllers can end up trying to push a block through the table in their effort to reach the target location specified. This is one example of the need for force-oriented rather than position-oriented control. Invent new communication primitives and modify your program for part 2 so that the final placement of a block is done under force control.

Problem 12-5

As it stands, the blocks-manipulation system can stop dead in its tracks with an error message when something goes wrong during execution of a PUT-ON. The plan and the property lists of all objects are left as they were at the time the error message is printed. Change the system so that instead of stopping, the plan and all property lists are reset to the values they had when PUT-ON was entered. Here is a hint: keep track of all changes as they are made and then undo those changes in reverse order when an error is encountered.

The PLANNER language provides mechanisms which automate the sort of backtracking required in this problem. The automatic mechanisms involved require a lot of remembering because circumstances may require undoing everything previously done. This means PLANNER tends to suffer from inefficiency.

FOR CHAPTER 13

Problem 13-1

Suppose we want a program which generates and explores some tree-like space like the one involved in previous map-traversal examples. Further suppose that each city is represented by an atom and all adjacent cities can be found in a list under the property NEIGHBORS. For the example shown in figure 17-13-1, the following illustrates.

```
(GET 'S 'NEIGHBORS)
  (A B)
```

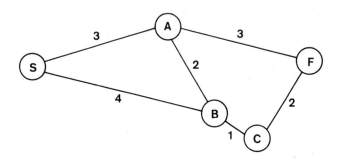

Figure 17-13-1

Write a function DEPTH-FIRST which accepts a start city and a finish city and returns a route as suggested by the following:

```
(DEPTH-FIRST 'S 'F)
  (S A B C F)
```

Depth-first search is to be used so the exact route returned will depend on how the cities are ordered on the NEIGHBOR lists. In the example, the particular route shown is not the shortest, of course.

Problem 13-2

Write a function BREADTH-FIRST which handles the city traversal task of the previous problem using breadth-first search. You will probably decide that depth-first search is easier to arrange in LISP.

Problem 13-3

Generalize the function BREADTH-FIRST to make BEST-FIRST which pushes forward from the city which has the shortest air distance to the finish. Assume city positions are found by referring to the property COORDINATES. Further assume that the earth is flat.

Problem 13-4

Write a function BRANCH-AND-BOUND which finds the optimal route from a start city to a finish city using the branch-and-bound technique.

Problem 13-5

One can think of representing a difficult management task as a network of subtasks in which an arrow between two subtasks mean that the one at the tail must be complete before work can begin on the one at the head. Of the many paths through such a network from start to finish, one is of particular concern to managers because it determines the time required to accomplish the total task. It is called the critical path. Should any subtask along the critical path be delayed, the entire project will be delayed.

Part 1. Write a function CRITICAL-PATH for computing the critical path for a task. Assume atoms represent subtasks. The relationships between subtasks are denoted through the property NEXT-TASKS and the times required through TIME.

Part 2. Can your function be improved using the idea of branch and bound?

Problem 13-6

BIGGEST and SMALLEST were combined into one function, MINIMAX. To be sure you understand what happened, repeat for BIGGEST1 and SMALLEST1.

Problem 13-7

In an earlier chapter a formula was given for limiting search by reducing the amount of branching allowed as depth increases and plausibility decreases:

<number of descendants>
$=$ <number of descendants from parent>
$-$ <rank in plausibility>

Modify the given version of MINIMAX again, this time so that the number of descendants considered at each node is the smaller of the number given by the above formula and the number returned by PLAUSIBLE-MOVES. Assume the list returned by PLAUSIBLE-MOVES arranges moves from most promising to least.

Problem 13-8

MINIMAX negates the NEW-VALUE and returns the results. How would play be changed if the negation were mistakenly omitted? Would there be more or less static evaluations on the average?

Problem 13-9

In many game trees different move sequences reach the same board position. Modify MINIMAX to take advantage of this observation. You may assume that board positions are stored as s-expressions so that two boards are the same if EQUAL returns T when applied to them.

Problem 13-10 (by Mark Lavin)

This search problem deals with a type of structure known as an IS-A network. It is often used to show the relation between various classes and subclasses of objects; an example is the Linnaean taxonomic system in Biology.

IS-A networks can be represented graphically as shown in figure 17-13-10-1. The network can be interpreted to mean, in part, a cat IS-A mammal and a dog IS-A mammal; it can also be interpreted to mean that the set of dogs and the set of cats are both subsets of the set of mammals.

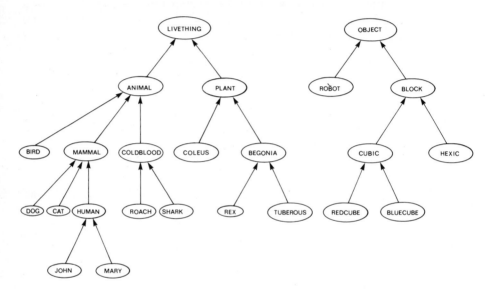

Figure 17-13-10-1

IS-A networks can be implemented in LISP structures in many ways. Assume the nodes of the network are repesented by atoms, and the IS-A relations are represented through the property-list mechanism. For the IS-A network given, something like the following have evidently been executed:

```
(PUTPROP 'DOG 'MAMMAL 'IS-A)
(PUTPROP 'CAT 'MAMMAL 'IS-A)
(PUTPROP 'MAMMAL 'ANIMAL 'IS-A)
```

NOTE! For Parts 1, 2, and 3 of this question, assume that for each node X in the IS-A network, there is at most one (and maybe not any) node Y in the network such that X IS-A Y; also, loops of IS-A pointers are not acceptable.

Part 1. Explain, in simple English, what the following LISP program does when given two nodes in an IS-A network as arguments; you may assume that the network is represented as described above, and has been previously constructed using lots of PUTPROPs. Assume the function ALLNODES returns a list of all atoms which represent nodes in the IS-A tree.

```
(DEFINE (IS-A-R NODE1 NODE2)
  (PROG (THIS1 THIS2)
        (MAPCAR '(LAMBDA (NODE) (PUTPROP NODE NIL 'MARKED))
                (ALLNODES))
        (SETQ THIS1 NODE1)
        (SETQ THIS2 NODE2)
        LOOP
        (COND ((AND (NULL THIS1) (NULL THIS2)) (RETURN NIL)))
        (COND ((NULL THIS1))
              ((GET THIS1 'MARKED) (RETURN THIS1))
              (T (PUTPROP THIS1 T 'MARKED)
                 (SETQ THIS1 (GET THIS1 'IS-A))))
        (COND ((NULL THIS2))
              ((GET THIS2 'MARKED) (RETURN THIS2))
              (T (PUTPROP THIS2 T 'MARKED)
                 (SETQ THIS2 (GET THIS2 'IS-A))))
        (GO LOOP)))
```

Part 2. This part deals with the IS-A network of figure 17-13-10-1. Indicate the result of evaluating each of the following expressions based on your explanation of the program in Part 1:

```
(IS-A-R 'JOHN 'MARY)
(IS-A-R 'HUMAN 'ANIMAL)
(IS-A-R 'CANARY 'CANARY)
(IS-A-R 'REX 'DOG)
(IS-A-R 'REDCUBE 'SHARK)
```

Part 3. One of the main reasons for using an IS-A network is that it is a convenient and compact way of associating *properties* with classes and subclasses. Consider figure 17-13-10-2. The properties could be realized in LISP by placing them on the property lists of the atoms which represent nodes:

```
(PUTPROP 'MAMMAL 'HAIR 'BODYCOVER)
(PUTPROP 'DOG 'ALPO 'FOOD)
```

A common convention is that properties are inherited from superclasses; for example, since (DOG IS-A MAMMAL), we can conclude that DOG has HAIR as the value of its "implicit" BODYCOVER property.

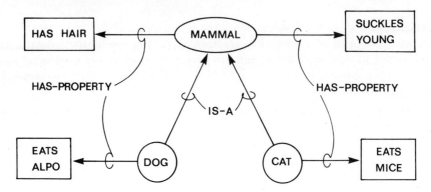

Figure 17-13-10-2

Write a *simple* LISP function called IS-A-GET, which works analogously to the standard LISP function GET, with the wrinkle described above; it should give results like:

```
(IS-A-GET 'DOG 'BODYCOVER)
  HAIR
```

Part 4. In Parts 1 through 3 we restricted the IS-A network to allow only single IS-A links to emanate from any node. However, we might choose to relax this restriction and allow multiple IS-A pointers. Argue for, or against, the feasibility and/or necessity of this modification to the IS-A scheme.

Part 5. Suppose, in spite of (or, in accordance with) your argument in Part 4, we decide to allow multiple IS-A pointers, realized by allowing the IS-A property to have a list as its value:

```
(PUTPROP 'SCOUT
         '(HERO MISER SAGE)
         'IS-A)
```

Describe briefly how this change would affect the IS-A-R program of Part 1 (our program) and the IS-A-GET program of Part 3 (your program).

FOR CHAPTER 14

Problem 14-1

The MATCH function given handles pattern and data items which are lists of atoms only. It cannot match pattern and data items which are more general lists of lists. Modify MATCH slightly so as to provide for the more general case involving nesting patterns and data. For example, the following should match:

```
(MATCH '(>A (>B >C) >D)
       '(L (M N) (O P Q)))
```

The value of A is to emerge as L; B as M; C as N; and D as (O P Q).

Problem 14-2

Use the basic MATCH apparatus with a little extra code to produce a recursive program which converts infix arithmetic notation to the prefix LISP notation. Assume the operators ∧, *, /, +, and − correspond to EXPT, TIMES, QUOTIENT, PLUS, and DIFFERENCE. S-expressions with the infix operators are to be converted to equivalent s-expressions with the prefix operators as in the conversion of this example:

```
(A * B * C ∧ D)

→

(TIMES A
       (TIMES B
              (EXPT C D)))
```

Undoubtedly you will use a COND prominently. Try using the first clause to terminate further action on elemental expressions consisting only of atoms. Then the second clause can handle lists with only one element and hence without operators. It simply funnels the recursion into the element. For example, ((A * B)) is an s-expression caught by this item and it results in a recursive call on (A * B).

The remaining clauses will test for the presence of various operators. Their order in the COND determines the precedence assumed for operators in the infix form. On finding an operator, a new expression is made out of the name of the corresponding prefix operator and the results of converting its arguments to prefix form as found through recursive calls to the program. For example, the s-expression (A * B + C * D) causes the following new s-expression to be constructed:

```
(PLUS <results of INFIX on (A * B)>
      <results of INFIX on (C * D)>)
```

or

```
(PLUS (TIMES A B)
      (TIMES C D))
```

Problem 14-3

We now develop a slight simplification of the matcher used in Evan's geometric-analogy program. Assume GEOMATCH is a function of two arguments, both of which are lists of relations such as this:

```
A1
  ((L ABOVE M) (L ABOVE N) (N INSIDE M))
A2
  ((X ABOVE Y) (X ABOVE Z) (Z INSIDE Y))
```

GEOMATCH must find the way of pairing the variables such that the two lists have the biggest intersection. GEOMATCH is to return the number of items in this maximal intersection.

Normally GEOMATCH would work on the output of the rule-generating functions which would look at numerical descriptions of the geometric figures. These rule-generating functions produce output that differs in two unimportant ways from the samples shown. First, there will be three sets of relations in each rule, not just one. Second, the atoms appearing will be funny-looking, internally generated ones like G0012, not alphabetic characters like L, M, and N.

Part 1. Write a function PICK which returns a list of the variables found in lists of relations like those above.

Part 2. Write a function which accepts two equally long lists of atoms and works out all ways of pairing them up. For each way, the returned value is to contain a list of two-element lists as suggested by the following:

```
(PAIR '(L M) '(X Y))
  (((L X)  (M Y))
   ((L Y)  (M X)))
```

Part 3. SUBST is a LISP function of three arguments which substitutes one s-expression for a second wherever it is found inside a third. Consider this:

```
(SUBST 'L 'X A2)
  ((L ABOVE Y) (L ABOVE Z) (Z INSIDE Y))
```

Write a function SUBSTITUTE which performs substitutions on a list of relations using a list of atom pairs. For example, the following is desired:

```
(SUBSTITUTE '((L X) (M Y) (N Z)) A2)
  ((L ABOVE M) (L ABOVE N) (N INSIDE M))
```

Part 4. Once substitutions are made, the LISP function LENGTH and the function INTERSECTION can determine the degree of match between two lists relative to the pairing used. Keeping this in mind, write GEOMATCH.

Problem 14-4

Sometimes a shorter list of atoms matches a longer list in that all of the elements of the short list appear in the longer list and they appear in the same order. Thus (A B C) match (A X Y B Z C) in the sense of match intended here.

Part 1. Write a function M which tests two lists in the way defined.

Part 2. Extend the function written for part 1 so that > and < type variables can be used in the shorter list. The > type variables are to pick up assignments and the < type variables are replaced by those assignments when encountered.

Part 3. Extend the matcher so that the elements of the two lists can be lists of atoms as well as atoms. Assume that > and < type variables may appear on either level. This kind of matching is required in an Elementary Production System whenever a production rule pattern is compared with short term memory.

Part 4. You probably wrote the matcher in such a way that the following results are produced.

```
(M '(>X <X) '(A B A))
   T
(M '(>X <X) '(A B B))
   NIL
```

It could be argued, however, that the second situation should also have a T result with the interpretation being that the first element in the longer list, the A, is ignored, X then picks up an assignment of B via the >X variable, and the <X therefore matches the final B. Extend your matcher so that both situations cited return T. It may help to recall how the *-type variable feature was implemented.

Problem 14-5

Consider the following algebra problem. Do not be upset by the absence of units — assume all numbers are given in compatible units.

```
(THE RAIN IN SPAIN IS TWICE THE DISTANCE BETWEEN TOLEDO AND
MADRID P THE RAIN IN SPAIN IS MAINLY IN THE PLAIN P THE
SPEED OF MY CAR IS 20 P THE TIME IT TAKES TO GO FROM TOLEDO
TO BARCELONA IS 7 P HOW MUCH IS THE RAIN IN SPAIN Q)
```

Show the set of equations that would be produced. List any aspects of the problem that would cause Bobrow's STUDENT program to employ information not contained in the problem. Will the program give the correct answer, an incorrect answer, or no answer at all? Explain.

Problem 14-6

In general terms, how could the matching functions be used to implement a GPS attack on some particular problem domain?

FOR CHAPTER 15

Problem 15-1

The furniture-moving production system has no productions which serve the function of MAKESPACE in the LISP blocks world manipulation system. Introduce a makespace function by adding productions which completely clear off the target object. Very little change is required.

Problem 15-2

Some production system interpreters permit users to specify that certain items must not appear in short-term memory if match is to succeed. Modify the interpreter in order to create such a feature. Assume that forbidden items are announced by preceding them in patterns by the atom ABSENT.

Problem 15-3

Bobrow's STUDENT program translates word problems into algebraic expressions in a two part process: translation of compound sentences into simple sentences and translation of simple sentences into LISPese. The first translation is done by looking for certain situations and responding accordingly:

```
(DEFINE (SEPARATE S)
  (PROG (R L W)
        (RETURN (COND ((MATCH '(IF *L
                                   C
                                   (RESTRICT >W QWORD)
                                   *R)
                              S)
                       (APPEND (SEPARATE L)
                               (SEPARATE (CONS W R))))
                      ((MATCH '(*L C AND *R) S)
                       (APPEND (SEPARATE L) (SEPARATE R)))
                      ((MATCH '((RESTRICT >W QWORD) *R Q) S)
                       (SEPARATE (CONS 'UNKNOWN R)))
                      ((MATCH '(*L P *R) S)
                       (APPEND (SEPARATE L) (SEPARATE R)))
                      (T (LIST S)))))))
```

Implement this action in a Production System instead of LISP. You may use a modified Production System matcher if you wish. Assume that the entire story to be translated resides in STM in a format of your own choosing. The result is to be written back into STM.

Problem 15-4

Write a compiler for translating productions into LISP code.

Problem 15-5

Write an interpreter for simulating Augmented Transition Networks. You may find this harder than writing the Augmented Transition Net compiler.

Problem 15-6

Criticize the following statements: (a) Language systems can be written in any programming language with the power of say PL/1, FORTRAN, APL, COBOL, or any good assembly language. (b) Computers can never be smart because the computer can only do what it is programmed to do.

FOR CHAPTER 16

Problem 16-1

Extend TEST and ASSIGN so that they can handle recursive pattern and data arguments.

Problem 16-2

Extend TEST and ASSIGN so they can handle ? and > variables in data items as well as in patterns. This is needed for implementing if-added and if-removed demons with those special symbols in their patterns.

Problem 16-3

Extend the DEFINE-DEMON function so that demons without names can be created. Assume such demons have NIL in the function name position.

Problem 16-4

Extend REMOVE so that it can handle ?, >, and < variables.

Problem 16-5

Implement if-needed methods. Note that the first job is to decide how the matcher should work.

Problem 16-6 (by Richard Brown)

Consider the following short story:

> Minnie Mouse lived under the cruel King Grump, and it was no worker's paradise, let me tell you. One day, while working in the fields, she heard a dragon crying. Upon investigation, it became clear that the dragon had a thorn in its wing. Minnie extracted it, and to show his gratitude, the dragon gave Minnie a magic lamp.
> "It will give you unlimited amounts of anything you want, but don't forget the magic words to turn it off."
> When King Grump heard of the action going on down in the fields, he decided to get a piece thereof. He took the lamp from Minnie and in the privacy of his castle he started making pistachio ice cream. But he couldn't stop the sticky green flow, and drowned.
> Finally, the river of green carried the lamp back to Minnie, who said "Foo" to stop it, and everybody lived happily thereafter.

Part 1. Characterize the twist of this story.

Part 2. Find and characterize the bug in the following program:

```
(DEFINE (FACTORIAL N)
        (PROG (TOTAL)
              (SETQ TOTAL N)
              LOOP
              (SETQ N (SUB1 N))
              (SETQ TOTAL (TIMES TOTAL N))
              (GO LOOP)))
```

Find a one line patch to be put after LOOP that will make the program work (assume that the program ought to do what its name indicates).

Part 3. Consider the following short story (based on an idea by Larry Niven):

> *Redford had accomplished his life's dream; at the stroke of midnight the demon had appeared in his pentagram. But a problem had arisen. It seems that a demon is required to fulfill any single wish its invoker may name, except that the wish may not demand more than 24 hours of the demon's time. After fulfilling this wish, the demon must appear inside of any new pentagrams which demand (via mystical inscriptions) its presence. A demon is not required to ever fulfill more than one wish per customer, and can appear in pentagrams arbitrarily quickly.*
>
> *If no new pentagrams call, a demon has free time on its "hands." This particular demon took a fancy to destroying people who invoked it.*
>
> *Redford, after much bargaining, gave his wish: the demon should remain immovable (relative to the ground) for 24 hours.*
>
> *Redford thought all night and the next day. It was now 11:45 p.m., and Redford had not figured out a solution to his problem. Staring at the demon, Redford snapped his finger, and with his magic marker smilingly drew a new pentagram.*
>
> *At midnight, the demon sensed a new pentagram, and started to appear inside of it. "Strange, this pentagram is smaller than I thought. I'll make myself smaller." But the pentagram was still too small, so the demon again made himself smaller, but the pentagram was still too small....*
>
> *Redford continued to smile while the demon shrank into nothing. He knew the demon would never quite make it into the pentagram he had drawn on the fat belly of the demon.*

Characterize the twist of this story.

Part 4. Find the bug in the following program:

```
(DEFINE (FACTORIAL N)
        (COND ((EQUAL N 1) 1)
              (T (TIMES N
                        (FACTORIAL (DIFFERENCE N
                                               1)))))))
```

Conjecture: There is a correspondence between bug types and story ideas. The above two stories correspond to the above two programs in the sense that the twist corresponds to the bug. The two above bugs happen to be bugs of control structure. Another bug is the well-known deadly embrace (a resource-allocation bug), for which the *Gift of the Magi* by O. Henry has a corresponding plot twist. The classic FUNARG problem (a control-structure bug) is illustrated in Hamlet by the Rosencrantz and Guildenstern business.

There are other classes of bug types; for example we have sequence bugs considered by Sussman. These can often be neatly summarized by giving morals of fairy tales.

Such observations suggest a technique for generating new plot twists.

Part 5. Select a program bug, characterize it, and then write a very short story, which should be original, which has that bug as its twist. Be sure to justify why the twist corresponds to the bug. Suggestions for bugs: typing error, wrong data type, unexpected side effect, missing prerequisite, and undefined label. Of course, if you can come up with an original bug as well, so much the better.

APPENDIX: SOME BASIC LISP FUNCTIONS

The following is a list of some basic LISP functions. In some LISP systems some of the functions have slightly different syntax or may have more or less generality. Arithmetic functions, for example, may be restricted to two arguments. Unless otherwise noted, all arguments are evaluated.

ABS
(ABS <number>) returns the absolute value of the number.

ADD1
(ADD1 <number>) returns the number plus one.

AND   [292]
(AND <s-expression 1> ... <s-expression n>) returns NIL if any of the s-expressions are NIL and returns <s-expression n> otherwise. It does not evaluate any of the arguments beyond the first NIL value encountered.

APPEND   [268]
(APPEND <list 1> <list 2>) returns a single list whose elements are the elements of the two lists strung together.

APPLY   [281]
(APPLY <function> <list of arguments>) operates on the arguments with the function given as if that function appeared as the first element in the list. The function may be a name or a LAMBDA expression.

ASSOC   [368]

(ASSOC <atom> <alist>) uses its first argument as a key and looks for that key in the alist supplied as the second argument. The value of the ASSOC is the entire element whose CAR matches the key. The value is NIL if the key is never found.

ATOM   [271]

(ATOM <s-expression>) returns T if the s-expression is an atom. Otherwise it returns NIL.

CAR   [266]

(CAR <list>) returns the first element of the list.

CDR   [266]

(CDR <list>) returns the list with the first element removed.

C-R, C--R, C---R, and C----R   [268]

All of these are equivalent to a series of CAR and CDR operations when As and Ds replace the hyphens.

COND   [273]

(COND <list 1> ... <list n>) is the branching function.

CONS   [265]

(CONS <s-expression> <list>) adds the s-expression to the list as the first element.

DEFINE   [275]

(DEFINE (<function name> <argument 1> ... <argument n>) <body>) defines a function. The function name is the value returned, but that is of little consequence. It does not evaluate its arguments.

DEFPROP

(DEFPROP <atom> <s-expression> <property name>) installs the s-expression as the given property of the atom. It does not evaluate its arguments as PUTPROP does.

DELETE   [265]

(DELETE <s-expression> <list> <number>) removes instances of the s-expression which appear as elements of the list. The number removed is determined by the third argument, if present. Otherwise all instances are removed.

DIFFERENCE

(DIFFERENCE <number 1> ... <number n>) returns the first number minus all the others.

DO

DO is the iteration function available in some LISP systems.

EQUAL   [271]

(EQUAL <s-expression 1> <s-expression 2>) returns T if the s-expressions are identical.

EVAL   [271]

(EVAL <s-expression>) returns the value of the evaluated s-expression.

EXPLODE   [328]

(EXPLODE <atom>) converts the atom into a list of single character atoms.

EXP

(EXP <number>) raises *e* to the power given by the number. This is not typically available in LISP systems.

EXPT

(EXPT <number 1> <number 2>) raises the first number to the power given by the second number. This is not typically available in LISP systems.

FUNCALL   [306]

(FUNCALL <function> <argument 1> ... <argument *n*>) operates on the arguments with the function given. Typically used when the function name is produced by some computation rather than by the programmer. Somewhat similar to APPLY.

GET   [289]

(GET <atom> <property name>) returns the value of the named property associated with the atom.

GO   [289]

(GO <tag>) is used with PROG.

GREATERP   [272]

(GREATERP <number 1> ... <number *n*>) returns T if all the numbers are in decreasing order.

IMPLODE   [329]

(IMPLODE <list of single character atoms>) forms the characters into a single atom and returns it.

LAMBDA [284]

(LAMBDA <list of arguments> <body>) is vaguely like define.

LAST

(LAST <list>) returns the list with all the elements before the last one removed.

LENGTH

(LENGTH <list>) returns the number of elements in the list.

LESSP [272]

(LESSP <number 1> ... <number n>) returns T if all the numbers are in increasing order.

LIST [273]

(LIST <s-expression 1> ... <s-expression n>) returns a list of n elements constructed from the n arguments.

MAPCAR [280]

(MAPCAR <function specification> <arguments>) applies a function to a list or lists of arguments. Returns a list of the results.

MAX

(MAX <number 1> ... <number n>) returns the biggest number.

MEMBER [272]

(MEMBER <s-expression> <list>) returns T if the s-expression is equal to a top-level element of the list.

MIN

(MIN <number 1> ... <number n>) returns the smallest number.

MINUS

(MINUS <number>) returns the negative of the number.

MINUSP

(MINUSP <number>) returns T if the number is negative.

NOT [272]

(NOT <s-expression>) returns T if the s-expression is NIL or NIL otherwise. Equivalent to NULL.

NULL [272]

(NULL <s-expression>) returns T if the s-expression is an empty list or NIL otherwise. Equivalent to NOT.

NUMBERP   [272]

(NUMBERP <s-expression>) returns T if the s-expression is a number.

OR   [293]

(OR <s-expression 1> ... <s-expression *n*>) returns the first non-NIL s-expression. If none are non-NIL then NIL is returned. No arguments are evaluated beyond the first winner.

PLUS

(PLUS <number 1> ... <number *n*>) adds all the numbers together.

PLUSP

(PLUSP <number>) returns T if the number is positive.

PRINC   [322]

(PRINC <s-expression>) is like (PRINT <s-expression>) except that PRINT inserts a carriage return before starting and a space when finishing.

PRINT   [296]

(PRINT <s-expression>) causes the s-expression to be printed out. The value is always T.

PROG   [289]

PROG is complicated. See the text.

PUTPROP   [289]

(PUTPROP <atom> <s-expression> <property name>) installs the s-expression as the given property of the atom.

QUOTE   [368]

(QUOTE <s-expression>) is entirely equivalent to ' s-expression.

QUOTIENT

(QUOTIENT <number 1> ... <number *n*>) returns the result of dividing the first number by all the others.

READ   [296]

(READ) returns the next s-expression typed by the user. The s-expression is not evaluated.

REVERSE

(REVERSE <list>) reverses the order of the elements in the given list. Note that reversal takes place only at the top level.

RETURN   [289]

(RETURN <s-expression>) causes the s-expression to be returned immediately as the value of the PROG it appears in.

SET   [270]

(SET <s-expression 1> <s-expression 2>) returns the second s-expression. The first s-expression must evaluate to an atom and that atom's value becomes the value of the second s-expression. SET in some LISP systems may take more than two arguments. See SETQ.

SETQ   [272]

(SETQ <atom> <s-expression>) returns the s-expression but has the important side effect of making the s-expression be the value of the atom. Note that the atom is not evaluated. SETQ in some LISP systems may take more than two arguments, in which case the odd-numbered arguments are atoms and each one's value is set to the value of the following even-numbered argument.

SQRT

(SQRT <number>) returns the square root of the number.

SUB1

(SUB1 <number>) returns one less than the number.

SUBST   [354]

(SUBST <s-expression 1> <s-expression 2> <s-expression 3>) substitutes s-expression 1 for all occurences of s-expression 2 in s-expression 3.

TERPRI   [322]

(TERPRI) causes a carriage return to be printed.

TIMES

(TIMES <number 1> ... <number n>) returns the product of all the numbers.

ZEROP   [273]

(ZEROP <number>) returns T if the number is 0.

INDEX

INDEX